AN OFFICER'S LETTERS TO HIS WIFE
DURING THE CRIMEAN WAR

GENERAL SIR RICHARD DENIS KELLY, K.C.B.

AN OFFICER'S LETTERS TO HIS WIFE DURING THE CRIMEAN WAR

With an Introductory Memoir

OF

GENERAL SIR RICHARD DENIS KELLY, K.C.B.

BY HIS DAUGHTER
MRS. W. J. TAIT

LONDON
ELLIOT STOCK, 62, PATERNOSTER ROW, E.C.
1902

To

MY BROTHERS AND SISTERS
AND THEIR CHILDREN

PREFACE

My dear Nephews and Nieces,

It is chiefly for your sakes that I have written this very short and imperfect outline of the life of your beloved grandfather. I have done so in the hope that it may help to keep his memory green in your hearts. Some of you knew him well, and are in no danger of ever forgetting him, but others of you are too young to have more than a faint recollection of him.

A noble example, a pure and upright life led in our midst, is a gift of God, for which we should be thankful, and for which we are responsible. All of us, his children, should give God thanks for the memory and good example of Richard Denis Kelly, but do not let us forget that we are also responsible. A good example, such as his, should be an inspiration.

> ' Whene'er a noble deed is wrought,
> Whene'er is spoken a noble thought,
>   Our hearts, in glad surprise,
>   To higher levels rise.
> The tidal wave of deeper souls
> Into our inmost being rolls,
>   And lifts us unawares
>   Out of all meaner cares.'

And his was emphatically a noble life; his aims were always high, his motives pure; he has left his children a legacy of untarnished honour, intrepid courage, and unswerving truthfulness.

I undertook my task without the slightest misgiving, for I knew that

> 'Whatever records leapt to light, he never would be shamed.'

The letters that form the bulk of this little volume speak for themselves; not only are they deeply interesting, giving as they do a graphic account of the historic siege of Sebastopol, but they breathe in every page the warmest affection, the deepest humility, and the most ardent devotion to duty. Your grandfather was a distinguished soldier, but he was more than that—he was a Christian man; he served his Queen and country, but he did more than that—he served God. And so his example is a beacon-light to us all, whatever may be our vocation in life.

The great lessons we may learn from his life, as from the lives of all who were as he was, followers of the 'true and only Light,' are — the inestimable value of love and the paramount importance of duty.

I am, my dear nephews and nieces,
    Your affectionate aunt,
        ELLEN CATHERINE TAIT.

CONTENTS

MEMOIR OF GENERAL SIR RICHARD DENIS KELLY, K.C.B. - - - - - - 1

LETTERS WRITTEN FROM THE CRIMEA BY GENERAL SIR RICHARD DENIS KELLY TO HIS WIFE:

CHAPTER
	PAGE
I. THE VOYAGE	103
II. AT BALAKLAVA	120
III. IN CAMP	131
IV. BEFORE SEBASTOPOL	154
V. IN THE TRENCHES	176
VI. A PRISONER OF WAR	205
VII. JOURNEY TO RUSSIA	228
VIII. LIFE IN CAPTIVITY AT RIASAN	257
IX. RELEASED	275
X. BACK IN CAMP	291
XI. SECOND CRIMEAN WINTER	334
XII. RUMOURS OF PEACE	385
XIII. THE ARMISTICE	418
APPENDIX	434

MEMOIR OF
GENERAL SIR RICHARD DENIS KELLY,
K.C.B.

RICHARD DENIS KELLY was born at Point de Galle, in Ceylon, on March 9, 1815. He was the eldest son of Colonel Richard Kelly and Anne his wife. His mother was of French extraction, being the daughter of M. François Thomè, son of a Huguenot refugee. M. Thomè was a merchant, and at one time wealthy; but his ships were wrecked and the freight lost, so he was reduced to comparative poverty. He married a Miss Montgomery, by whom he had two sons and three daughters.

Richard Denis Kelly belonged to one of the oldest families in Ireland, and he was able in the later years of his life to prove his claim to be The O'Kelly. His father was a very distinguished officer. He was gazetted to the 41st Regiment in 1799, and joined at Templemore at the time of the Irish Rebellion, from whence he was sent with orders to seize all the blacksmiths' bellows he could lay hands on, so as to hinder the making of pikes for the rebels. On March 6, 1806, he was gazetted Captain of the 2nd Battalion of the 66th Regiment, having raised a company, chiefly from among his father's tenants at Mucklon, county Galway. Upon the breaking out of war after the Peace of Amiens, his battalion embarked for Portugal in March, 1809. Captain Kelly was senior Captain; the Lieutenant-Colonel was on the staff in the West Indies, and the battalion was commanded by Major Murray. Major Lloyd, the junior Major, was drowned on the way to Cork, and so the battalion landed in Portugal with only one field officer, and thus Captain Kelly had to perform the duties of Major.

At the passage of the Douro the battalion was taken into action by Major Murray, and he being severely wounded, the command devolved upon Captain Kelly, who retained the command for nearly two years, and took the 66th into action at Talavera. Captain Kelly was specially recommended for a majority, but was to his great regret posted to the 4th Ceylon Regiment. He did not, however, relinquish the command of the 2nd Battalion 66th until early in 1811, and so was present at the Battle of Busaco, and also in the lines of Torres Vedras.

On his leaving the 66th, the officers of the 2nd Batatlion presented Major Kelly with a silver-mounted sword of honour, as a mark of their high esteem and regard, and 'to return their acknowledgments of his kindness to them while they had the happiness of serving under his command.'

Major Kelly received the gold medal for Talavera, but died before the issue of the Peninsular medal, to which he would have been entitled, together with three clasps for the Douro, Talavera, and Busaco.

On December 6, 1810, he was gazetted Major of the 4th Ceylon Regiment, and was sent out to aid in the suppression of the Kandian rebellion, in which he greatly distinguished himself, and received a highly complimentary letter from Sir Edward Barnes.

At the taking of Kandy Major Kelly became possessed of some interesting and valuable relics, among which were the King of Kandy's punch-bowl—afterwards used at the private baptism of his eldest grandson—the gold flexible chain that had encircled the waist of the King's infant son, and some very fine pearls, subsequently divided between his two daughters.

On the voyage out to Ceylon, which in a sailing-vessel viâ the Cape and St. Helena took nine months, Major Kelly became acquainted with Miss Anne Thomè, who with her brother Francis was on her way to India to visit her sister, Mrs. Stoddart, who was in bad health, and had written asking her sister to come out to her. The acquaintance ripened into friendship, and the friendship developed into love, so that before the nine months' voyage was over Major Kelly and Miss Thomè were engaged. On landing at Colombo, Miss Thomè received the sad intelligence that her sister, Mrs. Stoddart, had passed beyond the need of earthly help, but possibly her grief may have been assuaged by the prospect of her speedy union with the man she loved, who proved to her the best of husbands, as he was afterwards the best of fathers, revered and loved by all his children to the last hour of their lives. He was the first of three generations of men all bearing the honoured name of Richard Kelly, than whom no better in every relationship have ever lived.

On landing, Miss Thomè went to her kind friends Sir Harding and Lady Giffard, and was married from their house.

In Ceylon Major and Mrs. Kelly formed a friendship

that has lasted through three generations—that of Captain and Mrs. Cleather. While their husbands were engaged in suppressing the Kandian rebellion, the two wives lived in bungalows side by side on the beautiful lake of Kandy, and shared a buggy. Later their children became playfellows, and the friendship begun thus early among the spicy breezes of Ceylon endured through life. Sophie Cleather married the Rev. George Collinson, Vicar of St. James's, Clapham, and her children and those of Richard Denis Kelly, Major Kelly's eldest son, inherited the friendship of their parents.

Another friendship was formed by Major Kelly in Ceylon—that of Bishop Heber, author of the well-known missionary hymn, 'From Greenland's icy mountains.' He married the young couple, and some years later, during his second visit to Ceylon, confirmed Major Kelly at his own request in Ceylon Cathedral. To the influence of Bishop Heber is due the deep though unobtrusive religion that permeated the whole life and thoughts of Major Kelly, and which he transmitted to his eldest son, who resembled him much in character, mind, and feeling.

Colonel Kelly (as he now was) brought his family home in 1819, and took them over to Ireland, and in 1820 settled them in Bath. Here Richard was sent to a private school on Sion Hill, kept by a Dr. Allen. He had already learned to read, having to a great extent taught himself by asking the names of the letters over the shops in Colombo and Kandy, and astonished a friend by reading the newspaper aloud at five years old! He was all his life devoted to reading, and, having a wonderfully retentive memory, he was a perfect mine of information on all subjects that came within the scope of his reading. He read aloud most beautifully; it was one of his children's greatest treats to be read aloud to by him. His sister relates: 'I remember once, when we were staying at my father's cousin's, Dean Mahon, of Weston, near Mucklon (the family estate), there was a blind old gentleman on a visit there, who was very fond of being read to, and who was constantly calling out, "Richard, come and read to me." While the rest of us would rush away at the sound of his footsteps, dear Richard was always ready and willing to give up his game of play with us and read patiently to the old man and then lead him about wherever he wished to go.'

On Colonel Kelly's return to Ceylon, Mrs. Kelly settled at Teignmouth with her children. Here Richard attended a private school kept by a Dr. Eaton. His love of study, shown even in boyhood, his fine natural qualities and religious turn of mind, led his mother to hope that he would take Holy Orders, but she was too wise to cross his natural bent, for he was a born soldier. When Colonel Kelly came home from Ceylon after five years' absence, Mrs. Kelly took her eldest boy down to Portsmouth to meet his father, and his sister says that it was the sight of the regiment landing and the military parade that decided Richard's bent for a soldier's career.

Colonel Kelly remained at home about three years. Through the influence of Lord Hill, the Commander-in-Chief, he was exchanged into the 34th Regiment, and went to Halifax, Nova Scotia, in command of that regiment.

About this time, 1829-30, Richard went to Sandhurst, then more of a school than a purely military college, from whence he brought home prizes every holidays.

In the year 1834 Colonel Kelly returned from Canada and sold his commission, and then took his family abroad. The same year, in March, Richard was gazetted an Ensign in the 49th Regiment, passing straight from Sandhurst without purchase. On the 14th of the same month he exchanged into the 34th, his father's old regiment.

The young Ensign, a lad of nineteen, got six months' leave, and accompanied his family to the Continent. The following year, on May 5, 1835, the regiment embarked for Nova Scotia, whence it proceeded to Canada, returning home in 1841. It remained at home two years, and in 1845 embarked for Corfu, where it remained until 1848. During this time Richard had purchased two steps, those of Lieutenant and Captain.

Meanwhile Colonel Kelly and his family remained abroad, spending the winter at Geneva, where Francis, the second son, was at school, and afterwards visiting Florence, Rome, and Naples. On returning home, a year was spent between Mucklon, the family estate in county Galway, then in possession of Colonel Kelly's eldest brother George, and Dublin; a couple of years were spent at Ardmulchan, near Navan, and then, after another year of wandering about in search of a home, Colonel Kelly in 1842 took a lease of the house, grounds, and farm of the property known by the name of Weston, near Duleek, in county Meath. He at once began to enlarge the house, but died, ere the improvements were completed, on January 6, 1845. His remains were buried in the churchyard of the little village church of Duleek, built on the site of the first Christian church in Meath. For many years after his death the village children used to place holly and ivy on his tomb at Christmas, so truly was 'the good Colonel' beloved by all who knew him. The remains of his widow were placed beside him on October 3, 1861.

Colonel Kelly's will was found to be unsigned. Weston was left to the younger son Francis, Richard being heir to the estate of Mucklon. According to law, as his father had died intestate, he could have claimed the whole of the real and one-third of the personal property, but with characteristic generosity he wrote home from Corfu, where he was then stationed, to say that the will was to be carried out as it stood.

Weston is a charming old country house, not beautiful, but spacious and comfortable. It is entered by a porch gay with flowers; the front-windows look out on a lawn flanked with shrubberies, divided by a low iron railing from fields dotted with clumps of trees. Two avenues, each terminating in a lodge, connect the house with the highroad. Behind the house is a good-sized walled garden, famous for its gooseberries and peaches, and a charming old-fashioned flower-garden, the special care and pride of the youngest daughter, Annie, always a passionate lover of flowers and an enthusiastic gardener, a taste inherited by two of her nieces. This little flower-garden was divided into beds, and each bed was surrounded by a border of gentianella, making in early summer a series of sapphire rings round the flowerbeds.

In the same county of Meath, within an easy afternoon's drive, stood another and more dignified country seat—Lismullen, the property of Sir William Dillon, Bart., the representative of an ancient Irish family, being descended from a common ancestor with the Earls of Roscommon. The family then consisted of one son, Arthur, in the 74th Highlanders, and two daughters, Ellen Susanna and Louisa Wilhelmina. Several children had died in infancy, and one, Henrietta, in girlhood.

The Kellys of Weston and the Dillons of Lismullen were neighbours, and were destined to be united by a stronger bond than that of friendship. The young people of both families were good riders, which facilitated intercourse, and when young Captain Kelly was at home on leave he had many opportunities of meeting Miss Dillon, who afterwards became his wife.

Miss Dillon's earliest recollection of meeting her future husband was while she was still in the schoolroom. He was lunching at Lismullen, and when she rose to leave the room he jumped up and opened the door for her. She was struck by this chivalrous attention to a mere schoolgirl.

It was in 1847, the year of the terrible Irish famine, that Captain Kelly asked Ellen Susanna Dillon to be his wife, and was accepted. They were married on March 2, 1848, in Temple Keiran Church, in the parish of Skreen, county Meath. The marriage was an eminently happy one; no woman ever had a more tenderly devoted husband, and no man a more sincerely-attached wife.

Of this marriage there were seven children: Ellen Catharine, born at Lismullen; married, January 6, 1870, Rev. Walter James Tait, Fellow and Tutor of Worcester College, Oxford, eldest son of Rev. W. Tait, D.D., British Chaplain at Pau, France. Annie Louisa, born at Lismullen; married, January 7, 1875, Captain Charles Lacon Harvey, 71st Highland Light Infantry; died December 3, 1875. Sophia Henrietta, born in Grenada, West Indies; married, July 25, 1872, Lieutenant Hamilton William Wetherell Spooner, 11th Regiment. Arthur Dillon Denis Kelly, born at Weston, county

Meath; educated at Wellington College; entered the army, gazetted to the 34th Regiment in 1873, retired 1897 to reserve of officers; married, April, 1895, Henrietta, daughter of the late Hon. Chichester Thomas Skeffington, second son of Viscount Masserene and Ferrard. Richard Makdougall Brisbane Francis, born at 6, Waterloo Terrace, Dublin; educated at Marlborough College; entered Royal Academy, Woolwich, passed out from thence with distinction in 1877; married in India, on December 10, 1887, Mary Pearcy, only daughter of Major-General P. Bedingfeld, R.A. Beatrice Frances, born at Fyzabad, India; married, at Shrublands, Earley, Berkshire, on February 4, 1892, Francis Arthur, son of the late Captain Beauchamp, R.N. William, born at Suez, September, 1861; died when a few days old.

Two years after her marriage, while absent in the West Indies, Mrs. Kelly lost her father, and not long after her only brother, Sir Arthur Dillon, Bart., who caught a chill after playing cricket, which turned to pneumonia. On his death the title and estate of Lismullen passed to a cousin.

Out of Lady Dillon's ten children, only two now remained on earth, and of these one was married. From the other she was only parted when her own summons came in April, 1866. Louisa Wilhelmina Dillon married in 1857 Captain John Prevost Battersby, 60th Rifles, and died on January 27, 1898, only a few months after her brother-in-law, General Sir Richard Kelly, to whom she was sincerely attached.

About three weeks after Major Kelly's marriage, the 34th was ordered to Gibraltar. On arriving, Major Kelly learned that the Colonel had died on the voyage from Corfu, so that he landed as senior Major, and thus would be sent home to command the 4th Company

Depôt as soon as the new Lieutenant-Colonel arrived. He was thus in command of the 34th while in Gibraltar. Major and Mrs. Kelly lived in lodgings at first, and afterwards in quarters in the new barracks. They were three months at Gibraltar.

Major and Mrs. Kelly returned home in August, and after a short leave, which was spent at Lismullen, he joined the 4th Company Depôt at Nenagh, county Tipperary, where the young couple took a small unfurnished cottage. In October the depôt was moved to Boyle, county Roscommon. Christmas was spent at Lismullen, where Mrs. Kelly remained till after the birth of their eldest child on February 13, 1849. In 1850 the depôt was removed to Londonderry, and in the autumn of that year Major Kelly was ordered to join headquarters at Barbadoes in the West Indies. He sailed in H.M.S. *Apollo*, taking with him his wife and infant daughter, Annie Louisa, born at Lismullen, May 28, 1850.

Barbadoes was reached after a voyage of six weeks, in the course of which they touched at Madeira, where a few days were spent. After about six months in Barbadoes, Major Kelly was sent to command the troops in Grenada, where he remained till 1853, when he came home, joining the depôt at Preston in September of that year. At Grenada the third daughter, Sophia Henrietta, was born on December 23, 1851.

The eldest child had been left at Lismullen, under the care of her grandparents, Sir William and Lady Dillon, and Mrs. Webb (Auntie Heb, otherwise Aunt Anne), Lady Dillon's sister-in-law.

In 1851, the year of the Great Exhibition, Mr. George Kelly, of Mucklon, went up to London to see the show. He never returned. Crossing the street near the Marble

Arch, he was run over by a mail-cart, picked up insensible, and carried into St. George's Hospital, where he lingered for ten days without recovering consciousness.

The Kellys, in common with many other old Irish families, possess a 'banshee,' whose singing is supposed to presage the death of the head of the family. Major Kelly's sister relates that during Mr. Kelly's absence in London the wife of one of the tenants came up to the house in great distress, inquiring anxiously whether any news had been received about 'the master.' She was assured that he was well when they had last heard, and asked why she inquired. 'Och! praise the Lord!' exclaimed the poor old woman, 'I was afeart he was dead, for the Lady has been singing beautiful.' Next day the news of the fatal accident was received. On a subsequent occasion, when the report of Major Kelly having been killed in the Crimea reached Mucklon, it was not credited, on the ground that the 'Lady' had not been heard to sing. It would be interesting to know—but one could not inquire, lest evidence should be manufactured—whether the Lady sang her song of welcome in July, 1897.

On the death of his uncle, who never married, Richard Denis Kelly succeeded to the estates of Mucklon and Kilcash.

In September, 1853, Major Kelly was quartered at Preston. His wife and family did not join him there. His wife went to Weston with her children, and here, on December 5, was born the son and heir. He was baptized privately in the drawing-room at Weston (Duleek, the nearest church, being four miles distant), in the King of Kandy's punch-bowl, and given the name of Arthur Dillon Denis.

In February, 1854, Major Kelly went to Sheffield, accompanied by his wife and infant son, and soon after the regiment was moved to Portsmouth. In this year the ill-advised, disastrous Crimean War broke out. The ill effects of that unfortunate struggle are still felt in the Christian provinces of Turkey. Perhaps the only nation (Turkey cannot properly speaking be called a nation) which reaped any benefit from it was Italy, as the help afforded to the allied armies by Sardinia no doubt aided Italy in her struggle for independence. The headquarters of the 34th were sent to Corfu, and Major Kelly was sent to Plymouth to command the 4th Company Depôt. Here they took a house and furnished it, but they were only allowed to remain a few months, for after the Battle of Alma, September 20, the 34th were sent from Corfu to the Crimea, and Major Kelly was ordered to go out at once with a large draft. He arrived at Balaklava soon after the Battle of Inkerman. The Crimean letters give a detailed and deeply interesting narrative of Major Kelly's life during the next two years, and of the brave and honourable part he took in the war.

His wife and children meanwhile found a home at Weston. It is the earliest home of which his children have any recollection, beyond a few trifling incidents that stand out from a nebulous background. The house and its surroundings have been described. An attempt must now be made to delineate its inmates. First, there was the grandmother, an old lady over seventy years of age, with a sweet face and silver-gray hair, covered by a close-fitting white cap, tied under her chin, kind and indulgent, and much loved by her grandchildren. The uncle, kind and good-natured, always ready for a game of play with his little nieces, who nicknamed him the 'fun man.'

The two aunts, Kate and Annie, whom the children used to distinguish by Aunt Annie wearing curls. Aunt Kate, the elder of the sisters, was a most beautiful character; she was absolutely unselfish, tender-hearted, and sympathetic. She will live in the memories of those who knew and loved her, not for what she said or did, but for what she was, and we doubt not still is. Whittier's beautiful lines in 'Snow-bound' might, with some slight alterations, have been written for her:

> 'Next the dear Aunt, whose smile of cheer
> And voice in dreams I see and hear—
> The sweetest woman ever Fate
> Perverse denied a household mate,
> Who, lonely, homeless, not the less
> Found peace in love's unselfishness,
> And welcome whereso'er she went,
> A calm and gracious element,
> Whose presence seemed the sweet income
> And womanly atmosphere at home.
>   *   *   *   *   *
> 'For well she kept her genial mood
> And simple faith of maidenhood;
> Before her still a cloudland lay,
> The mirage loomed across her way.
> The morning dew, that dries so soon
> With others, glistened to her noon;
> Thro' years of toil and soil and care,
> From glossy tress to thin gray hair,
> All unprofaned she held apart
> The virgin fancies of her heart.
> Be shame to him of woman born
> Who hath for such but thought of scorn.'

A distant cousin of the family, a Miss Keys, lived at Weston; she was not fond of children, so was rather a lay-figure—certainly not an attractive person, from all accounts.

A nursery-governess was engaged for the children soon after they took up their abode at Weston—a Miss Lebel, niece of their mother's old governess Miss Lowe. To her the children soon became devotedly attached, perhaps owing to the contrast of her gentle manners to those of their baby brother's crabbed old nurse Mrs. Caffray, who might have been the model of Miss Sinclair's Mrs. Crabtree in 'Holiday House.' In the gardener the children had a devoted and loyal friend; John Kelly was always ready to help them in their little gardens, and play with them and talk to them by the hour.

Major Kelly was given the brevet rank of Lieutenant-Colonel in December, 1854, and was Lieutenant-Colonel of the 34th on March 9 (his birthday), 1855. On the night of March 22, 1855, Colonel Kelly was wounded and taken prisoner by the Russians while in command of the trenches before Sebastopol. The incident is fully described in his letters, and the following extract from Kinglake's 'Invasion of the Crimea,' written by my father for the second edition at the author's request, gives his own account of it.

'The field officer that night (March 22) on duty in the precincts of "Gordon's Attack" was Colonel Kelly; and of the 1,200 men he had under him, one half at first guarded the third or their foremost parallel, which (if reckoned with the trenchwork prolonging it) may be said to have crossed the whole breadth of the Worouyoff Ridge, from the Dockyard Ravine on his right to the Worouyoff Road on his left. These last 600 men were composed of detachments from several regiments, and stood ranged in the order here shown: Rifles, 90th, 34th, 88th, 77th, 97th. With 300 of his men Colonel Kelly had furnished the working-parties employed that night under the guidance of Colonel Tylden, of the Royal Engineers, and the remaining 300 he kept higher up in reserve. Colonel Kelly enjoyed an advantage which, of course, for one acting at midnight was beyond measure great, that of having at his side Major Gordon (the Directing Engineer of the Gordons or right-attack siegeworks), who thoroughly knew the ground.

'Marking all that through the darkness and storm the eye and ear could still tell him of the conflict sustained by the French, and learning thus that, though slowly, the enemy had carried their trenches, Colonel Kelly divined that the Russians would very soon turn to their right and try to make a sweep along the ground in his rear, where the 300 men he had furnished were busy with pickaxe and spade. To prepare against any such onset, Colonel Kelly made these dispositions, not disturbing at all the detachment composed of the 97th men, which formed the extreme right of the line and was critically circumstanced; but resorting instead to the two next detachments (troops furnished by the 77th and 88th Regiments), he shifted these both from their places in the advanced trench, and drew them up at right angles to the 77th men, foremost in skirmishing order, supported by the 88th men in line. To take up the positions thus vacated, there came down soon afterwards a fresh detachment, one furnished by the 7th Fusiliers.

'Directed by Ensign Zavalichine (whose force, though from English ground, had been hitherto poured on French troops), the attack planned against our right flank was opening with some shots from his skirmishers, when under the orders of Bondistcheff, and designed to take effect on our front, a heavier onslaught began.

'Greatly favoured, of course, by the darkness, but also by the roar of a wind overpowering the sound of their march, a body of Russian troops moved out from the lines of Sebastopol and ascended the Worouyoff Ridge. Undertaking a front attack on the extreme right wing of our advanced parallel, the column opposed its strength to the detachment of our 97th Regiment, a detachment composing no more than seventy or eighty men, but commanded by a brave, warlike officer, Captain Hedley Vicars. The column, advancing in silence, had seemingly come up so close as to be yet driving in the out-sentries, when it all at once fired a volley. Then instantly, awaiting no orders, entertaining no doubt, and listening only, it seems, to that gallant spirit of his which used always to prompt him in action, Captain Vicars sprang over the parapet, carrying with him the whole of the seventy or eighty men who formed his little detachment, and their ringing cheer, heard amid the darkness that gave to every sound a more than treble significance, was the cheer of the soldiery, not halted, but joyously attacking an enemy.

'With Gordon still at his side, Colonel Kelly was at this moment busied with the lesser affairs of the flank attack, but on ground not far from our advanced parallel; and at the sound of the volley, followed close by the cheer, they both of them sped off at once to the new scene of action, and were presently in the midst of the men of the 97th, who had newly sprung over the parapet. Gordon, sharing the fervour of the soldiery, was even lending his voice to the joyous tumult of war, when he received a wound from a musket-shot, which struck his right arm and disabled him; but Colonel Kelly running forward overtook Captain Vicars, and was presently moving down alongside him against the enemy's column. It is supposed that, baffled by the darkness, the Russians may have failed to divine the exceeding scantiness of the impetuous little force that assailed them with a strength we have already seen estimated at only about one to ten, for when the advance of our soldiery was becoming, or had become, what Englishmen mean by a "charge," the column fired a last volley, and then, still hanging together after the manner of Russians in flight, began to retreat at the double, its rear files turning, however, and firing back shots while they ran. By one of these Parthian balls, there was taken the life of the Captain who had ordered and led the charge. Whilst moving eagerly forward at the side of Colonel Kelly, and whilst listening, indeed, to his words, Hedley Vicars was stricken and killed. Our soldiery, in spite of the darkness, saw enough to be sure that their cheers were accelerating the flight of the column, and a brave little bugler of the 97th, whose irrepressible zeal kept him always far out towards the front, was unsparing in the use of a power with which he seemed to think himself armed. As he rightly or wrongly imagined, he made the retiring mass spring at the blast of his clarion, like a horse that is touched by the spur, and so kept the whole force at a gallop by sounding the advance in its rear. Colonel Kelly at last stayed the chase, and brought back the 97th detachment to its former place at the trench.

'With his men of the 77th detachment, supported by that of the 88th Regiment, Captain Rickman, after a well-sustained fight, and losing several men, defeated the venturesome column which Zavalichine had led, and drove it down the ravine. From this time—about midnight—until one other hour had passed there was peace on the Worouyoff Heights; but again at one o'clock in the morning the tumult of more and more fighting began to make itself heard, and the seat of conflict this time was a part of the ridge further west.

'With his newly-received detachment of the 7th Fusiliers now marching westwards by fours along the course of the foremost parallel, Colonel Kelly made what haste he could towards the sound of the firing; but the dark-

ness and the state of the trench—still unfinished and
encumbered with stones—made the progress of the
troops somewhat slow, and the Colonel himself, being
able to move at a faster pace, pushed forward impatiently
in advance of his men. Soon he met Lieutenant Jordan
with some men of the 34th (the Colonel's own regiment),
and by him was apprised that the Russians had seemingly entered a part of the trench further west. The
Colonel said that our people must try to drive the enemy
out, told Jordan to get his men together, informed him
that the detachment of the 7th Fusiliers was coming up,
and then once more hastened on towards the sound of
the firing. He had gone but a little way further when,
standing together in the trench, he saw a group of seven
or eight soldiers whom he took in the darkness to be
men of his own regiment, the 34th; so, going close up
to them, he directed these men to "fall in" with the other
men under Jordan. He was met by an uproar of out-
landish cries, and found he had been accosting the
enemy! He brought out his revolver, and, pointing it
at the head of his nearest foe, pulled hard, though in
vain, at the trigger, held fast by the safety-catch.*
Whilst lowering his weapon in order to draw back the
bolt, he was felled by numbers of blows laid upon him
by the butt-ends of muskets, and when on the ground
was bayonetted in the right shoulder, in the left hand,
and in the right leg; whilst also his assailants—not
Russians, but Albanians, engaged in the enemy's service
—were so emulous in the truculent work of pounding
and battering at him with the stocks of their firearms
that many of the blows they were levelling intercepted
each other, and the victim had not succumbed, nor even,
indeed, lost consciousness, when a young Russian officer,

* This little contretemps saved his life; had he killed one, he
would have received no quarter.

no less generous than brave, interposed. Standing over the prostrate Colonel, and so courageously shielding him as himself to become the recipient of some of the fiercely-aimed blows, this chivalrous noble at last proved able to make good the rescue, and caused the wounded Colonel—who, of course, became a prisoner of war—to be safely brought into the fortress, where he was treated with every kindness and courtesy.

'The misfortune which threw Colonel Kelly into the hands of the enemy was unknown at the time to our troops, and men supposed after a while that the field-officer of the night had been killed.'*

By some inadvertence Colonel Kelly's name appeared in the list of the killed. The terrible news reached Weston on the Wednesday following, and after three days' anguish, during which his poor wife could neither eat nor sleep and his family were plunged in the profoundest grief, to their intense joy and thankfulness, no less than nine telegrams were received by friends, saying that he was wounded and a prisoner, his life having been saved by a Polish officer in the Russian Army, who had protected him by throwing himself across his body as he lay wounded on the ground. This officer was promoted by the Russians for his brave conduct.

Sir Richard has described in his letters the incidents of his captivity; he has written warmly of the kindness he received from the Russian authorities. The name of Madame Braillard, wife of a Professor at the College at Kharkoff, occurs several times. The following extract, headed 'A Memory of the Crimea,' appeared in the *Westminster Gazette* of October 19, 1898:

'Mr. C. M. Courtenay writes a letter which will

* From 'The Invasion of the Crimea,' by A. W. Kinglake, vol. vii.

interest survivors of our soldiers and sailors who were taken prisoners in the Crimean War and marched to Kharkoff, who will regret to learn that the bright, kindly little Englishwoman, Madame Braillard, *née* Chillingworth, by whom they were met on arrival and accosted in their native tongue, has just died at Schloss Sayn, near Coblentz, at the age of eighty-two. Her husband, a Swiss, was at the time of the war Professor at the College at Kharkoff, and, being acquainted with the Governor of the gaol, she was allowed to go down there twice a week to meet the prisoners on arrival, and to visit them afterwards. Besides talking to them and being the means of communicating to their friends in England the news of their safety, she took them all the comforts she could—clothes, tea, tobacco, books, writing materials, etc.—collecting money for this purpose from her sister and wealthy friends in St. Petersburg. The officers on parole dined daily at her house. Her unselfish kindness met with no public recognition, but in her old age it was no small pleasure to her to reflect that, though so much of her life had been spent abroad, still, that when the opportunity had been given her she had shown herself a true-hearted Englishwoman.'

In August, 1855, after five months' captivity, Colonel Kelly, with three other officers, was exchanged for some Russian officers, and returned to the Crimea, arriving a few days after the fall of Sebastopol.

After the signing of the Peace of Paris, Colonel Kelly got leave and returned home, his wife going to Paris to meet him. There were great rejoicings at Weston—a bonfire, flags, etc. His daughter well remembers the old nurse, Mrs. Caffray, hanging all her coloured ribbons out of the nursery window as her contribution to the general rejoicing.

On their return from the Crimea the 34th Regiment was quartered in Edinburgh, in the grand old castle which dominates the city. Here a year was spent of happy domestic life. Colonel Kelly much enjoyed his stay in Edinburgh among the kindly, hospitable Scottish people. Here he formed a lifelong friendship with the Colonel of the regiment, Sir Thomas Brisbane. While in Edinburgh he also had the honour of dining with the Queen (Victoria), who spoke to him after dinner and questioned him as to his Crimean campaign.

His children's earliest recollections of their father date from their sojourn in Edinburgh Castle. How they used to climb on his knee and get him to draw the castle for them, and their eagerness to catch a glimpse of him if, while playing in the gardens, the regiment marched through Princes Street. But this happy period came to an end all too quickly, and was followed by five years' separation, and 'things were never the same again.'

In May, 1857, what is known in history as the Indian Mutiny, or Sepoy Revolt, broke out. Its origin and cause need not be entered upon ; the determining cause was the greased cartridges, but probably the real cause was more remote and deep-seated, and this was only a pretext. The revolt, which took the British by surprise, spread rapidly and assumed alarming proportions ; a large number of the native regiments had mutinied, and there was only a small number of British troops in India at that time. Reinforcements were urgently needed, and among the regiments sent out was the 34th, although it had only been a year at home since serving in the Crimea.

The leave-taking between Colonel Kelly and his family made a deep impression on his children, their mother weeping and their father walking alongside the railway-carriage as long as was possible, speaking words of hope and comfort.

His wife took a house in Waterloo Terrace, Dublin, and here her second son, Richard Makdougal Brisbane Francis, was born on September 24. He was named Brisbane after his godfather, Sir Thomas Brisbane, Colonel of the 34th, and Makdougal after Lady Brisbane, his godmother.

Colonel Kelly embarked with the regiment on August 7 in the *Golden Fleece*. The voyage was round the Cape, and was the quickest on record, though it took sixty-seven days. They landed at Calcutta and proceeded to Cawnpore, at which place they arrived in time to take part in the battle of November 26, 27, and 28. Unfortunately none of his letters during the year 1857 can be found, so that details of the voyage out, first arrival in India, and of his share in the Cawnpore Campaign and the Relief of Lucknow are not available. Information about this year is therefore necessarily very meagre—indeed, a bare outline.

The most tragic incident of the Indian Mutiny was the massacre at Cawnpore. Nana Sahib, the adopted son of a deposed Indian Prince, had been refused by the British Government what he considered an adequate pension, and was not recognised as the rightful heir of his adoptive father (according to Hindu custom). The Nana formed a deeply-laid plot of revenge. The British garrison under Sir Hugh Wheeler were entrenched in an almost indefensible position, and were being hard pressed by the attacking force of sepoys; the Nana was outwardly friendly and carried on negotiations with Wheeler; he offered an asylum to the women and children at his palace at Bithoor. Fortunately, his offer was declined, but still there was no suspicion of treachery, and when the Nana offered a safe-conduct to the garrison to Allahabad it was accepted. The offer was an act of the blackest treachery, intended to lure them to destruction. Slowly the miserable, emaciated garrison, accompanied by the women and children, walked down the long mile from the entrenchment to the river, where they found boats awaiting them to convey them, as they hoped, to Allahabad. Scarcely were they in the boats when the foul treachery of the plot burst upon them. The rebels opened fire upon them from the shore, the boats were set fire to, those endeavouring to escape were shot or sabred in the water. Efforts to shove the boats off were unavailing—they stuck fast in the mud of the bank; only one succeeded in getting afloat, and but four out of the whole number escaped. At last an order was issued to spare the women and children, and they were marched back again and imprisoned; but at the approach of General Havelock they were brutally massacred, and the dying and the dead thrown down a well, over which the beautiful monument of a stern avenging angel has been raised. Cawnpore was reoccupied by British troops, but the author of all the cruel treachery had fled for his life and escaped.

All this happened in July. In November Cawnpore was again the scene of a battle. The garrison was under the command of General Windham. The position was threatened by the revolted Gwalior contingent under Tantia Topi, the Nana's General. Several regiments of the newly-arrived reinforcements from England—among them the 34th—were sent to resist the attack. General Windham divided his force into two brigades. One was under the command of Colonel Kelly. This brigade did good service. The 34th repulsed a charge of the enemy's cavalry and temporarily disabled them. Colonel Kelly then led the 34th at the enemy's guns and captured three of them, upon which the enemy fled and were pursued for some distance. Unluckily, General Windham did not follow up his advantage, but, drawing his troops off, marched back towards the city. Tantia Topi took advantage of this retrograde movement to make a fresh attack. The 34th were sent to join Brigadier Carthew's brigade in defending the approaches to the town, but later in the day General Windham, finding his own position untenable, sent for the 34th to reinforce him.

In his 'History of the Indian Mutiny' Malleson says, writing of this incident : 'At this moment Windham, to protect his retiring movement, sent for the bulk of the 34th. This regiment, which had covered itself with glory by its repulse of the enemy, was accordingly sent to reinforce the left brigade. It found that brigade in considerable disorder. The two big guns had been for the moment abandoned, and the men were falling back disheartened. The 34th came up in time to take the initiative in dashing at the big guns, and, with the aid of the sailors of the *Shannon*, in bringing them in with the retreating column.'

Next day the 34th were again transferred to Brigadier Carthew's brigade, and gallantly held the bridge under a storm of fire poured upon them from the housetops. To quote Malleson : 'But the unconquered soldiers of that splendid regiment still held on. Twice did they clear the streets in their front, twice the church compound on their right; but the continuous storm of fire of which I have spoken would not allow them to hold the positions they had gained at the point of the bayonet. More than that, the enemy shifted their position so that Chamier's guns could no longer bear on any vital point, whilst the fire from the roofs caused the defenders to drop fast.

A strong reinforcement might still have saved the position; Carthew sent for it. Pending its arrival, this gallant leader went amongst the men, cheering them and keeping them up to their work. Even when the position had become practically untenable, when the enemy had all but turned his flanks, and when the party he had sent under Colonel Simpson, of the 34th, to keep open his communications was forced back, he still held on. Still the reinforcements did not come. At last, when it was absolutely certain that unless he were to retire he would be cut off, Carthew reluctantly gave the order to fall back on the entrenchment. I have already stated that Carthew had sent for reinforcements; he received them in the shape of two companies of the Rifle Brigade as he was falling back, just in time to cover his retreat. Had Carthew not begun his retreat, the reinforcement was too small to be of much avail. . . . A strong reinforcement an hour earlier might have saved the position. Under cover of the riflemen, Carthew fell back in good order within the entrenchment. It was then quite dark. He and his officers and men had been for thirty-six hours almost without food or sleep. . . . His efforts had been splendidly supported by all under his command. In the 34th alone three officers had been killed and eight wounded.'*

One of the eight wounded was Colonel Kelly. He was hit in the chest by a ball, but did not consider the wound serious enough to desist, and continued fighting until the end of the day, when, on retiring to rest, he found the bullet in his boot.

Meanwhile the Commander-in-Chief, Sir Colin Campbell, had arrived on the other side of the river from the second relief of Lucknow, from whence he had conveyed

* 'History of the Indian Mutiny,' by Kaye and Malleson, vol. iv.

the women and children of the garrison. His victorious army was close behind him, with which he was to retrieve Windham's disaster and finally subdue Cawnpore; but before engaging in any action it was necessary to send the women and children to a place of safety. The sacred city of Allahabad, to which law and order had by this time been restored, was the place chosen, and Colonel Kelly was selected to escort them. This duty he performed in a most efficient manner, and his sympathy and thoughtful kindness to those under his care won the love and gratitude of them all.

The convoy started on December 3, and returned on December 23. Colonel Kelly's movements after that date cannot be clearly traced. In the statement of his services issued by the War Office, and filled up by his own hand, is the following entry, under date of February, 1858: 'Present with Sir Hope Grant's force on left bank of river Ganges at capture of Meangunge, Oude.' There is no mention of this action in Malleson's 'History,' so no details can be given. The next entry is 'Siege and capture of Lucknow.' The three great sieges of the Indian Mutiny were Delhi, Lucknow, and Cawnpore; of these, Lucknow was the most protracted. The siege commenced on July 1, 1857, and the garrison was relieved by General Havelock on September 25; but the relieving force were not strong enough to drive off the enemy, and were themselves besieged until the final relief by Sir Colin Campbell in November. The sick and wounded, women and children, were brought away in safety, but the city itself was still in the hands of the enemy.

As soon as Cawnpore had been finally subdued, Sir Colin Campbell proceeded to besiege the city, which had so long been besieged by the rebels. When he had quitted Lucknow to march with his large convoy to Cawnpore, he had left Sir James Outram to occupy the Alambagh, or large royal garden, just outside the city walls. On January 23 he was reinforced by ten guns, escorted by part of the 34th Regiment. They were part of the advance portion of Sir C. Campbell's force which had started from Cawnpore on December 24, the day after the return of the carriages which had conveyed the women and children to Allahabad, so, doubtless—though this is but an inference—Colonel Kelly was in command of them.

There now succeeded a series of attacks upon the various places held by the rebels between the Alambagh and the city of Lucknow, ending in the capture of the latter on March 21.

The relief of Azinghar is the next action in which Colonel Kelly took part. Here is a brief summary of the events that led to it, from Malleson's 'History of the Indian Mutiny':

'Kunwar Singh, one of the few natives of marked ability whom the Mutiny had brought to the surface, when he saw how British troops were being hurried up from every quarter to take part in the attack on Lucknow, leaving the western frontier of the British provinces bordering Oude comparatively denuded of troops, resolved to make a push for Eastern Oude, and, combining with the numerous rebels still at large in that part, to make a dash on Azinghar, and, if successful, to push on to Allahabad or Benares. Fortune greatly favoured him. At the moment when he crossed into Oude Brigadier Rowcroft at Amorha was confronting the entrenched camp of the rebels at Bulwa. His inability to storm that position had singularly encouraged the enemy; they, too, had designs on Azinghar. Still holding their camp at Bulwa, they detached a considerable force to the south-east. With these troops Kunwar Singh succeeded in effecting a junction on March 17.

'The Azinghar district was then guarded by a small British force under the command of Colonel Milman (37th Regiment). On the afternoon of March 21 Milman received from Mr. Davies, magistrate of Azinghar, the intelligence of the vicinity of the rebels. He at once broke up his camp, marched all night, and at daybreak on the 22nd came upon the advanced guard of the enemy's force, not occupying the forts, but posted in some mango-groves. Without giving them time to recover from their surprise, he attacked and defeated them.

'The enemy being dispersed, Milman determined before advancing further to give the men their breakfast. He accordingly halted in the mango-groves whence he had expelled the rebels, and his men, piling their arms, prepared to enjoy the matutinal meal. But the proverb, "There's many a slip between the cup and the lip," was literally exemplified; the breakfast was almost ready, when information was suddenly brought to Milman that the enemy were advancing in great force!

'It was too true. At last the opportunity for which Kunwar Singh had longed through so many weary months had come to him. An enemy, though European, far inferior in numbers, worn out by a long march, by want of food and sleep—an enemy twenty-five miles from his base and with no supports!

'Milman, as soon as he received the tidings, galloped forward, followed by some skirmishers, and beheld the enemy in great strength. Still, hoping that a daring movement on his part would check their further progress, he ordered an advance. But the numbers of the enemy exceeded his in the proportion of eight to one. Outflanked, it was impossible to advance. Forced back, he at least maintained a bold front. The enemy, never attempting to charge, contented themselves with a steady advance and a steady musketry fire. Once, indeed, as the British troops neared the camp at Koilsa, which they had quitted the previous evening, the rebels made a desperate effort to outflank them, but the movement was frustrated. Then, worn out and wearied, having lost many men in killed and wounded, the survivors found their way into the camping-ground of Koilsa—not, however, to discover a refuge there. The rumours of their mishap had preceded them; a panic had seized the camp-followers, most of whom had fled, taking their bullocks with them. The foe was still near; the camp was not defensible; there was no food. Milman, therefore, abandoning the camp equipage, continued his retreat to Azinghar. He reached it the same day, and, while making every preparation to defend it, sent off expresses to Allahabad, Benares, and Lucknow for assistance.'

On March 28 Sir Colin Campbell received information of Milman's disaster. His movement to repair the misfortune was prompt. On the 29th Sir E. Lugard was despatched with a brigade of infantry, which included the 34th Regiment.

'Lugard left Lucknow on March 29. The distance to Azinghar was fifteen marches. Pushing on as rapidly as possible, he reached Sultanpore on April 5. The next stage on the march was Jampore, on the right bank of the Goomtee. A few miles north-west of it, on the direct road from Sultanpore, lies the village of Tigra. Within four miles of this village a rebel force of 3,000 men and two guns had appeared on April 10, threatening Jampore. On the afternoon of April 11 Lugard reached

Tigra, and heard of the vicinity of the rebels. He had made a sixteen-miles march; his troops were exhausted; the heat of the day was excessive. He therefore resolved to remain where he was till his men should have rested and the heat be less oppressive. Towards evening, however, he received information that the rebels were on the move. He at once turned out his men, dashed after them, caught and attacked them.

'The rebels attempted for a moment to stand, but they could not resist the terrible onslaught of the cavalry. After a short resistance they turned and fled, leaving eighty killed and their two guns on the field.

'Lugard marched on next day to Didagung, relieved the Ghurkas at Jampore, and then pushed on to Azinghar. On the 14th he was within seven miles of that place. Azinghar was still invested by the force under Kunwar Singh, computed to be 13,000 strong. On the approach of Lugard on the 15th, Kunwar Singh drew up his forces along the banks of the little river Tous, commanding the bridge of boats across it. Lugard attacked the rebels with great vigour, but for some time he failed to make an impression on them; they held the bridge of boats, and it was not until they had by their long resistance insured the safety of their comrades that they fell back. Lugard then crossed the Tous and sent cavalry in pursuit of the rebels. The pursuers had a gallop of twelve miles before they caught sight of them, and then, instead of a defeated and scattered host seeking safety in flight, they came upon a body of men retiring unbroken and in good order. But the pursuers did not hesitate; they charged, to make, however, no impression. "It was all we could do," wrote one of the officers engaged, "to hold our own against such odds. Immediately our cavalry charged they stood and formed square, and used to abuse and tell us to come on." The loss of the British was considerable.

'Lugard, after crossing the Tous, had pitched his camp, and, drawing to himself the garrison of Azinghar, was preparing to move actively against the rebels, but the moment he received the report of the pursuing column halted at Nathunpore he despatched reinforcements to it.

'Lugard remained at Azinghar, occupied in clearing the surrounding country, but, having heard that Kunwar Singh had crossed the Ganges, he set off with a portion of his brigade, crossed the sacred stream on the 3rd and two following days of May, and marched at once to the neighbourhood of Arah.'

Then followed a series of skirmishes, in which the British troops suffered much from heat and exposure to the sun, and Sir E. Lugard himself, wearied and broken by the unparalleled hardships of the campaign, was forced by the state of his health to resign his command and proceed to England. He was succeeded by Brigadier Douglas.

It was not till the end of the year that the districts under his command were completely cleared of rebels. The campaign had been more trying, more fatiguing, than many that are counted more glorious in their results. Never had troops in India made longer or more continuous marches. On one occasion the infantry marched twenty-six miles a day for five days.

The next and last entry on the official list of Colonel Kelly's services in India is: 'Defeat of rebels under Bala Rao near Bootwal, on the Nepaul frontier, 25th to 28th March, 1859.' Here follows an abstract of Malleson's account of this action:

'Sir Hope Grant reached Balranpore on December 16. There he learned that Bala Rao, brother of Nana Sahib, had taken refuge in the fort of Tulsipore with a number of followers and eight guns. Grant at once directed Rowcroft to attack Tulsipore. He found the enemy drawn up to receive him, beat them after a feeble resistance, but could not pursue them for want of cavalry. Hope Grant, fearing that they should escape, took up the pursuit himself, and, cutting off Bala Rao from Gorrockpore, ascertained that he had retreated with 6,000 men and six guns along the margins of the jungle. Manœuvring with great skill, and placing his columns in a position so that escape to any other quarter than Nepaul was impossible, Grant moved against them on January 4, 1859, and drove them across the border, taking all their guns. The province of Oude was now cleared of rebels and the Mutiny practically crushed out. The province was left under the military care of Sir H. Grant, who was instructed to keep the frontier of the border of Nepaul closely shut up, so as to prevent, if possible, the escape of any rebels into the lower country.'

From one side only—that of Nepaul—was further danger to be apprehended. The then ruler of Nepaul, Maharajah Jang Bahadur, was friendly to the British, and not only did he refuse to protect the rebels who took refuge in his territory, but allowed British troops to cross the border to disarm them. Under this permission Brigadier Horsford early in the year entered the Sonar Valley, and, crossing the Rapti, came upon a body of rebels and captured fourteen guns. Later on Colonel Kelly, of the 34th, caused the surrender of six guns after having chased the rebels with great loss under the hills. The events of 1859 are chronicled in the letters of that year. Here follows a brief outline of them :

After the capture of the guns on the frontier, Colonel Kelly was sent at the head of a large force into Nepaul to hunt for Nana Sahib, who had taken refuge there. He was not successful in actually capturing him, but the Nana completely disappeared, and has never been heard of since. He most likely perished miserably in the jungle.

The following letters and despatches refer to this campaign. The latter Colonel Kelly used to write sitting under the table in his tent, on account of the great heat.

Letter from Brigadier Carthew.

MOOSANUGGUR,
January 15, 1858.

MY DEAR COLONEL,

I arrived at this place, called Moosanuggur, this morning, and shall move to-morrow morning to Bhoogneepore. I just write this line to let you know where we are, and do not think we shall fall in with the enemy anywhere in our route, for as soon as they hear of our movements they are off elsewhere. The information now brought to the Collector is that they have all crossed back again into Calpee (?). During the night the Collector expects the return of the men whom he has sent out for information, and if anything particular is brought in I will let you know to-morrow from Bhoogneepore.

If not detained for any object, I shall the following day (Sunday, the 17th) proceed from Bhoogneepore towards Cawnpore.

All well in this camp, and I hope you and the 34th are the same.

Yours sincerely,
M. CARTHEW.

To Colonel Kelly, H.M. 34th.

From Sir Hope Grant.

LUCKNOW,
March 28, 1859

MY DEAR KELLY,

I congratulate you on your success in having taken four guns from the rebels at Bootwal (?). I sent —— and Colonel —— to catch them if they come as far up as these parts. I have received a telegram from the C.-in-C. directing me to order you to report to me direct for the future. In the event of your requiring any further instructions for your guidance in the prosecution of the services in which you are engaged you are to address yourself to me. I should hope this last licking you have given them will make them see the folly of holding out longer. I trust you are healthy still, and I do not fear any danger till the rains begin, but you must not allow your men to drink of the Terai waters.

—— must know also of your having turned out the army from Bootwal (?), and I shall telegraph to him. I have sent you 600 . . . of the 9th Punjaub Infantry, which must be near Gorrokpore by this. . . .

I shall be surprised if these rebels ever show their heads outside the jungle. I hear they are suffering much from climate (?), and are in a sad plight.

Let me know, please, how you are getting on, and if there is any chance of these scoundrels breaking up. Don't hesitate in sending part of Smith's force anywhere to the . . . into Oude should you think it necessary.

Ever yours sincerely,
HOPE GRANT,
Major-General.

MEMOIR OF GENERAL SIR RICHARD DENIS KELLY 35

Letter from Brigadier-General Carthew.

FUTTEHPORE,
April 24, 1858.

MY DEAR COLONEL,

I received your note yesterday, and hasten to reply to it in the best manner that I am able. It has been a great source of regret to me that my despatch of the operations of those three days was never published. I forwarded it to General Windham as soon as I was able, of which he acknowledged the receipt, at the same time telling me his own had already gone in, but that mine should be forwarded by express. It was, as you know, never published, nor was Major Walpole's, who commanded the other brigade on the 27th and 28th.

Had General Windham waited a little for these two despatches before he sent in his own, it is probable his would not have contained the misstatements and omissions which it did. I shall ever have a most gratifying recollection of the honour conferred on me by having the 34th placed under my command on the 27th and 28th. How could you suppose I could have any reason for not being perfectly satisfied with the manner in which the duties of those days were performed by your regiment? Far, far from it; nothing could have surpassed the steadiness and gallantry of the 34th on those days, particularly on that trying occasion on the bridge, when we were fired at the whole day without being able to get at an enemy.

I was supported throughout that day in the most able manner by yourself as commanding the regiment, and by your two next most excellent officers, Colonels Simpson and Gwilt, and every officer and man did his duty cheerfully and gallantly. But it has fallen upon us all that, because the result of the three days' opera-

3—2

tions was not successful, our services should not have been acknowledged.

General Windham's remarks on me were even more disparaging than if my name had not been mentioned at all, and on the 27th I am ignored altogether. He could not have known the full circumstances of the 27th and 28th when he sent in his despatch; had he done so, he would not have written as he did.

I should be delighted to have the pleasure of meeting you again. In the meantime, believe me,

Yours very truly,
M. CARTHEW,
Brigadier.

Lieut.-Colonel Kelly, commanding 34th.

Note on Back of Letter.—Brigadier Carthew, April 24, 1858, respecting Cawnpore affair of November 28, 1857.

From Sir W. Mansfield.

ALLAHABAD,
October 7, 1858.

MY DEAR COLONEL,

I enclose copy of instructions sent to Sir Hope Grant, who, as you will observe, has been directed to move on . . . in order that he may be in the best position to co-operate with you, and bring you the assistance of heavy guns. The 73rd is wanted for the defence of the district you are about to leave, and must on no account be diverted from it, as Brigadier Douglas is about to give the *coup de grace* at Sugdenpore (?). You should make over the command of your district formally to the officer commanding H.M. 73rd Foot on leaving Azinghar. Major-General Campbell has been requested to send you a staff officer, who, I presume, is *en route* to join you; a commissariat officer is also on the road. I do not understand whether Mr. Elliot belongs to Azinghar or to Oudh; let me hear on this point.

There is a great difficulty about the steamer plan, as no one knows the river, and it appears to me a very doubtful advantage for a vessel to be groping and sounding when she might at any moment have to go into action. However, it will have the attention of the Commander-in-Chief and of the Government.

I hope you have all you want. It is much to be regretted we were not previously informed about the country on the right bank of the Gogra. We were told that the . . . (word illegible) of a few hundred men and two guns of the Akbusson . . . (word illegible) was all that was required. Otherwise the arrangements we made would have been ordered before.

I hope to hear that you will have started by the 9th.

Yours very truly,

W. MANSFIELD.

Colonel Kelly, C.B., Azinghar.

N.B.—The 9th is the day I have indicated to Sir Hope Grant as the day likely for you to start. I enclose copy of telegraphic message sent you this morning.

From Sir W. Mansfield.

ALLAHABAD,
September 23, 1858.

MY DEAR COLONEL,

Major Gryll's battery will be attached to you *pro tem.*, and we are sending you a regiment of irregular cavalry. When joined by these two bodies, you will advance to Akberpore, in Oudh, so as to tighten the cordon and clear the whole country of rebels. The officers commanding at Sultanpore and Fyzabad will both be told to look out and aid you to your right and left in attacking rebels who may be driven westward by your movement.

You will, of course, communicate with Fyzabad and Sultanpore, announcing the date of your march and scope of your instructions. You should also, to save all chance of mistake, communicate with Mr. St. George Tucker, the Deputy-Commissioner of Fyzabad. Colonel Payn, H.M. 53rd, commands a small column about ten miles from the left bank of the Goomtee, between Sultanpore and Fyzabad.

You will have the goodness to make him also acquainted with the date of your advance.

Captain Needham, 10th Foot, whom you propose as a staff officer, is the . . . of the Dinapore Division. You should have some man who can talk the language well, and is acquainted with the native manners and ways.

Lord Clyde desires me to say he is much pleased with the prudence and discretion with which you have lately managed your command.

I shall be obliged to you to write to me privately about all your operations and instructions. This becomes necessary in anticipation of public despatches, that no harm may be incurred in the communication of alteration of instructions from the Commander-in-Chief.

A full instruction will be sent you through Brigadier-General Campbell at . . . (name illegible).

            I am, my dear Colonel,
                  Yours very truly,
                      W. MANSFIELD.

Colonel Kelly, C.B., Azinghar.

Telegram from Headquarters.

From Headquarters, Meeran, the Terai, March 12.
From the Quartermaster-General's Office.
To Fyzabad. To Lieutenant-Colonel Kelly, commanding Field Force on the Gomdack (?). Words 146, S.R.

FYZABAD ELECTRIC TELEGRAPH OFFICE, 4 P.M.,
March 13, 1859.

Lord Clyde has received your letter of March 8 and telegram of same date. He entirely approves of your having sent Colonel Simpson to Nichloul (?), and of your remaining yourself at Buguhaghat until you have ascertained that the means used by the rebels at Leeranlieghat had either been removed within our territory or destroyed. The Nepaul Durbar has given full authority to cross the border. Ascertain from the civil officer who accompanied you if operations in the Terai can be conducted during the next fortnight without seriously risking the health of the troops; if they can, you have permission to attack the enemy in any position which would not involve the necessity of your remaining more than a few days in the Terai.

Send copies of all your letters and telegrams addressed to headquarters to General Sir H. Grant.

From Brigadier Rowcroft.

GORROCKPORE,
March 31, 1859.

I send you a thousand congratulations on your grand success over the rebels on March 28; also to your good officers and good troops, and to Sheikh Khywodeen. I received your letter of 28th, and Khywodeen's this morning. As I have orders now also to report by telegraph intelligence to Government, Calcutta, I sent off a telegram this morning to Calcutta, to Quartermaster-General, Army Headquarters, and to Grant, Lucknow; also to Lieutenant-Governor, Allahabad, and Wingfield, Chief-Commissioner of Oude, at Seetapore, just now. The following is a copy:

'Colonel Kelly's force attacked the rebels again on March 28, near Bootwal, with great success, capturing 6 elephants, 30 camels, 300 horses and ponies, a great deal of baggage, many prisoners, and a quantity of arms thrown away by the rebels; about 400 rebels killed. The mass of the rebels driven over the first hills; others fled westward. The Begum, Kula Rao, and Nana supposed to have gone to second hills. Mirzah Nallir with 50 followers surrendered after the action; several chiefs wrote wishing to surrender. British loss: 5 killed and 9 wounded!'

I also learned later to-day, through Mr. Morgan's letter to officer commanding, that the —— of Fyzabad and one of the Begums of Lucknow, with one or two other influential persons, had given themselves up as prisoners to your civil officer, Dr. M. Khywodeen, and had been sent to Fyzabad under escort. This goes off by telegram this evening. . . .

You must have had a deal of perplexing bother; and you can now fancy what I went through all last year and the end of 1857. I hope you have found Khywodeen useful; I thought he would be so in various ways to you; he had . . . so much to do here I had some little difficulty for a day or two in getting him sent up to you.

I am very happy your loss has been so slight, and that by God's blessing you have been able to do so much in such a difficult country, and under many other difficulties, and that you all appear to keep healthy. Your letters of 24th and 26th came in at last only yesterday morning. I sent them off at once, and explained to Grant their miscarrying. You wrote me you were going to blockade the rascals a little longer on your ground near Bootwal. I was going to write to you I thought it was a good plan, as the troops kept healthy; but I hear you will be at Lotem to-day with your whole force, perhaps a matter of supplies, as all the rebels have cleared away over the hills.

Yours sincerely,
ROWCROFT.

To Colonel Kelly, C.B.,
    Commanding Field Force.

From Sir Hope Grant.

May 30, 1859.

MY DEAR KELLY,

    I don't see any objection to your forwarding an application for leave of absence for the four or five officers whom you wish to go. The crisis is, I think, now over. I think it is but fair that your officers should get a little leave. With regard to the officer who is D.A. Quartermaster-General of the Dinapore Division, I should think there will now be no objection to his joining his appointment, but you had better make an application to that effect and I will forward (it) to the C.-in-C. I shall be happy to allow you to go for two months to Calcutta.

I think we have driven out the rebels from this country, and I hardly think they will venture to enter it again. After taking Bala Rao's two guns, we went up the Jerwa (?) Pass to Guruchee (?), but I found it of such a difficult nature that I gave up all idea of crossing the force into Denkur (?).

I am now on my way to Lucknow, where I shall get on the 4th inst.

                Am [yours] very sincerely,

                          HOPE GRANT.

To Colonel Kelly, C.B.,
   Commanding 34th Regiment, Fyzabad.

From Sir Hope Grant.

                    NEAR BURRUMPORE,
                          May 6, 1859.

MY DEAR KELLY,

With regard to Simpson's force, should you think it advisable you can move it higher up, wherever you may think best; but I would like you to shut up these jungles principally to the south and east. Rowcroft writes that there are still portions (?) of rebels along the upland frontier as far to the east as Bootwal, and he thinks it better to let Henry's force remain at Jotum (?). I have told him to do so, and he wishes also to know if, in case of emergency, he might take any (of) Murray's force from you. I have told him that you must have the management of that force for the present, but that as soon as the country is clear you can make it over to him. He wishes the Jât Horse with Murray to go to Henry, and to be replaced by Pinckney. I have told him he (may) make this change, but to write to you about it. I hear you have got the jungles about you pretty nearly cleared, and I expect to join Pinckney in a few days and get them drawn out of the Nepaul frontier. I should have been at Bulrumpore to-day, but have been tied down by the heavy rain of last night.

                Am yours very sincerely,

                          J. HOPE GRANT.

To Colonel Kelly, C.B., commanding at Bungaon.

Note from Colonel Kelly.

BUNGAON,
May 8, 6 *p.m.*

DEAR BRIGADIER,

I send you this, just received, which please return. I think it would be very inexpedient at present to withdraw Murray from Doomeria (?), as it appears to me that his is the only post now on the Raptee or in that part of the district, all the others having been withdrawn. I do not think there can be any large force of rebels near Bootwal, as we have heard of so many of them going W. I should have thought a small force would have sufficed at Jotum, but Mr. Piper naturally likes to have a force near his property.

Please let me know what force is at . . . (three names, all illegible).

Yours truly,
R. D. KELLY.

DESPATCHES.

Extract from General Orders, Military Department, dated Fort William, April 21, 1859. *No.* 558 *of* 1859.

His Excellency the Governor-General in Council is pleased to direct the publication of the following letter from the Deputy-Adjutant-General of the Army, No. 93 of the 17th inst., with enclosures reporting the recent operations of a column employed under Colonel Kelly, C.B., of Her Majesty's 34th Regiment, against the rebels who had taken refuge in the borders of Nepaul.

His Excellency in Council highly commends the conduct of Colonel Kelly and of the officers and troops employed on the occasion.

No. 93 : *From the Deputy-Adjutant-General of the Army to the Secretary to the Government of India, Military Department.*

HEADQUARTERS CAMP, DELHI,
April 6, 1859.

SIR,

I have the honour, by the desire of the Commander-in-Chief, to transmit for the information of His Excellency the Governor-General in Council, documents as per margin, relative to the recent operations of a column employed under Colonel Kelly, C.B., of Her Majesty's 34th Regiment, against the rebels who had taken refuge in the borders of Nepaul.

Lord Clyde considers that Colonel Kelly has discharged the duty entrusted to him in a most successful manner, and that he and the officers and troops employed under him are deserving of the approbation of the Government.

I am to beg you will submit his Lordship's recommendation in favour of the men of the Jât Horse, whose gallantry is reported by Colonel Kelly. . . .

I have, etc.,
(Signed) H. W. NORMAN,
Major, Deputy-Adjutant-General of the Army.

List of Documents referred to.

I. Despatch (in original) from Colonel R. D. Kelly, C.B., dated March 26, 1859, with returns of casualties and captured ordnance.

II. Despatch (in original) of Colonel R. D. Kelly, C.B., dated March 28, 1859.

III. Copy of a telegram from Brigadier Rowcroft, C.B., dated April 4, 1859.

No. 176 A.: *From Colonel R. D. Kelly, commanding troops, Nepaul Frontier, to the Chief of the Staff, Army Headquarters Camp, near Bootwal.*

NEPAUL,
March 26.

SIR,
With reference to my letter No. 156 of 24th inst. to the Quartermaster-General of the Army, I have now the honour to report for the information of his lordship the Commander-in-Chief that I left Kajooreah at 4 a.m. on the 25th inst., for the purpose of attacking the rebels, said to be in force at a place called . . . (name illegible), in the heart of the Terai, with the force named in the margin. [Margin: J Field Battery R.A.—4 officers, 88 non-commissioned officers and gunners; 4 guns. Jât Horse—4 English officers, 23 native ditto, 464 sabres. 3rd Sikh Infantry—4 English officers, 18 native ditto, 766 non-commissioned officers and privates. 7th Punjaub Infantry—4 English officers, 15 native ditto, 573 non-commissioned rank and file.]

2. At Beturhe (?) I halted the column for about an hour, whilst I went forward with a troop of cavalry to reconnoitre the jungle about three miles in our front, but could see nothing of the enemy's outposts, although the villagers told me they had been there early that morning.

3. I accordingly advanced the column, and, covered by a strong line of skirmishers of the 3rd Sikh Infantry, we proceeded through a thick jungle, with occasional open spaces, where a resolute enemy might have occasioned us heavy loss.

4. On reaching . . . (name illegible) we learnt that some of the rebels had proceeded west, while others had gone on towards Bootwal. I determined to continue my march

towards that place, being of opinion that the majority of them would try to escape by a road running west from Bootwal through the jungle under the first range of hills, being the same by which they entered Nepaul.

5. Here I was obliged to leave the detachment Her Majesty's 13th Light Infantry, as, by some misapprehension, they had not brought cooked rations with them, and had to halt to give the men a meal; and I considered the force with me sufficiently strong for pursuit, and was anxious to lose no time.

6. When within two or three miles of Bootwal, about 4 p.m., the cavalry flankers on our left reported the enemy as being in force in some topes in the open country on our left skirting the jungle.

7. I immediately desired Captain Rennie to cover our advance in that direction with the 3rd Sikhs thrown out in skirmishing order. I formed the rest of the column in line to the left: the four guns of the J Field Battery, R.A. being on the left of the 7th Punjaub Infantry, and a squadron of Murray's Jât Horse on each flank of the line, and in that order proceeded towards the enemy.

8. I left the baggage in rear in charge of two companies 7th Punjaub Infantry and one troop Jât Horse. I also sent an express to . . . (name illegible) to bring up the detachment 13th Light Infantry, who, although they used every exertion, were not able to arrive till after the affair was over, much to the regret of Lieutenant-Colonel King his officers and men.

9. After proceeding about half a mile, we came on the enemy, posted in a good position, his right resting on an elevated ridge, and his line extending through topes strongly occupied by infantry, to the jungle on which their left rested, and in which they had large bodies of men. They had guns on both flanks, which were all

covered by strong bodies of cavalry, of whom they had at least 1,200 in the field, with about 4,000 infantry visible. Indeed, prisoners have since informed us that the whole of the rebel army was on the ground under the command of Bala Rao. The ground in their front was intersected by nullahs and deep irrigation channels, which offered great obstacles to the rapid progress of the guns.

10. The skirmishers of the 3rd Sikhs, ably directed by Captain Rennie, soon drove the left of the enemy into the jungle, while the sharp fire of Major Henry's guns made them leave the topes. Their cavalry on each flank made an attempt to turn our flanks and get at the baggage in our rear, but were promptly stopped on our right by the fire of the two companies of the 7th Punjaub Infantry under the command of Lieutenant Gordon, H.M. 61st Regiment, the second in command, whom Captain Stafford had most judiciously ordered to change front to the right, and by a dashing charge made on them by Major Murray with a squadron of Jât Horse.

11. The rebel cavalry on the left were similarly dispersed by a charge which I directed Lieutenant Chalmers, second in command Jât Horse, to make on them with his squadron, which he led most gallantly, killing two men with his own hand. The squadron then wheeled to the right and took a gun on the ridge, and a general advance of the whole line and guns drove the enemy across the nullah into the jungle, several of them being cut down in the open plain by our cavalry.

12. On the edge of the jungle, the Sepoys made a stand for some time, and their fire, I regret to say, caused several casualties among men and horses of our cavalry, who were then in advance; but the skirmishers of the 3rd Sikh and 7th Punjaub Infantry, and the discharge

of some rounds of case from the guns which rapidly came up, inflicted heavy loss on them and put them to flight.

13. It was now nearly six o'clock, and would soon be too dark to act in the jungle; the men and horses had been out since 4 a.m., and had marched from eighteen to twenty miles, mostly under a burning sun, besides being engaged for two hours. We had taken four guns on the field, besides two which were found the following day abandoned by the enemy, together with sixteen cart-loads of ammunition and a gilded howdah, supposed, from the royal fish of Oude carved on it, to have belonged to the Begum.

14. I accordingly pitched my camp, having previously sent patrols of cavalry along the road leading west. The rebels retired through the jungle into the hills, where we saw their fires burning at a considerable elevation. Their loss must have been severe in killed and wounded, judging from the bodies found in the open plain and the number stated by native reports to be in the jungle. Our casualties amounted to thirty-six, of which I enclose a numerical and nominal return, together with a list of captured ordnance.

15. It only remains for me to draw the attention of His Excellency to the admirable manner in which officers and soldiers of all ranks, both British and native, behaved in their steadiness under fire, and their patient endurance of heat and fatigue, and to bring to the favourable notice of Lord Clyde the name of Major Henry, R.A., commanding J Field Battery; Major Murray, commanding Jât Horse, to whom I am particularly indebted, not only for the able manner in which he commanded his corps on this occasion but also for the zeal and readiness which he has invariably displayed since he has been under my command, in reconnoitring

and procuring intelligence; Captain Rennie, commanding 3rd Sikh Infantry, a most admirable Light Infantry corps; Captain Stafford, commanding 7th Punjaub Infantry; Lieutenant Cochrane, Her Majesty's 34th Regiment, my staff officer, who is always most indefatigable in the discharge of his duty; Lieutenant Fitzgerald, Her Majesty's 13th Light Infantry, who acted as my orderly officer.

16. I have also to express my sense of the exertions of all the medical officers of corps in their attention to the wounded, particularly Assistant-Surgeon MacWellar, Jât Horse, the senior present, and whose corps had by far the greatest number of wounded. Major Murray also mentioned his being most useful and active in carrying orders for him during the action.

I must also mention the name of Ensign Hennessy, Her Majesty's 24th Regiment, Adjutant of the Jât Horse, a most promising young officer, and who, by remaining on the piquet for three days, watching the enemy's outposts, before I entered the Terai, was able to furnish me with reliable intelligence and a sketch of the country.

I am also much indebted to Mr. Piper, Deputy-Magistrate, who accompanied me into Nepaul, for the very useful information he has afforded me respecting this part of the country. Sheikh Khywodeen Achmed, Deputy-Magistrate, attached to this force, has also been most useful in procuring intelligence.

17. Major Murray has also brought to my notice the names of the following native officers and men of the Jât Horse who particularly distinguished themselves on this occasion on charging a gun, viz., . . .* and I trust they may be suitably rewarded.

I enclose Major Murray's letter, forwarding their

* Here follows a list of names.

names, and also a letter from Major Henry, R.A., detailing the proceedings of the J Field Battery during the day.

> I have, etc.,
> (Signed) R. D. KELLY,
> *Colonel 34th Regiment, commanding troops Nepaul Frontier.*

(Here follows a table showing the actual state of the field force under his command, and a detailed nominal list of the killed and wounded.)

From Colonel R. D. Kelly, commanding Field Force, to the Quartermaster-General of the Army, Army Headquarters.

CAMP NEAR BOOTWAL,
March 28, 1859.

SIR,

I have the honour to report to you, for the information of His Excellency the Commander-in-Chief, that, the force under Lieutenant-Colonel Simpson having joined me yesterday, I carried out my plan of attacking the rebels in the first range of hills, whither they had retreated after their defeat on the 25th.

At daylight this morning, having established a chain of piquets of infantry, cavalry, and artillery skirting the jungle, in order to cut off their retreat, I formed two columns composed of the 3rd Sikhs and 7th Punjaub Infantry respectively, 100 rank and file of Her Majesty's 13th Regiment Light Infantry being attached to each, which ascended the hills at different points, and beat the jungle to the summit of the ridge, driving the mass of the rebels completely over the first range of hills, killing from 300 to 400 of them, and taking a quantity of arms of all sorts, 6 elephants, and about 25 camels and 300 horses and ponies.

The columns were most ably led by Captains Rennie and Stafford, commanding respectively the 3rd Sikhs and the 7th Punjaub Infantry, and they deserve the greatest credit for the manner in which they so successfully carried out my instructions. All officers and men engaged were animated with the greatest ardour, and seemed entirely to disregard the toil of fighting their way up a steep hillside covered with dense jungle, under a burning sun, and opposed by a numerous if not a resolute foe, who had also the advantage of a superior position. I trust soon to be able to transmit for His Excellency's information a report of their proceedings from Captains Stafford and Rennie. Our casualties amounted to, I regret to say, five killed and nine wounded; among the latter was Lieutenant-Adjutant Ballie, 7th Punjaub Infantry, a most excellent officer. He received a severe scalp wound on the back of his head from a musket-ball. The wound, I am happy to say, is not considered dangerous, and he is going on well. The mass of the rebels are, I hear, now between the first and second ranges of hills, where they will find it difficult to get food, which I hope will soon oblige them to surrender. The Nawab Mirza Nadir of Lucknow gave himself up to-day with about fifty followers, and Mahomed Hossein has sent in to ask for terms. The health of the troops continues very good.

I have, etc.,
(Signed) R. D. KELLY,
Colonel commanding Field Force.

Gorrockpore, April 4, via Fyzabad, April 5.
From Brigadier Rowcroft, C.B., to the Quartermaster-General of the Army, Army Headquarters, Delhi.

Mahomed Hossein, with his nephew Mahomed Nawaz, and with three other followers and six elephants, surrendered on March 31 ; also some ninety Afghans and Persians, mostly cavalry, laid down their arms and came into Colonel Kelly's camp.

True copy.
(Signed)   H. W. NORMAN,
Major, Deputy-Adjutant-General of the Army.

Extract from General Orders, Military Department, dated Fort William, May 3, 1859. No. 609 of 1859.

His Excellency the Governor-General in Council has much satisfaction in publishing the following letter from the Officiating Adjutant-General of the Army, No. 932 of April 17, 1859, forwarding detailed reports of the attack made on the insurgents in the forest range of the Nepaul hills on the 28th ultimo, by the troops under Colonel Kelly, C.B.

His Excellency in Council, while concurring with the Commander-in-Chief, in the approbation expressed by his Lordship, desires to record his thanks to Colonel Kelly, and Captains Rennie and Stafford in command of columns, and the officers and troops employed on this occasion.

No. 932 : *From the Officiating Adjutant-General of the Army to the Secretary to the Government of India, Military Department.*

HEADQUARTERS CAMP,
April 17, 1859.

SIR,

In continuation of my letter of the 6th inst., No. 93, I have the honour, by the direction of the Commander-in-Chief, to transmit, for the information of His Excellency the Governor-General in Council, detailed reports of the attack made on the insurgents in the first range of the Nepaul hills on the 28th ultimo, by the troops under Colonel R. D. Kelly, C.B., of Her Majesty's 34th Foot.

2. Lord Clyde desires to record his approval of Colonel Kelly's arrangements, and to recommend to the favourable notice of the Governor-General Captains Rennie and Stafford, in command of columns, and the officers and troops employed.

3. His Lordship further solicits the bestowal of the Third Class of the Order of Merit upon the native officers and soldiers of the 3rd Sikh Infantry and 7th Punjaub Infantry who are specially brought to notice.

I have, etc.,
(Signed)   H. W. NORMAN,
Major, Officiating Adjutant-General of Army.

Extract from a letter from the Secretary to the Government of India, Military Department, to the Chief of the Staff, dated Council Chamber, Fort William, May 19, 1859.

2. The Governor-General in Council highly appreciates the good judgment of the officers and the discipline of

the troops which have marked the conduct of their troublesome and harassing operations.

3. His Excellency in Council never for one moment attached any importance to the stories which were circulated from Nepaul respecting the burning of villages and other flagrant acts of violence attributed to the British troops. It was certain from the beginning that false complaints of this nature would be made by one or other of the factions into which the Nepaulese are divided, and this was one of the reasons which made it desirable to avoid sending our troops across the frontier, if this had been possible.

4. The Governor-General in Council fully concurs in the opinion that no time should be lost in sending the troops into quarters.

5. The Chief Commissioners of Oude will be instructed to make arrangement immediately, in concert with Major-General J. H. Grant, for guarding the frontier as effectively as may be possible by the police and the native services.

True extract.
(Signed) H. W. NORMAN,
Major, Officiating Adjutant-General of the Army.

True copy.
W. P. LEESON,
Lieutenant-Adjutant, H.M. 34th Regiment.

During this campaign Colonel Kelly contracted jungle fever, which left him so weak that those who assisted him into his dooley never expected to see him again. He was taken to the house of a friend, and the rest, together with his wonderful recuperative powers, so restored him that in a few days he felt so well that he wrote to Sir H. Grant, requesting that he might be allowed to rejoin, which he accordingly did.

Colonel Kelly was thanked by the Governor-General in Council on May 19, 1859, for the judgment shown by him in the operations of the troops under his command employed in Nepaul. He was also mentioned in the despatches of General Windham, Sir H. Grant, Sir E. Lugard, and Lord Clyde. The Chief of the Staff says in a letter to the Military Secretary to the Government of India: 'Colonel Kelly acted in accordance with his instructions and with great spirit; he advanced with rapidity, pressed the enemy hard, and defeated him twice with considerable loss, taking seven guns, and eventually turning the whole body to the westward.'

Meanwhile, in October, 1858, his wife went out to join him, leaving their five children under the care of Miss Lowe, who had formerly been Mrs. Kelly's governess, assisted by the nursery-governess, Miss Lebel (Mia), who was her niece. A house was taken in Dublin, where they lived for one year, going to the seaside in the summer. They then removed to Guernsey, going by sea to Southampton, and I have never forgotten, after a lapse of more than forty years, coming on deck in the morning while the vessel was anchored in Falmouth Harbour, and seeing a field of golden corn sloping down to meet the blue waters of the harbour, all flooded with brilliant sunshine.

When Mrs. Kelly arrived at Bombay, she heard the unwelcome news that her husband had been ordered to take the field again, and it was quite uncertain when they should meet. This was a most distressing situation for her, as she had no friends in India; but she was not long left in loneliness. Her cabin companion on the voyage out was a Mrs. Mackenzie, who had friends in

Bombay, Mr. and Mrs. Spooner. He was Commissioner of Customs. To them she told the sad plight of her friend left high and dry on the shores of India, and with characteristic Anglo-Indian hospitality they despatched her to the hotel, where she found Mrs. Kelly weeping in loneliness and sadness of heart. Mrs. Mackenzie bade her dry her tears, gave her the Spooners' hospitable invitation, and insisted upon her returning with her to their house as their guest. Here Mrs. Kelly remained for three months, and formed a lifelong friendship with her kind and hospitable host and hostess—a friendship afterwards cemented by the marriage of Mr. Spooner's younger son to Mrs. Kelly's third daughter.

It was not till the following year, 1859, that Mrs. Kelly left the Spooners and went to Calcutta, where she stayed with Mr. and Mrs. Money, at 7, Old Post-Office Street, Calcutta, until her husband joined her in June.

While at Calcutta she was one day driving round the Maidan, when Sir James Outram came up to her and said: 'Your husband is doing splendidly, Mrs. Kelly.' And during her stay in India she frequently met ladies who had been among those escorted from Cawnpore to Allahabad by her husband, and who spoke in terms of warmest gratitude of his care of them and kindness to them on that journey.

Soon after Colonel Kelly joined his wife at Calcutta they went to Fyzabad, where the 34th were quartered; here, as the officers' quarters were too small and there was no bungalow available, they built a house, which was named Ellenville, and here, on November 14, 1860, their youngest daughter was born.

In India an intimate and lasting friendship was formed with Captain Wyse, of the 34th, and his wife. Captain Wyse was a Roman Catholic, and one day at mess someone spoke disparagingly of Roman Catholics in his presence; the speaker was sharply rebuked by Colonel Kelly (though himself a strong Protestant), who thereby earned the lasting gratitude of Captain Wyse, who was a deeply-religious man.

In 1860 Colonel Kelly was made a K.C.B., in recognition of his services in defeating the rebels in Nepaul.

While in India he had the sorrow of losing his mother, to whom he was much attached.

About three years were spent in Fyzabad, and then the regiment was moved to Seetapore, from whence Sir Richard and Lady Kelly returned home in 1862. It was an unfortunate journey. Lady Kelly was near her confinement, and the child was born prematurely at Suez, and only survived his birth a few hours, and when at last they reached Jersey they were weather-bound there for a week.

It was a pouring wet day in October when Sir Richard and Lady Kelly arrived at Fosse André, Guernsey, and the family was once more united. In joyful anticipation of this long-looked-for event we had decorated the house; but the 'Welcome,' cut out of gilt paper, was torn and battered by the wind and rain, and our efforts were unnoticed; it was altogether a disappointing homecoming, so different to what we had looked forward to.

The spring following their return from India Sir Richard and Lady Kelly went for a three months' tour in Italy. It was during this tour that Sir Richard paid his first visit to Rome. He was very fond of travelling, and was a most conscientious sight-seer, never satisfied unless he understood what he saw, and saw it thoroughly; this, combined with his wide reading and retentive memory, made his mind a perfect storehouse of information upon a large range of subjects.

The following spring Sir Richard and Lady Kelly took their children abroad for a month's tour in Normandy and Brittany. It was their first visit to the Continent, and a great event in their lives. The following summer they paid their first visit to London with their parents, and stayed with their father's old friend, Mrs. Collinson.

The following year Sir Richard and Lady Kelly left Guernsey and went abroad; the winter was spent at Brussels.

Sir Richard enjoyed his life in Guernsey; the people were most kind and hospitable. He was fond of walking, and would take long walks with his children through the roads and lanes of the beautiful little island. His sister Kate paid them long visits in summer, staying two or three months at a time. This was a great delight to us all, for we were devoted to her. She used sometimes to come out walking with us, and we would dispute the privilege of walking beside her. Nothing was too trivial to interest her; we were always sure of her attention and interest and sympathy.

The family left Fosse André, the villa taken on first coming to Guernsey, soon after the return of the father and mother, and moved into a larger house in Euston Terrace, looking down Vauvert Road. The little back-garden, where the children each had a patch of her own, was a source of great pleasure to them. They were fond of Guernsey, but it was then very isolated, and their parents did not care to settle in so small and out-of-the-way a place.

In the summer of 1867 Sir Richard's eldest son, Arthur, who was at Wellington College, got an attack of pleurisy, followed by slight inflammation of one lung. When well enough to be moved, he left the school, to which he never returned. The doctor recommended a winter in the South of France, and someone advised Pau; so it was settled to go there in the winter. The summer was spent between Paris, Tours, and Aix-la-Chapelle, and in October they reached Gelos, a village about a mile outside Pau, where they shared a house—the Villa Dampier —with two old ladies, who were the owners of the villa, and from whom they rented part of it.

Pau, like Heidelberg, is built on the dividing-line between flat and beautiful country. On the north side of the town stretch the monotonous *landes*, while across the Gave, a mountain stream, commence the *coteaux*, or low hills, which spread like a rippling sea of green to the foot of the magnificent snow-clad range of the Pyrenees.

The south rooms of the Villa Dampier looked across the intervening *coteaux* to this glorious range of mountains, which stretches from end to end of the horizon; in the centre the range falls apart, as it were, and the Pic du Midi rises in solitary grandeur. At times the mountains looked so near that it was difficult to believe they were thirty miles off.

A carriage and pair was hired for the winter months, but it was chiefly used for shopping and visiting in Pau. Sir Richard used to take long walks in the *coteaux*, and his eldest daughter was usually his companion. He was very fond of walking, and a good walker; they were generally accompanied by Bob, a bull-terrier given to Sir Richard by his brother-in-law, Colonel (now General) Battersby, when he was ordered out to India. No dog could have been more beloved than Bob, nor more truly mourned when he died the following summer, poisoned by a vindictive old woman in revenge for his having killed her cat.

The English chaplain at Pau was Dr. Tait. The

family attended his church; Lady Kelly and two of her daughters sang in his choir. His wife was a great invalid, but a very charming woman, and her drawing-room was always crowded when she was well enough to receive visitors. There were two sons, both at Oxford, one Fellow and Tutor at Worcester College, the other an undergraduate at Queen's.

The summer was spent at Biarritz, where the Taits also had a villa, and the two families saw a good deal of each other.

The next winter the Kellys had a house in the Rue Porte Neuve. It was there the eldest daughter first met her husband, Dr. Tait's eldest son. The following summer, which was again spent at Biarritz, they became engaged.

The family left Pau in the autumn, and took a small flat in Paris, where they spent the winter, and where, on January 6, 1870, the eldest daughter was married in the ballroom of the British Embassy to the Rev. W. J. Tait, M.A. They spent a week at Fontainebleau, a few days in Paris, and then went to Oxford, where their married life began.

The family left Paris and went to Bonn, and afterwards to Homburg, where Mr. and Mrs. Tait joined them in the summer.

There were rumours of war afloat, and many people were seriously afraid of a French invasion; war was actually declared while they were at Homburg, which broke up the party, and Sir Richard took his family to England.

A letter from Sir Richard to his brother may fitly come in here, in which he very accurately predicted the result of the war which had just broken out.

3, LUDWIG STRASSE, HOMBURG-LES-BAINS,
July 25, 1870.

MY DEAR FRANCIS,

I was very glad indeed to get your letter of the 20th inst. yesterday, just after I had posted a long letter to Annie giving her the news about ourselves, and, as no doubt she will tell you, that we are all, thank God, safe and well, although, as the Yankees would say, ' very much up a tree,' as for a few days to come we shall not be able to get away, for all the Prussian railways near this are now exclusively occupied in taking troops to their stations, and they say it is very uncertain whether the boats are now running on the Rhine; but it is very difficult to learn the truth, as you can't telegraph, and there are no end of reports flying about, very few of which are credible. I think, however, when the first of the war passes by this neighbourhood, we shall be able to get away more easily—if it does not overwhelm us, which is not likely, as all here say it is one of the safest places in Germany, for at the end of the last war they say a Convention was made exempting all these Bads from having actual hostilities carried on in them, and they are to be reserved for invalids and wounded, and I dare say the destiny of the Kursaal here will be to have its splendid saloon turned into hospital wards—perhaps a much better use of them than at present is the case; besides, this place is of no strategetical importance, as the only railway from Frankfort here leads nowhere else, and the town is too small to accommodate many troops or to furnish large contributions. I think it very probable that the French will pass near this, and that, if we can't leave very soon, we may at least hear the cannonade of a battle; for I have no doubt that for both political and strategetical reasons the French, if they win the first battle, will try to occupy Frankfort, a perfectly open town, and nine miles from this. I think it likely that if the French advance from their bases of Metz and Thionville, and that the Prussians do not stop them at Saar-Louis, they will try and cross the Rhine either at Bingen, in which case they would pass through Wiesbaden and circle round to the right on Frankfort, having their left flank covered by the Taurus Mountains, or, in order to avoid being interrupted by the strong garrison of Mayence, they might cross still higher up, somewhere near Mannheim. I dare say they will also make a diversion from Strasbourg; if they do not cross below Mayence it will be the better for us, for then the Dutch steamers, being neutral, will continue to run down the Rhine so long as actual fighting is not taking place along the banks, and if so, when we are ready, we will drive to Bibrich, as the railway from thence to Frankfort will be occupied, and there embark in a Dutch steamer, and go either to Cologne or Rotterdam, according to circumstances, and go home either via Ostend to Dover, or to London from Rotterdam. If we can't get down the Rhine we must try a circuitous route by rail to Rotterdam, via Giessen, Wesel, Dortrecht and Arnheim, which I hope may be open: they say there are only now about thirty English left in Homburg, of whom one tenth are Generals in H.B.M.S.

Ellie and Walter left here yesterday at 8 a.m. for Frankfort, that being the last day for some time to come for the railway being open for the public; and will you tell Annie that, since closing my letter to her yesterday, Mr. Reins, who went in with them to Frankfort, returned and told us that they were so fortunate as to start at 10 a.m. by the last public train that would be allowed to start for Heidelberg, and that they hoped, but were not sure, to reach Stuttgart that night; and that they would push on as fast as they could till they got to the Lake of Constance, when, being out of the probable theatre of war, they would rest a little if fatigued, and then go on through Switzerland by Zurich, Neuchâtel and Geneva to Lyons, whence they can easily go to Biarritz, where they will join the Tait family?

Last night, between ten and eleven, we all went out to see the 82nd Prussian regiment quartered here go off by rail for Frankfort and Landau (?); they turned out upwards of 1,000 strong, and almost all Hessians, I was told. Almost all the town accompanied them to the railway, and they marched through the streets singing patriotic songs in chorus; they looked a fine able-bodied set of young men, physically stronger than the French, although perhaps not so active, more like our own men, but very heavily laden. Although of the lately acquired subjects of Prussia, their detestation of the French is something extraordinary. We spoke to several of the soldiers, and they said this war was not a 'Bruder-king' like the last, but that they would give their King the last drop of their blood rather than that the French should have an inch of their Rhineland. Even at Frankfort, where till this declaration of war the Prussian soldiers were detested, they were received when passing through last week with the greatest enthusiasm by the inhabitants, who gave them brandy and other comforts as they passed along the streets. In fact, Napoleon by his arrogant and uncalled-for declaration of war has united Germany like one man against him. The French may perhaps get success at first from their better organization as an army, and the rapidity and force with which their first blows will be dealt; but I think the German firmness and resolution in the defence of their native land will prove victorious in the end. If France should prove unsuccessful, I think it will be the end of the Emperor's dynasty, and that his son will never succeed him, and that the King of Prussia will be declared Emperor of Germany, as he deserves to be. But as I think the power and resources of the two countries are so nearly matched, it will be a long, bloody and exhausting war, and that it will be difficult for neutral nations to avoid being entangled in its complications. . . . I think the Emperor has justly forfeited the sympathies of . . . Europe for causing so much bloodshed and misery of all sorts by declaring war without any just cause, *pas pour une idée même*, and I hope he will get soundly thrashed, as he deserves.

The weather has been lovely for some time past, and the corn is nearly all ripe for cutting; some has been already, and I wish it were all, so that it might escape being trodden down by the hoofs of the horses and wheels of the cannon.

5 *p.m.*—Just got a telegram from Walter; dated Zurich, 2.20 p.m., to say they had got there safely, which is a great comfort, as now we need no longer be anxious about them.

There is no doubt, from what you say in your letter, that the late Colonel F. E. Kelly was the same person I always thought he was, and was in no way related to our family. Annie told me in her last you were making great improvements in Weston, painting and doing up the house, and I am sure when finished they will recompense you for all the trouble and inconvenience you have been put to. . . . I am very glad to hear that you and poor old Donolly got compensation from the county for the malicious burning of your lodge, and I only wish the incendiary could be made to pay for the damage.

Walter, Ellie and Arthur all came to us together on the 2nd inst.; the latter, of course, goes home with us, and the others would have stayed with us at least a month only for this unfortunate war; and this was such a pleasant place and such a beautiful neighbourhood, and we were all enjoying it so much and had met so many friends.

We met a very nice old lady here, the Hon. Mrs. Hamilton, daughter of Lord Castlemaine, and sister of Colonel Handcock, who married a daughter of our old friend Lady Stannus. . . . Mrs. H. is the widow of General Hamilton, son of Hans Hamilton of Sheephill; he commanded the 97th Regiment in Ceylon for a long time, where Mrs. H. told me she knew our father, and spoke of him in the highest terms; she also told me that the daughter of Sir Everard Kennedy, and the widow of the late Sir Henry Lawrence, was her niece; is she not also a cousin of Kate? Thank you for your information about the rate of subscription to the Church Fund. I will reserve my determination on the point until I return home.

July 26.—Ellen drove in yesterday to Frankfort with two other ladies to do a little shopping, and she heard that the Dutch steamers are still going down the Rhine, and will continue to do so till stopped by actual hostilities; also that the railway on the right bank is still open, and that even if they are transporting troops, they in general (?) put on one or two passenger carriages; so as soon as I get a remittance that I expect from England, either tomorrow or next day, we will try to get to Bebrich, to embark there in a Dutch steamer for either Cologne or Rotterdam, the former if we can get on from thence to Ostend. If we arrive safe in England, we intend taking lodgings at Southboro' to be near the Prevost Battersbys till October.

With our united kind love to Kate,
Believe me,
Yours affectionately,
R. D. KELLY.

After spending a few months in England, partly in the pretty little village of Southborough, near Tunbridge Wells, where Colonel and Mrs. Battersby also had a house, Sir Richard and his family went to Dublin, and took a house at 27, Clyde Road, where they lived for three years.

In 1871 his son-in-law, the Rev. W. J. Tait, accepted the living of Long Benton, a Pit village near Newcastle-on-Tyne (in the gift of Balliol College, where he had been an undergraduate). Here Sir Richard paid them a visit, and was much interested in going down a coalmine. It was about the time of the engagement of his third daughter, and Sir Richard, who was a great letter-writer and scrupulously conscientious about answering letters, had an extra amount of correspondence; the post went out at four o'clock in the afternoon, and he used to say he was 'tied by the leg' till that hour. One day, however, he was persuaded to come for an expedition to Alnwick Park, which he much enjoyed in spite of the bad weather.

On July 25, 1872, his third daughter, Sophia Henrietta, was married in St. Bartholomew's Church, Dublin, to Hamilton William Wetherell Spooner, younger son of his old friend Mrs. Spooner, widow of Mr. Spooner of Bombay.

In the autumn of that year his son-in-law, the Rev. W. J. Tait, was given the living of Tavistock in South

Devon, by the then Duke of Bedford, on the recommendation of Dr. Jowett, Master of Balliol.

In the year 1873 the autumn manœuvres took place on Dartmoor, and Sir Richard stayed with the Taits at Tavistock for them. He was naturally much interested in them, and I remember he was rather disgusted with me at the march-past, because I thought the magnificent white billy-goat of the Welsh Fusiliers the most interesting feature of the spectacle!

In 1870 Sir R. D. Kelly succeeded to the rank of General, and in 1874 he was given the command of the Cork district through the recommendation of his old friend and brother officer, Sir Richard (afterwards Lord) Airey.

Sir Richard appointed his son-in-law, Captain H. W. W. Spooner, his A.D.C. His Deputy Assistant Quartermaster-General was Captain Charles Lacon Harvey, 71st Highland Light Infantry, who on January 7, 1875, married Sir Richard's second daughter, Annie Louisa.

There was no General's house at Cork, so Sir Richard rented Sidney House, a large old-fashioned house with a good garden, and he had the happiness of having his two daughters living quite near him.

At the close of the year 1875 a great sorrow fell upon him and the whole family. At the end of November a little girl was born to Mrs. Charles Harvey. At first all went well, but a few days after the birth of her child she developed scarlet fever. From the first there was little hope of recovery, and on December 3 she breathed her last; her baby followed her ten days after, and their earthly forms lie together in the cemetery at Cork. It was a crushing blow to her husband, her parents, and her brothers and sisters. It was virtually the first break in the home circle, for we had never seen our infant brother, and did not know of his existence until after he had passed over.

Annie Harvey was a singularly beautiful character, most unselfish and warm-hearted. She was the favourite of all her family, and no wife was ever more truly mourned; and though her husband has remarried most happily, and is surrounded by sons and daughters, her memory has never faded, nor has his love for her weakened, while his affection for her family has remained unchanged.

A memorial window was placed by her sorrowing parents in St. Luke's Church, Cork.

Such a gloom had been thrown over Cork by this great and unexpected sorrow that Sir Richard and Lady Kelly were anxious to leave it, and in 1877 the Eastern District falling vacant, Sir Richard applied for and was given it.

Meanwhile, in the summer of 1876 they went abroad for two months, and were joined by their younger son Richard, then at Marlborough College, during his school holidays. A foreign tour had been planned for the following winter, but owing to a scare of war with Russia all officers were refused foreign leave, so Sir R. and Lady Kelly, with their youngest daughter Beatrice (the only one at home now), went to London for Sir Richard's leave. They took lodgings in Sloane Street to be near the Royal Military Asylum, of which Colonel Battersby, who had married Lady Kelly's only sister, was Governor.

In February, 1877, they returned to Cork. Soon after their return their younger son met with a severe, and what but for the mercy of God would have been a fatal, accident. He and his youngest sister were starting for a ride; the horse he was riding was very fresh, and before he could get his foot into the stirrup it bolted and flung him on the road, dashing his head against the kerb. He was picked up insensible, and carried into the house of Mr. Leycester, where he remained four or five weeks, and from whom he and all the family received unbounded kindness and hospitality. He had fractured the base of his skull, and for some days lay between life and death. By God's great mercy he recovered and was restored to unimpaired health and strength. The debt of gratitude which his family owe for his preservation will be appreciated by all who know him, and know what he is to everyone connected with him.

In April of that year Sir Richard and his family left Cork, not sorry to quit a place which had been the scene of so much sorrow and anxiety, and Sir Richard took over the command of the Eastern District at Colchester. At Colchester Sir Richard rented White Hall, a pretty country house with a nice garden a mile or so out of the town. Captain and Mrs. Spooner lived about a mile off at Donyland Lodge. They remained at Colchester till the autumn of 1878, when the command expired, and went abroad for the winter. They went first to Paris, and then to the Riviera, spending Christmas at Nice. On the way thither they stopped at Avignon, where Sir Richard was interested in the old palace of the Popes, which has been turned into barracks. He also went to Nimes to see the very perfect colosseum there. From Nice they went along the Riviera to Genoa, where they stayed for a few days, and from there went on to Florence, where a month was spent. Here they were joined by their youngest son, who was now at the Royal Academy, Woolwich. From Florence they went to Rome; after a stay in Rome of about six weeks they proceeded to

Naples and Sorento, and spent Easter at La Cava. They next went to Amalfi and back to Naples. They then returned to Rome for a few days, from whence they visited the Falls of Terni. Then to Perugia, Siena and Milan, then through the Mont Cenis Tunnel to Aix-les-Bains. Here Sir Richard much enjoyed long walks through the beautiful surrounding country. From Aix-les-Bains, where Lady Kelly went through a course of waters and baths for incipient rheumatism, they went to Geneva, made a tour through Switzerland, and came home through Paris.

It was about this time that Sir Richard began to show symptoms of weak health, which continued more or less during the remainder of his life, and which but for his splendid constitution and wonderful recuperative powers might have shortened his life. It is supposed that the jungle fever, contracted while pursuing the rebels in Nepaul, was never completely eliminated from his system. He became subject to attacks of sickness and giddiness, which would come on quite suddenly, causing much anxiety to his wife and daughter; this lasted a few years, and then gradually disappeared under treatment.

He also suffered increasingly from deafness, which was probably partly congenital, as his mother and both his sisters were very deaf. It first became noticeable in him after his return from India, but grew much worse as time went on; the hearing in one ear was completely gone, and that of the other very defective. It was a great privation to him, as he could not hear general conversation, but the affliction was borne most patiently, and even cheerfully; his deafness did not make him morose or suspicious, as it is often said to do; he very rarely asked to have things repeated to him, but sometimes, when a ripple of laughter went round the family circle, one would see a wistful look in his eyes, and then whoever was nearest to him would tell him what was interesting us. One always tried to remember good stories to tell him, and repeated to him any little joke or related a humorous incident, which, with his keen sense of humour, he thoroughly appreciated.

But his deafness was not only a deprivation to him; it was also a very great loss to his family. He was naturally silent, reserved and unobservant (thoughtful persons are rarely very observant), and as he seldom heard anything that was not directly addressed to himself, many things passed in the family circle of which he was not fully cognizant, or, if so, only at second-hand, so his well-balanced judgment and strong sense of justice had not full play; it was like looking at the home life through glass, and sometimes through coloured glass.

Although naturally silent, no one could talk better on a congenial subject and to sympathetic listeners, and no one more thoroughly enjoyed real conversation; his love of reading and retentive memory enriched and stored his mind, and was a great solace to him in his declining years. He was not the least bit pedantic, and never obtruded his wide knowledge, and he never talked of himself. No one could tell a good story better or with a more keen appreciation of its humorous side, but he equally enjoyed hearing others tell their stories.

His favourite reading was history and biography, and he was a diligent newspaper-reader, for he regarded the newspapers as contemporary history. He was not a great novel-reader, nor did he care much for poetry, with the exception of Shakespeare, whom he knew intimately.

In the autumn of 1879 Sir Richard and his family settled near Reading. They rented Berkeley House, a villa on the Bath Road, and resided there till the summer of 1883. They liked the neighbourhood of Reading, and had made many friends there, and in the summer of that year Sir Richard purchased a house in the parish of Earley, about two miles from Reading. It was a pretty two-storied house, with a conservatory and veranda, coach-house, stables, and gardener's cottage, standing in six acres of garden and meadow-land, nicely wooded, with a very pretty lawn in front of the drawing-room windows. They named it Shrublands. My father became very fond of this little property; it was a great source of interest and pleasure to him in his declining years.

In the autumn of that same year (1883) his son-in-law, the Rev. W. J. Tait, was appointed Rector of St. Edmund's, Salisbury. That winter Sir Richard and his wife and daughter went abroad after Christmas—first to Biarritz, where he met his old friend and school-fellow, General Robertson. They made expeditions together from St. Jean de Luz to the various battlefields of the Peninsular War, Bayonne among others.

A tour through Spain was then made: Madrid, Seville, Barcelona, and Saragossa were visited; at the latter place he was much interested in seeing painted up in the cloisters of the cathedral the words 'Ninth Company' in English, evidently a relic of the Peninsular War. He also visited Granada, where he was enchanted with the ruins of the beautiful Alhambra, of which he brought home some exquisite models. A legend over one of the entrances greatly interested him; on the keystone of an arch is carved a hand, and below it a key, and the legend runs that when the hand reaches down and grasps the key the Moors will return and regain possession of the kingdom.

Christmas of the years 1886 and 1887 was spent at

St. Edmund's Rectory, Salisbury. In the summer of 1884 Sir Richard joined his eldest daughter and her husband in a little driving tour to Savernake Forest. They went in their own carriage, a Stanhope phaeton, drawn by their sober old mare Peggie. They drove by Avebury, where he was much interested in the monoliths, similar to those of Stonehenge, but scattered about in fields. They visited Marlborough College, and there he had the gratification of seeing his youngest son's name in gold letters among the list of honours hung up in the hall. (He had passed direct from Marlborough into Woolwich.)

They stayed at a charming little inn in the Forest, and saw the magnificent avenue of trees which is the only part of Savernake which at all rivals the New Forest. Some old friends of Sir Richard, Captain Beauchamp, R.N., and his wife and daughters, were then living in a house on the outskirts of the Forest; he took this opportunity of calling on them and introducing them to his daughter and her husband. They little thought then that they should one day be connected with them by the marriage of their sister with Captain Beauchamp's youngest son.

It was a very enjoyable little trip, without any contretemps, and very pleasant to look back upon, one of those periods of life that give one a sense of possession.

> 'So memory brightens o'er the past,
> As when the sun, concealed
> Behind some cloud that near us hangs,
> Shines on a distant field.'

In 1887 (the year of Queen Victoria's Jubilee) Sir Richard and his wife and daughter, accompanied by their old friend, Mrs. Wyse, went abroad for some months—first to Holland, where they were delighted with the sight of the fields of hyacinths in bloom; then to Berlin; then Dresden, where a month was spent; then to Teplis, where Lady Kelly went through a three-weeks course of baths for rheumatism. From there they went to Prague, and then to Vienna, and from thence by boat to Buda-Pesth. Then by steamer down the Danube, through the Danubian provinces as far as Rustchuk. From Rustchuk they took the Orient Express to Varna, and crossed the Black Sea to Constantinople. This was the first time Sir Richard had been there since the Crimean War, and he was naturally much interested in revisiting it. From Constantinople they went to Athens, and from thence through the Grecian Archipelago to Trieste. They landed at Corfu; Sir Richard was much pleased to see the lovely little island again, which he had not visited since he had been quartered there as a Subaltern. From Trieste they went to Venice, then over the Brenner Pass to Innsbruck. From Innsbruck they visited Botzen and Meran, and then crossed the St. Gothard to Lucerne.

Sir Richard, who was anxious not to lose any of the grand scenery through which they were passing, stood out in the corridor between all the tunnels, and the draught brought on a bad attack of eczema, which detained them some weeks at Lucerne. From Lucerne they went to Strasburg, Stuttgart, and Mayence; then by the Rhine railway to Cologne, and home viâ Rotterdam and Harwich.

The following summer Sir Richard went abroad for the last time. In July he and his wife and daughter, accompanied by Mrs. Wyse, went to Switzerland. They spent some weeks at Pontresina and the Maloja, crossed the Brigalia Pass by Chiavenna to the Italian lakes, where some weeks were spent. While they were at Menaggio the Lake of Como rose beyond its normal

level, and the hotel in which they were staying was
flooded. At Bellaggio a fête was held to celebrate the
vintage. I remember receiving a long letter from my
father, giving a graphic description of it. They returned
home by Munich and Paris.

Travelling was a very great pleasure to Sir Richard,
on account of his appreciation of historical associations,
his love of seeing everything thoroughly and in detail,
and his retentive memory, which made the retrospect
almost as enjoyable as the actual tour. In the autumn
of this year his younger son, Major R. M. B. F.
Kelly, R.A., was married in India. His wife, Miss
Bedingfeld, went out to him, and was married from the
house of her uncle, Major Hayne.

In 1889 Sir Richard had the honour of being made
Colonel of his old regiment, the 34th, or Border Regiment, as it is now styled. The two following letters
refer to this:

SHRUBLANDS,
March 26, 1889.

MY DEAR FRANK,

Many thanks for yours of 19th, congratulating
me on having been offered the colonelcy of the 34th. I
have not been gazetted yet—indeed, in last Saturday's
paper I saw a paragraph stating that the vacancy was not
to be filled up, but would be absorbed; but the enclosed
kind note from Harman (which I send you to read, and
then to forward to Annie to be returned to me) will show
you that they intend keeping their promise. It is, of
course, most gratifying to become, which I hardly
expected, chief of the regiment in which I served so
long, and if I am appointed (which is customary) the
day after poor Maxwell's death, on March 8, I get it

not only on my birthday, but on the thirty-fourth anniversary of my getting the lieutenant-colonelcy.

*　　　　*　　　　*　　　　*　　　　*

I am sending you with this the history of the 66th Regiment, in which our father's name is often mentioned, to read, as I dare say you may like to see it.

All here join me in love to you and Kate.

Ever yours affectionately,
R. D. KELLY.

General Harman's Letter.

HORSE GUARDS,
WAR OFFICE, S.W.,
March 18, 1889.

MY DEAR KELLY,

I was quite sure it would be a great gratification to you to be Colonel of the old regiment, as I (am) sure it will be to all who have served, and also to those still serving, in the regiment. The Duke was quite pleased to make an exception to the general rule in your favour, and certainly the circumstances and curious incidents you mention to me in your note fully warrant it.

I can show your note to H.R.H.

Hoping you may long be spared in health to preside at our annual regimental dinner,

Yours sincerely,
G. HARMAN.

To General Sir R. D. Kelly, K.C.B.

In the year 1890 Sir Richard's health began to decline. He had a bad attack of influenza, which mysterious malady was at its worst that year. The attack passed off, but left him considerably weakened, and he never completely recovered power over his limbs, which was a great privation to him, as he had always been a good walker and was very fond of the exercise. The weakness was chiefly muscular, but it gradually increased till, towards the close of his life, he could not walk without support.

In the spring of 1890 his son-in-law, the Rev. W. J. Tait, resigned the living of St. Edmund's, Salisbury, and in the autumn he and his wife went out to India for a tour of eighteen months. During the summer they joined Sir Richard and his wife and daughter in Scotland, first at Strathpeffer and afterwards at Kinggussie. It was a very wet summer, and during the fortnight spent at Kinggussie there was only one day without rain. This was a great disappointment to Sir Richard, who had been looking forward to enjoying the beautiful Highland scenery.

In the spring Sir Richard had gone to Hastings for change of air, after his attack of influenza. One day, while walking in Fairlight Glen with his eldest son, he stumbled, and before he could recover himself he fell heavily to the ground on his field-glasses, which he was wearing over his coat with a strap. The fall jarred and shook him, and made him realize for the first time the feebleness of old age. His words to his son, as he helped him to rise, were: 'My bolt is shot.' Yes, it was too true; but it did not fall till seven years later.

In the spring of 1891 Sir Richard and his wife and daughter went to Brighton, and in the summer to Harrogate. In August of that year Sir Richard had the first of a very alarming kind of seizure to which he was subject during his remaining years. It came on quite suddenly, usually at night, lasting from five to fifteen minutes, and leaving him very weak. He was quite unconscious of it, and suffered no pain.

On February 4, 1892, Beatrice Frances, youngest daughter of Sir R. and Lady Kelly, was married in St. Peter's Church, Earley, to Francis Arthur, younger son of the late Captain Beauchamp, R.N.

Their home was in London, and from that time Sir and Lady Kelly took a house in London every year for the winter months.

A great sorrow fell upon the family this year. On May 1 Sir Richard's elder sister, Miss Catherine Elizabeth Kelly (Aunt Kate) was taken from us by death. She and her widowed sister, Mrs. Battersby, had lived together all their lives, and to the latter (Aunt Annie) it was like a second widowhood. The death of his sister was a great grief to him. He had very warm affections, and was deeply attached to all the members of his family.

The winter of 1892-93 Sir Richard and Lady Kelly shared a house—56, Ladbroke Grove, Notting Hill— with their son-in-law, the Rev. W. J. Tait, and his wife. It was a good-sized house, comfortably furnished, and close behind it was a private garden, where my father took a short walk every morning when he felt able and the weather was favourable. He could not walk alone now, and only very slowly, but he had brought his carriage and horses up to town, and enjoyed driving. He also occasionally went to tea with his youngest daughter, who was then living in Cambridge Terrace. His eldest son, who was a Captain in the 34th, spent part of the winter (his leave) with us at Ladbroke Grove.

On January 10, 1893, in the middle of the night, my father had a bad attack, which alarmed us all very much. The doctor thought his case very serious, and said he must have a nurse. He wrote a note to a nurses' home for one. She came at twelve o'clock that day (January 11). She has been in the family ever since (Nurse Davies). My father was unconscious and seriously ill when she arrived. By five o'clock that afternoon the danger was past, and next day he was almost himself again. He had wonderful recuperative power, and was as a rule a good sleeper. He took to Nurse Davies at once, and always retained a warm affection for her.

On January 27 his little grandchild, Marjorie Beauchamp, was born. She was a great joy to him in his declining years. He was very fond of children, who always took to him. He suffered greatly from depression, partly caused by his deafness; and when he became too feeble to take interest in his accounts or to write letters, two favourable occupations all his life, he had no resource but reading, of which he, fortunately, never tired. But, however impressed he might be feeling, he always brightened up when Marjorie came in, and was never tired of talking about her to Alice, as he used to call Nurse Davies.

The winter was diversified by visits from friends—his sister Mrs. Battersby, his daughter Mrs. Spooner, etc.; and he saw many friends passing through London, as well as those living in town.

In March he had a great pleasure. His daughter-in-law sent him a copy of a very complimentary letter from the Commander-in-Chief (Lord Roberts) with reference to the work of his younger son, of whom Sir Richard was justly proud; there had always existed between them a very strong bond of trust and affection. The joy of receiving this letter was so great that he could scarcely sleep the following night.

In April he left London and returned to Shrublands,

where he spent the summer. He was very glad to return to the country, as he did not like London; the gloom depressed him, and he was very fond of Shrublands.

In July of this year he drove in the wagonette to meet his eldest daughter and her husband, who were breaking their journey from Leamington. In driving up from the station one of the horses took fright, and they bolted. After running away for a couple of miles, just at the top of a steep hill one of them got its leg over the trace, which stopped him, and all the occupants of the carriage got out. He had sat quite unmoved, and seemed rather surprised at everyone getting out, so much so that his daughter thought he could not have realized what had happened, and said they were running away. 'I know,' he replied. He had quite realized the situation, but had not even felt apprehensive.

In November he came up to London for the winter to a small house in Lansdowne Road (No. 97). He was twice ill during this winter, and attended by Dr. Schofield, but owing to his marvellous recuperative power he was able to throw off the malady quickly.

On November 4 he went with his son-in-law, the Rev. W. J. Tait, to a matinée, and on March 22 to see the exhibition of 'Constantinople.' He also lunched with him on three different occasions at his club, and was able to go to tea and dinner with his daughters.

In April, 1894, he returned to Shrublands. In October of that year he again came up to London for the winter, and took a house in Campden House Road (No. 41). He was wonderfully well during the first part of the winter; walked to Kensington Gardens and back one day; went out to luncheon and tea; dined with his eldest daughter and her husband on January 6, 1895, on the occasion of the silver wedding, when there was a large family gathering, and came to an 'at home' in their flat next day.

In February he was seriously ill, and, unfortunately, his nurse was ill at the same time. It was the time of the influenza epidemic, and there was great difficulty in getting a nurse, but eventually one was procured. This illness lasted about three weeks; the recovery was complete, and he was able to go out to lunch and tea again.

On April 17 his eldest son, Major Kelly, 34th Regiment, was married in St. Mary Abbot's Church, Kensington, to Miss Skeffington. The excitement and interest of the occasion had a most beneficial effect upon Sir Richard. He walked up the aisle of the church without assistance, to the astonishment of his family.

On April 27 he returned to Shrublands. In September he had the great pleasure of paying a visit to his younger son, Major Kelly, R.A., at Sheerness. Nurse Davies accompanied him; they broke the journey in London, staying a night with his eldest daughter and her husband in their flat, 131, Ashley Gardens, Westminster. On the return journey he stayed two nights, and enjoyed a drive with his daughter round Battersea Park.

In October he came up to London for the winter, to 33, Lansdowne Road. This was the most comfortable house they had had in London; it was in a cheerful situation, the rooms were large and comfortably furnished. Early in November he had a slight attack of congestion of one lung, but by the end of the month he was well again, and able to go to luncheon with his daughter.

His two daughters living in London, and their husbands, always dined with him on Christmas Day. This Christmas his children made him a joint present of a large wicker easy-chair, with which he was much pleased; he always used it from that time till his death.

On March 9, 1896 (his eighty-first birthday), he had several letters of congratulation, and a telegram from his regiment, which gratified him very much.

In April he returned to Shrublands. He enjoyed sitting out on the veranda, and going to his club to read the papers. Writing was beginning to be a trouble to him, but reading he was as fond of as ever. One wet Sunday, while his eldest daughter and her husband were staying at Shrublands, his son-in-law read the service in the morning-room, and he volunteered to read the lessons, which he did as clearly and beautifully as ever.

In November of this year he came up to London as usual. The house taken was No. 9, Hereford Square. It was the least comfortable of all their temporary London residences; there had been great difficulty in finding a house, and it had been practically 'Hobson's choice.' The house faced north, and never got a ray of sun, which intensified the gloom inseparable from a London winter.

Up to Christmas he was as well as usual, able to go out to luncheon, and on Christmas Day he was very well and bright, taking great interest in the distribution of the Christmas gifts. Letter-writing, which used to be a source of much enjoyment to him, and for which he had a great gift, had for the last two or three years become a severe tax upon his strength and energy, and had to be relinquished; but on December 19 he wrote a short letter to his third daughter, Mrs. Spooner, asking her where he could get a watch-bracelet like hers, as he wished to give one as a Christmas present to his wife. This was the last letter he wrote.

On New Year's Day, 1897, his two daughters and their husbands dined with him, and he was very bright and well.

On Sunday, January 7, his son-in-law, the Rev. W. J. Tait, administered Holy Communion to him and his family. It was the last time he partook of it.

On January 28 his last illness, which continued with intermissions five months, commenced.

By February 7 he was better and able to be downstairs, but felt very weak and low, was disinclined to take solid food, and was anxious to go away for a change; for a few days he fluctuated, but on February 21 he was too ill to get up. He began to have bad nights, and was restless and uneasy during the day; the doctor gave no hope of recovery, and the rest of the family were sent for. The next ten days was a sad and anxious time for all his family; the days were spent at Hereford Square, and each morning one dreaded to hear that he had passed away in the night.

In himself he was most peaceful and happy; believing himself dying, he had not the slightest dread of the great change. He liked having those he loved near him, and, though naturally undemonstrative, he seemed to hunger for expressions of affection; his son-in-law's prayers were a great comfort to him. One day he asked his daughter to read the Bible to him; she read the fourteenth chapter of St. John, the chapter that had comforted her beloved sister on her death-bed. When she had finished, he said: 'What a comfort those words are to me!'

At times he seems to have had visions of the departed. One day he said to Nurse Davies, 'There's Jordan!' pointing to a particular spot in the room. Nurse thought he meant his old friend General Jordan, who lived in Reading, but he said quite impatiently ' No, no—

Edward Jordan!' meaning the young fellow who was killed in the trenches the night he had been taken prisoner in the Crimea. Then he added: 'There's darling Annie, too.' One day while his wife was sitting with him he opened his eyes and said, 'Kate!' and Nurse Davies said he spoke again of seeing his dear sister Kate, and that he added, 'So many people!' putting out his hand to beckon to them.

One of his most alarming symptoms was the Cheyne-Stokes breathing, the breath coming intermittently, with pauses between each breath.

On February 28 he was at his lowest ebb. He spoke with difficulty, and the Cheyne-Stokes breathing was very marked; none of his family expected to find him alive next day; all had a superstitious dread of March, his fateful month. He himself had once said he supposed he should die in March. Contrary to all expectation, and in defiance of the doctor's verdict, on the first day of March—his lucky month—he began to improve! The evening before, when his daughter went up to see him before leaving for the night, she thought he looked more natural, and the pauses between each breath seemed shorter. When she came over next morning, hardly expecting to find him alive, she heard a much more hopeful account: he had had a good night, the breathing was better, the pulse stronger, and both nurse and doctor hopeful! When she went up to see him he was lying quietly asleep, breathing regularly, and looking quite like himself.

The recovery was slow and fluctuating, and never quite complete; there was great difficulty in getting him to take sufficient nourishment.

He was very thankful for his recovery, and quite realized how marvellous it was. He wished to mark it by a service of thanksgiving and a present to his devoted nurse.

On March 9, his eighty-second birthday, he was wished 'Many happy returns of the day' by three different papers. When told of it, he said: 'It is for my father's sake; he was such a good man, everyone respected him.' Such was his beautiful humility and self-forgetfulness, and his intense love for his father.

In April he was able to travel down to Shrublands in an invalid carriage which conveyed him from door to door without any change. He bore the journey well, and recovered a certain amount of health and strength in the country air and congenial surroundings of Shrublands.

His eldest daughter and her husband paid him a short visit in May. He was able to be downstairs, and even to sit out on the veranda.

Towards the end of June his health began to fail again, his sleep forsook him. On July 1 all his children were summoned. On the morning of July 2 he rallied a little, and knew those around him. Early in the afternoon the change began. He grew restless, and his breathing became difficult; then blessed unconsciousness came on, from which he never emerged, and at 4.30 he breathed his last with his hand in that of his son-in-law, the Rev. W. J. Tait. At the moment of his passing the sun shone out brightly; it had been a gloomy day till then.

On Saturday, July 3, his old friend General Bedingfield, whose only daughter his younger son had married, died. There were obituary notices of both in the same column of the *Times*.

On Tuesday, July 6, all that was mortal of Sir Richard Kelly was laid to rest in the pretty little churchyard of St. Peter's Church, Earley. The coffin was covered with floral wreaths and crosses, among them a beautiful wreath from the Border Regiment, and at the head on a black velvet cushion his medals were arranged. The service was read by the Rev. W. J. Tait; the hymn 'O Perfect Peace' was sung in church, and 'Now the labourer's task is o'er' at the grave.

Just as the coffin was placed on the bier in the chancel, a ray of sunshine fell upon it. The coffin was carried from the church to the grave by non-commissioned officers of his own regiment.

An Irish cross of white marble has been placed at the head of the grave by his widow and children. I.H.S forms a medallion in the centre, surrounded by a wreath of laurel leaves which is continued down the centre, doubly appropriate as being the emblem of the Border Regiment. The cross bears the following inscription:

> 'In loving memory of
> GENERAL SIR RICHARD DENIS KELLY, K.C.B.,
> The O'Kelly of Mucklon, County Galway,
> Colonel 34th Cumberland Regiment.
> Born March 9, 1815.
> Entered into rest July 2, 1897.'

Round the coping-stone run these words:

> 'And his Lord said, Well done, thou good and faithful servant; thou hast been faithful over a few things: I will make thee ruler over many things.'

The following are among some of the letters received by his widow after his death:

THE LETTERS OF CONDOLENCE.

From Mrs. Battersby.

LISTOKE, GUILDFORD,
July 7.

MY DEAREST ELLEN,

You are so much in my thoughts to-day that I feel I must send you a line to tell you what a comfort it was to me to be with you yesterday, and how I hope you had some sleep to rest your poor weary brain, and that you are taking more nourishment to-day than you did yesterday. I trust none of you are the worse for the terrible trial of yesterday. Oh, how my heart ached for you all, and how impossible one felt it to do or say anything to lighten such sorrow!

God alone can speak peace to the broken heart.

With deepest sympathy and fond love to all,

Ever your attached sister,
LOUISE.

From Colonel Harvey.

44, GROSVENOR PLACE, S.W.,
July 8, 1897.

MY DEAR LADY KELLY,

I could not express to you all my sympathy and sorrow for you in your great affliction when I came to you on Wednesday. Indeed, it is useless to stir up old memories and to give way to grief, but we were together in mind of our last mutual sorrow, when darling Annie was taken from us.

I so well remember Sir Richard coming into the room where she lay, and with a sob he said: 'She was the flower of the flock.'

No words can avail to mitigate your feeling of loneliness after having, been forty-nine years bound up in thought and interests with dear Sir Richard; he was such a grand example of chivalry, justice, and high-mindedness, but to those who survive him it is a happy thought that he lived so happily in full possession of all his faculties, and able to see his children all doing well, and following his lead in uprightness and good lives.

The last service was most impressive; Walter read

most beautifully, and felt all he said. I admired him for his wonderful control of his feelings; most of us felt the hot tears trickling down silently, as the service and choral singing brought back all the cherished memories of his dear and precious life. Almost the most trying part was when the colour-sergeants of his dear regiment —the 34th—carried him on their shoulders to his last resting-place, followed by the Colonel and all the officers in uniform. It was just what he would have wished. General Jordan, Colonel Dyson Laurie, and other old comrades, were present.

I do not write this to disturb your much-needed rest, expecting any letter; you must not write to me at present, but all I want you to know is that I am with you in my thoughts and feel for you very deeply.

On Thursday I attended at Windsor the funeral of my old friend General Bedingfield. It is very sad for all, and Mary felt very much her double loss; she is now at Sheerness.

We leave London on July 15 for Exmouth, where we intend to settle for a while. Later on I will write and tell you. I wish you could try some cure and massaging for your rheumatism.

Please remember me most kindly to good Nurse Davies; she was so devoted to him. On that Wednesday all feelings were upset and confused, so that to her as to others I could not express all I felt.

Good-bye, dear Lady Kelly; bear up in your great trial.

    Believe me ever,
      Yours very affectionately,
        CHARLES LACON HARVEY.

From Mrs. Burnaby.

ST. MARY'S VICARAGE, BEVERLEY,
July 5, 1897.

MY DEAREST AUNTIE,

I have only just this moment heard from Birdie that our dear uncle passed away on Friday, and I feel I must tell you how very, very deeply I feel for you all in your sad loss. Indeed, we have all lost one whom we loved dearly, as everyone must have done who knew his sweet unselfishness and wonderfully beautiful humility.

I have none but the very happiest and sweetest memories of his unceasing thoughtfulness and kindness whenever we were with you all; and I am so glad to think that I saw him once again last year, though it was only for one day. God help you, my dear, dear Auntie; you will miss him sorely, but your great love will comfort you with the thought of how much better it is for him to be at rest from all weariness and suffering.

Please give my love and deepest sympathy to dear Bee if she is with you.

Ever your very loving niece,
BUSY BURNABY.

From Mrs. Busby.

98, LEXHAM GARDENS, KENSINGTON, W.,
July 10.

MY DEAR ELLEN,

Kindly forgive me for sending you a few lines from Fanny and myself, to say how deeply we have felt for you in the very sad loss you have so lately sustained. Only those who knew dear Richard well, and knew what a very lovable and noble character he was, can enter into the loss he will be to you all, and particularly to you, as your devoted attention to him must have greatly assisted the doctors in prolonging his life for a time.

I was so glad to hear from dear Beatrice that all his children were around him except Richie, who could not arrive in time, and this must have been a great sorrow to him, poor fellow! as he was so deeply attached to his father.

I have been down several times to see poor Annie Battersby. She has felt this sad loss greatly; I can see the blow has struck her very deeply. We are both very anxious to hear of you, how you are and how you have been supported in this sadly trying time, and I should be so much obliged by someone with you sending us a very few lines to tell us how you are.

With our united very kind love,
        Ever, dear Ellen, believe me,
            Affectionately yours,
                MARY BUSBY.

From Mrs. Francis Kelly.

WESTON, DULEEK,
July 17, 1897.

MY DEAR ELLEN,

I did not like sooner to intrude upon you in your sorrow, and when you must be overwhelmed with letters and business of all kinds; but I knew you would understand how much I felt for you through all the sad time, and the sudden cessation of all the care and love after many years, by which I am sure, under God, the dear life was prolonged. It was a comfort that he was saved from pain and suffering at the last, and that he had all his loved ones about him.

I hope, dear Ellen, you have not suffered in health

from it all. I was glad to hear you have Arthur and Henrietta to be with you and help you.

Francis felt deeply the loss of a brother he was so much attached to, and to me he was always so kind and affectionate. Francis is well for him, and is now busy at the hay, for which the weather is splendid while it lasts, and joins in love with

>Your affectionate sister,
>
>KATH. KELLY.

My sister sends her kind remembrances.

From Mrs. Spooner.

>TILLINGTON COURT, HEREFORD,
>*July* 28.

MY DEAREST LADY KELLY,

I have not ventured to write to you before, but my whole heart has been with you, dear, dear old friend, and I have prayed God to be with you and give you the sorely-needed strength to submit to His will. Your constant anxiety and watching are at an end; but, oh! the sense of being alone is very, very hard to bear. You know where to look for consolation. I feel as if I had lost someone very dear to me, as all who knew dear Sir Richard could not help loving and respecting him, so good, so unselfish, so kind as he was. I never knew Hammy to feel anyone's loss as he did Sir Richard's— not even his brother's or sister's. His letter telling me of it was very touching.

You are not going to live at Shrublands, I hear, and it would be painful to do so. I hope you will sell or let it soon. Helen joins me in much love to you.

>Always affectionately yours,
>
>M. SPOONER.

From Mrs. Beauchamp.

ELMHURST, EARLEY, READING,
July 11, 1897.

MY DEAR LADY KELLY,

Before leaving home I must write a few lines to tell you how much I have thought of you, and with the deepest sympathy, for I know all the sorrow you have gone through, and will suffer. The great blank in your life—may our Heavenly Father comfort and support you.

I have been thankful to hear that you have not suffered so much pain from rheumatism; may you be strengthened in every way.

I am very sorry that it will be a few weeks before we see you, but I hope we may do so then. Annie and Alice beg me to say how much they, too, think of you and feel for you.

Leaving home seems a great effort to me, but it must be done.

I shall ever think of dear Sir Richard as one of my kindest friends, and I feel honoured to have had his regard.

It is a comforting thought that those who are gone from us are nearer to us than we think.

With much love and sympathy from us all,

Believe me, dear Lady Kelly,

Ever yours affectionately,

A. L. M. BEAUCHAMP.

From Anna, Countess of Moray.

DOUNE LODGE, DOUNE, N.B.,
July 26.

MY DEAR LADY KELLY,

I was so exceedingly grieved to hear from one of my sisters of your terrible sorrow, and of the death of our dear old friend Sir Richard. We were all always so fond of him, and he was our mother's oldest friend; and then to you, dear friend, I know his loss must be unspeakable, you were so devoted to him, and he was such a noble, unselfish, beautiful character: you must feel as if half your life were gone.

Please accept my deepest sympathy, and may God in His love and mercy strengthen and help and comfort you and your dear children in this great sorrow.

With my love, I am, dear Lady Kelly,
Ever affectionately yours,
A. MORAY.

From Miss Vessey.

EDENHAM VICARAGE, BOURNE,
July 20.

MY DEAR LADY KELLY,

Thank you very much for your letter. Ever since dear Bee wrote to tell me of your great sorrow I have wished to write to you, but, knowing well the shower of letters you would get, did not, as I myself received more than a hundred.

Dear Lady Kelly, words are so weak and inadequate in the midst of your grief, but I must say how we all feel we have lost a dear old friend, who we shall always remember with the warmest affection. The beauty of his unselfish life and simple kindness is not dead, but will always live in the hearts of those who had the honour of knowing him. For you the loss is terrible; no children make it up, however devoted, as I well know my own mother always felt. I hope dear old Bee is stronger; if she is with you give her my dear love. I am so specially sorry for her; I know how devoted she was to her father, and how very lonely she will feel—that dreadful blank feeling!

Ask Bee to send me a line when your plans get more settled; I'm always very much interested to hear. And, with much love from us all,

Ever, dear Lady Kelly,
Yours very affectionately,
MARY VESSEY.

From Mrs. Dalton.

47, LANSDOWNE ROAD,
July 8.

MY DEAR LADY KELLY,

I have just heard through the little girl who works for Mrs. Beauchamp that the blow has fallen, and that you have had to part from the best of men. Dear Sir Richard! I can't tell you how I loved and respected him and how truly I shall mourn him. I lose not a moment in begging you to accept for yourself and all your children our sincerest sympathy. For you, dear Lady Kelly, I do feel deeply, and I know what a terrible blank it must be to you to be without the dear object of all your loving thought and care, so devoted as you have been. For him we can only rejoice, for he has entered into Paradise, his long life of usefulness ended here, but to continue in the presence of the Master he had served, and he will meet all our loved ones who have entered into rest eternal. But I do grieve for you and his children; I too well know what it is to mourn such a father.

I should so much like to hear how you are; perhaps Mrs. Tait or Mrs. Beauchamp will let me know.

With kindest love and true sympathy,

Believe me ever,
Yours affectionately,
AMELIA DALTON.

From Colonel Ransford.

44, CHAUCER ROAD, BEDFORD,
July 6, 1897.

DEAR LADY KELLY,

I trust you will allow me to join with my wife in expressing my deepest sympathy for you in your great loss. I had the honour of serving under Sir Richard Kelly when I was attached to the 34th for duty at Seetapore in 1862. Sir Richard was my first commanding officer, and always showed kindness and consideration to us all. I am quite sure that the officers of the 34th who served under Sir Richard will all regret his loss.

Believe me, with much sympathy,
Yours sincerely,
C. RANSFORD.

From the Rev. George B. Vessey.

DEAR LADY KELLY,

Our own recent sorrow has shown me what a trouble letters may become in their multitude—hence my delay in writing to assure you of my sympathy and that of my brother and sisters with you in your trouble.

But I cannot let this occasion pass without writing to tell you how much I valued and esteemed him who has been called away.

My dear father and mother had a great regard for him, and so I am sure must everyone have had who knew him.

From the time when I was a boy at Eton I have received many kindnesses from him, and my impression of him was that of a courtly, kindly, unselfish gentleman, in the highest sense of the word, and a soldier who nobly filled his place in the world.

Your loss is great, but could you wish it otherwise? Our holy religion assures us not only of the resurrection of the body and the life everlasting, but also of the Communion of Saints; and he who has gone from you has gone to be another link to bind you to the things eternal.

Few men have had a nobler sense of duty towards man or towards God; and God has called him, and like a true soldier he has obeyed.

Sorrow, yes! That remains to lead us to the Cross, to the Crucified. The Man of Sorrows is still the Light of the world. In Him alone can we see the meaning of sorrow; through Him alone can we find consolation.

Please accept the sympathy that is poorly expressed but truly felt, and don't trouble to answer this.

Sincerely yours,
GEORGE B. VESSEY.

From C. W. Tait, Esq.

26, COLLEGE ROAD, CLIFTON, BRISTOL,
July 3, 1897.

MY DEAREST ELLIE,

What can I say? I know what a blank this will make in life to your loving heart, although you could hardly have wished your dear father to have lingered long in his shattered and increasingly infirm state. For him the change is all for the good. Of all the men I have ever known, he stood as the representative of a kindly, quiet, and beautiful life, and I shall look upon his memory, and be grateful that I was privileged to know him.

If it is not obtrusive, I should much like, if possible, to be allowed to come to the funeral, in memory of my gratitude to that good man.

Give my affectionate wishes and sympathy to your mother and to you all.

Yours ever most affectionately,
C. W. A. TAIT.

From the Same.

26, COLLEGE ROAD, CLIFTON, BRISTOL,
July 7, 1897.

MY DEAREST ELLIE,

Of course I quite understood that something had happened to the letter. I am sure that you knew how truly I felt anything that I wrote, and how real my feeling towards your dear father was. Well, he has left us an example which will not soon pass away into forgetfulness.

With kind love to you both,
Yours most affectionately,
C. W. A. TAIT.

This little memoir would be incomplete without an attempt to delineate those features of my father's character which so greatly endeared him to his family and friends.

I think the most leading traits of my father's character were unselfishness and love of justice. He was entirely free from self-seeking of any kind, always thought of others before himself in small things as well as great, so much so that one who knew him well once said of him: 'I think Sir Richard sometimes forgets that there is such a person as himself.'

Unselfishness is the root of all the most winning virtues; hence he was most genuinely humble, he disliked talking about himself or hearing his own praises. He had much self-respect, but very little self-esteem, hardly any ambition, but much aspiration—which is ambition turned

Godwards: his highest ambition was to do his duty, and to make those he loved happy.

He was very liberal, always ready to give to any good object, and to help anyone who had any claim on him, and he delighted in giving presents. He was most generous, always ready to forgive, never bearing resentment and not easily offended. Though he had a high standard and could be severe on any failure of duty or honour, he judged the faults of others leniently, and was never heard to say an unkind word of anyone, nor could he bear to hear anyone else do so. He was perfectly courteous, with that genuine courtesy which springs from a kindly nature. Not only did he observe the outward forms of courtesy, but he carefully refrained from wounding the feelings of others, especially of those in an inferior position; and in society he would devote himself to the most obscure or neglected of the company. He had very warm affections, and anything like family dispeace or contention grieved him beyond everything; he could not be happy till harmony had been restored. Without seeking it, he won the respect and affection of all who knew him, and he never lost a friend.

His sense of justice was very keen; he could not bear injustice even to himself, for he had the highest regard for truth, and injustice is untruth in action. He would never have resented an injury, but he could not remain quiescent under injustice, so when the credit for the repulse of the Russians on the night of March 22, which he had organized and commanded, was given to his subordinate officer, he remonstrated, and though the mistake (while acknowledged) was not fully repaired, the true version of the affair will go down to posterity in the standard book on the Crimean War, 'The Invasion of the Crimea,' by Kinglake.

On one occasion his younger son had been unfairly treated by the authorities at Woolwich, and he took an infinity of trouble, and wrote numberless letters, until the mistake was rectified. In another case he insisted upon justice being done though it was against his own interest.

He was very patient under suffering. During his later years he had frequent attacks of eczema, which affected his eyes with extreme irritation; he bore this trial most patiently, and was always full of gratitude to those who ministered to him. His deafness was a great privation, but it did not make him suspicious or exacting; he could not enter into general conversation, but he never asked to have it repeated to him, he so disliked giving trouble to others.

His temperament was quiet and reserved and undemonstrative; he had a very keen sense of humour, he loved a good story, but his innate refinement of mind made him loath the least approach to coarseness.

He was deeply religious, but he very seldom talked about his religious convictions even to those with whom he was in closest sympathy, and he disliked controversy. He was very loyal both to the forms of religion in which he had been brought up and to the institutions of his country, and affectionately loyal to his Sovereign. One day, towards the end of his life, he was driving in the Park when the Queen's carriage passed; though very feeble, he insisted on standing up to take off his hat, and was rewarded by a gracious bow and smile directed towards himself which made him very happy.

He was very fond of children, and they always took to him. His grandchildren were very fond of him, and nothing pleased him better than a visit from them, or interested him more than hearing of their sayings or doings. His youngest grandson, Charlie Spooner, was in his room an hour before he died.

He was also fond of animals. Bob, the bull-terrier left in his care by his brother-in-law when the latter went to India, was a great favourite; so was his cat, Jack, who always shared his breakfast; and his little dog Snap was the last creature he spoke to on Earth.

Punctuality and accuracy were leading characteristics. His children used to say: 'We cannot be late if papa is with us.' Accuracy was part of his innate truthfulness, and it was also shown in his exact keeping of accounts and in his correspondence. He was a delightful correspondent, always answering letters punctually and sympathetically, and giving vivid and interesting descriptions. His most marked taste was for reading, of which he never tired. History was his favourite subject, including the daily papers; he had a very retentive memory, and one seldom appealed to him in vain for information. He also read aloud extremely well.

He was fond of walking, and up to the last ten years of his life a good walker. He was also a bold rider and fond of hunting. He was very fond of travelling, and liked seeing everything, such as galleries and churches, thoroughly; a cursory view never satisfied him. He was fond of making plans for travelling, and liked to adhere to them when once made.

He was a good whist-player, but did not care much for any other game except chess. He was naturally silent, but could talk very well to a sympathetic listener, and he could listen well, a much rarer gift.

He was absolutely fearless, but he loved life, and was always thankful for deliverance from danger.

A member of his household in Edinburgh once remarked in the hearing of his eldest daughter, then a child of seven, that she always thought of 'the Colonel' when she read the ninety-first Psalm. Ever since his daughter has called the ninety-first 'his Psalm.' Her little memoir of him may be fitly concluded in its words.

Psalm XCI.

Whoso dwelleth under the defence of the most High: shall abide under the shadow of the Almighty.

I will say unto the Lord, Thou art my hope, and my strong hold: my God, in Him will I trust.

For He will deliver thee from the snare of the hunter: and from the noisome pestilence.

He shall defend thee under His wings, and thou shalt be safe under His feathers: His faithfulness and truth shall be thy shield and buckler.

Thou shalt not be afraid for any terror by night: nor for the arrow that flieth by day.

For the pestilence that walketh in darkness: nor for the sickness that destroyeth in the noon-day.

A thousand shall fall beside thee, and ten thousand at thy right hand: but it shall not come nigh thee.

Yea, with thine eyes shalt thou behold: and see the reward of the ungodly.

For Thou, Lord, art my hope: Thou hast set Thine house of defence very high.

There shall no evil happen unto thee: neither shall any plague come nigh thy dwelling.

For He shall give His angels charge over thee: to keep thee in all thy ways.

They shall bear thee in their hands: that thou hurt not thy foot against a stone.

Thou shalt go upon the lion and adder: the young lion and the dragon shalt thou tread under thy feet.

Because he hath set his love upon Me, therefore will I deliver him: I will set him up, because he hath known My Name.

He shall call upon Me, and I will hear him: yea, I am with him in trouble; I will deliver him, and bring him to honour.

With long life will I satisfy him: and will shew him My salvation.

LETTERS WRITTEN FROM THE CRIMEA BY GENERAL SIR RICHARD DENIS KELLY TO HIS WIFE.

CHAPTER I

THE VOYAGE

The 'Adelaide,'
December 28, 1854, 11 p.m.

Dearest Ellen,

We are now getting up steam, and have just fired a gun and burned a blue light to recall Campbell and Worthington, who went ashore. I hope they will return in time, as we are to be off at twelve o'clock. I am writing to you before I go to bed, as I find the pilot will leave us at the Ram Head, which is only an hour's steaming from this. You will be glad to hear that the purser has made my cabin very comfortable by putting up some hat-pins on which I can hang up my things; he has also had my lamp fixed up, and given me a looking-glass, as that mirror was inconveniently placed, and, thanks to your kind forethought in sending me the bit of carpet, I shall be as snug as possible. Mr. Collyer has not sent the padlock as he promised. Did I tell you that the purser is going to let us have brandy from the ship's stores to fill our jars with? I have just seen on board the *Times* of Friday last, that we were so anxious to see, and I find that Lord Ellenborough asked Lord Harding, as they were going to double the number of captains and subalterns in a regiment, if they were also going to double the number of field-officers; otherwise it would make the promotion to the upper ranks very slow. I copy Lord Harding's answer, which is very satisfactory: 'Lord Harding begged to state in answer to the noble Earl that there would at once be an additional Major, and eventually, as soon as the numbers reached anything like what they were expected to be, there would be a second Lieutenant-Colonel.' I wish I could send you the paper so much, but it was only lent to me. But there is no doubt of their intention now, and I dare say the end of January will see me a Lieutenant-Colonel. I hope to send my next from Malta. I trust you will not be knocked up with all your exertions and anxiety; but cheer up, for I really think our prospects are brightening. They have all come on board, and we shall be off directly. Kiss the darling pets, and tell them always to pray to God for dear papa and mamma, that we may be mercifully spared to one another. Goodnight; God bless you.

Ever your affectionate
RICHARD.

Give my warmest love to dear Kate.

THE 'ADELAIDE' AT SEA,
TWENTY MILES SOUTH OF LISBON,
New Year's Day, 1855, 3.50 p.m.

MY OWN DEAREST ELLIE,

As this is the first New Year's Day that we have not spent together since we have been married, I cannot let it pass without commencing a letter to you, hoping that, through God's goodness, we may be as mercifully spared and blessed this year as we have been during the many happy ones we have passed together; and that we will not be unmindful of the great mercies that He has vouchsafed to us, and how little we have deserved them, and I humbly trust that, by the assistance of His grace, we may be led to improve this year more than those that are past. We have been hitherto most fortunate in our weather, not having had a drop of rain, and especially in having had smooth water in crossing the Bay of Biscay, where we most wanted it. Yesterday (Sunday) is the only rough day we have had; there was a good deal of swell, which discomposed some of our stomachs, mine among the rest, but to-day I am all right again. This is a most lovely day, the air as mild and balmy as in June at home, and the sea quite smooth; it is like summer sailing. You can judge by our position to-day what a good run we have made, although on the evening of the 29th we had to stop the ship to repair the engines, one of the bolts having come out of the boiler, and the sea being smooth, the engineer thought it a good opportunity to make a survey of the whole of the engine, which caused a delay of four hours and lost us about fifty miles; we have, however, made up for it well since, going between ten and eleven knots an hour, and expect to reach Gibraltar to-morrow, which will be a very rapid passage. I am writing on the chance of our being able to communicate with Gibraltar, although not very probable, as I am afraid we shall pass it in the night. If we miss Gibraltar, however, I am in hopes that we shall touch at Malta for coal, as we have been burning ours at a great rate; we consumed no less that 44 tons yesterday. It will be a great treat to us all if we do, as we shall have an opportunity of sending letters, and perhaps of getting them; we shall also hear news both from England and Sebastopol; from the latter place I hope the accounts may be more cheering than those we have lately received. I shall try to get at Malta the very few things I still want for my kit, viz.: a padlock and key for my brandy-jar, which Mr. Collyer did not send on board as he promised, also another picket-rope, as I think only one was sent round the saddle-box; a book or two to read on the voyage would also be acceptable, as there is a great scarcity of them on board, and their want is greatly felt. Our time passes, as usual on board ship, chiefly in eating, drinking, sleeping and walking the deck; we find Captain Gray a very agreeable, gentlemanly person. We have some agreeable officers on board besides our own; Captain Massy of the 19th, and Lieutenant Balfour of the Rifles, are the nicest; the latter is a capital draughtsman, and I am sure is a good officer; he was out with the army at Varna before, and has given me several useful hints. I do not think the *Adelaide* is well suited either for a troopship or for passengers on a long voyage, as the hurricane-house, which contains the saloon, the captain's and my cabin, cuts up the deck greatly and gives very little space for exercise. She is an iron ship of 1,800 tons and 450 horse-power; she is built in compartments, which also limits the space below, and our men are consequently rather crowded; fortunately, the fine weather has allowed them to be a great deal on deck. The *Adelaide* is, however, both a fast and easy ship, although she has a very heavy cargo on board of large iron guns, with quantities of ammunition. With the exception of our draft, the rest are very young soldiers, chiefly recruits, and those of the 88th a very troublesome lot. The poor horses are getting on much better than I expected, and continue to eat well; it was so lucky the first two days of their being on board were so smooth, as it broke them in to the rolling of the ship. Leander takes it much more quietly than the mare, who kicked greatly last night when it was so rough, and smashed the side of the horse-box, which has since been mended; these boxes are so warm that they don't want their hoods. Chatfield is very attentive, and rubs down their legs every day except yesterday, when he could not stand. Leander has cast a shoe, and I suppose I shall not be able to get it on before I get to camp. I wonder if you left Plymouth to-day as you intended, and if you went by sea or land; if by sea, I hope you have as calm and lovely a day as this, and that you, the dear pets, and Kate may reach Weston safely. I hope you had no trouble in giving over the house at Plymouth, and that you have made out your long journey prosperously. You, I know, my dear love, will try and cheer up my dear mother, and not let her feel downhearted, as, at her time of life, it is a great object to prevent her feeling nervous if possible. You can't tell what a consolation it was to me to see you bear up so well at the trying moment of our parting, although I well know what a bitter trial it was to you, and how keenly you felt it. You are all constantly in my thoughts and dreams, and always in my prayers. It may perhaps please God that we should all meet once again before the close of this year, and, oh, what a happy thought that is! it will cheer me in many an hour of danger and distress. But should that not be the Almighty will, still more should we hope and pray that, being redeemed from our sins by the blood of His Son, we may be prepared for the great change, and meet again in a better world never more to be parted.

January 2, 11.39 *a.m.*

Another lovely day. We have made a good run since yesterday; we passed Cape St. Vincent about ten last night, and are about sixty miles from Gibraltar. I am afraid there is but little chance of sending a letter ashore, but I will have this ready, and if I fail it will go from Malta, I hope.

OFF ALGIERS,
January 4, *noon*.

We ran through the Straits at 6 p.m. on the 2nd, with a splendid breeze, and saw Europa light, and, as I expected, did not communicate; so this must be kept for Malta, where I hope and think we shall touch. We passed two steamers homeward bound in the Straits, but did not learn their names; they have promised to report us in England. The weather continues lovely and the sea very smooth; we could not desire a finer passage, and expect to be at Malta on the 6th. I, thank God, am as well as possible, still deaf in the right ear from cold; the doctor has, however, lent me a syringe, which I use, and it will, I trust, cure it. I hope to post this at Malta; till then adieu. Love to all and kisses to pets.

OFF CAPE BON,
Saturday, January 6.

We expect to reach Malta about nine to-night, and will coal next day, leaving in the evening. Being Sunday, we shall not be able to get anything in the shops, but it is a great pleasure being able to send a letter, which I hope you will get about the 17th or 18th. Our lovely weather still continues; indeed, I never remember having such fine weather at sea for a continuance; we have not had a drop of rain since we left Plymouth, and, with the exception of Sunday last, the sea has been almost without a ripple, and the air as mild and balmy as in June at home; it has been hitherto quite a pleasure trip. This day week I suppose we shall be at Balaklava. I will, D.V., finish this at Malta; till then adieu.

MALTA,
Sunday, January 7, 8 a.m.

We arrived off this island at three this morning, and got into harbour at daylight, and have commenced coaling already, as we are to leave this evening at four. I shall go ashore after breakfast and post this. I hear a mail left this yesterday viâ Marseilles, but a steamer is expected in here to-day from Alexandria, when another mail will leave four hours after for Marseilles, which I hope will take this. The postage is 1s. 1d., which I have not prepaid, as I am told I had better not, and it is not necessary. The news from Sebastopol that we got here on arrival is, I am sorry to say, gloomy— the army still in want of everything, and 7,000 sick in hospital. The Russians surprised the 50th lately in the trenches, while rolled up asleep in their blankets, and destroyed a great number of them, although repulsed afterwards themselves. The Duke of Cambridge left here yesterday *en route* for England. General Adams' body is here; he died on his way home. The *Britannia*, with Admiral Dundas on board, is here repairing; he has given up the command of the fleet to Sir E. Lyons. The *Neptune* has arrived with the 72nd, and the *Mauritius*, I hear, embarks the 14th for Balaklava to-morrow. I can give you no description of the town here, as I have not landed. The harbour is very fine, and the fortifications appear impregnable. I will now conclude with warmest love to you all, and prayers to Almighty God ever to protect and bless you. Kiss all the pets for me, especially darling baby; do not let them forget me. My fondest love to my dear mother, K. A. and F., and kindest regards to Miss Keays. Remember me to Mrs. Caffrey.*

> Ever your affectionate
> RICHARD.

P.S.—My next will be from Constantinople, I hope.

January 7, 1 p.m.

P.P.S.—I have just returned from St. Paul's Church, founded by Queen Adelaide, where I went with Campbell, It is a beautiful building, but I was too deaf to hear the sermon. I called at the post, but got no letters; as, however, I did not expect any, I was not disappointed. I am writing this from the club. We have taken on board here Captain Hamilton, R.N., to join some ship in the Black Sea. We leave this evening as soon as we have finished coaling. Adieu; God bless you all.

> THE 'ADELAIDE' AT SEA OFF THE ISLAND
> OF NEGROPONT, GRECIAN ARCHIPELAGO,
> *January 10, 1855, 9 a.m.*

MY OWN DEAREST ELLIE,

My last letters to you were posted at Malta on the 7th, to go next day viâ Marseilles, and I hope you have got them both, as one of them, written only two hours before we started, contained a pair of black lace Maltese mittens which the purser kindly spared me, and I hope they will fit you. I wish they had been long ones instead of short, as I believe they would have been more correct for dress, but I was glad to be able to get any to send you. Two or three hours before we left Malta the English mail arrived, and it was very provoking that we could not wait to get our letters, as I have no doubt there were letters for some on board. I did not expect

* The children's nurse.

any, as on leaving England it was not thought that we should touch at Malta; therefore you probably did not write. Captain Hamilton was the only one on board who got letters, and his came out with the Admiralty despatches. I like Captain H. very much; he is a very agreeable man, and has none of the pomposity of his brother the Governor; he goes with us as far as Balaklava, his ship, the *Leander*, being at Eupatoria. The Duke of Cambridge I think I told you was at Malta, but I believe is going to England; he keeps very quiet, and does not go out at all; they say he is very much annoyed at all that has appeared in the papers about him. Sir G. Browne's wound is nearly healed, and he is most anxious to rejoin the army, which he hopes to do in three weeks. There were a number of officers on sick-leave at Malta, but some that I saw were looking as well as possible. All that I spoke to said it would be impossible to get up anything from the camp from Balaklava unless you carried it yourself; for that reason I will try and get two pack-saddles at Constantinople, as I know one horse won't carry all my things, and if we succeed in taking Sebastopol, and have to march through the country in the spring, I shall require two baggage-horses, as I will have to carry my tents in addition to my own things. I hear you can get pack-saddles at Constantinople for £1 each, and they make capital seats in the tent. I intend walking myself, and shall fill my haversack with some cold meat from the ship, brandy-flask, knife, candles, matches, etc. I *intend filling the saddle-box*, when I have taken out the saddle, holsters, etc., with what things I least require, in case of being obliged to leave it behind. We did not leave Malta till 9 p.m. on the 7th, as we waited for the moon to rise, and a most fearful accident took place almost immediately after our leaving the harbour to an unfortunate man of the 38th, who was sitting over the hatchway leading into the engine-room, which, unfortunately, had no grating over it, as it ought to have had, and while in this position the unfortunate man fell asleep, and fell backwards down the hatch, and struck his head on the engine, which was stopped immediately, but not before it had made one or two revolutions, crushing his body in a fearful way. The poor man's death, however, must have been instantaneous on his striking the engine, as his brains were dashed out by the shock, and he never uttered a groan. It was a most fearful accident, and I trust he was prepared for the great change. We committed his body to the deep next day; it was so mangled that they were not able to strip the body of his clothes. We are still favoured with a continuance of the same lovely weather that we have enjoyed the whole voyage; we have not had a drop of rain since we left Plymouth, but since leaving Malta we have felt a sensible change in the weather, which has become much cooler, still very pleasant, and I do not find it cold enough for a pea-coat on deck. We made the Greek coast yesterday, and passed close to Cape Matapan, and had a fine view of Mount St. Elias, its summit covered with snow; the whole coast is rugged and barren, with a few small villages and an occasional monastery perched high up in the hills to be out of the way of the pirates. We passed Cerigo, the southernmost of the Ionian Isles, yesterday evening, and entered the Archipelago last night. This morning we were off Negropont, the hills on it covered with snow. We are now (1.30 p.m.) just past Chios, famous for its wine; we expect to reach the entrance to the Dardanelles to-night, and if the Turkish authorities will allow us to go up by night, we may expect to be at Constantinople by the middle of the day to-morrow; and if so, we shall probably not leave till next day, as we shall have to land a few sick at Scutari, and most likely have to coal again, as we only took in 300 tons at Malta, all they could spare us, the supply there being very short. We shall probably arrive at Balaklava on the 13th; this I intend posting at Constantinople. The 14th were to leave Malta for Sebastopol to-day in the *Emen* (?), as also the French with 250 mules got from Spain, not before they were wanted. I will now say adieu till to-morrow; the horses are well and eat well, but the mare has lost a shoe by pawing, as well as the horse, which is a bore.

January 11, 1 *p.m.*

Last night we arrived within twenty miles of the entrance of the Dardanelles, and as ships are not allowed to go up by night, we lay to till morning, and at eight we were abreast of the first Turkish town, Castro, on the island of Tenedos, a very wretched-looking place with a picturesque castle. On our right were the celebrated Plains of Troy, distinguished by two large mounds called the tombs of Patroclus and Achilles, with Mount Ida in the distance. At about nine we entered the Dardanelles, which at the entrance are about four miles wide and defended on each side by two strong forts, called respectively the New Castles of Europe and Asia, and mounted with very large guns throwing immense stone shot of several hundred pounds weight. We passed numerous batteries on each side going up, some of them quite new and built since I was here last in 1847; generally there is a small town or village close to the fort, with a mosque and burying-ground and grove of cyprus. The shore all along the strait is very steep, and the scenery is very fine, if we could only have seen it, but to-day the weather has been wretched—a cold wind, with continual rain and sleet—a foretaste, I suppose, of the weather we may expect when we get into the Black Sea. However, we must not complain, as it is the only bad day we have had since we sailed. If the weather continues as thick and bad as it is now we are to anchor for the night at Gallipoli, at the entrance of the Sea of Marmora, and if so, we may expect to reach Constantinople to-morrow evening, and leave for Balaklava on the thirteenth. It must be blowing pretty fresh now in the Black Sea. I have been occupied to-day in stowing away in one portmanteau all the things I can best dispense with, in case I can only bring up one to camp. How I long for your next letter, which will tell me, I hope, of your safe arrival with the dear pets at Weston!

AT ANCHOR OFF POINT PESQUIERES AT
ENTRANCE TO SEA OF MARMORA, ABOUT
FIVE MILES SOUTH OF GALLIPOLI,
January 12, 2 *p.m.*

Soon after closing my letter to you yesterday the weather became so thick, and with such heavy showers of sleet and snow, that the pilot thought it prudent to anchor, especially as we could not see any great distance ahead and it was blowing pretty fresh. We were then just passing Cape Abydos, and ahead of us were two French steamers close to the shore, and just as we anchored a boat with an officer came off to us to say that one of them, the *Foulton*, bound with 200 Zouaves to the Crimea, had run ashore the night before last, and that her consort *Euminède* had failed to get her off, and they therefore asked our aid, as we were as large as them both put together. So we agreed to stay where we were for the night, and try and pull her off in the morning. The Frenchman's boat broke adrift while he was on board, and he was obliged to dine and sleep on board us. We found him an agreeable man, lost in admiration at the comfort our officers and men enjoyed on board so fine a ship. His ship, the *Euminède*, had left Sebastopol about three weeks ago, and he gave a very wretched account of the state of affairs—the siege not progressing at all, the weather very bad, and the men in the trenches up to their knees in water, and that several of the Arab troops had lost their feet; the only consolation was that the Russians were rather worse than we were, and that they had heard from pretty good authority—the French Consul—that Austria had actually declared war against Russia, which I hope will make a diversion in our favour. Yesterday was certainly a bitter day: a keen wind and the air full of sleet, which before night covered our decks with snow, a portion of which entered my cabin, the door having blown open in the night. This morning early (12th) we weighed anchor and came up with the French steamers, and after a good deal of dodging about— as from the strong wind that was blowing and the current we were afraid of getting ashore ourselves—we succeeded in getting a hawser fast to the *Euminède*, which was attached in a like manner to the poor *Foulton*, and we both steamed and tugged away for half an hour, but as yet without success, for although her stern is afloat, yet her bow is buried 4 feet in the mud; luckily for her the wind is blowing off shore. At 3 p.m., however, we are to have another try with a double hawser, when, perhaps, we may be more successful. The weather to-day, though cold enough, is fortunately clear, and we have no snow in the air, although the ground is thickly covered with it. The French troops were all landed out of the *Foulton* in order to lighten her, and they have formed a camp ashore close to the water's edge with their little *tentes d'abris*, one of which is carried by every four men; this morning we saw them running about to keep themselves warm, and a short time ago they were lighting fires and cooking their dinners. A steamer has just been signalled coming up the Dardanelles which is supposed to be H.M.S. *Gorgon*, which left Portsmouth with a company of the Rifles on board just a week before we did; if it should be her, Captain Hamilton, as the senior officer, will give an order that she should take a pull at the Frenchman along with us, and if we are unsuccessful, to stay by her while we pursue our voyage. I shall now say good-bye for the present.

CONSTANTINOPLE,
January 13, 9 *a.m.*

DEAREST E.,

The steamer which we yesterday supposed was the *Gorgon* turned out on approach to be the French war-steamer *Tesiphone*, so we, after taking another pull at the poor *Foulton*, which was unsuccessful, as she was buried too deep in the mud, left her to the care of the two consorts, and at 6 p.m. steamed off for this place, where we arrived at seven this morning, and before we go ashore are waiting orders as to whether we are to go on at once or wait to coal. The wind is excessively cold, the houses and ground covered with snow, and everything wears a most wintry look; it is, however, better than rain. We are now about thirty-nine hours' run from Balaklava, as if we leave this evening we shall reach it the middle of the day on the 15th. This place presents a very different aspect at this season from what it did when I saw it in the summer; there are a number of sailing men-of-war here, both French and English. We have anchored off the immense barracks of Scutari, now occupied as a hospital by our troops. The Captain has just gone ashore (10.30) to get our orders.

SCUTARI, 4 *p.m.*

I have just landed to report myself to the Commandant. We are to sail at daylight to-morrow. It has been blowing so hard we could not cross to Constantinople, and I must only try and get one on this side of the water. I must close this. Adieu; God bless you! Give my fondest love to my dearest mother and all at Weston. Kiss the darlings for me.

Ever yours affectionately,
RICHARD.

THE 'ADELAIDE,' FIFTY MILES FROM
SEBASTOPOL,
January 15, 1855, 1 *p.m.*

MY DEAREST ELLIE,

This afternoon we expect to arrive off that renowned fortress which for so long has claimed so large a share of the world's attention. We do not expect, however, to make Balaklava before nightfall, and shall therefore not enter it before daylight to-morrow, when I suppose we shall disembark immediately and march up to camp. We arrived at Constantinople on the 13th, and I wrote to you from there two letters, one on the 13th and one on the 14th, both of which I hope you got. I told you in mine of the 13th, which I finished in the barracks at Scutari, that I had landed there to see about getting Minié rifles for some of the drafts. We went ashore in a caique, and on returning to the wharf found it blowing so hard that the boatmen refused to take us off again. Indeed, it was just as well they did, for a boat was upset close to our ship and one man drowned, so we returned to the barracks, or, rather, hospital, where we were hospitably received by Major Tillery, the Assistant-Commandant, who gave us a dinner quite in camp fashion and a shake-down on a divan in his room. There were 5,000 sick and wounded at Scutari alone, besides those at Kulali, on board ships in harbour at Abydos in the Dardanelles; and they are now sending them to Corfu. Besides the stables being full, sick men were ranged in every passage and corridor in the barrack. Those I saw had bedsteads, and appeared pretty comfortable. Colonel Mauleverer, of the 30th, who was wounded, told me a good deal of news. Poor Major Sharp, of the 20th, is dead; they had not heard of his wife's arrival. Captain Daubeny had gone home. The nurses were of great use to the sick, and Miss Nightingale was indefatigable. She even attends amputations, and supports and cheers the patients under them. She is a most noble character. I also saw Sergeant Hinds, of our regiment, who is in charge of our sick in the hospital, sixteen in number, of whom five are wounded. We have also had some men killed in the trenches, and some have died, among them poor Farrel, from dysentery. I pity his poor wife, and should be glad if we could do something for her. Young Byron was wounded and taken prisoner in the trenches during a sortie on Christmas Day. I must try and get his parcel of warm clothing sent to him. Goodenough and Maxwell were both laid up in camp. Westhead is supposed to be on his way home, as he was heard of at Constantinople, although we did not see him. It was not known whether the detachment left at Corfu under Jordan had joined or not.

Our regiment was attached to the light division temporarily. I was fortunate enough to get from the Paymaster at Scutari, an old friend, a pack-saddle, the property of a deceased officer, for £1, which will enable me, I hope, to bring up a good part of my baggage. I also paid the purser 15s. for a pair of overall trousers, 1s. for boat-hire, and 7s. for a Turkish scarf to go round the waist, which everyone gets here, as it keeps your loins very warm, and is useful to carry things in. I was, however, greatly cheated in the price, as, not being able to go to Constantinople myself, I had to trust to a commissionaire. I could not get a padlock, and shall not therefore bring up any brandy. I am very sorry I did not bring the fisherman's boots I got at Plymouth. It was a great mistake, as all the Government boots are so immensely large. I am going to mess with Dr. Dwyer, whom I like very much. We heard at Constantinople that the French about three weeks ago pursued Lipsardi's corps for sixteen miles on the road to Simferopol, but they retired without fighting, and the French then returned and destroyed their camp.

The huts for our men have mostly arrived, but they are strewing the beach at Balaklava instead of being brought up to camp. We took on board at Constantinople an officer of the 62nd, with despatches for Lord Raglan from the Commander-in-Chief in India, stating that the 10th Hussars, 83rd and 86th regiments were to proceed overland from India to the Crimea. I am afraid you could hardly read my last from Scutari; it was written in such a hurry and so blotted. This is but little better, as the ship since entering the beastly Black Sea has rolled more than during her whole voyage before. The weather is cold, but clear, which I am glad of, and I hope the frost will last. We left Constantinople at 2 p.m. yesterday, Admiral Boxer being in a great state of excitement at our remaining so long, and after a lovely sail up the Bosphorus entered the Black Sea at 4.30 p.m., and have been tumbling in it ever since.

CHAPTER II

AT BALAKLAVA

BALAKLAVA,
January 17.

MY DEAREST LOVE,

Here we are at last. We got into harbour at seven this morning, and are now only waiting for orders for disembarkation. We were off this place yesterday early in the morning, but it blew such a gale of wind that the Captain did not think it safe to enter, and we beat about all day within sight of the place. It was a most dreadful day—a bitter north wind and heavy squalls of snow every hour. We could see the tents of the poor fellows on the bare, exposed hills above Balaklava, and I am sure they must have suffered greatly in the night. As soon as it got dark, although it was a bitter night with snow, we could see every now and then the sky illuminated by the flashes of the guns from Sebastopol, showing that the firing was carried on in spite of the elements. To-day, I am glad to say, is a lovely one after the storm—quite calm and a hard frost, with bright sun. I hope this weather will last, as it will put the roads in good order and enable us to get up our baggage.

I have heard from officers who have just come on board that the siege, as far as we are concerned, is virtually suspended; no firing at all from our batteries, it being impossible to get up ammunition.

7 p.m.

I have just returned from reporting myself to the Assistant-Quartermaster-General at Balaklava, and we are not to disembark till we get orders, and I hear that some drafts remain on board ship for weeks before they are disembarked. The 39th, who have been here for some days, are on board ship still. It is so difficult to supply the troops that they don't want to send up more than they can help. Our men have now to carry up their own rations and warm clothing, and even their tents. The commissariat can do little or nothing; they have no means of transport, and their horses are either dead or can scarcely crawl. Balaklava is crowded with stores of all sorts, and our men are perishing in the camp for want of fuel and clothing. I hope to be able to get up to camp to-morrow, as I must go up to take the command. The only officers I have seen are Shiffner, who is still in command of the draft. He came out in the *Charity*, and is in camp near Balaklava. I also saw Rowan and young Cochrane foraging for a dinner in Balaklava. I heard from them that Goodenough had only sprained his ankle by a fall in the trenches, and that it was not of much consequence. Maxwell has not been ill at all, and stands it very well. Farrel, I am glad to say, is not dead, but is in hospital at Balaklava. I also saw Dr. Evans, 16th Lancers, brother of Mr. Evans, of Duleek, and you may tell him that he is as well as possible. He has been in medical charge of our regiment, but now that he has been relieved by Dwyer he expects to be sent to Scutari. He tells me that out of about 500 we have nearly 189 on the sick-list; our men are, however, in very good spirits, and say they are better clothed than any regiment in the army. I saw young Ward of the 42nd and gave him his box. He looks as strong as a horse, and was wearing his kilt as if it was summer. I did not see Major Eveleigh, but sent word to him that I had got boxes for him, and he sent his servant on board for them and got them. I have not yet got any letter from you, although I hope to have the pleasure of finding one on arrival at camp, as I know well you have written.

You have no idea what an extraordinary scene Balaklava now presents. Its little harbour, which is completely landlocked, is crowded with vessels of every size and shape—men-of-war, steamers, sailing-vessels, lying in tiers two or three deep, and the streets of the wretched little village are more crowded than the busiest part of London. The narrow streets are almost impassable, from the number of dromedaries, mules, and horses; fatigue parties from every regiment, carrying provisions and stores; and officers in uniform, or rather winter dresses, of all sorts and descriptions, so it was impossible to tell to what regiment or even branch of the service many belonged. Several French officers and soldiers were in the crowd. The day was so fine and warm that almost all the camp came down to Balalava to market; the road to camp was one living stream. The road from camp to town, however, presented a more melancholy scene; long trains of sick men were being brought down to the ships, no less than 150 of them suffering from frost-bites.

THE 'ADELAIDE,' BALAKLAVA,
January 18.

As soon as I have closed this I am going ashore to post it, and to see the Commandant about going up to the camp. To-day the wind is from the south, with every appearance of a gale, and the weather is mild and threatens rain; it will be a good thing in one respect —that it will hinder the Russian reinforcements from coming up, 2,000 of whom have already arrived within the last week from Odessa. There is one point I have omitted mentioning before, which is, that when at Scutari I spoke to Major Sillery about officers' wives coming to see their husbands when in hospital. He strongly advised no one to attempt it, as he said they could not be put up in the hospital, as there was literally no room to put them in, there being three wounded officers in each, and that there is no hotel nor any accommodation in Scutari to go to. Under these circumstances, therefore, I think it best, my dearest Ellie, that you should forego your generous resolution of coming out to attend me in case of my being obliged to go to Scutari; you would only, perhaps, after a long and fatiguing journey and great anxiety, find on arrival that you could be of no service to me. I must now conclude as my paper is nearly exhausted. I trust I may find letters from you in camp to cheer me, for affairs here are as gloomy as they well can be. The reinforcements received have not done more than fill up the gaps caused by disease and death; the effective strength of our army is not greater than it was at Inkerman. Give my love to my mother and sisters and Francis; kiss the dear pets for me, especially darling baby. I long to hear how you made out your journey to Weston. There is a rumour I have just heard that there will be peace in two months. God grant that it may be so; everyone is tired of this work. God bless you, my pet! I pray that we may soon meet again.

Ever yours most affectionately,
RICHARD.

THE 'ADELAIDE,' BALAKLAVA,
January 19, 1855.

MY OWN DEAREST ELLIE,

As I find that the mail for England does not close till 8 to-night, I intend to give you another line in order that you may hear the latest news. I went ashore yesterday to learn our destination, and was informed that it was customary now in this place to keep all drafts on board ship for some time after their arrival, as it has been found that if the recruits, of which the drafts are now chiefly composed, are sent to the trenches or put on duty soon after their arrival, they fall sick and die off very fast. The 39th Regiment, who arrived a fortnight ago, are still on board ship, as also are the drafts on board the *Robert Low*, under command of Lieut.-Colonel Moorsom of the Guards, who have been here some weeks. They are employed in the first instance on fatigue, carrying stores and provisions to the camp, and we have 290 men employed on that duty to-day. I went out yesterday and walked up to the defensive line thrown up by us round Balaklava, and visited the camps of the Artillery and Turks. The breastworks in front of them appeared very weak, and as if any active man could run up them; they are, however, well flanked by batteries we have thrown up. I wish there were more guns planted on the heights on which the *Genoese* (?) is situated, on the right of the harbour as you enter, and which commands it completely. If the Russians were to carry these heights, all the shipping in the harbour and stores in the town would be at their mercy. Besides the troops defending the lines, we have, however, at least 2,000 men on board ships in the harbour, and the *Emen* (?) was signalled yesterday as being outside the harbour with the 14th Regiment on board from Malta; so we have, fortunately, a strong reserve. The Russians have also, no doubt, received strong reinforcements within the last few days, and I dare say they will attempt something. The French have received large reinforcements, and their men are in better order from being better supplied than our men; they have given us great assistance on the right towards Inkerman by taking up some of our outposts, as our regiments have been so reduced in strength that they could not hold them all. The 68th, which landed here 1,000 strong, can't now find 59 men for duty, and have been struck off in consequence; 14,000 of Omar Pasha's army have been landed at Eupatoria, and more are expected. As that is too large a force merely to defend that place, it is supposed they are going to invest Sebastopol on the north side, and till they do that effectually Sebastopol will never be taken. The French and Russian batteries fire at each other all day long, and I heard several salvos when I was out. Ours never fire a shot, and they consequently let us alone except occasionally firing a few volleys of shells into our trenches at night, just to keep us awake, but the men are so used to them that no one cares for them; they, however, make a sortie nearly every night, and frequently catch our sentries napping, and thus surprise the pickets. I saw Lord Raglan, Sir J. Burgoyne, General Airey with all their staff, come into Balaklava yesterday. It appeared to be quite an event in the place, for he hardly ever stirred out, and they all complain greatly of his apathy; he was, however, looking very well. I saw Airey for a few minutes, but he was too busy to speak long. I wore the long Government boots yesterday, and found them excellent articles and completely waterproof; they were well put to the test, as our walk was chiefly through deep half-thawed snow, and afterwards I waded nearly up to my knees to get on board a boat, and my feet were not the least wet. By wearing two pairs of stockings and my slippers in them I can walk in them very comfortably, and find them not a bit too large for me. The price of everything here is tremendous: long boots, £5 a pair; 4-lb. loaf, 2s.—and wretched bread it is; packet of envelopes, 2s.; mould candles, 3s.; and everything else in proportion. If you should have an opportunity of sending me a box, send eatables of some sort in it, as they say you require something to eat with the salt pork to prevent your getting scurvy, which is often the case with the men, especially if they eat it raw, as they frequently have to do for want of fuel to cook it with. There is no carriage on parcels sent in ships freighted by the Government. I saw Major Eveleigh yesterday; he was looking very well, and seemed to bear roughing capitally. He told me that he goes out with his axe and saw and cuts his own fuel. He has built himself a hut, and asked me to sleep in it for a night or two before going to camp, as it would break me in for sleeping in a tent, which I should find rather cold at first. I have just seen Rowan, who has come down from the camp, and tells me that there are no letters for me in camp, which is a great disappointment, for I fully expected to receive some. I hope I may get some by the next mail.

I hope you will send me occasionally a few papers, as often you hear more of what is going on here from the papers than you do on the spot. The rumour in camp to-day is that a special messenger arrived yesterday with despatches of great importance for Lord Raglan, the purport of which will not be known for two days; it is hoped that it is relative to peace. I saw on shore the lady of Balaklava, Mrs. Duberly, wife of the Paymaster of the 8th Hussars. She is an extraordinary person—wears a very long gown, which she does not mind holding up pretty high, and discloses a regular pair of trousers lined with leather.

Believe me, ever your affectionate
RICHARD.

I shall have to pay 3s. 6d. a day for my living for every day I am on board, commencing on December 28, and you must, therefore, leave a sum in Cox's hands sufficient to meet it. Our daily ration at camp is 1 lb. salt meat, 1 lb. biscuit, $1\frac{3}{4}$ oz. sugar, 1 oz. coffee, 1 gill rum, 2 oz. rice, 12 lb. charcoal, 12 lb. barley, and 8 lb. hay for each horse. Sergeant Reay is recommended for an ensigncy. Major Simpson expects to go home to the depôt. Our men have to carry everything up to the camp; they therefore don't bring up much charcoal, as they can't carry everything, and trust for fuel to the roots of trees, etc. Adieu!

THE 'ADELAIDE,' BALAKLAVA,
January 21, 1855.

MY DEAREST ELLIE,

All the drafts for the light division (19th, 34th, 88th, and Rifles) are ordered to disembark at 9 a.m. to-morrow and march to camp, and as the mail closes to-morrow, unless I write to-day I shall have no time to do so to-morrow. The roads are at present in a dreadful state, owing to the thaw which has prevailed since the 17th and has melted all the snow, and I am afraid all the men, with all the heavy loads they have to carry, will not be able to make out the march (seven miles in one day), as, in addition to the usual heavy marching order load, they have to carry each two blankets, waterproof capes, and two days' provisions, besides camp-kettles and bill-hooks. The roads were never worse than they are at present—full of mud-holes, in which you sink above the knee. I am, therefore, afraid of overweighting poor Leander, and shall only put on him two portmanteaus and my carpet-bag. I sent up to-day my bedstead, canteen and tin of butter; my bed-basket and saddle-box I have left in the stores, and must get them sent up the first opportunity. Our camp is in front of the light division, and we are the most advanced regiment in the army, being about half a mile from the batteries, and we have a most splendid panoramic view of Sebastopool and the harbour from the summit of the hill on which our camp is placed, which overhangs the Valley of Inkerman. The French are on the opposite ridge, on which they have established a battery, and between them and the Russians a good deal of firing goes on.

The night before last there was a continual rattle of cannon and musketry, occasioned, I believe, by the French attacking and taking a redoubt. We hardly fire at all now except an occasional shot from the sailors' battery, where Lieutenant Spalding of H.M.S. *London* was killed to-day; indeed, we have nearly given up fighting, the time and energies of the men being fully employed in guarding the trenches and getting food and clothing, and occasionally fuel, from Balaklava. The commissariat can do nothing in the way of transport; they will give you almost anything you like to ask for, from a hut to a preserved potato, if you only can carry it up; but there is the difficulty. The commissariat horses are as a race nearly extinct, and their carcasses strew the roads in every direction. The cavalry division of ten regiments cannot muster 800 live horses, and not half of them are fit for work, and they are almost solely employed in carrying the unfortunate sick from camp to ship-board, and not a day passes but from 200 to 300 of these poor fellows are thus brought down, and most of them obliged to be supported on their horses. If we were to have an action to-morrow, the artillery could not horse twelve field-pieces. Balaklava is stocked with stores both on shore and on board ship; from want of room they stand in the open air, liable to be stolen or destroyed by the damp, yet two miles away the men are suffering the greatest privations for want of common necessaries. I was told by a staff officer that one regiment for three days ate their pork raw, for want of fuel to cook it with. The sickness and mortality among the men, especially the new-comers, from overwork and want of rest, is something frightful; with all our reinforcements we cannot muster 12,000 effective men. The extinction of the 4th Division, the medical officer in charge of it says, is a mere question of time; he gives them about six weeks more to exist; a company with ten men fit for duty is considered very strong. The 63rd Regiment landed in the Crimea, in September last, 1,030 strong; yesterday when they marched into Balaklava for embarkation for England (having been struck off duty) their strength was nine officers and twenty-five men. Our regiment, compared with others, is very well off, and I never saw the officers looking better, and the men that I have seen are in very good spirits, and say they have plenty to eat, and are close to wood and water, but that the duty is cruelly hard. The whole army is full of the report of some astonishing piece of news, which Lord Raglan has received within the last few days, and which is to be promulgated to-morrow, and is to surprise and gratify both army and navy. All sorts of reports are of course afloat, from the declaration of peace to the storming of Sebastopol; and I believe that either of these would be better than our present position. Everywhere you hear the greatest complaints of the apathy of Lord Raglan and his staff, who seem to look after nothing; but everything is conducted on the happy-go-lucky system: you must look after yourself, for no one will do so for you. The weather is delightfully mild at present, and this thaw will stop the advance of the Russian reinforcements. My paper is exhausted; I will therefore say adieu till next mail, when I hope I may have to answer a letter of yours. Adieu; love to all, kisses to pets.

Ever affectionately,
R.

CHAPTER III

IN CAMP

> LIGHT DIVISION CAMP,
> BEFORE SEBASTOPOL,
> *January* 25, 1855.

MY OWN DEAREST ELLIE,

We disembarked from the *Adelaide* at 10.30 on Monday morning, the 22nd, and although the distance was only seven miles, yet the main body of the draft—70 out of 108 who started—did not reach the camp till 4 p.m., and the remainder not for two hours afterwards, so heavily were the men loaded, and the state of the roads such as to baffle all description, owing to the thaw of the few previous days. The main or Woronzoff road is not used, for although the Russians, under Lipandi, have retired from the valley, yet their Cossacks have pickets on the opposite ridge; we had therefore to take a track that led through some steep ravines, along which there was a constant stream of men and horses, and occasionally artillery waggons, both going and returning, which converted the road into a regular quagmire of mud, in which the poor men sank up to their knees, and frequently had their long boots dragged off. Brown Bess struggled through very well, but was very much startled at the sight and smell of some dromedaries she met coming out of Balaklava. Leander, however, does not seem to approve of campaigning in the Crimea at all; he wouldn't carry up my bed at all, and I was fortunate in being able to have it transferred to one of the ponies carrying the tents. He didn't arrive till very late, and about the middle of the night, being alarmed, I suppose, by the firing—it happened to be pretty sharp —he broke his chain and galloped off, and I of course thought he was lost to me for ever, as horse-stealing is thought nothing of here; anyone that finds a stray horse tries to sell it immediately, and at Balaklava is sure to find a ready market and a good price. I sent round the camps of our division next morning to make known his loss, and most fortunately two of our men met him with an artilleryman on his back, on his way to Balaklava, no doubt for sale; they, however, made him dismount, and brought him back to me, clothing and all, and I have had him since made more secure with a rope. We are encamped on a tongue of land running between two ravines; in our front is a redoubt occupied by the French, from which you have a splendid view of Sebastopol, distant about a mile and a quarter. The town, from the number of Government buildings in it, all built of white stone, has a very handsome appearance, and looks as clean and fresh as possible, and the forts as formidable as ever. Immediately in our rear are the camps of the remainder of the 1st Brigade Light Division, viz., 23rd, 33rd, and Rifles; on the opposite side of the ravine, on our right, lies the battle-field of Inkerman, and on it are encamped the 2nd Division and Brigade of Guards. Our regiment is supposed to be encamped on the healthiest ground in the army, and very conveniently situated for wood and water. I have a double tent, which is much warmer, although darker, than a single tent, and it is now tolerably comfortable; I am having the floor paved and then covered with sand. I have been fortunate enough to get four blankets, and, indeed, you require them all, for it freezes hard every night. But we have been most fortunate in the weather, which, although cold, has been dry and calm, and the sun has shone brightly, which raises one's spirits. Goodenough and Simpson kindly asked me to dine with them the two first nights, and very good dinners they gave: soup, fish, meat, and pudding; but they live very extravagantly, and have a man constantly foraging at Balaklava for whatever he can get. Harman also messes with them, and he told me that their total living, from December 10 to the present time, cost them about £79. Dwyer and I had our first dinner on our own account yesterday, of good salt pork and biscuit, and we are to have the same to-day, with the addition of preserved potatoes, a ration of which has been served out to-day, and will be a great treat. I take essence of coffee for breakfast and find it very good. I have sent to town to-day for charcoal, and hope I shall be able to get some, as a fire inside your tent this cold weather would be a great luxury. I am now enjoying the comfort of one in Roach's tent, and writing on a regular table, which he contrived to bring up, and kindly allowed me to make use of; my hands and feet were so cold in my tent I could hardly write. I must now tell you of the happiness I had of getting your dear letter the day I arrived in camp, and you can imagine what a thrill of pleasure I felt in seeing your dear handwriting once again and learning from you that you and the dear pets were all well. I am so glad you made up your mind to go by Liverpool, and trust that you all made out the journey without fatigue. I am sure you must have had a hard job packing up all the things and giving up the house. I hope you had a smooth passage across; I long to hear of your safe arrival at Weston, and how you found them all there. You did very well in leaving our heavy baggage with the Buckleys, as it will be easy to get them from Plymouth. I am glad, my dearest love, that, in spite of the hard trials you have to undergo, *you still keep up* your spirits and put your trust in the only true Source. God has mercifully protected us through many a danger and difficulty, and will continue to do so still, I have no doubt.

I am so glad you have received good accounts of my dear mother. I am sure your presence will cheer her up more than anything else. How generous Catherine Keys has been! I hope the bracelets are handsome. I hope the darling children continue well. I should like to have seen darling baby crawl upstairs and step into the portmanteau. I am glad you have got a maid for the children, but I hope Mrs. Caffrey will not leave you; remember me kindly to her. Thanks for sending me the spurs. Major Eveleigh told me that the box was to come out by the *Malacca*, which I see has arrived, so I suppose I shall soon get them. I wish I had a second pair of long boots for a change, as one pair frequently gets frozen. I wish you would send me by the first opportunity a pair of strong laced shooting-boots, made double at the toes, and wide and easy, so as to admit three pairs of stockings, and, if possible, with waterproof soles. I am very badly off for boots; common Wellington boots are of no use; the only ones I have to depend on are my Government ones. Please also to send me, if you can, some cases of preserved soups—Gamble's are the best; also some more of that soluble chocolate, some split peas for soup, and some biscuits. What a kind, feeling letter that is from

Richard Lloyd! Will you tell him how much I am obliged to him for it? Nothing has been heard out here yet of the articles sent out to the army by the Crimea Fund. Our life in camp is as follows: The whole army turns out an hour before daylight, and stands to arms till every object is distinctly seen. I then breakfast, first (as the morning air makes us all so hungry) on essence of coffee and biscuit. The former is capital, and I wish you would send me some more of it, as it is so difficult to grind the green coffee. After breakfast I wash and indulge in warm water, as that brought us from the river is invariably frozen. After breakfast a fatigue-party is sent to Balaklava to bring up warm clothing for the men and buffalo-skins to lay on the ground in their tents. We have been promised a hut for our hospital, if we can carry it up; it will take seventy-nine men four days to do it. My horses go into Balaklava every day to try and bring up forage and charcoal, and they return without either. I have got all my baggage up except the saddle-box, which I must try and get up to use it for a cupboard; the basket put on a portmanteau makes a capital table, just the right height for me when sitting on my bed. My lunch, as yet, has been Bologna sausage and biscuit, and at two I generally take a walk, dine at four, take a cup of coffee at seven, and in bed by eight. The men always sleep with their belts on, and I have only taken off my boots. I never saw the officers as a body looking better, especially Roach and Maxwell; the latter is getting quite fat. Mrs. Roach is living at 43, Summer Hill, Dublin, with his sister, Miss Roach; I am sure you will try to see her if you can, or write to her. My turn for the trenches has not come yet; I shall probably be on to-morrow. We furnish about one hundred men with a Captain and Subaltern every night, and, although the

Russians fire a good deal in the daytime and when you are going out of the trenches, we have not had a casualty among our men since I arrived. The French and the Russians are almost always at it, and they keep up a lively cannonade through the night. The wonderful news I spoke of in my last has ended in smoke, although we hear through Vienna that the Emperor has accepted the four points and that peace may be expected, but I don't believe it. Lord Raglan and staff are looked at by the army as very incompetent. Love to all and kisses to pets.

> Ever yours affectionately,
> RICHARD.

On the 27th I walked over part of the field of Inkerman. A number of dead horses still remain unburied, but I only saw two corpses, both Russians; one was under a ledge of rock by the side of a steep ravine, and I suppose had been forgotten. I see no reason why the other should not have been buried; they both presented a ghastly sight. The field was strewed with cannonballs of all sizes, some at least 109 pounds weight, much larger than any in our service. I picked up a few musketballs. Both English and French have erected strong batteries on the heights of Inkerman, in order to command the harbour and Russian ships, but only one French battery is armed, and we are waiting for the fine weather to carry up our guns. The Russians have established batteries on the opposite side of the valley, and were firing at the French works while we were there, but did not do any mischief. I walked yesterday to the Gordon or 21-gun battery on our right attack. Most of the guns are so much injured by the Russian guns, or worn out by their own fire, that they will have to be replaced by fresh guns before we can do anything. I hear they are beginning to-day to try and get up fresh guns. I have not been in the trenches yet, but suppose my turn will soon come. 890 men are furnished by each division for the trenches in the night, and 700 by day, and they are relieved every twelve hours just at dawn. The day trenches are the best, as they never make a sortie by day, and, although they keep up a constant fire, yet, if you keep under cover, they don't do you much harm. Poor Byron's parcel of clothing, which I got from his uncle, was sent to him to-day by a flag of truce; he is to be removed from Sebastopol to the interior. I have not seen Frederick Smith yet, but I hear he is very well. I must now conclude, with affectionate love to my mother and all the dear circle at Weston, and kisses to the dear pets.

Believe me, dearest, to be,
Your most affectionately attached
RICHARD.

LIGHT DIVISION CAMP,
January 31, 1855.

MY OWN BELOVED ELLIE,

Last night the English mail arrived, and I had the happiness of getting your affectionate letter of January 11 to 13, and two papers—the *Times* of January 5 and the *Dublin Evening Mail* of the same date; many thanks for them. I am sure we lose half our papers, as I have only received the *Times* of the 4th, 5th, and 6th. You can well imagine what a consolation it is to me to get your letters, every line of which breathes such affection and devotion for me. God bless and reward you for it. The reports in camp about the probability of peace are much stronger since the arrival of the mail. Lord B——, one of Lord Raglan's A.D.C.'s who is son of Lord Westmorland, our Ambassador in Vienna, says that his father has strong hopes of a peace being concluded; but I think Sebastopol must fall first. The French would be mad if they were foiled in taking the place, after all their preparations and exertions; their batteries are all armed, and ready to open fire with about 150 guns. They only wait for us. We have to exchange most of the guns in our batteries, some from being disabled, and others for guns of larger size. For the last two days they have been bringing up guns to our 21-gun battery—bringing them just out of range in the day-time, and slipping them into the battery at night. We have also to arm our batteries at Inkerman, which are to mount very heavy guns and mortars, and are intended to destroy the Russian ships. If this fine frosty weather continues, I suppose the guns will be got up, and ready to open fire in about a fortnight, when it is supposed that a heavy fire for three days, from 259 guns, will completely destroy their defences; and then if they don't surrender the assault will be given. The French, I believe, will take the principal part in this; we shall be in reserve to check any diversion attempted to be made by the Russian army outside. I hear that our depot is likely to be sent to Preston, where a depot battalion is to be formed. I suppose, if six companies are to be in England, the Lieutenant-Colonel will be there also, and the Major sent to Malta. Nothing is known yet as to which Major is to go home; some think it will be the senior, and some the junior; we must only have patience. If I am ordered to go, I will go, and if not, I will remain and do my duty here, as I know all is ordered for the best; and if it is the Almighty will,

I can be preserved in the midst of danger as well as if at home.

I am glad you think my dear mother looking better since her illness; I am sure having you and the children with her raises her spirits and does her a great deal of good, and prevents her from feeling so nervous. Tell her, with my fond love, that I shall be delighted to hear from her, whenever she feels inclined to write.

We have been most fortunate in our weather since our arrival, for although very cold with hard frost, yet it has been dry and without wind; we have had rain only for a few hours one night; this had a very good effect on the health of our men, and I believe we are the healthiest regiment in the division. Most of the regiments have got up huts for their hospitals, and in some few cases, also, two or three for their men; our regiment, from being so far in the front and having no 'bat' horses attached to the regiment, have not as yet been able to bring up any huts; but we have been promised to be lent some commissariat horses in a few days, when I hope to be able to get up one for the hospital. It takes ten horses four days to bring up a hut from Balaklava to our camp, so I don't expect ever to see our men hutted. My tent, being a double one, is much warmer than the others. I have now, besides, abundance of bedclothes, having been served with seven blankets, of which I have four over me, and I assure you it is not too much, for the frost is intense at night; I have also had my sheepskin coat exchanged for a Turkish fur coat, which is a most comfortable wrapper to put on when you sit in the tent, for it reaches down to my heels, and is made like a dressing-gown; the fur, which is inside, is black lambskin, and the skin outside is embroidered in silk. We have also received from Government two jerseys, two pair flannel drawers, two pair socks, two pair woollen gloves, and one pair ammunition boots, same as the men's; so we are very well off for warm clothing, and I must also say that all the time I have been here our rations have been most ample and good; and we have enjoyed with great relish some very fair pea-soup. I have not yet tried the portable soup, but hope to be able to do so in a few days.

February 1.

Yesterday a most curious accident occurred here, showing the extreme carelessness and want of foresight and vigilance which has characterized our proceedings during the whole campaign. In the French works and batteries no one is allowed to enter, not even an English officer, without an order from their General. In ours anyone that likes goes in and out just as he pleases, no questions asked, and the consequence was that a Russian spy yesterday went through the whole of our Gordon battery, speaking to some of the officers who were on duty there, and then through some of the camps and back to Sebastopol, with all his information, without being arrested; he was dressed in the costume usually adopted here by English officers, having as little as possible of uniform on, viz., a blue pea-coat, long boots, and forage-cap. He must have got through our chain of sentries in front—no difficult matter, as we have an immense extent of ground to cover and very few men. When asked who he was, he said he was a medical officer of the 2nd Division, and although he spoke with a foreign accent, nothing was suspected till he had left the battery and was seen going towards Sebastopol, when the sentries were ordered to fire on him, which they did, but missed, and he reached a picket of his own men in safety, who received him with three cheers. An order is issued to-day that no one is to enter the batteries, except on duty, without a pass. Last night there was very heavy firing on our left, and to-day we hear that the Russians made a successful sortie on the French, killed a Lieutenant-Colonel and Major, and took several officers and men prisoners. The two young Grand-Dukes are in Sebastopol, and it was thought we should have had an attack this morning, but none took place. A Russian steamer, however, amused itself by shelling a redoubt which the French have constructed on the brow of Shell Hill, just in front of our camp and about 500 yards from it; they threw twenty-eight shells, and made very good practice, some of them falling right among the tents of a French picket about half-way between the redoubt and our camp, but, strange to say only two men were wounded. This lasted from about nine to ten; then they left us and shelled the redoubts on the Inkerman hill, on the opposite side of the ravine, but did no mischief, although they pitched one shell right into the ravine in front of our camp; it did not burst, however. I saw Linton to-day, who inquired kindly for you; he looks very much aged and fagged. Our camp is pitched in ground just like a ploughed field at home; the traffic has been so great that not a vestige of grass or turf remains; the ground was once covered with a copse-wood of dwarf oak, but not a tree is now to be seen, all having been cut long ago for fuel, and the men have now to dig up the roots for that purpose. Two ships with part of the material for the Balaklava railroad, and the navvies to work on it, have arrived, and land has been surveyed, and I hear they have commenced laying down the sleepers for the rails. A ship has also arrived laden with articles from the Crimean Fund, but it has not yet been settled how they are to be distributed. You would never tell, from the appearance of our troops, that they were British soldiers, such extraordinary costumes do they appear in: some in sheepskin coats, others in Turkish, and some in large watch-coats with hoods, most with long boots up to the knees, and all wear fur caps of one pattern or another. When they go into the trenches at night they are loaded with so many coats and blankets, one over the other, to keep themselves warm, that it is hardly possible for them to move, and I don't know how they would use their arms when required.

February 2.

Last night passed off very quietly, with less firing than usual, and to-day they have only thrown a few shells at our batteries on Inkerman. To-day the weather is very mild, with slight rain; our weather has latterly been very favourable to our operations, and we certainly ought to take advantage of it to hasten them and bring this tedious siege, of which everyone is tired, to an end. My box fell off the horse and got broken coming up; I have had it repaired, and it makes a seat and cupboard. A bottle is my candlestick, except on windy nights, when I use the lanthorn. So you see I am very snug and comfortable, and, thank God, I enjoy excellent health—the first of blessings—so you need not be the least alarmed or anxious about me.

    Believe me, dearest,
        Ever your most affectionate
            RICHARD.

LIGHT DIVISION CAMP,
February 5.

MY DEAREST ELLIE,

Last night I had the pleasure of receiving your affectionate letter of January 16, also a letter from my dear mother and Kate dated the 17th, and a *Times* of the 12th; thank you all for them—they are my greatest consolation here. Our weather here continues very fine, but very cold, with hard frost. On the 3rd and 4th the thermometer was at 10 degrees, with a sharp wind; I have never been in a place where the wind changes so much as here. On the night of the 2nd we had steady rain till eleven, when the wind shifted suddenly to the north, and it froze hard, with heavy snow, and our poor fellows had a miserable night in the trenches, as their clothes were first wet through and then frozen.

The next day was bitter cold, with frequent snowstorms, and I was for the trenches in the night, and thought I should have passed a very unpleasant one, and, accordingly, put on such an amount of clothing that I could hardly waddle under the weight of it. Our division and the 2nd Division formed the guards of the trenches for the right attack, and their strength by day is 700, and by night 800; they are commanded by a Lieutenant-Colonel and a Major; the Lieutenant-Colonel commands in the battery, and the Major in the advanced works, about 500 yards in front of it; they consist of a ditch with a parapet in front, constructed of gabions filled with earth, and sand-bags on top of them, and there is a step inside to allow the men to fire over the parapet. On the right this work communicates, by a covered way, with the Gordon or 21-gun battery in the rear; and the left rests on a steep ravine, called the Valley of the Shadow of Death, from the heavy fire that was poured up it at the commencement of the siege, and it is literally paved with shot; across this is a breastwork, and behind it is stationed a picket, the sentries from which communicate with the sentries in front of the advanced work, and complete the chain. We throw out in the advanced works from forty to fifty sentries, according to whether the night is light or dark, and they are posted about fifty yards in front of the works, and relieved every hour. The guards of the trenches are always relieved in the dark, that the enemy may not see you. We started from our camp at 5 p.m., and all assembled at the rendezvous opposite the Marine camp, from whence it is nearly three miles to the trenches; it was a most disagreeable night when we started, blowing and snowing, and so dark that you could hardly see before you, and we missed our road in consequence once or twice. We reached the trenches about seven, and the wind and snow soon ceased, the moon came out, and it was a most lovely night, although cold. Our right trenches are nearly opposite the Russian Round Tower, which we destroyed at the commencement of the siege, but under which they have constructed most formidable batteries. Our Gordon battery is very much exposed to capture, if it should be attempted by a large body in a determined manner, for it is nearer Sebastopol than the nearest camp from which assistance could come, and we have only 800 men to guard it; fortunately, the Russians don't know how weak we are. The risk is considered so great that, as we are not using the guns at present, we have actually spiked them ourselves with wooden spikes, in order to prevent the Russians doing it more effectually, should they get temporary possession of the battery. The night was so clear that we could plainly see the Russian sentries, who are about 500 yards in our front, and are about three times as numerous as our own, being posted five or six together, instead of merely double ones, as ours are, but we haven't men enough for that. Their sentries and ours never fire on one another, however close they may be, except when an attack is made; but directly it gets light their rifle-men come out and fire at everyone they can get a glimpse of, either inside or outside the parapet; and therefore our outside sentries are always brought in at daybreak, and the guards and pickets are supposed to be relieved at the same time, while it is still dark. Owing to a neglect of that, and the relief being late, four men of the Royals who were on picket in the ravine on my left which I spoke of were picked off the morning I came off. We were fortunately relieved very early, and hadn't a shot fired at us; indeed, there was very little firing the whole night, although we occasionally saw the fiery track of Russian and French shells crossing one another on their errands of death and destruction. I was walking about a good deal in the night, visiting the sentries, etc., and so did not find it so very cold. An officer of the 19th also brought down some charcoal, and made a very nice fire, and boiled some chocolate, of which we all partook; so we spent rather a pleasant night than otherwise. We don't put much faith here in the reports of peace, as we think the Emperor of Russia is only negotiating to get more time for his reinforcements to come up. I see Sardinia has joined the alliance against Russia, and the *on dit* is that we are to be joined by 15,000 Sardinians, which if the case will be a valuable reinforcement, as they are good troops. I hope the dear pets' colds are better. I had such a kind letter from my mother and Kate. Thank them both warmly for it, and say I hope I may be able to answer it by next mail; but letter-writing is very difficult here, there are so many interruptions. Since I began this I have been called away by the General of the division, General Codrington, the Brigade-Major, and the Assistant Quartermaster-General, besides interruptions from officers and sergeants every half-hour.

You seem to have a severe winter; I hope you don't feel it more than you did last. Here the water frequently freezes solid in my tent at night. I have generally a charcoal fire in the day, but even then it is very cold if you sit long. I have done as yet with the stores you supplied me with at Plymouth, and I have a great quantity left, and peas and onions are all I have bought at Balaklava. I use the chocolate at breakfast, and find it very good, and so easily prepared; I wish I had more of it. The essence of coffee is capital also, and so is the butter, which keeps so well this weather. I generally lunch on the cheese. I have not yet touched the potted meats. I used the portable soup for the first time yesterday, when the doctor and I had a grand dinner, as we had a ration of fresh mutton and rice (the second time of issue), which was made into a hash, and to wind up we had fried plum-pudding, Westhead's father having kindly sent out a box of them to the officers. One of Lord Blantyre's ships is expected shortly, and I hear each regiment is to send in a list of what they require, when they will be sold at cost price, and if so, I will procure some, I hope. The two companies of our regiment that were left at Corfu arrived here along with the 71st, in the *Medway*, on the 3rd. Warry was in command of our detachment, and I suppose they will soon be sent up to camp. Fred Smith called on me the other day; he is not looking well, and he is very much pulled down He says he has been suffering from rheumatic fever, but hopes soon to get his promotion in the other battalion; he was, however, in very good spirits, but not strong. Dr. Evans is very well, and is still with us, but expects to be appointed to the 8th Hussars. I must now conclude with kisses to the pets, and affectionate love to all.

Believe me ever your attached
RICHARD.

LIGHT DIVISION,
February 7, 1855.

MY OWN DEAREST ELLIE,

Last night I had again the happiness of getting your dear letter of January 19, with the *Times* of the 15th and 16th; it is a great comfort indeed to receive your letters so regularly. Many thanks to you for writing so often. I trust you have received all mine equally regularly; the mail closes in camp every Monday and Friday evening, and generally is sent from Lord Raglan's quarters to the mail-steamer in Chersonese Bay. Sometimes, however, if his lordship has anything particular to communicate, he sends off the mail before the time, as I am afraid was the case on the 5th, and that all our letters were late for that mail. You must not, therefore, be anxious if a considerable delay sometimes takes place in your getting my letters; you may rely, my love, on my writing at least once a week, if possible, for it is not only my duty, but also my greatest pleasure to write to you; but occasionally I may be prevented by business or duty, so you must not get into a state of mind if sometimes you do not hear from me when you expect to. I am so glad my letters from Malta at last turned up, and that they afforded you such pleasure. It was just as well that you did not write to me to Malta, as the English mail only arrived a few hours before we left,

and most probably we should not have got our letters.
I am glad you like the mits, and hope they fit; had it
not been Sunday I could have got a pair for each of the
ladies at Weston, but if I am spared to return home
that way I hope to bring some with me. I am glad you
keep up a correspondence with Mrs. Bourke, as she
would always be able to let you know about the depôt
and how they are increasing in strength, for till they are
near their establishment (1,000 rank and file) I am afraid
they won't appoint a second Lieutenant-Colonel, and I
dare say it will not be till April. The general order
came out yesterday about what officers were to go home;
each regiment is to have three Field-Officers and eight
Captains present, and only those in excess of that
number are to go home; so we three Majors must stay
out here a little longer, and only the three junior Captains
go home. As some set-off to this disappointment
I was agreeably surprised, and no doubt you also, at
seeing last night in the *Gazette* of the 19th both Goodenough's
and my name appear as Brevet Lieutenant-Colonels,
my commission being dated December 12 and
his January 6. Is it not extraordinary what a close race
we have run each other? The advantage to me will be
that from the 22nd instant, when I shall have been in
actual command of the regiment for one month, I shall,
as long as I continue in command, receive 17s. a day,
and commence counting for the three years' service necessary
to complete before promotion to the rank of Colonel.
We, of course, consider it a great honour to be in the
Light Division, and I believe are indebted for it to
General Airey. We are commanded by Major-General
Codrington, formerly of the Guards, who is a particularly
gentlemanly person, and very active, and I like
what I have seen of him very much. We are in the

1st Brigade, composed of 7th, 23rd, 33rd, 34th, and 2nd Battalion Rifle Brigade, and commanded by Colonel Lawrence, of the Rifles. The 2nd Brigade, under Colonel Shirley, of the 88th, consists of the 19th, 77th, 88th, and 90th. They are not going to form a 5th Division. The regiments are too weak for it. General Barnard has the brigade in the 3rd Division, formerly commanded by Colonel Bell, of the Royals. I am sorry to hear Louisa has got influenza; she has been a great sufferer. I am sorry indeed that I omitted to mention her name and your mother's in my last, but it was not from want of remembering them, for they are constantly in my thoughts, and tell them so with my love. I hope your mother's sciatica is better; she is indeed to be pitied with all her trials and troubles. I hope you will always take every good opportunity of making her some little present. I hope on your return to Weston that you found the coughs and colds of the pets better. I am sure they were delighted with the baskets for their dolls' clothes. I hope dear Kate has quite got over her fatigue, and that Mrs. Caffrey is also quite well again.

I paid a visit to-day to Major Eveleigh, who has by far the most comfortable abode I have seen. He has built for himself a hut sunk 4 feet in the ground, with good thick mud walls all round, with a wooden roof covered with tarpaulins, a regular fire-place and chimney, two windows and a door, and inside no end of furniture—table, two chairs and a bed—and you can't think how snug and comfortable he is; the floor is as dry and hard as pavement, from having sand and ashes frequently thrown on it and rammed down with a tent-mallet. A tent is worst in windy weather. The night before last it blew very hard, and I was very much afraid the tent-pegs would have been dragged out. We have commenced getting up huts, and have two nearly finished, which are intended for the sick; it takes, however, a week to bring up all the materials for a hut and then to put it up, at which rate it would take a month before all the men were hutted, and then would come the turn of the officers. I gave your message to Boyce, who was very glad to hear of his family, as he had not heard from them yet. He had rather a narrow escape a short time ago. He was looking with a glass from over the parapet of one of our batteries at Inkerman, and was watching the movements of a Russian steamer, when she commenced shelling the battery, and he had just stepped down when the first shell went over his head just where he had been standing, and burst about fifty yards behind, but happily without doing any mischief. Young Clayton was nearly shot the night before last by a French sentry. He was on picket, the sentries from which communicated with the French, and on visiting them to see that the chain was kept up, a Zouave took it into his head that he and his patrol were Russians, and, by way of making sure, fired at him when he was within 10 yards, and then cried, 'Qui Vive?' and Clayton had a very narrow escape of not being able to answer the question, as the ball whizzed close by his ear. The French are certainly capital troops, and understand soldiering in all its branches, and in intelligence, method, and arrangement, and in everything but sheer pluck and endurance, and perhaps discipline, are superior to our men. We have a regiment of Zouaves encamped not far from us, and they have a very fine band, who play very often as they pass through our camp every day to relieve a strong picket they have on a redoubt about 400 yards in front of our camp, which they have named Victoria, and which I am glad to see they have armed with five heavy guns, which will make our position on this side a good deal stronger than it was before. These Zouaves are fine, picked men, and are dressed as Arabs, in red petticoat-trousers, shoes, and gaiters, blue capots with hood and red fez. They keep their arms beautifully bright and clean, and every three men carry between them a little *tente à l'abris*, in which there is just room for three men to lie down and be sheltered from the weather. I have not been at Balaklava since my arrival in camp, and don't intend to go unless absolutely obliged; it is such a filthy place, and the road to it so bad. I hear Lord Raglan has turned out all the shop-keepers from the town in order to make room for the stores of the Crimean Funds. The shop-keepers have removed to tents outside the town, where a sort of bazaar is held, the prices in which are now regulated by Lord Raglan, and they have been much reduced lately, so that you can now buy a loaf of bread for 1s. 6d., and a bottle of porter for the same. I am waiting, however, for the Crimean Fund things, which are to be sold at cost price. Whenever you send me a box put up some candles in it, wax or sperm, as from the draught in the tent they burn very quickly. Many thanks to my mother for the parcel she has sent for the use of our men; they will be very acceptable. I got a letter from Mrs. Whately, wife of the Archbishop of Dublin, stating that the Irish Ladies' Crimean Clothing Fund had despatched three bales of warm clothing for our regiment through Hayter and Howell, army packers, Mark Lane, London, who are empowered by Government to forward parcels for officers and men in the Crimea by any steamer or transport free of expense, and that will be your best way of sending anything. I shall now say, Good-night! and God bless you. I took a walk the other day with Drs.

Evans and Dwyer over the field of Inkerman, and the former, having been in the action, was able to point out all the interesting spots. The position is now made very strong, several redoubts and batteries having been thrown up; the Russians would find it difficult to establish themselves there again. The view of Inkerman valley, through which the Tchernaya flows, is very pretty. At the end near the harbour of Sebastopol it is bounded by very high cliffs of sandstone, in the sides of which have been excavated caves, and a sort of church or castle, but by whom tradition does not mention—some say by the early Christians. The hills on our side of the valley are uniformly covered with a sort of thick copsewood, or dwarf oak, but almost all of these have been cut down, and even their roots dug up for fuel by the troops. The great want in the scenery about here is wood; the country about is just like a brown, barren, rocky moor, without a blade of grass or tree to be seen, and those parts of it that are within range of the town batteries thickly strewed with shot of all sizes and fragments of shell. The plateau is intercepted by numerous deep and steep ravines, all running down to the harbour. The sides of these ravines were formerly clothed with vineyards, which I hear were very productive, but they have been long since rooted up for fuel, and the houses of the owners unroofed and gutted; but this is one of the least of the many horrid evils of war. The *Princess Royal* has, I hear, arrived in Chersonesus Bay with drafts, chiefly of the 14th, 17th, 39th, and 89th Regiments. Captain Peel has, I hear, volunteered to come out with the draft; a younger brother of his is out here *en amateur*, and I believe is to be appointed to our regiment. I see in orders that your cousin, Captain Dillon, 30th, has been recommended by a Medical Board for recovery of his health.

February 9.

We had very heavy rain last night, which was unfortunate, as the ground was just beginning to get dry. This morning, however, the wind has shifted again, and we have a lovely mild day with bright sun. There was very heavy cannonading last night on the part of the Russians; as the night was dark there was a very pretty display of fireworks, the Russians being very fond of throwing large shells fitted with small ones; it is very pretty to see them all bursting. They kept up the diversion till past eleven, when they kindly let us go to sleep. It is now reported that they have received orders to take Balaklava at any cost, and they say 30,000 of them have returned to their old ground outside Balaklava, in the upper valley of the Tchernaya. There was an alarm there the night before last, and the garrison was out under arms till 6 a.m.; the Guards are to be sent there to increase the former. If they were to take Balaklava, we should be done for; but with the force defending it, I think that would be improbable. Will you tell dear Kate, with my love, that my paper will not admit my answering her kind letter to-day, but I hope to do so next week? Dr. Evans has been sent to take charge of the 1st Regiment; we are very sorry to lose him, as he was a very nice person, as well as skilful. Colonel Denney, 71st, who came from Corfu with our two companies, has quite lost his head from excitement, and is to go home. They have kept our detachments at Balaklava, and I don't know when they will come up. I have just returned from the Royals' camp, where I went to see F. Smith, but he was out; I saw Dr. Hearne, who said he was much better. The bag is closing; I must therefore say adieu, with kisses to pets, and love to all.

Ever yours affectionately,

RICHARD.

CHAPTER IV

BEFORE SEBASTOPOL

Light Division Camp,
February 10.

My own beloved Ellie,

Many thanks for your kind congratulations on my promotion, which you will see by my last letter, however, that I learnt by last mail. I am glad that on your return you found the colds of the dear pets better, and hope they will soon recover their looks and loss of flesh. What a darling dear baby must be! I should like to hear his attempts at speaking; but, please God, that may be the case yet before very long, although at present I see no immediate prospect of my return home. I told you in my last of the advantages I would gain by promotion to Brevet Lieutenant-Colonel as long as I remained here in command of the regiment; another local advantage is that Lieutenant-Colonels command the entire guard of the trenches, and are stationed in the battery instead of the advanced works, and you are thereby more sheltered from the weather, and have less distance to go, which is some advantage, which I shall have the benefit of to-night (February 11), as I am going on the battery for the first time. I am afraid it will be a wet and boisterous night, as the wind is now very high, and it threatens rain. Last night it rained very heavily, and the ground about the camp is a sea of mud. I only hope it will not turn to snow before morning. From my short experience of Crimean weather, I have not yet found it generally so cold as I expected, although we have had some sharp days; but the weather is extremely changeable, and we are constantly in a state of variation from hard frost with dry ground to rain, snow, and slush, which is decidedly worse, as inside your tent everything gets damp and mouldy, and outside is like a ploughed field. Bullock is certainly not much of a cook, although he has not had much yet to test his skill, beyond boiling and frying pork, and making coffee and pea-soup. The butter you sent me is excellent, and I enjoy it at breakfast and at lunch with a bit of cheese. One day that we got a bit of pork which we did not fancy, on account of its being all fat, we fell back on one of the pots of potted meat, and found it excellent. I have not been to Balaklava since I came to camp, and therefore I have not made any purchases, but I dare say you have despatched a box off to me before this. I have not sunk my tent, as the labour of doing so is very great, and our men are very hard worked as it is. No one knows when the assault is to take place, or whether there will be an assault at all. We shall not be ready to open fire for at least a month. General Jones has just come out in the *Princess Royal* to take charge of our engineering department, and no one knows what his plans may be. General Palissier, one of their African Generals, has also arrived to take command of the French *corps de siège;* and they place great confidence in his skill, and they say they intend before long to take the Round Tower by assault. It is also reported that General Bosquet with his division is to go to Eupatoria and aid the Turks in investing Sebastopol on the north side; but there are so many reports flying about one can't believe half. What is certain, which you can see with your own eyes, is that the Russians work night and day strengthening their position, and adding battery to battery, and meet with no opposition from us, as we are afraid of provoking their fire, not being at present able to return it. I am glad you wrote to Mrs. Turner to congratulate her on her husband's promotion. I see he is now Lieutenant-Colonel, so he is fast catching me up. I am glad Colonel Ward has got Gibraltar; it is where he wished to go to. It is time for me to get ready for the trenches. It is a most desperate night; within the last quarter of an hour the wind changed round from W. to N., and we have now hail and snow, and very cold.

February 12, 8 a.m.

I came off the trenches at six, and laid down for two hours, as I find I am for a court-martial at eleven. I must bring this to a close, as the mail closes at two. Last night turned out better than it promised before starting, as the snow ceased soon after we got to the trenches; but the night was very dark, and as I had to walk about a good deal, I kept floundering into holes full of mud and water, which the Engineers are pleased to call drains, and my clothes were in a terrible state on my arrival. We had a very quiet night—only one turn-out, caused by one of our sentries seeing, or fancying he saw, three men creeping among the bushes, whom he fired on, which caused a general alarm which ended in smoke. I have not half answered your letter, but must conclude abruptly, as if I don't finish now the mail will probably be closed before I return from the court-martial. In great haste, adieu; love to all, and may God bless and protect you; kisses to pets.

Ever your fond
RICHARD.

LIGHT DIVISION CAMP,
February 13.

MY OWN DEAREST ELLIE,

This is a most miserable wet day, and I can't employ it better than writing to you. Owing to my being on a court-martial yesterday, and not knowing how long I might possibly be detained, and the mail closed at 2 p.m., I closed my letter very hurriedly without saying all I wished to. This is dear Ellie's birthday, and she is six years old. God grant that she is as well and happy as I wish her, and that she may grow in grace as she does in years! Kiss her for me, and give her my fondest love. Let me know in your next how Weston is looking, and if there have been any improvements or changes in the house or furniture. Yesterday was a fine day after all the snow and sleet on Sunday; but last night it blew a heavy gale from the S.W., which shook our tents not a little, and put them in jeopardy of being blown away; fortunately, however, they all stood it. The gale continued till six this morning, when it was lulled by a rain which has continued to pour almost without intermission ever since, and has converted the ground into a perfect quagmire. To-night the wind will probably shift to the N., and we shall have frost and snow again. The worst of this damp is that your clothes get damp, your provisions mouldy, and your razors, knives, etc., rusty. Our two companies that arrived from Corfu, and which have been encamped at Balaklava ever since, are to come up to our camp to-morrow. Poor fellows! it is a bad time for their moving, as they will have to pitch their tents literally in mud and water. We lost a man to-day from fever, the first that has died in our camp for a month, so we have been most fortunate as regards health. Our sick have moved into the hospital hut, where they are more comfortable than in the marquee. I now breakfast always on coffee and biscuits and butter, and have a tin of hot coffee every evening before going to bed, which I enjoy very much. I have not drunk any tea since I have been in camp. I tell you how I was dressed to keep out the cold when I went to the trenches last Sunday night, which promised to be a desperate night, and I put on accordingly as many clothes as I could possibly walk under. I had first a flannel vest, then a chamois one, and over that my shirt. On my feet I had first a pair of silk socks, then a pair of lambswool, then chamois, and over them a large pair of soldier's socks, given by Government. Then I had my flannel drawers, and over them my chamois ones; then came my regimental trousers with my long blue knit stockings drawn over them. Over my shirt, and outside my trousers, I put a blue sailor woollen jersey, given by Government; it is very elastic, and fits tight from the throat to half-way to the knees, and is very warm. Over my long stockings came my long boots, with a pair of cork soles in them; the boots are perfectly waterproof, and with the soles keep my feet dry and warm. Over my boots and trousers I draw on a pair of sailor's flushing-trousers, without which my others would have been ruined by the mud. Then came Mr. Philipson's coat, with a comforter round my neck instead of a stock; over that my great-coat, with sword and revolver round my waist, and over all my mackintosh. On my head over my red night-cap was a black glazed leather cap, with fur ear-covers (also served out by Government). On my hands I had a pair of kid gloves, then a pair of worsted, with fur ones over all; a comforter round my chin, a spirit flask, and a little cheese and biscuit completed my equipment, and you may fancy what a load I had to stagger under, and what hot work it was walking there and back, and going round the sentries, but yet if I sat down for any time I found it cold. Of course, when the alarm was given, I had to throw off my great-coat and cloak to be ready for action. I write you all this stuff as I have no letter of yours to answer till the next mail comes in, which we expect to-day. I am glad to see they are beginning to send the Militia to the Mediterranean to relieve the regiments there, as we shall want large reinforcements by the spring. I do not think we will, or can, do much till the fine weather sets in, but must be content with holding our ground. There is a rumour afloat that the Russian army, which has resigned its old position outside Balaklava, is to be shortly attacked by General Bosquet's division, assisted by an English one; but there are so many rumours spread about that you can't believe them all. I walked yesterday with Maxwell to a hill overlooking our batteries, and commanding a fine view of the town and harbour; and while there Gordon's battery fired one gun at the Russian Redan Fort, probably at a working party. The Russians at first appeared annoyed at our audacity, as we fire so seldom; but they soon opened fire from about thirty guns, and then shelled us with mortars. Their practice was very good, most of the shots striking the battery, and the shells bursting over it. The only casualty, however, was an artilleryman struck on the head by a stone displaced by a ball, and which stunned him for a time. General Jones, who has just come out as commanding Engineer, came to the battery while the firing was going on. It is reported that he says that we have no chance of taking the place by assault, as we have allowed them to make it too strong, and that our only hope of success is by closely investing it on the north side, and starving them out if possible, which will be a tedious operation, and I dare say last the whole summer. A few mornings ago a party of the 33rd were on sentry in front of the advanced works, and on account of the morning being very foggy it was thought to be earlier than it really was. The sentries were not withdrawn as soon as they should have been, when all at once the fog cleared away in an instant, and they saw about 200 yards in their front a line of Russian rifle-men, each man lying in a pit with a wall built in front, through the chinks of which they fire at everyone they see, and right good shots they are; and if our sentries had tried to run back into our works they would have been shot, every man; so they, together with an officer who was with them, had to lie down under cover of heaps of stones, that we have built for our sentries, and stay there quietly without anything to eat till dusk that evening. Fortunately, the day was not very cold, otherwise they would have suffered severely.

It must have been a melancholy satisfaction to poor Mr. Winter to have even his son's horse and servant return. I asked Dr. Evans, who was present at the battle, the particulars of his death. He says that he was seen wounded and bleeding, and some time after his horse came in without him, covered with blood; his body was never found, as the Russians held the ground on which the action was fought, and buried all the dead.

February 14.

Yesterday I had the happiness of getting your letter of 25th and 27th, together with the *Times* of 23rd and 24th; many thanks for them. Thanks for the box you are so kindly preparing for me. I shall not want any more warm clothing, as the winter will be over before it can arrive, but preserved soups and meats, cheese, butter, chocolate, and candles, will be acceptable. I never have a charcoal fire in my tent when closed, so you see I am very cautious; indeed, the weather since our arrival has not been so cold as I expected. I am glad to hear the dear children and all at Weston continue so well. You do not say anything of yourself, but I trust you are not suffering from pains in your legs, or any other ailment, and that you do not over-fatigue yourself about the house, as your general custom is. Tell dear Annie that the Russian bear has not come near papa yet, and that, please God, he will not touch him. . . . Sir G. Brown has joined from Malta, his wound having healed. Colonel Deverell, of 90th, shot himself in the stomach the other day by fiddling with his revolver.

February 16.

Yesterday it blew a gale of wind, which has had the effect of drying up the ground. I have never yet seen it in such good order, which is a fortunate thing for our two companies who join us to-day from Balaklava. I must now conclude with kisses to pets and fond love to all at home.

    Believe me,
      Ever your affectionate
        RICHARD.

LIGHT DIVISION CAMP,
February 17, 1855.

MY OWN DEAREST ELLIE,

Last night I was greeted by your long, affectionate letter of January 29, and the *Times* of 26th and 27th. I am very glad you got my two letters from Constantinople which you were so anxiously expecting, and I trust that you have received all that I have written since, as I am happy to say that I have not yet missed a post. Our regiment is considered far the healthiest in the division, and since my arrival we have had but one death in camp, and either nine or ten at Balaklava and Scutari that have been reported to us; yet we have 200 sick out of 808; of these 101 are in hospital at Scutari and Balaklava, and 99 in camp. Of these latter, however, more than half are trifling cases—colds, etc.; our men have now plenty of warm clothing, and their rations ever since I have been here are good and ample. For fuel to cook them with they have to go some distance and dig up roots of trees with pickaxes, and a scarcity of these picks, so many having been broken in this work, is become a serious evil. What tells most against our men now is the hard duty, as they never have more than thirty-six, and often only twenty-four, hours off the trenches, and it is from this cause that the sentries in our army have been so often surprised—they are worn out with fatigue. On the 15th we had a balmy south wind; it was a most delicious day, and I saw several crocuses *bloom about* our camp. Yesterday and to-day, however, the wind has again changed to the north, and this evening it has commenced to snow again, and I suppose we shall have a white world again to-morrow. We continue to receive articles of clothing from Government. I think I told you I had a pair of soldier's boots given to me, and a great comfort they are, and I wear them when the ground is dry, with three pairs of socks, and keep my long boots, which are rather heavy, for wet and muddy weather. I also got a pair of leather mits, lined with flannel, and to-day they brought me a pea-coat made of tweed and lined with fur inside. I am afraid it is not waterproof, but it will be capital to wear out on a frosty day or when sitting in one's tent. I was also offered a pair of wooden shoes, but these I declined. What we are to do with all these things when we move I can't tell. The poor horses are well, but begin to look out of condition; they want hay greatly; I sent four times to Balaklava for it, and was not able to get any. The debates in the papers are most interesting; how we must be lowered as a nation in the sight of all Europe, such confusion and mismanagement has prevailed, both at home and abroad! Blunders and mistakes have been made by nearly everyone, and it is hard to say who is most to blame. I say Government decidedly were, in the first instance, for not having taken Odessa before they attacked this place, and for attempting this expedition without being sufficiently acquainted with the strength of this place and the resources of the Russians, and especially for not having sent out a proper siege-train and proper means of transport of ammunition and provisions, for the want of which the greatest sufferings of the army have arisen. I think, however, that the worst is now past with us, and that the condition and efficiency of our army will improve every day, and that if we can only invest Sebastopol on the north side we shall eventually take it, but not for some time or without heavy loss. We are now constructing new batteries for 18-inch mortars (of which we have not one in position) on the right of our advanced works of the right or

Gordon's attack. The Russians are also hard at work fortifying their already immensely strong position, and adding battery to battery; their working-parties work openly in broad daylight, and are not molested by us, so fearful are we of drawing the Russian fire on us, and having our batteries demolished before they are finished; they are not equally forbearing to us, as they fire upon every party of ours they see working, and to-day they kept up a very heavy fire on our workmen in the right attack, and killed one and wounded three of the 77th. Puget also got a sharp rap on the head from a stone displaced by the bursting of a shell; Boyce had charge of the party, and had a narrow escape, as some of the men's shovels were broken by the fire, and eventually they had to give up working. I am sure I need not tell you that I never wish any of my letters to appear in the papers without my express permission. I should be greatly annoyed if they did.

Sunday, 18th.

This is a fine bright day, the ground as hard as iron and a keen north wind blowing. There is to be service to-day performed by the chaplain of the division for the first time since my arrival, as I have always had to read prayers myself till now. What a fine child baby must be—God bless him!—to be able to toddle, and trying to speak already! No one expects ever to see Colonel Browne out here; he must either sell or retire on full *pay.* What a blessing that dear baby cut two double teeth without any teething fit! I am afraid you have just as severe a winter at home as we have, and that you feel it more than you did last. I have just heard that our draft in the *Canadian,* under Ramsay, arrived in Balaklava to-day, all well, and I suppose will join us in a week. They must have had a quick passage, as I believe they only left England on January 29. Dr. Worthington also returned from Scutari, where he had been on a month's sick-leave, and is looking much better. I hope you have started off a box of provisions for me, as my stock is beginning to run low. Bouilli and ox-tail are the best of the preserved soups, as they are both meat and drink. I suppose W. Smith had no idea the 22nd had gone to the Crimea when he exchanged. We hear that the 83rd, 86th, and 10th Hussars are, besides, ordered from India to the Crimea. I am glad Francis has got such a nice pin given him by C. Keys, and I hope he often wears it. Try all in your power to keep up my mother's spirits. You must not believe all you read in the letters published in the *Times*, for although there is a good deal of misery, yet I think some of the statements are exaggerated. Our regiment, compared with others, is particularly well off, and we are much healthier than our neighbours. We are to be inspected on the 29th by Major-General Codrington, a very nice, gentlemanly man; he still commands the division, although Sir George Brown has arrived. We are exchanging our smooth-bore for rifles. I myself don't think the change is advisable, as our men have had very little experience with the Minié, and will find them awkward at first. I heard that the firing on our battery yesterday was brought on by an officer of the 7th firing at and hitting a Russian officer—I suppose an engineer —who was seen to come out of the town, and, with a measuring-tape in his hand, coolly begin to trace a work outside.

The gifts of warm clothing from the ladies of Ireland were, I believe, shipped in the *Canadian*, and if so I suppose we shall soon get those intended for our regiment.

I received a large parcel, I don't know who from, containing two sets of the *Leisure Hour* for the last two years, and also some numbers of the *Sunday at Home*, a new work. I have distributed them among the sick in hospital, who were very glad to get them. At Divine service to-day the chaplain did not read Litany, Psalms, nor Communion Service, only the Prayers and Epistle, and preached a short, practical sermon on 1 Cor. xiii. 1 on charity and brotherly love. Although the mail does not close till to-morrow evening, I must finish this to-night, as I find I am for the battery to-morrow morning. We have to start at 4.15 a.m., and don't get relieved till 6 p.m., which makes a long day of it, and we must have our meals sent down to us. I will therefore conclude with kisses to the darling pets, affectionate love to my dear mother, Kate, Annie, Francis, kind regards to Miss K. Remember me to Mrs. Caffray, and with warmest love of all to yourself, and praying that God may bless and preserve you, and give me the happiness of soon being restored to you,

    Believe me,
      Ever your affectionate
        RICHARD.

      LIGHT DIVISION CAMP,
       February 24, 1855.

MY DEAREST AND MOST BELOVED ELLIE,

When I concluded my letter to you yesterday evening, I was in expectation of going into the trenches, and had all my warm extra clothing on, and was just going to dinner, when I was told it was a mistake, and that it will not be my turn till to-morrow morning. I had hardly finished my dinner, when the mail came in, and brought me your dear affectionate letters of February 7 and 8, with the curly lock of baby's hair, which I have safely put up, and the box of opium pills, and the three papers. Major Eveleigh kindly sent me yours of 5th this morning; many thanks for all these. How kind of you and my dear mother to pack up such a quantity of things for me, and just the things that would be most useful and acceptable! I long for the box to come, and I hope Boyce will find an opportunity of sending it on from Malta. Indeed and in truth, I do feel most grateful to God for having given me such an affectionate wife and mother, sisters and brother, who are always thinking of me and doing all in their power to contribute to my comfort. I am so glad you got my long-expected letters from Balaklava; and, as you have been aware before this, I have received all yours. We are apt to be too impatient at first, at not getting letters exactly when we expect them; but from this out I hope we shall get each other's letters in general twice a week, but we must both occasionally expect to be disappointed from mails being late, etc., sometimes by our being prevented writing, which, however, I trust will not often be the case. My brandy is all right, as I have put the padlock on the jar; the valise padlock was a great deal too small, it would not have gone over the hasp. I always drink brandy-and-water at dinner, as it would not be safe to drink the water plain; but when I go into the trenches I make snow-punch overnight, and fill my flask with it, and drink it cold, and find it very good. I am very glad indeed to hear that the poor Bourkes' baby is recovering, and I trust that he may be spared to them. I wonder Mrs. B. does not accompany Captain B. to Malta, for, as far as one can see, there is very little chance of his being sent on here, as a vacancy among the Captains would be filled up by the senior subs., who are all out here. I am much obliged to him for his kindness in offering to take a box for me to Malta, and I hope he will soon get a chance of sending it on, but there I am afraid will be the difficulty. With your usual activity, you did not let the grass grow under your feet, and, thanks to my mother's generosity, you have made a most capital selection, and all the contents will be most acceptable, especially the preserves, which will be capital to eat with biscuit; I have, however, about one third of mine left still—I never tasted better. We have had fresh meat twice this week—also potatoes and onions, which are a great treat; as we have had an issue of each of these articles to-day, an Irish stew is ordered for dinner. We also now get an occasional issue of stearine candles from Trieste, and very good ones they are; and I as field-officer get double allowance. Tell C. Keys that I am much obliged to her for the books she is sending to me, and that they will be a great treat to me, as I always read for some time before going to bed. Many thanks, also, for the box you intend sending me through Hibberd. The things you mention are what are most required. I have warm clothing enough to last the winter; but a good pair of strong and wide-laced boots would not come amiss; they should be double at the toes. Some of the Crimean Fund ships have arrived, and the prices of articles are, I hear, very moderate; as yet nothing has been issued, but I suppose we shall get our share. The Turkish shawl was by no means cheap, as for half the price I would have got a better article at home. Alt (?), who bought it for me, was taken in in the purchase. The over-alls I found very useful.

To build a hut, my dearest pet, you require timber for the ridge-pole and rafters; and for miles round you could not cut a walking-stick. Major was fortunate enough to fall in with the captain of a ship whom he had formerly sailed with, who gave him a ridge-pole and planks for rafters, and also made him a door and windows. I am glad the Ministerial interregnum is over, and that Palmerston is Premier; he will carry the voice of the country with him, and I trust will carry on the war energetically. Lord Panmure will make a good War Secretary, I should say. If, unfortunately, I should be wounded, I only hope I shall not be sent to Scutari to recover—as the air there, they say, is very unfavourable for wounds—but either to the new hospital at Smyrna or, better still, to Corfu, where they now talk of sending sick, and where, if I should unhappily require your aid, I would be delighted to see you. I am sorry to hear that Turner's promotion has involved so disagreeable a change of residence. It is the common lot of military men—no sooner comfortable than you are moved.

I hope they were all well when Mrs. Turner wrote. I hope the ball at Beabeg went off with *éclat*. Mrs. Rainsford is catching you up very fast in the number of her offspring, but, with all her boys, I don't think any of them will surpass dear baby; what an intelligent, affectionate creature he must be, and how you must love him! They are all indeed darling children, and I trust they may increase in the fear and love of God, as they do in years. I suppose Ellie and Annie read words of two syllables now fluently. Has pet Sophie ever yet shown any inclination to learn her letters? The horses, I am glad to say, are doing uncommonly well. Brown Bess has been greatly admired; she keeps her coat so well while the other horses look rough and shaggy; she is in high spirits. Old Leander does his work, too, uncommonly well, and goes to Balaklava twice a week for forage and charcoal. I don't think there is any need for you posting your letters earlier, as since January 22, I have never missed getting a letter by every mail. When you are sending a box again, you might send four towels, as those I have are getting very ragged. I would also like a good stout piece of tarpaulin or waterproof cloth, which I might wrap round my basket, so as to keep all the things dry in it, as it would be very light and easily carried on a horse, if we take the field next spring, as we probably shall do; a pair of waterproof leggings, like those I saw at Plymouth, I should also like, as the leather ones I have would not be comfortable after having been more than twice wet; also some more horseshoe nails and some tooth-powder; I don't think of anything else at present. Fancy your nailing and cording the box all yourself—just like you! Many thanks to you for the trouble you have taken about it.

I suppose the Colonel will make Sergeant Mortimer sergeant-major, as he has done his duty as acting-sergeant-major exceedingly well. I am sure there will be no peace till Sebastopol is taken, and when that will be no one can form an opinion, as they seem to be making it stronger and stronger every day. I must now tell you what happened this morning. At 2 a.m. we were all roused by a tremendous rattle of musketry in our front, and the heavy Russian guns soon joined in the chorus. We were under arms directly, and I had the regiment formed in quarter-distance column in front of our camp ready to move if required, when General Codrington came up and told me it was an attack made by the French on a battery which the Russians have just constructed (but not armed) opposite the Victoria Redoubt in front of our camp. We remained under arms about an hour, during which the rattle of musketry and cannon was almost incessant; the fire was altogether on the side of the Russians (the French only using the bayonet), which opened from almost all their batteries, and as it was dark we could see the fiery track of their shells crossing and recrossing in all directions, and often bursting in the air. It was a grand display of fireworks; none of them came near us, and we heard afterwards that, with all this tremendous firing, the French suffered very little from shells. I suppose they were thrown at random, the enemy not knowing exactly where their opponents were. The French, I am sorry to say, met with heavy loss, and did not succeed in the object of their attack; their force was too small, only consisting of 1,800 Zouaves, supported by 1,200 Infantry of the line and of the Marine. The Marine, we hear, did not behave well, but bolted; the Zouaves behaved most gallantly, and carried the battery with the bayonet, and even charged the defenders to the water's edge; but here they were met by a tremendous column of Russians, a reserve, they say, of 20,000 strong, who not only drove them back, but clean out of the battery before they had time to demolish it. The French loss, we hear, was 9 officers and 60 men killed; 12 officers, including General de la Monnaye, who commanded, wounded; and 60 missing. They brought back 50 Russian prisoners. The Russians might either have had information or suspected an attack, as they were quite prepared for them. There are strange rumours going about camp that the French General Forey has been detected sending information to the Russians, and that he is to be sent to Paris to be tried; a quarrel with General Canrobert about someone having been promoted over his head is assigned as the reason. I don't, however, credit the report. I will now wish you good-night, as I must go to bed early, for at 4.30 to-morrow I must go on the battery, and will therefore, D.V., finish my letter on Monday.

February 26.

MY DEAR LOVE,

I came off the trenches yesterday evening rather earlier than usual, as, being a fine moonlight night, I had Brown Bess down for me to ride home on. Yesterday was a very fine, pleasant day, part of the forenoon quite warm. The Russians hardly molested us, and fired one shot at us the whole day. They were very busy, however, sinking a second line of vessels across the harbour, commencing from Fort Pasel, which, if you have a plan of Sebastopol, you will see is on the west side of the dockyard creek—that is, on the right hand entering the creek from the main harbour. We saw them sink a frigate early in the morning. A number of sailors from the merchant-ships from Balaklava, as usual on Sundays, came up to stroll through the batteries. I, however, turned them all back, as there is no saying who they might be, and when going away one of them must actually have had the fool-hardiness to light with his cigar the fuse of an unexploded shell, for we saw them running away, and presently we saw a shell burst some way to the rear of the battery, and, as none had been fired by the enemy, one of them must have set fire to it. Fortunately, no one was hurt. I was looking with my glass at the battery the French attacked on the 24th, but could see no damage done to it. Mr. Fyffe, who was formerly in our regiment, kindly sent a box of warm clothing for the regiment, consisting of mits, comforters, shirts, stockings, etc.; it was very kind of him remembering his old comrades. I have had part of the box made into a table and stool for my tent; the former is a great comfort, as the basket now occasionally is a little rickety. I trust that after all the trouble you have had about the box, which I am afraid has been great, it will arrive in time. How kind and thoughtful of you, my pet, to send me a letter through Major Eveleigh lest I should not get yours by post! He kindly rode over here on Saturday to ask if I had got it, and said he would have sent it the night before, only he was in the trenches. We afterwards rode out together. I like him very much. He has frank, engaging manners, and he is a capital soldier. He is expecting to get a brevet lieutenant-colonelcy for Inkerman. It was a great shame he did not get it before, as he brought the regiment out of action, and was mentioned by the officer commanding the regiment in his despatch for his gallant conduct; but it has been the system to give promotion to all the staff, and as little as possible to regimental officers. Roach is very well and in good spirits, as he has heard that Annie has been put to a good school at Aberdeen, and Winship is preparing for his entrance examination at Sandhurst. Our only sick officers are Marsh, at Scutari, Bale, who has been suffering from his liver, and Chapman, from an affection of the kidneys.

Your ever devotedly attached

RICHARD.

LIGHT DIVISION CAMP,
March 2.

MY OWN DEAREST ELLIE, ANNIE, AND SOPHIE,

Dear mamma will read this to you, and tell you how glad I was to hear when she last wrote that you were all well and had no colds, although the weather was so severe, and that Annie and Sophie had no toothache. I hope that Ellie was taking her cherry-wine, and was getting fat and strong from it. I was still more glad to hear that you were good children, and I hope you all pray to God to keep you good, and to send His Holy Spirit into your hearts to prevent your doing or saying any naughty thing, for we are none of us good by ourselves; we are all inclined naturally to be naughty and wicked. I hope, therefore, you are kind to each other, and that you do all that dear mamma and grandmamma tell you. As dear baby can't understand this letter yet, you must tell him that papa sends him his love and a great many kisses, and that he is glad to hear he can walk, and that papa has got the lock of his hair that mamma sent quite safe. I will now tell you about poor papa. He is more than 3,000 miles away from you, with the soldiers that are fighting with the Russian bear, and I am sure that you will all pray that God will protect him and bring him home safe from the war. Papa does not live in a house like Weston, but in a tent which is made of canvas, like what the sails of a ship are made of; there is a long pole in the middle to keep it up, and it is fastened to the ground by pegs; and this tent keeps off all the rain and the snow and the wind, and at night you can shut it up quite close. And inside papa has a bed and a table and a stool, and a fire when it is cold; so you see he is quite snug and comfortable. The country about looks now very bare and ugly; once on a time there were plenty of trees about, and in the valleys were vines with grapes growing on them, but they have been all pulled up and burnt by the soldiers, and the trees cut down, and the soldiers have now to go a long way to look for roots of trees for fuel to cook their dinners with. There is a fine large town near this called Sebastopol, which the English and French want to get into, but the Russians won't let us if they can help it. I hope it will soon be taken, as then papa hopes to be allowed to go home and see you all again. What a happiness that will be to us all! I hope Ellie and Annie are getting on with their reading, and that little Sophie knows her letters now, and that she will be able to read to papa when he comes home. I hope Mrs. Caffray is quite well; remember me kindly to her. Good-bye, my darlings, and remember that I am always your affectionate Papa, who loves you all dearly.

CHAPTER V

IN THE TRENCHES

> LIGHT DIVISION CAMP,
> *March* 1.

MY OWN BELOVED ELLIE,

Last night I had the pleasure of receiving your welcome and affectionate letter of February 29, together with the *Times* of 6th and 7th; many thanks for them all. You seem to have at home an even more severe winter than last year, but I am so glad to hear that none of you have taken cold from it, and trust all of you may escape. On the 27th we had a most delicious day, as warm as the end of May at home—a balmy south wind blowing, and the crocus also; and it was also quite hot in your tent, and you could not bear anything over your shell-jacket. Yesterday it was cool and misty, last night it began to rain, this morning the wind chopped round to the north and we have hail and snow, and are wrapped up in furs once more. I am so glad to find that as yet all my letters have reached you, and I hope you may continue to get them, as I have not, and trust shall not, miss a mail. We have indeed, amidst all our troubles, many blessings to be thankful for, that we both, the children, and all our dear ones in Dublin, have been spared, and permitted to enjoy good health, and that I have been mercifully protected from all the dangers that everyone out here is exposed to, more or less; and I humbly trust that, by God's grace, I may be enabled to feel that my gratitude proceeds, not from my lips only, but from my heart.

The regiment, I am thankful to say, still continues healthy, and although we have a number of men on the sick-list, yet we had only four deaths in camp yesterday; not more than we might fairly have expected, in the same numbers, if we had been at home. We were inspected yesterday by General Codrington, our Brigadier, who expressed his satisfaction with the appearance of the men, and said they looked very healthy. Our men, like the rest of the army, present a very motley appearance; very few, except the last draft that came out, have shakos, but most wear leather caps with fur ear-covers; some have fur caps. Those that came out lately from England have long boots; others have leggings made of blanket over their trousers; all have beards that can grow them, and every man has either a fur coat, or a capote, which is a coat made of very thick cloth, with a hood, to wear in the trenches. The belts are of a dirty brown colour, and stained through and through. The whole army is without pipeclay, a loss which Sir G. Brown seems greatly to deplore, as he has ordered our division to take immediate steps to get a supply, and to get everything ready to take the field in the spring. He inspected our hospital on the 27th, and said the men appeared very comfortable. The sick get fresh meat every day, and preserved soups and wine are given to those who require it. We have had a box of oranges sent up for them. The prevailing complaint is dysentery. We have also a few cases of low fever. Sergeant Baker is a most valuable man out here, so kind and attentive to the sick.

I have recommended him for the medal and gratuity which is to be given to each sergeant from each regiment out here. Within the last few days we have had the first distribution of the articles sent out by the Crimean Fund. The prices affixed were very moderate, such as 6d. per lb. and £1 per cwt. for bacon. The greater proportion of these we, of course, gave up to the men; and although the quantity was considerable, when divided among so many, the share of each was not great. We gave the men all the bacon, butter, cheese, tea, herrings, candles, and tobacco, and kept for the officers the wine, spirits, and chocolate, which were divided equally amongst us; and twelve cases of potted venison were raffled for, but I did not win a prize; my share came to three bottles of port, for which I had to pay 2s. each, two of brandy at 2s. 6d., and one of sherry at 1s. 6d., and seven cakes of chocolate, the price of which I don't know. We are glad to get these things, even by paying for them, as the prices are moderate. The sherry and brandy are excellent, but the port has suffered from the frost and the shaking coming up. I have been laying out a little money on preserved meats, at prices which no doubt you will think most extravagant; but you can't get them for less here, and a change sometimes from salt diet is absolutely requisite. I paid for a 6 lb. tin of boiled beef, which is capital, 9s.; a tin of hare soup, 4s.; and one of bouillon, 3s.; the tins of soup are just enough for two persons to make their dinner off. I also paid 2s. for a pot of strawberry jam, which would be 1s. at home; so you see I have been taking very good care of myself. I see by the papers that Bourke sailed from Plymouth in the *Indus* on February 10; so I trust the box was in time. How kind of you all at Weston to make me a plum cake! it will be most acceptable; but all of you are always thinking of me and how to contribute to my comfort.

I see by the papers that the regiments out here are to be made up to twelve companies of 139 each, which I am afraid puts an end to all our hopes of a second Lieutenant-Colonel and a reserved battalion. But we must only have patience, and trust in God's goodness, that it may be His will to bring things to a happy issue for us; He knows what is best for us, and it may seem good to Him that we should have our trials, in order that we may draw closer to Him in our distress. We received many blessings from Him, and we must not repine if we are now made to taste the bitter drop. Don't be alarmed about the position of our camp; it is certainly within range of the enemy's guns, yet, as they can't see us from their battery, they don't know exactly the position of it, and, accordingly, never have fired on us, although random shells have been thrown at the redoubt in our front, and have fallen pretty close to the camp. The night before last we had a very grand spectacle; the French were throwing rockets into the town from the Victoria Redoubt in our front, and some of us went to the top of the ridge to see the practice. It was a lovely calm night; first we saw a tremendous blaze of light, and then heard the tremendous rush of the rocket, and could trace it for some way along its fiery path, by the long train it left behind. The Russians were not slow in returning the compliment with shells, one of which fell right into the redoubt, but fortunately did not burst. On returning to the camp that night, I had a Providential escape from one of them; I heard the report of the mortar, and, looking up, saw my friend travelling through the air at a pretty good pace, and judging by the direction that it would fall pretty close to me, I threw myself on the ground, and soon heard it fall there also, with a good whack, and after a suspense of a second or two had the satisfaction of hearing it burst, without receiving any injury. It was too dark for me to see how far off from me it fell, but it was close enough for me to be covered by the earth it threw up, and you may be sure I was thankful for my escape. I only mention this to you because I tell you all that happens to me, and not by way of boasting, as there is not an officer out here that has not had an equally narrow escape some time or other. We never heard the astounding piece of news that I mentioned to you in my last from Balaklava; I fancy it was a rumour of peace—it was much talked of in the camp at that time. Rumours of all sorts are flying about every day; the last is that Sir E. Lyons was confident of peace, and that General Airey, and even Lord Raglan, is to be recalled. I am glad Lord Seton is coming to Ireland; I think he will be very popular there. Tell the dear pets, with my love, that I am so delighted to hear that they are all good and well, and do not forget poor papa, and are glad to hear of him, and that he hopes that God will soon bring him back to them. I am glad poor Annie has no toothache now; I was afraid she had been suffering from it. I am very much distressed at hearing that my poor mother still continues nervous and anxious about me, as I am afraid that it will have a bad effect upon her health. I hope you do all in your power to cheer her up and raise her spirits. I enclose a note for her in this, which I hope may dispel her anxiety about me. The farriers here charge a tremendous price for shoeing—a shilling for putting on each shoe, you finding the shoe and nails!

March 2.

This is the anniversary of our happy wedding-day, during which we have enjoyed seven years of almost uninterrupted happiness. We have been blessed with children, and have loved each other more than ever. God be thanked for all His mercies to us, and grant that we may be permitted to pass the next anniversary together with our children.

With love and kisses to the children,

Ever your attached
RICHARD.

LIGHT DIVISION CAMP,
March 7.

MY OWN BELOVED ELLIE,

Yesterday I had the happiness of receiving your two dear, affectionate letters of February 13 and 17, together with the *Times* of 8th to 14th; many thanks to you for all. I hope Major Johnson will be able to bring me out the box; what a feast we shall have on the good things it contains on his arrival, which I shall soon hear of, as the 33rd are in the same brigade with us, and their camp no distance from ours. Captain Prettyman, 33rd, our Brigade-Major, told me to-day that they have been expecting Major Johnson for the last month, but they heard by this mail that he was actually embarked, so I hope we shall soon see him. I am sure the cake will be excellent, and will be a great treat out here, although I am not yet tired of the biscuits. I was glad to hear from my mother that dear Ellie's birthday passed off so pleasantly, and that she got such nice presents. Your accounts of the darling children and their affectionate recollection of me filled me with such joy as you cannot think. Poor little Sophie! what an endearing pet she must be! And darling baby—to think of his having so much intelligence and affection! How I long to see them all again! and if I am spared to do so I trust it may be our last separation. I see by the papers the Thames has been frozen over—what a very severe winter you seem to have had at home! much worse than we have had out here—since I have been out, at least. I trust you have all escaped cold, though I am afraid you must have suffered very much, exposing yourself on an outside car in such weather, and all for my sake, too; but I beseech you not to run such risks again, as my getting a box a few days earlier would be no compensation for you being laid up with a severe cold, so I hope you will be more prudent in future. I am glad the pets, except baby, did not go out in that severe cold; what a fine, hardy little fellow he must be to stand it! Our weather here for the last few days has been quite delicious. Yesterday the sun was quite hot, and to-day it is mild and balmy; it would seem as if spring had commenced, if we do not get a return of winter. What a number of letters you wrote to all sorts of people about my box! But there was one letter you told me nothing about. I heard from Roach that on February 17 Mrs. Roach had got a letter from you, wanting to know what had become of me, and in a great fright because you had not heard from me on the 14th. It was just like your usual anxiety about me, and that anxiety makes me so afraid lest by any chance there should be delay in the receipt of my letters. We have just been all greatly astonished by the information, sent to Lord Raglan by telegraph from Lord John Russell at Vienna, of the sudden and unexpected death of the Czar, on the 2nd instant, caused by a rush of blood to the head, which, perhaps, is only another term for his having been strangled. Lord

Raglan sent in a flag of truce to Sebastopol to communicate the news to the Governor, which they had not received, and would not credit. I wonder if it is possible that it can be true, or another canard, like that of the fall of Sebastopol last year. If true, it seems like a special interposition of Providence for the purpose of putting an end to the war by the removal of the person who was the greatest obstacle in the way of peace. Alexander, the heir to the crown, is, they say, peacefully inclined ; but it is supposed that his accession may be disputed by his warlike brother, Constantine. I dare say a revolution will be attempted in Russia; we must only hope and pray that it will be the means of bringing this horrid war to an end, and that I shall soon have the happiness of being restored to you all again ; that I am longing for more and more every day. There was not much firing to-day, but Sergeant Willitt, who came out with me, was slightly wounded under the knee by a splinter of a shell. Our batteries are very nearly completed and armed, and would be soon ready to open fire if required ; but we shall probably wait to know what effect the death of the Czar may have on the negotiations for peace. Yesterday morning one of our batteries at Inkerman opened with hot shot on a Russian steamer at the head of the harbour, which used to annoy us greatly by throwing shells at long range ; they put eight shot into her at a distance of 1,800 yards, and must have damaged her machinery, for although she had her steam up, she was obliged to set sail to get out of range.

March 8.

Another most lovely day, which promises to be warm. I am getting my tent dug out and sunk about 2 feet, as not only will that give me much more room, the banks of earth round it serving as a shelf, but it will also be cooler in hot weather; and should my tent be even blown away in a gale, my kit would be sheltered by the hole. The sand that we get in the ravine near this is capital for covering things, and makes it so dry. The horses are in capital condition; Leander's swollen hock has greatly gone down, and the exercise of going into Balaklava twice a week does him a great deal of good, and the roads are now in capital order; I never saw Brown Bess looking better. Many thanks for the cotton socks and jerseys you are sending me; they will be just the things for the hot weather, which seems to be beginning.

Our first parade every morning is now at a quarter to six. We have now regular parades for drill, and are trying to get the men into some sort of order again and to shake off the winter clothing—in the daytime, at least. Sir G. Brown has also ordered that pipeclay and blacking should be got out from England, and the stick reintroduced. He is very fidgety and particular, wishing that the men that are every other day in the trenches should appear the same as in England. The whole division would prefer General Codrington, who commanded our brigade, being at their head; he is such a gentlemanly, nice, kind-hearted man and a capital soldier. We have a very strong force of French now in our rear—at least 10,000 men—and they furnish all the advanced pickets on the side of our position. The general opinion in camp is that the death of the Czar and the junction of Prussia with the allies will certainly bring about peace. I suppose you have read Lord Panmure's speech on February 29. I should think that there was little doubt now but that I should soon get my lieutenant-colonelcy, and, I trust, soon be ordered home. But that may depend on the arrival here of Colonel Browne; we hear that he has expressed an intention of joining soon, and I hope that may be the case. He has not yet received my letter offering him £1,000 to retire on full pay, and I suppose he has no intention of doing so; to tell you the truth, one of my chief reasons for making him the offer was that, in case of anything happening to me, both you and the children would get much better pensions if I were a regimental Lieutenant-Colonel; however, I trust that I shall now get the step for nothing. I hope the new staff people they are sending out will infuse a little vigour and system into the army out here, which it wants very much.

My buffalo robe has been my counterpane hitherto, and I have found it most comfortable; but if this warm weather continues I shall have to dispense with it. The waterproof blanket retains the perspiration, and is bad on that account, unless you actually are sleeping in the open air. Since I have been in camp I have never taken off when I went to bed anything but my coat and boots, and always slept in my dressing-gown and trousers. My Turkish fur coat is, I am afraid, so large and cumbersome that I shall not be able to pack it in any of my portmanteaux, but my tweed jacket lined with fur I hope to bring home for you, as it will be just the thing for a lady to wear in winter. I intend, of course, to bring home my Inkerman relics, with some buttons taken from the coats of some of the Russian 34th, whom we found lying dead in the field. I have often used the portable soup, especially when I went on the trenches, and found it very good. I do not think myself I shall require two pairs of long boots; one will be ample. What a quantity of good things you are sending me out! I hope, at the same time, that I shall not stay here till they are all finished. The patent fuel was most useful in lighting fires. Thanks to the brazier you got made for me by Mr. Carrold, I was always enabled to have a fire in my tent during the cold weather. I am sorry that you do not receive better accounts of dear Louisa; she has suffered greatly. Give my love to her and your mother. I have a great deal more to say to you, but my paper is near its end, and I must reserve it for my Monday letter, D.V. Our draft from the depôt has arrived from Malta in the *Crecy*, and Captain Peel expects to come on here immediately. I send two violets from the garden of our ravine villa in the front of our camp, just under Inkerman; the house is now occupied by the French pickets. I am going to shift my tent and remove into the hole. Love to all, kisses to the dear pets.

Ever your affectionate
RICHARD.

LIGHT DIVISION CAMP,
March 10.

MY DEAREST ELLIE,

Although I do not expect to get another letter from you before the close of the mail on the 12th, yet I will not let it go off without writing to you; in fact, I was not able to answer yesterday all your dear, long letter of February 21. After finishing my letter to you yesterday, I walked with Maxwell over to Inkerman, and met Colonel Maulever, 30th Regiment, whom I had last met at the hospital in Scutari, and I went with him to his tent, and, coming away, a man ran up to me grinning and asking how my honour was—that he came from Mucklon, his name was Lee, but his mother was *née* Flinn, that he had helped to lick the *Rooshians* at Inkerman without getting a scratch, and that he was then servant to the Adjutant, and doing very well. Although I did not remember the man nor his name, yet I was glad to find that Mucklon had produced one hero, and gave him, accordingly, all the loose silver I had about me, which, unfortunately, only amounted to 1s. 9d. The evening of the 8th, just as your letters arrived, the French commenced rocket-practice on the town from Victoria Redoubt, which the Russians returned with shells, as usual, several of which burst near our Grenadier tent without doing the slightest mischief; so altogether that evening we had rather pleasing excitement. It is extraordinary the number of shells they throw, and the trifling loss they occasion; several of them don't burst, owing to their fuses being bad. The French set some buildings on fire with their rockets, but it was soon put out. The railroad is going on very rapidly, although the ground presents more difficulties than they expected.

We are all anxiously waiting to learn what effect the death of the Czar will have on the war, and trust it will tend to peace. They have received the news at last at Sebastopol, and the two young Grand-Dukes, Michael and Nicholas, have left for St. Petersburg. Menschikoff was wounded in the leg, at the attack on Eupatoria, the other day. I should hardly think the Emperor of the French would come to the Crimea; I don't think it would be prudent for him to leave France just at present. The debates in Parliament are just now very interesting. I see the Foreign Enlistment Bill has proved a failure, and that we must rely on our own population to recruit for the army; and I am sorry to hear that we are not getting them, especially from the militia, as fast as it was expected, and I accordingly think it is a very good measure allowing men between the ages of twenty-four to thirty-two to enlist for shorter periods than ten years.

Our weather still continues lovely; last night we had some rain, but to-day it is as fine as ever, and quite warm, so that I went about to-day, for the first time, with nothing over my shell jacket. Hurst has made quite a garden on the bank that goes round the tent; he has crocuses, violets, and hyacinths growing on it. To-morrow morning at a quarter past four I go into the trenches, and will therefore say good-night and God bless you till Monday, when, D.V., I hope to resume my letter.

March 12.

DEAREST E.,

You will see that, thank God, I have returned from the trenches safe and sound, for, although it was Sunday, we opened a heavier fire from our battery, and of course had a still heavier in return, than on any day since I have been here. It arose in this way: we arrived, of course, at the trenches at dusk, and yesterday morning was thick and rainy, so we could not see clearly for any distance till past seven, when, on taking our usual glance at the Russian works, I was surprised to see that during the night they had begun to throw up a work on a hill, about 1,500 yards in front of our battery, called Gordon's Hill, because Major Gordon, of the Engineers, wished to make his battery there, as being so much nearer the town, but was overruled by Sir James Burgoyne. At the time we were looking there were a great number of men at work on it. I immediately sent a report of it to General Codrington, the general officer of the week, who forwarded it on to Lord Raglan; in about two hours down came Major Gordon, commanding Engineer of the right attack, and takes a look at it through his glass, and did not like the look of it, as it was on a spot on which we had

IN THE TRENCHES

intended some time or other, to erect a battery ourselves, but, with our usual procrastination, allowed the Russians to forestall us. Then came an order for every gun in this battery, that could bear on the spot to be opened on it, and an additional number of artillerymen were sent down. About an hour after this order is cancelled, and the gunners sent back, I suppose by an order of Lord Raglan, as not a gun can now be fired from the batteries without his authority. Soon after arrived General Jones, our chief Engineer, and General Bizot, of the French Engineers, with all their staff, and there was a little more looking through telescopes and shaking of heads and talking, and at last they came to the resolution that it would not do to let them go on working with impunity, that we really must disturb them and open fire. This decision brought back the extra gunners once more, and with them came Colonel Ward, commanding the Artillery, Colonel Dacre, do., and all their Staff; and after more telescopes and more talk it was discovered that only two guns in the whole battery could be brought to bear on the spot and for the most effective of these, a large 13-inch mortar, there were no fuses in the battery, as there ought to have been, and it could not, therefore, be used. However, at 4 p.m., after a delay of eight hours, which the Russians, no doubt, made the best use of, we actually did open fire from a 10-inch mortar, one 68, and one 24 pounder, till about 6.30, during which time we fired about fifty rounds, and the practice was very fair, most of the shots striking the works and damaging the parapet. The shells from the mortar were at first rather wild; our first shot scattered the working party, but they afterwards returned. The Russians gave us about 120 rounds from the Round Tower, but their practice was certainly anything but good, for, wonderful to relate! they did not touch a single man out of the fifty that were in the battery, nor did any damage to our works, for with a few exceptions their shot and shell either fell short of the battery or too far beyond. They made some good shots, of course, and Major Maxwell, who was with me, had a most wonderful escape from one of them. He had just stepped from the main into a cross trench, when a round shot came through a sally-port in the main trench, and struck the opposite bank at the very spot he had just quitted, covering him with the earth it threw up.

The erection of this battery by the Russians, which when finished will annoy Gordon's battery greatly, and impede the siege operations in general, has bothered our Engineers very much, so much so that that same night they began tracing out a battery to oppose it, and as I was riding home last night, on being relieved, I saw the ravine filled with men from the Light Division, so I knew there was something up, and this morning I heard we began constructing our new battery. Last night and as a preparatory measure, with this extra force in the ravine, consisting of detachments from all the regiments in the division (ours was 160 men under Warry and Hurst), we drove the Russian riflemen out of their pits, and filled them up, otherwise our men could never have worked exposed to their fire; the Russians did not stand at all, but took to their heels and ran, after giving one volley. I trust, now that we have destroyed their places of shelter, that we will not allow them to be reconstructed, for more men have been killed in the trenches by the firing of these riflemen than by shot or shell. I have not heard what our total loss was, but we had one man killed, Private Collaghan of the Grenadiers, who, I regret to see, leaves a widow and two children; I have returned his death to the Secretary of the Patriotic Fund, and they will be sure to get relief. As I intend writing a note to Kate, I will conclude with kisses, and affectionate love to my pets, Ellie, Annie, Sophie, and darling baby, and above all to you, my pet.

From your affectionate

RICHARD.

March 14.

We hear that the Grand-Duke Alexander has been proclaimed Emperor, and to-day we have a telegraphic despatch that the death of the Emperor has been announced to both Houses of Parliament. I trust it may bring peace; there is also a camp rumour to-day, that the new Emperor is desirous of having an armistice while the negotiations for peace are being carried on; but we don't put much faith in it.

The batteries, at all events, are firing away just as merrily as ever. Captain Craigie, Royal Engineers, was killed last night in the middle ravine as he was returning home from the trenches by a splinter of a shell which struck him in the side; he was buried to-day in the ravine below our camp. Major Gordon's Engineer camp being next to ours, I have often been on with him in the trenches; he was a good officer and much liked. Our weather is now perfectly beautiful and the ground in capital order; but I am afraid if we remain here the summer we shall find this place very hot, and that our men will suffer a good deal. Thank your mother for her kindness in sending the box to Cork for me, and give my love to her, Louisa, and your aunt, and say how much I sympathize with poor Louisa's sufferings from earache, and trust that she may soon get relief. I am very much surprised to see that Lord John Russell is in the Cabinet again after his treacherous and cowardly behaviour before. In the *Illustrated London News* of February 4 there are two very good views, one of the artillery camp Light Division, and the other of the Siege Depôt, Right Attack; they are both very like, especially the latter, which is directly in rear of our camp, Major Gordon's camp of Sappers being between. The plan in the *London News* is also good, and if you can find marked on it Right Lancaster or 5-gun Battery, then you may judge the position of our camp, which is about 500 or 600 yards to the rear and left of that battery. We are on a plateau called Shell Hill, between the white house picket ravine on the right and the middle ravine on the left. The plateau on our left (looking towards Sebastopol) is called Picket-house Hill, and where you see marked on the plan Left Lancaster Battery we are now throwing up a battery for two sea-service 19-inch mortars of very long range for the purposes of general annoyance; in front of Picket-house Hill is the 21-gun battery. I have not time to sleep after eight o'clock, even if I came off the trenches that morning, as the work of signing and sending in reports begins at that hour.

Sir G. Brown came and looked at our regiment while on parade to-day, and the first thing he thundered out was: 'I see a man without a shako, sir: where is it?' I explained to him that during the severe weather in December, when the regiment first arrived here, shakos were not worn by any regiments, and that the men, being so hard-worked, and having no place to keep their shakos but a wet and muddy tent, several of them got damaged and some lost them. Sir G. Brown during all this hard weather was at Malta recovering from his wound, and didn't know half what the men suffered and went through then, and I believe our regiment has worn shakos more than the rest of the Light Division put together. However, nothing would satisfy him, and he roared out: 'Try him by court-martial, sir! Try all those that have lost their shakos!' His next bellow was: 'Your belts are brown, sir, not white; have you no pipeclay?' I remarked that, considering the men almost lived in their belts, always sleep in them, and pass almost every other night working with them on in the muddy trenches, and that, all the supply of pipeclay they brought with them being exhausted, and there being no more of that article to be got in Balaklava, it was not very surprising that the belts looked rather whity-brown, but that I had sent for a supply, and expected soon to get it. This mollified him a little, and he growled out: 'Your men look very healthy, sir; they are a nice-looking regiment, and I hear they are a smart one, and I want you to be the pattern regiment of the division.' I then suggested, as there were some signs of returning good-humour, that if the men paid for the shakos they lost, there might be no necessity of trying them for it, when he grunted out: 'You may do as you like about it, sir; you had better come and dine with me to-morrow—I dine at six.' And he trotted off, and so ended my first interview with 'Ursa Major.' He is a regular hard-hearted old soldier of undaunted courage and iron frame as well. I have heard that he has done very kind things occasionally, but has no regard for anyone's feelings or strength where duty is concerned.

His creed seems to be that without pipeclay, blacking, sticks, and plenty of drill, to be used under all and every circumstances, the British Army will go to ruin. Since Sunday last, when we began our new trenches, we have had to furnish every other night from our division an extra covering and working party of 800 men, which is a great increase to the already hard duty of both officers and men; and to make it still more severe he has ordered that in future an officer shall be sent with every twenty-five men instead of fifty-nine as before, although there are not officers in that proportion in any regiment. The consequence is that officers who have come off the trenches in the morning have to go on again the same evening, and the result will be that the weak officers will not be able to stand this work, and that soon, instead of having an officer to twenty-five men, we won't be able to furnish one to a hundred. General Codrington, our Brigadier, is such a contrast to Sir G. Brown, he is so able and gentlemanlike; he tries to do all in his power to serve both officers and men, and is a capital officer at the same time; he is beloved by everyone. I have just been warned for the covering-party for the working-party at the new trenches at — p.m., so I must be quick and get dinner, and hope, D.V., to finish this to-morrow, so adieu, my pet, for to-night.

March 15.

You see, my own love, that—thanks be to God for His mercies and gracious protection!—I have been preserved from all danger, and am enabled to give you an account of our proceedings last night. At six I proceeded with my covering-party of 300 men (which should have been 500, only those furnished by the 2nd Division, through some mistake, never made their appearance), and followed by the working-party, to the pickets in the middle ravine, and we had just arrived there when a very heavy fire of musketry commenced over our heads on the plateau to the right of the ravine, and shot and shell from all the Russian batteries that would bear flew over

IN THE TRENCHES

our heads in numbers; every now and then a shell would occasionally drop short, and burst in the ravine or strike the edge and roll down. A poor man of ours of the name of Gately was killed just in our rear by the splinter of a shell. I was accompanied by Major Gordon, of the Engineers, who commands the right attack, and who has the disposition of the working and covering parties, and, as neither of us knew whether this attack was on the part of the Russians or the French, we deemed it best to move some way up the ravine in order to repel an attack, if any attack should be made in that direction, as, of course, every ravine is an opening into our position. However, in about an hour, the fire having ceased, we moved off to the trenches where our work was to be.

We afterwards learned that all this row proceeded from an attack made by the French with three battalions on two rifle-pits made by the Russians in front of the French trenches, extending from the front of the 5-gun battery on the right to the middle ravine on the left, where they are to be joined by our trenches, extending from the left of the advanced works in front of Gordon's battery. The French drove the Russians out of the pits, and had partly filled them up, when they were attacked in their turn by the Russians, who not only drove them out, but constructed two more before morning. We had scarcely reached the scene of our labours, which is in front of Gordon's battery, when the cannonading and musketry commenced again, mingled with yelling and cheering and bugling and drumming; and all this was going on on the plateau on the opposite side of the middle ravine, and was the Russian counter-attack on the French. As the night was so dark, we could not see much, except indistinctly, when revealed by the flashes of the guns; I saw large masses of men, and, as I was uncertain whether they might not cross the ravine and attack us, I threw back my right at right angles to the trench, so as to have part of my force facing the ravine in case they should come up that way; however, their attack was confined solely to the French, and they never crossed to our side of the ravine, although lots of their bullets did, and came whirling about our heads, and cutting up the ground on all sides. Fortunately, however, our men were lying down, and I am thankful to say we had only one man of the 88th hit in the leg. Several of our men, being very young soldiers, directly they heard the musketry on the other side of the ravine, began firing too, without getting any orders or knowing what they were firing at, and I had some trouble in making them cease.

After this little excitement was over, we posted a line of sentries in front of the working-parties, who went on with their digging, and the rest of the night passed off quietly, except the usual exchange of shots between the Round Tower and our battery, all of which passed harmlessly over our heads and had a very pretty effect; the night, fortunately for us, was lovely, as we should have had no shelter had it been wet. The failure of the French to destroy their rifle-pits is not only discreditable to them, as having failed to do with three battalions what we have done with less than the same number of companies, but it is unfortunate for us, as these pits, which are only 70 yards in front of the French trenches, directly enfilade our new trenches, and a man of ours was shot there this morning, and two men of other regiments wounded. They say the French are to try and take them to-night, when I hope they will be more successful. Dwyer, I am glad to say, has extracted the ball from poor Bates' ribs, and he has been doing better since; his left lung is, however, injured, and he only breathes through his right; he is, therefore, in a precarious state, but I trust he may recover. Sergeant Baker, you will be glad to hear, has been granted, at my recommendation, a silver medal and an annuity of £29, of which he is most deserving, as his kindness and attention to the sick has been unremitting. Poor Roach, I am sorry to say, has been suffering from diarrhœa more or less for the last eight or ten days, but I am glad to say he is now much better and able to go out again. Our trench duty, commencing to-day, is to be for twenty-four hours at a time, instead of for fifteen by day and nine by night; as the weather has been so fine, I think it will be better for the men, as it will make the intervals of duty longer. There has been a good deal of desertion from the Russians lately, chiefly Poles; and during the confusion of the attack last night an English sailor managed to make his escape from Sebastopol. They all unite in describing the distress as very great in Sebastopol, and all the garrison, with the exception of the sailors, (are) greatly discouraged and apprehensive of an attack by us; each man is provided with three days' provisions to take with him in case of their being driven out of the town; they say also that the rockets thrown by the French had set fire to several buildings in the town, and that our fire had done a good deal of mischief in the new works they are constructing. Their batteries are all manned by sailors, and the Round Tower commanded by an Admiral. I will now conclude for to-day with my love, as it is time for me to dress for dinner with old Brown, who, they say, gives very good dinners, as they go in camp.

March 16.

DEAREST E.,

Our dinner-party last night was pleasant enough. It consisted of Sir G. Brown and his staff, viz.: Lieutenant-

Colonel Brownrig, of the Guards, Assistant Adjutant-General of the division, and his three Aides-de-camp—Major Whitmore, 30th, Captain Pearson and Captain Markham, of the Guards—and Captain Burton, of the new Transport Corps. The General was chatty enough, and told a lot of anecdotes. We dined in his hut, half of which he occupies himself as bed and dressing room, and the other half he gives up to his staff. The dinner was plain and good, consisting of soup, stewed beef, roast fowls, haricot mutton, and something sweet, our vegetables—potatoes—which were a great treat, and the liquors, sherry and brandy. The best piece of news I heard was that the English mail had arrived yesterday, although, unfortunately, the Light Division bag had been left behind at Kamiesch (?), but I trust it may arrive today sufficiently early for me to reply to your letter before the mail closes. As no papers had been received by the mail, I did not hear any English news. There was a good deal of firing early this morning, I am told, but, owing to my vigil of the night before, I slept so well that I did not hear it, but it was reported that the French were successful in their attack on the pits this time. I trust that I shall soon have the happiness of getting my letters, with good accounts of you all at Weston.

Light Division Camp,
March 18, 1855.

My own beloved Ellie,

I commence this letter to-day in the hopes of having another of your letters to answer before posting this to-morrow. I think in my last I touched on most of the points of yours of February 28, but I will look over it again to see if I have omitted any. It is a very great comfort to us both that we receive each other's letters so regularly, and that, as yet, we have not missed one, and but very few papers. Let me know in your next how my mother is, and how she has borne the severe winter you have had; I trust she has not had any increase of her bronchitis or rheumatism. Please also tell me about Annie and her school, and say, with my love, that I hope both are going on well. Has she as much writing to do as formerly? How is the little dog Vic? and has she any other pets? I should like also to hear about Francis's farming, whether he has made any more improvements, and how Salmon and Garballagh are getting on; has he laid down any more land? I hope he is getting good prices for his oats. There has been a great change in the weather within the last few days, the wind having chopped round to the north. It has become very cold again, with hard frost at night; the ground is, however, hard and dry, which is a great matter. Our sick-list is, I regret to say, increasing a little, owing entirely to the extra work our men have now to do on account of the additional line of trenches we have just constructed; the guard of the trench hitherto used to be (for right attacks) 700 men by day and 80 by night; it has now been increased to 1,200 day and night, and the only relief we have had is the discontinuance of the middle ravine picket of ten men, which the French are to take in future. This makes a daily increase of 300 men to the duties of our division, which is sensibly felt by our already hardworked men. Colonel Yea is a good officer, and looks after his men, but he bullies his officers, and is very rough in his manner, and not very popular. He is now on sick-leave on board the *Royal Albert* in Kamiesch Bay.

We were all under arms last night from about nine to twelve, and our brigade was marched to Picket-house Hill to be ready as a support if necessary. There was another struggle between the French and the Russians for the old bone of contention—the rifle-pits in front of the trenches of the former—and I am sorry to say that the French not only failed in their attack, but were driven back into their own trenches by the Russians, who came out in great force; and this morning I observed that the Russians were in possession of the pits, and firing away from them as usual. The French, I am afraid, suffered heavy loss, as some of their wounded were taken into our hospitals, and we lent a stretcher to carry home a wounded French officer, whom we found in the ravine. The fire of musketry was very sharp for some time, but the Russians did not keep up their usual cannonade—I hear their ammunition is failing them. It is extraordinary how the French have failed in all their attacks lately. There were races yesterday, got up by the 4th Division, which afforded some amusement. I did not, however, go to them, as I was more interested watching our artillery practice from Gordon's battery on the Russian rifle-pits, which was excellent. They stood it for some time with great fortitude. At last a round shot bounded into their largest pit, and, I suppose, must have knocked some of them over, for they all bolted like rabbits and ran as hard as they could back to their works, and, extraordinary to say, although the whole of the men lining the French trenches opened fire on them when they were only about 10 yards off, and they had to run the gauntlet for at least 400 yards, we did not see a man fall, and there were at least sixty of them, which doesn't say much for the French being good shots, nor for their boldness in not occupying the pits themselves when we had turned the Russians out of them.

I haven't been able to see the *Gazette* of March 3; I wonder if my promotion is in it. Whenever I am

IN THE TRENCHES

ordered home, I suppose I shall have to report myself at the Horse Guards, and I hope I shall have the delight of either meeting you at Portsmouth or Southampton. I find the portable fuel very useful in lighting fires; I have a great stock of it still left. Since our band have arrived from Corfu they have played regularly; they are also employed in turn to take stretchers to the trenches in case anyone should be wounded. Divine service is to be performed with our brigade by the chaplain of our division this afternoon, and it is only the second time he has done so since I have been out here.

March 22.

MY DEAREST ELLIE,

All the troops in the front were this morning under arms from daylight till 7.30, by order of Lord Raglan, in order to support, if necessary, another attack made by the French against their old foes in the rifle-pits. There was some cannonading and a lively musketry fire for about twenty-nine minutes, and we have since heard that the attempt has only proved another failure, and that the officers could not get their men to advance the way they ought to do, and we begin to suspect that our friends the French, although their system of organization is admirable, are not equal to the Russians in the field. We have thrown up a battery for some field-guns at the advanced works, which command the rifle-pits and keep down their fire very much. Indeed, our artillery practice, since they opened on the 11th, has been excellent, and has done the enemy a great deal of mischief. A Polish Engineer officer deserted to us two or three days ago, bringing with him plans of the fortifications, and has given some valuable information. Since the death of the Czar a series of misfortunes seems to have befallen the garrison of Sebastopol. Their redoubted

Commander-in-Chief, Prince Menschikoff, is dead, it is supposed, poisoned; their chief engineer, who must have been a very able man, was killed by one of our shells while superintending the new works they are throwing up on the Mamelon; their last reinforcement of troops they received mutinied on the road while coming from Nicolaieff, and shot two of their Generals; the garrison, they say, are suffering very much, and are very harshly treated, and discontent prevails. He gives as the reason for the battery remaining comparatively silent their wishing to reserve their fire till we open on them, which they expect will shortly be the case, as they know we have been bringing up ammunition, etc.

Our new mortar battery opened fire on Picket-house Hill yesterday evening, and sent the first 'whistling Dick' right on to the square of the arsenal, clearing the place of the crowd that were collected there; the next was sent into the Mamelon, and blew down a large portion of the parapet. I shall be glad to see the daylight let into some of their fine barracks and arsenals and stores, which look now so beautiful and in as good order as the day they were built, as from some mistaken notion we have hitherto spared them, although they have annoyed us as much as possible; we are also constructing a mortar battery in the middle ravine, which will play into the Round Tower, so we are preparing annoyance for them. Lieutenant Mitchell, of the 27th Regiment, was wounded in the Woronzoff ravine by Russian riflemen on the 18th, all owing to the inconsiderate conduct of two naval officers, who, having strayed in the ravine *beyond our sentries*, were fired on, and lay down behind some stores to shelter themselves, and, being seen by our picket-men, were supposed to be Russian deserters trying to escape, when this officer volunteered with a few men to go and bring them in, and in attempting it he was shot through the lungs, and the fire on them was so heavy that, although wounded, he with the rest of them had to hide behind stones till dusk, when he crawled back to the picket. I am glad, however, to say that he is doing well.

Although Bullock is not an artiste, yet I would not wish to part with him, for he is very civil and willing and always in the way, and as honest as the sun. I wonder who took Growney after we left; whoever did got a good servant. I prefer the sunk tent very much, as it gives me much more room, and, I think, will be drier, as, if we have heavy rain, I can cut channels which, as the ground is on a slope, will carry off the wet; but we have had no rain for a length of time to test it, as this is the first wet day we have had for weeks. Yesterday was a lovely day, and I walked with Maxwell along the ridge overhanging the Tchernaya, as far as the Col de Balaklava. The day was very clear, and on the opposite side of the valley we could see the Russian batteries and entrenchments thrown up to protect the pretty bridge over the Tchernaya. We did not see that these were occupied by many troops, as we only saw a few Copeck videttes, but no doubt they had strong supports in the rear. A number of fresh French troops have come up and encamped in rear of 2nd and Light Divisions; they belong chiefly to their 10th Division, just arrived from France, and among other regiments contain our namesake and former antagonist in the Peninsular, the French 34th. Poor Captain Craigie met his death under very melancholy circumstances. It was his last night for duty in the trenches, as he was to have gone home on promotion, and, sad to say, was to have stopped at Corfu on his way to be married. What heart-rending news awaits his poor bride! God, I trust, will support her in her affliction. Poor fellow! he was so anxiously expecting the relief that night, little knowing what was before him. How true it is that 'Man proposes, but God disposes!' When we think we are quite out of danger we may be the nearest death, and that ought to make us endeavour to be prepared for it, come when it may.

General Simpson has arrived, and has assumed his duties as Chief of the Staff, which has thrown the Adjutant and Quartermaster-General quite in the background, and must be considered as a slap in the face by them. Have you read Lord Lucan's letter? I think he comes out of the mess with flying colours, and clearly shows that he could have done nothing else than obey the order from the way in which it was given, and upon Lord Raglan alone must fall the heavy responsibility of that dreadful and perfectly useless sacrifice of life which took place by the cavalry charge at Balaklava.

I must now conclude with my fondest love to all at Weston, and kisses and love to the dear pets, and the largest share of all to you, my dear Ellie. May God bless and protect you, and grant that I may soon return to you, is the constant prayer of your ever devoted

RICHARD.

CHAPTER VI

A PRISONER OF WAR

HOSPITAL, SEBASTOPOL,
March 23, 1855.

MY DEAREST ELLIE,

I regret to have to tell you that early this morning I was made prisoner, during a sortie of the Russians on our advanced trenches, and also slightly wounded in the left hand, by a bayonet, which has not injured any bone, and they say will soon heal. I also got a couple of blows from the butt-end of a musket, which, however, do not signify, and although this occurrence must be considered as a great misfortune to us both, I feel most thankful that my life was spared, and we must feel sure that all has been ordered for the best by the Great Disposer of events, in whom alone we must put our trust. You must not allow this to depress your spirits, but rely on the prospect of my soon being restored to you, please God. They dressed my wounds directly on arrival here, and I now hardly feel them. The authorities have shown me every attention that I could reasonably expect, and Prince Gortschakoff was good enough to send his A.D.C. to inquire after me. As soon as my wound has healed, which I trust will be in a few days, I expect to be removed from this into the interior; I will, if possible, let you know my destination, in order that you may write to me. I am sorry to say I believe that on being made prisoner of war, my pay ceases from that date. I have, however, written to Roach to send me my money, which I fortunately left in my tent, together with whatever field allowance is due to me. I have also directed my horses to be sold, so with all I shall have sufficient to last me for six months, before which time, I trust, we may be permitted to meet. They have kindly promised to send in a flag of truce, to enable me to get my clothes, and other things I require, which will make me more comfortable. My greatest loss was your last letter, which was put into my hand just as I was going into the trenches, and which I had intended to read as soon as it was light this morning, and put into my pocket for that purpose, when it was taken out by my captors, together with everything else I had, except my watch, which escaped their observation. When I was taken prisoner, I was surrounded by eight or ten Russians, who leaped into the trench as I was passing to form up the men, having come from some distance on the right (where we had repelled another attack) as soon as I heard the firing commence. I owe my life, under God, to a Polish soldier of the name of Stein, who prevented me from being bayonetted after I was on the ground. Do not be the least uneasy about me, as my wound is really not severe, and I feel very well. You will understand that, my letters being sent open, I cannot express half I wish to say. I will now conclude, with fond love to my dear mother, sisters, and Francis, and kisses and love to all the dear children.

Ever, my dearest Ellen, your affectionately attached
RICHARD.

Fort Nicholas, Sebastopol,
March 27, 1855.

My dearest Ellie,

As a flag of truce is to be sent in to-day to our camp, I don't wish to lose the opportunity of letting you know how I am getting on, as I know only too well how anxious you are about me. It will relieve your anxiety to learn that I am going on, thank God, as well as I can possibly do. I have been visited every day by an American doctor, in the Russian service, who tells me that the wound in my left hand is going on as favourably as possible, and that it will heal with the first intention; most fortunately, the bayonet passed through without touching a bone, and there is no inflammation, and it gives me no pain at all. He has made no change in my diet, and I merely bathe it in Goulard lotion, and keep it bandaged on a splint. My other wounds I do not feel at all, they are of no consequence. I enter into all the details in order to relieve the anxiety that I know you will be in about me, and you may rely on my having stated my case exactly; what I feel most, and which weighs down my spirits, is the thought of the long separation from you, and all those I love most on this earth, which must ensue in case this war should be protracted or that my exchange does not take place. We must put our trust in Him who alone can bring about events which, to man, seem impossible. We expect before very long to be sent into the interior of Russia, where the English prisoners are kept. The towns are situated about ten miles beyond Moscow, and 700 from this. I will try and let you know when our destination is fixed, and trust that we may be permitted to write to each other, which will be our greatest comfort. I regret to say I have had no tidings of your letter which was taken from me the night I was made prisoner. Everything I had with me but my watch and the clothes I had on were taken by the soldiers; but I felt the loss of your letter more than all the rest put together. Baron Osten Sacken has been so kind as to promise to send you my sword, if it can be found, which as yet has not been the case. We get our meals from his table; Captain Montague, R.E., shares my captivity. I must say adieu, with fond love and kisses to my darling Ellie, Annie, Sophie, and baby.

> Ever your affectionately attached
> RICHARD.

> FORT NICHOLAS, SEBASTOPOL,
> *March* 30, 1855.

MY BELOVED ELLIE,

I have but barely time to give you a line, to say that, thank God, I am as well as possible, and that my wound in the hand is healing fast. I had the happiness of receiving last night, together with my effects from the camp, your most affectionate letter of 9th, which was indeed a consolation to me, after having been so unfortunate as to lose your last. I am afraid to think what you must have suffered when you received Major Simpson's letter, enclosing mine of the 22nd, written just previous to my going into the trenches, and saying that I was missing, but that probably I was a prisoner. I trust, that, with that hope to catch at, the Lord mercifully supported you till you received my letter of the 23rd, which, I hear, Lord Raglan was kind enough to enclose in one of his own. This long-protracted separation which possibly may ensue, if peace be not speedily made, is the bitterest trial that we have as yet had to undergo; but we must not permit our faith to be shaken by it, but continue to put our trust in that Giver of all good who alone can bring to pass what we are anxious for; God grant that my captivity may be shortened, and that I may be restored to you, the dear children, and all I love. One of my boxes arrived in the camp on the 27th, brought by Major Johnson, I suppose. They have sent me from it some cotton socks, jerseys, and a bottle of lemon-kali; the eatables it contained they did not send, as they thought they would not be required. We continue to be very well treated, although not on our parole, but I believe we shall be when sent into the interior. We receive our meals from the kitchen of Baron Osten Sacken, the Commandant of the garrison, and one of his A.D.C.'s, a gentleman of the name of Roumin, has been excessively kind and attentive to us; he calls every evening and sits with us for some time, and takes care that all our wants are supplied, and offered to lend us money if required.

I have received £50 from Roach, and expect soon to get more from the proceeds of the sale of my horses, and this, I hope, will last me for eight or nine months. I dined yesterday with Prince Bariatinsky, a Captain in the Russian Navy, who gave us an excellent dinner quite in the Russian style, and passed a very agreeable afternoon, as some of the officers spoke English, and all French, and were very polite and attentive.

Kiss dearest Ellie, Annie, and Sophie, and darling baby, and give my fondest love to my dearest mother, Kate, Annie, and Francis,

   And believe me,
     Ever your devotedly attached
          RICHARD.

Fort Nicholas, Sebastopol,
March 31, 1855.

My beloved Ellie,

I wrote to you yesterday a very hurried, and I am afraid unsatisfactory, letter, as I had only half an hour's notice given me of a flag of truce going in. I would not, however, for worlds have missed the opportunity, as no doubt when we are removed into the interior the opportunities of writing will not be so frequent. I dread to learn the effect that the unfortunate intelligence of my having been missing on the morning of the 23rd must have had on you, for I suppose that you fancied me to have been killed, and I know well what your feeling and affectionate heart, as those of the rest of the beloved circle at home, must have suffered from that dreadful suspense, till the arrival of the next mail, which brought you, I trust, my letter of 23rd enclosed in one from Lord Raglan, and I have written to you twice since, on the 26th and 30th, all of which I hope you have received. It has been my constant prayer since I have been taken that our gracious Father, who was mercifully pleased to preserve my life at a time when I least expected it, would also vouchsafe His support to you in your distress, and that you would both seek and find Him a sure refuge in time of trouble, and to be a Friend that sticketh closer than a brother. Although it was done with the best intentions, I regret that Simpson wrote to you on the 23rd that I was missing, as I had taken care before going to the trenches on the night of the 22nd to write you a letter for the mail of the next day, so you would not have been uneasy at not hearing from me, and by the next mail you would have heard from me that I was made prisoner and doing well, and you would thus have escaped all the dreadful agony of suspense. I shall be most anxious till I hear from you how you have borne the news, and what effect it has had on your spirits; but although a dark cloud seems to hang over and obscure our prospects, which but a short time ago seemed so bright and cheery, yet we must not allow ourselves to be cast down or our faith to be shaken in that merciful God from whose hands we have so often received the sweet as well as the bitter; we must not forget that every cloud has a silver lining, and I trust that there are still many happy days in store for us.

I have great reason to be thankful. At the time I was made prisoner I was alone and in advance of my men, and was surrounded by eight or ten Greeks in the Russian service, and after an ineffectual resistance was knocked down, and would probably have been despatched by their bayonets if an officer of the name of Stein had not humanely interfered to save my life. You will be glad to hear that the wound in my hand is going on very favourably, and I think will be quite healed in about ten or fourteen days; it gives me very little pain or inconvenience. It is seen every day by an American doctor; he now only applies a simple cerate, and I wear a splint under my hand and carry the arm in a scarf. Fortunately the bayonet passed between the bones of the hand without touching them, so I think I shall not even have a stiff hand. The contusions I received on my head and right shoulder from the butts of the fire-locks are quite healed, and I also found on taking off my clothes a day or two after that I had received another bayonet wound in my right arm; but it did not penetrate deep, and is now nearly healed. We continue to be very well treated; we receive our meals daily from the kitchen of Baron Osten Sacken, and his Staff are very attentive to us, and one of his A.D.C's generally pays us a visit every morning, and asks us if we want anything. We have the gallery of the Fort, which is very extensive, to promenade in, and they have lately given us a young English soldier of the 47th, who was made prisoner, to attend on us as a servant, and he brushes our clothes, etc.

This morning a French officer has been placed in the same room with us. I should have preferred remaining alone with Captain Montague, but there is no help for it. We have not yet heard when we are to be moved into the interior. I fancy Kaluga will be our destination, which is about 900 miles from this, a long journey to make. I trust we may be able to continue our correspondence from there; your letters will be my greatest consolation. Till you hear from me where I am to be sent to I would advise you to continue to direct your letters to me to the British Army, as before, for then they will be sent to me here; and if I should have left they will no doubt be forwarded to my destination. It was very kind of Lord Raglan to write to you; I should like to know what he said. I wrote to him yesterday to thank him for his kindness, and to express a hope that, should there be an opportunity of exchanging me, I would not be forgotten; for else, unless the result of the negotiations at Vienna is peace, I can only look forward to a long captivity and separation from those whom I hold most dear on Earth. But I must not murmur; God's ways are past searching out, and He will dispose of us as seems best to Him. I think I told you I had received on the 29th a portmanteau and carpet bag with the greater part of my clothes, including the cotton socks and the jerseys you were so kind as to send me, and which arrived very apropos. They, however, made some omissions of useful articles, such as flannels, dressing-gown, slippers, sponge, neckerchief, which I have written for, and which I hope to get in a day or two. Roach sent me £20 in gold. . . . The balance of £11 8s. ½d. Roach will stop from the proceeds of the sale of my horses, which I have directed to be sold, as no longer being of any use. You see, therefore, that I shall not require any money for a long time to come; I trust it may serve me till we have the happiness of being restored to one another. But as for you, my darling, it grieves me to think how you will manage on having my pay, which is your chief support, cut off. I am afraid that it will be stopped entirely as long as I am a prisoner of war, but you must write to Cox, and ask him to inform you.

I am so glad you got both my letters of 19th and 23rd March together; I am afraid that by the previous mail you did not get one, but am not sure, as I was not able to read your letter. No doubt at present it appears to us a great misfortune (more so now than ever) that I did not go home to the depôt instead of Goodenough, but in every way it was his turn; I had just left the depôt, and I could not, consistent with my duty, have given up the command of the regiment in the field for the purpose of going to the depôt. Under all my misfortunes I am consoled with the sense that I have done my duty to the best of my ability. The night I was made prisoner I had already, two hours before, repulsed one attack on the right of our trenches by charging the assailants with the bayonet with part of the guard. Of the five officers who accompanied me, two were wounded; one of them, Captain Hedley Vicars, 97th, was hit close by my side, and when the attack was made on the left I was hastening thither with a party of the 7th Fusiliers to try and repel it in the same manner, when I was taken prisoner. You will, of course, now stop sending me any more things, as I cannot expect they will reach me when in the interior of Russia. I kept a diary in pencil in the pocket-book you gave me at Plymouth up to the day of my being made prisoner, but they have not sent it to me from camp. I have, however, written for it, as I will try to keep it up.

To Major Simpson, 34th Regiment.

HOSPITAL, SEBASTOPOL,
March 23.

MY DEAR SIMPSON,

Early this morning I had the misfortune of being taken prisoner and wounded in the second attack which the Russians made on our advanced works. I received a bayonet-wound through the left hand, which is doing well; a smart blow on the head from the butt of a firelock, which knocked me down; and another on the right shoulder, neither of which signify much. My wounds were dressed immediately I was brought in, and I have been very well treated by the Russian authorities, and have received every attention I could expect. I enclose a letter to my wife, which please have sent by Monday's mail. I will also thank you to try and get my bed and bedding, and my two portmanteaux and leather bag filled with my clothes, including my shell-jacket, boots, dressing-box, brushes, writing-case, Bible, Prayer-book, pocket-book, and anything else you might think useful to me. I have some clothes in a valise at the head of my bed. I have a quantity of fire-lighters in my portmanteau, and which I beg you will take. I also wish you would send me my money, which you will find in a belt, and portmonnaie in my box—Dwyer has the keys. Also ask Roach to be so kind as to give you, for the same purpose, whatever balance he has in hand of my field-allowance, command-money, etc., after deducting my ship and shore rations, and paying Bullock 25s. and

Chatfield 20s., the balance of their wages to March 31; also drum-major 8s., and Mr. Alt 2s., for things that they got for me at Balaklava. Will you also have the kindness to have my two horses sold, together with saddle, bridle, clothing, and other stable requisites, of which you will find a lot new in my basket, and the cash remitted to me by first opportunity; also my buffalo-robe and small black-leather valise? Anything, such as my pistol-case, which you don't either sell or send to me, please have packed up in my box and basket, they could be sent to my address at home by the first opportunity. I left my great-coat and waterproof in the advanced works; they both had my name on them. Should they have been recovered they would be useful, especially the latter. Don't forget my forage-cap, as I lost the one I had on in the struggle. They tell me here that two other English officers were taken last night—one a Lieutenant-Colonel of Engineers—but I can't learn their names. Hoping you will kindly excuse the trouble I am giving you, and with kind regards to all the officers,

Believe me,
Yours truly,
R. D. KELLY.

P.S.—I left in my tent two or three official letters, which were put in my hand just as I was starting for the trenches.

From Lord Raglan, Commander-in-Chief, to Mrs. Kelly.

BEFORE SEBASTOPOL,
March 31, 1855.

Lord Raglan presents his compliments to Mrs. Kelly, and begs to transmit to her a second letter from Lieutenant-Colonel Kelly, who, she will be rejoiced to hear, is doing very well, and is very kindly treated. He hopes that the account the Colonel first gave her relieved her from all anxiety respecting him.

[*Next letter missing.*]

'THE VALIANT,' SEBASTOPOL,
April 16, 1855.

MY DEAREST ELLIE,

My last letter to you I finished on the 11th, and gave it to Captain Rumine (?), together with one to my mother, which he promised to send to the camp, with my letters written on April 8—viz., one to you, one to Cox, and one to R. Lloyd—by the first opportunity, but, unfortunately, the bombardment commenced early on the morning of the 8th, and has continued almost without intermission, and is still going on, which, of course, has prevented any communication between the town and our camp. Captain Rumine, however, kindly promised, in case he could not send them to our camp, to forward them viâ Berlin and Warsaw, and I trust that by one way or another you will receive them safely. On the 11th we were removed from our quarters at Fort Nicholas to the *Ville de Paris*, a ship of 120 guns lying in the harbour, where we were very comfortably put up in the Admiral's cabin, and treated with great attention. Yesterday evening we were moved again to Port Cevernaia, on the north side of the harbour, but as on arrival there was found to be no room for us, we were taken on board the vessel from which I write this; and this morning we have been just told that we must prepare to-day *to start for the interior*, and this sudden order must plead my excuse with you for not being able to write a longer letter. Our destination is to be Kaluga, but on the arrival on board of the officer with the order I shall be able to give you more positive information in a postscript. Kaluga is distant from this 1,579 Russian versts, or about 850 English miles. Kaluga is the capital of the government or province of the same name, and is situated on the river Oka, about one hundred and twenty miles south-west of Moscow, and I think this description will enable you to find it on the map. Three French officers accompanied Captain Montague and myself, together with twenty French and seven English soldiers. We are to travel in the covered waggons of the country without springs, and as we do not travel post, we can only make short stages, and they say we shall be from one month to six weeks on the journey, which will be tedious enough. I will endeavour, if possible, to write to you *en route*. The principal towns we pass through are: Simpheropol, Perrekoff, and Pultawa, and as I shall be so long on the road I trust on arrival at Kaluga to have the happiness of finding letters from you, as the date of your last was March 21, which appears an age. God grant they may bring me good news of you and all the dear ones at Weston! You must direct your letters to me as follows: ' À Monsieur le Gouvernour de Kaluga, pour être remise à Colonel Kelly, prisonier de guerre.' You, of course, will make all the necessary inquiries about the postage; the best route is, I fancy, by Berlin and Warsaw, by which I send this.

You will be happy to hear that my wound is going on as well as possible, and that the flesh is skinning over, and I trust it will soon be healed. I hope also by using my hand gradually soon to recover the complete use of it. I never felt in better health; the only thing that preys on me is the thought of the long separation that may ensue between me and all those I hold most dear on Earth should this war be protracted; but we still indulge in the hope that the negotiations at Vienna may terminate in peace. God grant that our hopes may not be frustrated. I have written a note to Major Simpson to be forwarded to our camp by flag of truce, requesting him to forward any letters that may have arrived there for me to Kaluga. How I long to hear news of you, the dear children, and all at Weston! I have written to you twice a week since I have been made prisoner, and I trust you have received some of them, and that your apprehensions about my state have been quieted by them. I must now conclude, as I have not time to say more. God bless you and the dear children; may we all be mercifully spared to one another, soon to meet again! Kiss all the dear pets for me, and give them all at Weston my most affectionate love and kind regards to C. K. and Mrs. Caffray.

Believe me, dearest Ellie,
Ever your most affectionately attached
RICHARD.

P.S.—An A.D.C. of Prince Gortschakoff has just come on board, who asked us to dine with the Prince at 4 o'clock this afternoon, and I fancy from that that we shall probably not start till to-morrow morning. We shall learn there our destination, and also how to send our letters, all of which information I hope to give you in a P.S. Till then, adieu!

7 *p.m.*—I have just returned from Prince Gortschakoff, where I learned that the destination of the French officers is Kaluga; that of the English is still further, being the town of Yaroslaff, capital of the government of the same name, and situated on the Volga; it is beyond Moscow. Mr. Von Kotzebue, the Director of the Prince's Chancellory, has been good enough to take charge of this,

and has promised to send it viâ Warsaw; he has also given me the name of the principal towns on the road, which are: Ekaterinoslaw, Kharkoff, Toula, and Moscow, so I hope that with this itinerary you can trace our route; we start early to-morrow. The weather is now very fine, and I hope will continue so, although we cannot expect it during the whole of our long journey. I am afraid the roads in the interior will be in very bad order, on account of the breaking up of the snow. Once more, adieu, and God bless you!

Ever your affectionately attached

RICHARD.

General Buterlin, whom I met at Prince Gortschakoff's, has kindly promised to give me an introduction to his brother, the Lieutenant-Governor of Yaroslaff.

SIMPHEROPOL,
April 19.

MY OWN DEAREST ELLIE,

My last letter to you was dated the 16th, the day before our departure from Sebastopol, and in it I told you, as I was informed myself, that our destination was Yaroslaff; but on our arrival here I was informed by the Commandant that we are to be sent to the town of Riasan, which is not quite as far off as Yaroslaff, being on this side of Moscow, otherwise the route is very nearly the same. I have lost no time in acquainting you with this change in our destination, in order that you may direct your letters accordingly. Mr. Von Kotzebue charged himself with the forwarding of my letter to you, and I hope to have this forwarded by the Governor of this town, Count Adlahberg. We reached this about 8.30 in the evening of the 17th, having left Sebastopol, distant about forty miles, at 9 a.m. on the 17th. We travelled in the covered waggons of the country without springs, and drawn by three horses each, and as the roads are not very good, although never in better order than at present, you may easily imagine that we were pretty well jolted; however, the weather was delicious, and we enjoyed the drive very much, our party consisting of two English and three French officers, and three soldier servants, occupied two waggons, and we were escorted by an officer and six Cossacks. Our road, except when we crossed the valleys of the Balbek and Alma, lay chiefly over extensive steppes covered with grass, but perfectly treeless, and almost houseless; the valleys that we crossed, especially that of the Balbek, were very beautiful, and were covered with vineyards and orchards, and every description of fruit tree just bursting into blossom. At every step we met long lines of waggons loaded with provisions, forage, and stores for Sebastopol. At one we halted for a few hours to dine and rest the horses. Here, as I must say has been always the case wherever I have met with Russian officers, we received from them every attention. General Chaletzky, in command of a regiment of cavalry there, gave me an introduction to his daughter, who resides at Kharkoff, through which we pass, and begged me to call on her.

Batcheterai is the ancient capital of the Crimea when it was in the possession of the Tartars, and is as dirty a town as you can well imagine; the ancient palace of the Khans of Crimean Tartary still exists here, and is in good preservation, although at present converted into a hospital; there are numerous fountains throughout the building, and the gardens are in good order. We reached Simpheropol, the present capital of the Crimea, rather late, and as most of the houses in the town are occupied by the sick and wounded transported from

Sebastopol, there was some difficulty at first in procuring proper accommodation for us, and we were accordingly lodged that night in a sort of prison, which was certainly rather uncomfortable; but the next day the Commandant called and took me in his carriage to the hospital, where we were lodged in a much more comfortable room, and in the afternoon we all dined with him, and tasted some excellent wines of the Crimea, one of which resembled very much champagne, and another Frontignac. Since our arrival here we have been placed on an allowance, out of which we have to defray the expenses of our living; mine, as Lieutenant-Colonel, is $1\frac{1}{2}$ roubles, or about 5s. a day, which will be sufficient to support me in this country, I dare say. Since writing this I have heard that where we are lodging now is not the hospital, but the house of Mdlle. Radzewitch, who is distinguished for her kindness to the English and French prisoners; her servants market and cook our dinners for us. Captain Montague and I are to travel by post, and are to go together, and are, I believe, to start on the 21st, and shall be separated from our French companions, one of whom, a M. Martin, having been severely wounded, is returning to France, viâ Odessa. You will be glad to hear that my wound is now, thank God, completely healed, and I have now entirely discarded bandages and splints, and have begun to use my hand, which, although a little weak now, will soon recover strength, I hope. The only thing I wish for now is to be restored to you and the dear children, and I trust that may soon take place, for I feel that this life is quite a blank without you. God grant that peace may soon take place, and that we may be once more happy together! I have not heard from you since the 6th, and shall not be able to do so before my arrival at Riasan, when I trust I may have the happiness of finding letters with good accounts of you all; it is a long time to wait, but I must have patience. With fondest love to my dear mother and all at Weston, and kisses and love to the dear pets,

>Believe me to be,
>>Ever your affectionately attached
>>>RICHARD.

SIMPHEROPOL,
April 20.

MY DEAREST ELLIE,

As I found that my letter could not go off yesterday, I have taken advantage of the delay to add a postscript to my letter to let you know the way we live here, etc. I have already told you that Mdlle. Radzewitch has been so kind as to procure and cook our meals for us at the very moderate rate of two roubles, or 6s. 8d., a day for the five of us (of course, if we got them from a restaurant it would cost us double); for this we have four meals a day: breakfast at 7.30, dinner at 12, tea at 5, and supper at 8. Our breakfast is always very light, consisting only of tea, which is generally good in Russia, and bread. The samovar is to be found in every Russian house, and takes the place of our tea-urn, and is certainly superior to it; the water is kept hot by a pan of burning charcoal at the bottom of the urn instead of our heater, so the water, instead of getting gradually colder, becomes hotter and hotter, and on the top of the urn is a stand on which the teapot is placed to keep it warm. The tea is served in tumblers and drunk without milk, but with plenty of sugar. Their white bread is light and good; but their black, or rye bread, although they are so fond of it, is, I think, detestable. Our dinner generally consists of soup and bouilli, a *rôti* cut in slices, and some light dish, such as macaroni, or eggs and spinach, and something sweet. Tea and supper are a repetition of breakfast and dinner. When we leave this it will be necessary to take provisions, such as hard-boiled eggs, bread, tea, sugar, etc., with us, as, except at the large towns, nothing eatable except black bread is to be found on the road.

We went yesterday evening to see a M. Andriani, a Piedmontese officer in the French service, and A.D.C. to General Canrobert, who was severely wounded and taken prisoner at the Battle of Balaklava, where he charged with our cavalry, and spoke with the highest enthusiasm of the devoted gallantry of our brave soldiers. M. Andriani has been confined to his bed ever since his wound, a period of nearly six months. While at the hospital we witnessed the funeral of a Russian Colonel of Artillery who had died of typhus fever; he was buried with military honours: a band preceding the coffin, then came the cross and lighted candles, followed by two officers carrying the decorations of the deceased on velvet cushions; after them was borne the lid of the coffin, on which were placed his helmet, sword, and sash; then came the coffin, with the corpse dressed in full uniform, with the face uncovered—a ghastly sight, as the features were extremely thin and attenuated by illness. Immediately after the coffin followed, in the deepest grief, the poor widow, who had only arrived from Odessa two days before. Altogether it was a melancholy spectacle.

We next visited the poor wounded prisoners in the hospital, among whom were twelve English—almost all of them cavalry soldiers wounded at Balaklava, and most of them very severely, and seemed to have suffered greatly. I hear that there are two unwounded men of the 34th here, who were taken the same night as myself; I hope to see them to-day. I must not forget to tell you that we had yesterday a visit from an English lady, a Mme. Sevigny—young, pretty, and a widow; her husband, a Prussian, only died two months ago. I have not heard her maiden name, but she is from Wiltshire, and although only four years from England she speaks English now with quite a foreign accent; she also, I hear, has shown great attention to the prisoners. I must now conclude with affectionate love to you all, and fervent prayers for your welfare. God bless you, my dearest Ellie!

Your affectionately attached husband,
R. D. KELLY.

P.S.—As I shall not have an opportunity of writing to you except from the large towns, you must not expect to hear from me for some time, as the next large town to this is Ekaterinoslaw, which we shall not reach for some time, as we must expect detentions on the road, and it is not even certain that we start to-morrow.

SIMPHEROPOL,
April 25.
MY DEAREST ELLIE,

If my last letter, written on 19th and 20th April, has reached you before this one, you will be surprised to learn that we are still here; but the reason of the delay is owing to the reinforcement of the troops that have been constantly arriving here for the last week, and which have employed most of the horses, and there is therefore some delay in getting horses for us. Captain Montague and I expect to start positively to-morrow or early on Friday at the furthest. We are to be accompanied by a Russian officer, who, I am glad to say, speaks French, and will interpret for us on the road. We are to travel post, and so far will be more fortunate than the French officers, who have to travel with the rest of the prisoners, and will have to go by slow stages. My time, if I could divest myself of the idea that I was a prisoner, and still more that I am likely to be long separated from all those whom I hold most dear on earth, would pass pleasantly enough, for we continue to receive every attention. We dined yesterday again with the Commandant, where we met a larger party than before, and among the rest two Russian Generals, one of whom was a very agreeable person. In the evening, after a walk on the boulevards, we drank tea at the house of a Mrs. Jackson, widow of an English officer in the Russian Service, and who acted for some time as secretary to Prince Woronzoff, and was drowned two years ago in the Caucasus; she had two daughters, the eldest of whom speaks English very fairly, and she favoured us also with some Russian songs very prettily sung. They were kind enough to ask us to accompany them in a drive to see the gardens of Prince Woronzoff, which are near the town, but I am afraid we shall not have time before our departure. I mentioned in my last having witnessed the funeral of a Russian officer, but in that I was mistaken, as what I supposed to be the funeral was merely the ceremony of taking the body to the church, where it remained all night, and the funeral took place next day. This service was performed in the Lutheran church, of which the deceased was a member, and we arrived whilst it was going on, the coffin, with the lid off and showing the face of the corpse with flowers strewed all round it, in front of the Communion-table, or rather altar, for there were candles burning on it, and there was also a lighted candle at each corner of the coffin; the clergyman, when we came in, was reading in German a long discourse, or sermon, part of which was a eulogy on the character of the deceased. The poor widow knelt during the whole of this long discourse, and the ceremony concluded with singing and prayer. Then came a most painful scene—the poor widow taking leave of the remains of her husband, and kissing the cold lips of the corpse, and it was with difficulty that they were able to remove her from it; and when she heard the sound of the hammer nailing down the lid of the coffin she fell into hysterics, and her screams were heart-rending; it was altogether a painful spectacle. She was supported by Mdlle. Radzewitch, who seems to be the friend of the unfortunate, and happy when relieving the distresses of others. She has been very kind to us during our stay here; she is one of the Demoiselles d'Honneur of the Court, but resides here, as she has a property in the Crimea.

The Colonel of the 33rd Regiment has given me an introduction to his family at Moscow should I be able to visit that city. An American doctor in the Russian service lent us *Galignani* to March 23, which was a great treat. I saw the death of my cousin, Major Blackhall, announced in them. We went this morning to the market to buy provisions for the journey, as, except in the large towns, it will be difficult to get anything to eat on the road. Things were dearer than I had imagined. The following were the prices: Fowls being dear, we bought for 2s. 6d. a pair of bustards, about the size of guinea-birds, and very like in plumage—these we intend to have roasted; twenty-nine eggs 1s., to be boiled hard; one pound of cheese, 1s. 1d.; a smoked tongue, 1s. 4d; one pound of rusks, 1s. Tea is excessively dear; for a quarter of a pound I paid 3s. 4d., and for four pounds of beetroot sugar 4s. The morning we start, which I hear is to be positively Friday, we take a few loaves of fresh bread and two or three bottles of light Crimean wine at 1s. a bottle, so, on the whole, we shall not fare badly. At night we shall sleep in our waggons, as infinitely preferable to the post-houses. I hope to write to you again from Ekaterinoslaw; till then, adieu! God bless and protect you in all your troubles and anxieties, and send us a happy and speedy meeting! Kiss all the dear children for me, and give them my fondest love, as well as to my dear mother, sisters, and Francis, and believe me, dearest Ellie, to be

Your ever most affectionately attached

RICHARD.

CHAPTER VII

JOURNEY TO RUSSIA

Hotel Mauritz, Ekaterinoslaw,
May 7, 1855.

My dearest Ellie,

My last letter to you was dated April 26, from Simpheropol; we then expected to leave the following day, but from want of horses or some other reason we did not start till April 30, and reached this about eight last night. Before giving you an account of our journey, I must relate to you all the hospitality we met with before our departure. The day I wrote to you we were invited to dine with Count Adelberg, the Governor, and we found the Countess, a Prussian by birth, a very agreeable person. In the evening we drank tea with a Sister of Charity, who occupied a room in the house where we lodged, and who used to come every evening to dress the wounds of a Russian officer sleeping in a small room off ours; he was an officer of the Guards, and a very gentlemanly young man, and acted as our interpreter and looked after our wants, and the good lady used frequently to feel our beds in passing through to see if they were properly made, and if we wanted clean sheets or pillows. The following day we had a farewell dinner with the Commandant, Colonel Soukaroff, who was excessively friendly, and came frequently to see us. In the evening we drank tea with Mrs. Jackson. The 28th we dined with our excellent friend, Mdlle. Radzewitch, and were there introduced to Mr. Demetrieff, the officer who escorts us to Riasan; we also met there Miss Crim-gheri, the daughter of the last of the ancient Sultans of Crim-Tartary; her father was, I believe, brought up in England, where he married a Scotch lady, a Miss Nelson. The daughter, although she does not speak English, understands it, and is a very lady-like, well-brought-up person; she sketches in pencil very nicely, and after dinner took very good likenesses of two of our party—Captain Montague and a French officer of Zouaves. The following morning she asked us to breakfast, and, it being the fête-day of the Emperor, she wore her order as Demoiselle d'Honneur—a bow of blue ribbon fastened to the left shoulder by the Empress' cipher in diamonds, surmounted by a crown.

In the afternoon of the 30th, after a luncheon *à la Russe*, with porter for the special use of the English, given us by Colonel Ylopkin, of the same regiment as Mr. Demetrieff, who was a daily visitor of ours, and gave me a letter of introduction to his family at Moscow, we at last started in two telegas, or post-waggons of the country, which are open carts with seats shelving inwards, these only giving room for two persons to sit abreast. Our servant and the driver sat in front on the luggage, and the cart was half filled with hay for us to lie on if we liked. As these vehicles are entirely without springs, and the roads are mere tracks crossed by ruts in every direction, you can imagine how our poor bones were shaken; yet these are the vehicles that must be used by all who do not travel in their own carriages. The Governor advised me to buy a *caleche* while at Simpheropol, which might be had for a bagatelle of 2,400 francs; the Commandant, however, kindly provided us with a seat with stuffed arms and back, which was very comfortable so long as it lasted; but, unfortunately, it broke down the third day, and although we got it repaired at Perekop the jolting was too much for it, and it has become a total wreck, and we intend only taking on the stuffed back with us and sit on that. It requires one to be in good health and to have a strong constitution to travel far by post in this hot weather, and with the exception of having my face tanned, have suffered neither from the sun nor jolting, although Captain Montague has suffered a good deal in his back from the jolting of the cart.

I found your down pillow the greatest comfort to sit on, and, indeed, my bed altogether has been most useful to me on the road, for in most of the small post-houses there is but one small room, furnished with a sofa and four or five chairs covered in leather, which we sometimes found preoccupied with other travellers; so I always slept on the floor on the mattress, and gave Montague the stretcher and ground-sheet to sleep on. The whole distance between Simpheropol and Perekop you travel over nothing but steppes—vast grassy plains, on which hardly a house (for the wretched Tartar villages are few and far between) and not a tree is to be seen. It is like being on a green sea—nothing but sky and grass to be seen. The sky was very clear and the sun hot; we saw frequent mirage, looking in the distance exactly like a lake with wooded islands. Herds of cattle, sheep, and a few camels were to be seen occasionally; also in the villages storks on every house-top. We were constantly meeting long trains of carts laden with supplies of every sort for Sebastopol. We reached Bilkoff, a wretched village, about noon on the 2nd, but were detained till ten for horses. We there saw on either hand the Black Sea and that part of the Sea of Azov known as the Putrid Sea, with the isthmus of Arabet beyond it.

On the 3rd we crossed the Dnieper, about two miles wide, in a ferry, at the small town of Beroslaff. The country here, although still consisting of vast plains, commences to be more rolling, and the monotony of the scenery was broken by the plains being intersected by glens and ravines, in which were the only trees to be seen, and through which rolled tributaries to the Dnieper, which, studded with wooded islets, was generally to be seen some distance off as we kept ascending the right bank. In one of the prettiest of these valleys we halted for the night, at a considerable village, the property of Prince Woronzoff, with about two thousand peasants, also his property. All the houses looked exceedingly comfortable; they were all wooden cottages, with thatched roofs, each standing in a little garden, enclosed by a neat wattle fence; some of them were almost cottage *ornés* belonging to rich peasants, who let them to residents. Altogether, I did not expect to find so much neatness in Russia, but it must be allowed that Prince Woronzoff is extremely rich. We here met with more Russian hospitality, for the Prince's Intendant, a Mr. Sarkoff, who, of course, had the best house in the village, called on us on arrival, and wished us to sleep at his house. When we excused ourselves as having to start early next day, he insisted on our supping with him, which we did, and found his house a very good one and very nicely furnished. We were introduced to the ladies, some of whom were on a visit. The ladies all spoke French, and were very agreeable. When we

entered the room Mdme. Sarkoff was seated on the sofa,
and behind her was a lovely boy of about two years old,
with his little hands crossed before him, and sleeping
sweetly in spite of all the noise in the room; she was
shading him from the light, and the tears came into my
eyes when I thought how like you and dear baby it was.
Shall I see you and him in that position in God's good
time? and I trust that is not far off. Mrs. S. showed
me a splendid bracelet she had just received from the
Grand-Duchess Hélène, wife of the Grand-Duke Michael,
who had stayed at their house on his way to Sebastopol;
it was of gold and black enamel, and the centre contained
a beautiful little watch set in diamonds. We had an
excellent supper, and spent a very agreeable evening,
and were invited to breakfast next morning by a Mr.
Ruttenman (?), a [word illegible], with whom I managed
to converse a little in broken German. The meal commenced with tea and bread-and-butter served in a neat
bedroom, and ended with a substantial one *à la fourchette*
in the dining-room, which he wished us to wash down
with more wine than we thought was good for us. We
reached this at eight on the 6th, and found here Mr.
Clarke of the 5th, who was taken the same night as
Byron, and had been thirty-three days on his road
from Simpheropol, he having accompanied the soldier
prisoners who marched, as field-officers alone have the
privilege of travelling post. He told me that poor Byron,
who is [word illegible], took typhus fever between this
and Kharkoff, and was sixteen days in hospital, but is
now quite well, although weak; he also told me that the
prisoners may expect soon to be exchanged. I also saw
in the *Journal de Frankfort* a copy of Lord Raglan's
despatch of 26th, by which I was gratified to find that
my conduct on that unfortunate night had been approved

of. We leave perhaps to-morrow for Riasan, 600 miles off, and they say here I shall go on to St. Petersburg. I shall be glad of it, as I shall get your letters quicker. I hope I shall hear from you at Riasan. How I long to have news of you! God grant it may be good! I will write, D.V., again from Kharkoff, the next capital. I am quite well, and do not want for anything. I must close, as this goes to-morrow. Love to all, kisses to the dear pets.

Ever your most affectionate
RICHARD.

POST HOUSE, RIASAN,
May 25, 1855.

MY DEAREST ELLIE,

We arrived at this place, which is to be our destination if we are to remain in Russia, at half-past two this afternoon, and, as you see, I have lost no time in writing to you, although as yet I have not much news to tell you. The Russian officer who conducted us here wrote immediately to the Governor, who lives a mile out of town, to report himself to him, and was to have brought us our letters should any have been received for us; but, unfortunately, the Governor was out, and he is to call again to-morrow, when I trust he may bring me the letters I have been so anxiously looking for, and God grant they may contain cheering accounts of you and all I love so devotedly! There are five other English officers here besides ourselves—viz., Matthews, 8th Hussars; Mr. Chadworth, 17th Lancers; Captain Frampton, 50th; Mr. Duff and Byron of the 36th. Mr. Clarke, 50th, is also on his road here. They live, we are told, in different parts of the town, and as yet we have not seen them, nor can we ascertain where they live; but before the post goes out on the 28th I hope we shall have seen them, and that I shall be able to give you some news about our prospects of being exchanged, and other interesting subjects. My last to you was dated from Voronezh, the 19th. We remained there till the 21st. We made no acquaintances there, and found it a dull, uninteresting town. It is full of churches, and in the cathedral are deposited the relics of St. Metrofaney, which are supposed to be of great sanctity, as on the road to the town we met crowds of women going there on a pilgrimage. We went into the cathedral, and found it so surrounded with peasants that we could not stir if a Mass was being celebrated, and we could not see the relics.

We went one evening to the Botanical Garden, which was prettily situated about a mile from the town, but we did not observe that they contained anything very rare; it was, however, refreshing to get into the shade out of the dust, and to hear the nightingales, of which the gardens were full, sing so sweetly. We left Voronezh on the morning of the 21st, and had a tedious journey to this place of 270 miles, across a flat, uninteresting country, but very fertile with grain-crops. We passed through a great part of the government of Tabuloff, of which so much was spoken during the debate on the Repeal of the Corn Laws, as being able in itself to supply us with corn, it was certainly an immense tract, covered with wheat and rye, but wanted rain greatly, of which we have hardly had a drop since we left Simpheropol on April 30, and the dust has been in consequence very annoying. The only rivers of importance that we crossed were the Don, which was still in its infancy, and the Vorona, which was tolerably large. We found the roads as we got into the interior getting worse instead of better, and the jolting of the carts was consequently very great; and with all that we did not find they drove quick, and the pace rarely exceeded six English miles an hour, and we never changed horses, which involved a change of carts and consequent repacking of baggage, under half an hour. We have been twenty-six days on the road from Simpheropol, eighteen of which we were actually travelling, and we halted three at Ekaterinoslaw, three at Kharkoff, and two at Voronezh; and the distance we have come is 940 miles, and from Sebastopol 980. I will say that if the travelling has been somewhat uncomfortable, our living has been very moderate, for our whole expense during that time, including hotel bills and drosky-hire at the different towns, has not exceeded twenty-six roubles each; the value of a rouble is just four francs, which would make our expenses amount to a little less that £2 each, which is very moderate.

May 26.

DEAREST ELLEN,

The other English officers called on us last evening at six o'clock, and we drank tea with them in a house they have taken; but you may imagine my disappointment when they told me there were no letters for me, as all letters for the English were left at the police-office; indeed, only one of them had received a letter from England since they had been taken. This certainly has been a bitter disappointment to me, for I relied, too confidently, perhaps, on my getting letters on arrival here, as I know full well you have written frequently to me, but I suppose they have not been forwarded. I must only trust in the mercy of our gracious Father, who has been so merciful towards us, that you have been all spared to me, and that you continue to enjoy good health, and that ere long we may have the happiness of meeting again. You may possibly have directed some of your letters to Yaroslaff, as in the letter I wrote you on April 16, just before leaving Simpheropol, I told you, as I was informed myself, that we were to be sent there. Directly, however, on our arrival at Simpheropol I learned that we were to be sent to Riasan, I wrote to you to that effect.

In a letter I wrote to you from Sebastopol, on April 7, I told you that I had directed Cox to place to your credit the balance of the amount of the sale of my effects, which I hope he has done. You may rely on my continuing to write to you on every opportunity, and I only hope you may be more fortunate than I have been in getting the letters. All the officers here confidently expect soon to be exchanged. God grant that my name may be included with the rest! But this I shall learn from the Governor, I suppose, when I see him. They expect to be sent to England by way of Moscow and Warsaw, which latter is about a hundred miles from this; but they say the roads are good and that there are diligences, and from Warsaw there is a railroad to Berlin by Cracow, and from thence my route to England would be by rail to Ostend. I must go to London to report myself and get some clothes, and decide on my future plans, and in order to have the benefit of your advice on the latter point I should like greatly that you could meet me there. You might leave the children at Weston; I would telegraph immediately on my arrival in England, and you could do the same to me, and tell me when you could arrive. I could have a lodging taken for you, and meet you at the train. If you can't get an escort, bring Mrs. Reilly with you. Bring some shirts for me, as I shall want them. It is very pleasant indulging in these castles in the air. I only trust that, please God, they may be realized!

1 p.m.

I have just returned from the Governor's, who received me very kindly; but, alas! there were no letters to be found for us. I could hear nothing certain about our exchange. I think if you were to write to Cox you might get some information on the subject. We have an idea of taking a house close to where the other officers are—so close that we have only to step across the road to take our meals, and only sleep in the other house. I must now conclude, as I hope to write to you soon again. Give my love to my mother, K., A., and F., and kiss the darlings for me.

Ever your most affectionately attached
RICHARD.

RIASAN,
June 4.

MY DEAREST ELLEN,

We arrived here from Simpheropol on May 25, and on the following day I wrote to you saying that I had found no letters for me here as I expected, but that Count Buterlin had been so kind as to write to Mr. Anderson, the agent of the English prisoners at St. Petersburg, to know if any letters had been received by him for me; the answer arrived yesterday, and, to my great disappointment, I learned that none had arrived.

Riasan is not a very lively place, nor is there much society just now, most of the upper classes being in the country at present. The Governor, M. Novosillekeff, is very friendly and hospitable; he keeps open house, and would like us to come and dine with him every day. I have been there three times, and have found the parties very agreeable. He lives in a country house about half a mile from the town with pretty grounds about it, which are thrown open to the public. The country about Riasan is flat and not very interesting; the situation, however, they say is healthy. Last week we had cool weather with rain, but the hot weather has recommenced, and they say that during the summer we may expect great heat. We have taken a small house with one sitting and three bed rooms for a month, for which we pay 11 roubles, or £1 16s., but I believe Government will repay us the rent. The bread is excellent here and very cheap; the meat not so good as in England, but much cheaper, being only 2d. the pound of 12 ounces; tea and sugar are, however, very dear, the former being 11s. 6d. for 12 ounces. We are able to borrow both English and French books here, which is a great treat.

I live in the hope that I may soon hear from you, with good accounts of yourself, the dear children, my mother, and all I love at Weston, and that you have been all well and as happy and comfortable as circumstances will admit of. I must now say adieu. Kiss the dear children for me, and tell them not to forget their papa, who is continually thinking of them. I suppose baby is beginning to talk now. Give my love to my dear mother, K., A., and F., and kind regards to Miss Keys. God bless you and spare you to me, my dearest love, and believe me to be ever

Your most affectionately attached husband,

R. D. KELLY.

RIASAN,
June 8, 1855.

MY OWN BELOVED ELLIE,

Thank God I have at last had the happiness of hearing of you, although not yet from you. Yesterday

I dined by chance at the Governor's, for we have no special invitation, but dine there just when we like, and I met there Mme. Narischkin, who had just arrived from Moscow, and she told me that her governess, Miss Pole, had a message for me from Mr. Gray, the clergyman at Moscow, and on going to the hotel after dinner I saw Miss Pole, who told me that our kind friends the Maxwells had written to Mr. Gray about me, and also that he had heard from you, making inquiries about me. She did not know the date of the letter, but I have to-day written to Mr. G. begging him to forward the letter to me, that I may once more have the pleasure of seeing your handwriting, as I have no later date from you than your letter of March 21, which was sent to me to Sebastopol from our camp on April 7. You may fancy my delight and gratitude to the Giver of all good at knowing that you are still spared to me, for I felt so disappointed at not finding any letters for me on my arrival here, which I fully expected, that I began to imagine that perhaps you had been taken from me, and the thought has made me feel very sad and wretched; but, thanks be to God! I have still the hope of being one day again united to you, the dear children, and all the loved circle at Weston. Yesterday evening I also had the happiness of hearing of you through another source. Mrs. Braillard, an English lady, and wife of a gentleman who showed us a great deal of attention during our stay at Kharkoff *en route* here, in writing to one of the officers here mentioned in the postscript that she had heard from a Mrs. Merillies from St. Petersburg, who said you had written to her inquiring about me. I am sure you must have been very anxious about me, and am afraid that you have not received all my letters, for this is the thirteenth letter I have written to you since being taken, besides writing to my mother, R. Lloyd, and Cox. I have never lost an opportunity, and wrote to you from each Government town through which we passed on our route here. . . .

RIASAN,
June 11.

MY BELOVED ELLIE,

You may fancy my happiness at receiving your letter of May 14, forwarded by Mr. de la Chaumette, the first I have received since April 9. The Governor sent me a message to-day requesting me to dine with him, and on my arrival handed me your letter, which I was delighted to get, and to find that at that date, thank God! you, the dear children, my mother, and all at Weston, with the exception of poor Kate, were quite well. Your letter of May 8, forwarded through Lord Clarendon, I have not yet received, but I suppose it will be sent on to me from Yaroslaff. That unfortunate mistake of M. von Kotzebue, Prince Gortschakoff's Chancellor, in telling us we were to be sent to Yaroslaff, has caused, I am afraid, great delay in the receipt of my letters. I trust you have received my subsequent letters from Simpheropol in which the mistake was corrected, and that you have since addressed your letters to Riasan. On the 9th I got a letter from a Mr. Merillies, a merchant in St. Petersburg, stating that he had heard from a friend in London who was making inquiries about me on your behalf.

I had no idea, till I got yours of May 8, of the agony *and sorrow you all* suffered on my account from that report of my death. I was in hopes that you would have heard by the same mail that I was a prisoner, but the Lord mercifully supported you in your affliction, and your mourning was turned into joy. I have but little space to send more, as I send this under cover to a friend who has been most kind and hospitable to all the English prisoners, officers and soldiers. I will not give the name lest this may be opened, but I have mentioned it in a former letter she sends through her sister in London. I have not drawn anything from Cox since I have been abroad, nor do I want money, and have provided myself with all I want. Adieu! God bless you! Love to all at Weston, and kisses to the dear pets.

Ever your most affectionate
RICHARD.

RIASAN,
June 27, 1855.

MY BELOVED ELLEN,

I have the unspeakable happiness of being able to convey to you the gratifying intelligence that we are to be exchanged, and that much sooner than we anticipated. We only received this news to-day, and I believe we are to start by the diligence that proceeds to Moscow on July 1. I can hardly realize the idea that I shall so soon (D.V.) be on my way to rejoin you and all the other dear ones I left behind me (six months ago to-morrow). How I long for that happy moment to arrive when I shall see all your sweet faces again, and thank you for the warm and affectionate sympathy that you have all shown for me during my absence! How grateful we should feel to our merciful Father for all the mercies and bounties He has bestowed on us, especially lately! Not a long time back I had the prospect before me of either spending a dreary winter here without you or exposing you to the necessity of leaving your children and undertaking a long and fatiguing journey for the purpose of joining me, which, thank God! is not now necessary.

We go round by Moscow for the special purpose of allowing us to see that celebrated city, and I shall take the opportunity of sending this letter from thence through Rev. Mr. Gray, as no post will leave this before July 1, the day of our intended departure.

I forgot to tell you that instead of going home viâ Warsaw and Berlin as we had hoped, we are to proceed viâ Odessa; but what matters the road so long as it leads to you? Our journey, however, will be long; it is about 200 versts from this to Moscow, and 1,200 versts (809 miles) from thence to Odessa. From this to Moscow is one day's journey, and I suppose we shall remain at least two days, and from thence to Koursk, which is as far as the *chaussée* extends in that direction, is about 400 versts, which we shall travel in the diligence in two days. The remaining 800 versts from Koursk to Odessa we must post, going through Orel and Kharkoff (all over our old ground again), and then starting off to the right to Odessa through Nicolaieff. What with stoppages on the road this will take us at least ten days, and then we shall probably not arrive at Odessa before July 16. We may expect at least a week's detention at Odessa before the arrival of a British man-of-war to take us all on board. What orders she may bring as to our ultimate destination it is impossible to say. We may have to proceed, in the first instance, to Balaklava, or, which is much more likely (as we all require new outfits before we take the field), we may go on to Constantinople *en route* to England. In that latter case we might hope to leave Constantinople for England about August 9, and arrive about the 15th; not earlier, I think. I shall endeavour, if possible, to write to you *en route* from Kharkoff, where I shall be able to send it through Mme. Braillard. At Odessa I shall find an old Corfu friend of mine; the Chevalier Kischione is Austrian Consul, and perhaps I may be able to send a letter through him; and from Constantinople you may depend on my writing.

If the Weston party still intend going to Paris about that time, I am afraid I shall not be able to join them there now as I had once hoped to have done, if I had returned home viâ Berlin, as, of course, from Constantinople we shall be sent home in a returned transport viâ Malta. You may depend on my telegraphing my arrival to you as soon as I land in England, and I hope we may have the happiness of meeting you in London (where I must go, in the first instance) soon after. Lodgings will then be cheap, as the season will be over, and we will indulge ourselves in the pleasure of visiting the Collinsons at Clapham and the Crystal Palace at Sydenham. An answer to this written at once, and directed to the British Ambassador, would probably catch me at Constantinople before I left. You must take care to put on it 'To be left till called for,' or they would forward it probably to Balaklava, where, indeed, you might send me another on the chance of my being sent there. My last letters to you were on the 22nd, when I sent you two, one long one through the Governor and one by private hand. In them I acknowledged the receipt on 19th of yours of May 26, and on 20th of my mother's of the same date, sent to Orel, and of your darling letter May 8, sent through Danish Minister. I have received none since, and as no posts will arrive before our departure, do not expect to get any more while in Russia.

June 28.

DEAREST E.,

I wrote the last sentence because they told me yesterday no letters had arrived for me by the post, but fancy my delight at getting at last three letters—viz., a kind letter from Turner of June 2, dear Kate's affectionate letter of June 9, and your own dear letter of 6th and 7th. Yours of May 31 I have not got, nor can I expect to now. Many thanks for them all. I am so glad you got my letter from Ekaterinoslaw; Mme. Rodi enclosed it for me in one of hers to her friends at Bonn, and begged them to forward it. The lady whose letter about me you saw in the *Times* was Miss Hardcastle, governess in the family of the late Governor of Kharkoff, who died a short time before our arrival; I met her at Mme. Braillard's, at whose hospitable table we dined each time we were there. I am glad you saw the paragraph, as it relieved you from all anxiety about me. The letters we send through the Governors always will arrive late, for they are translated and copied before being sent off.

Kate gives me a charming account of all the dear children and of their being so well and happy, and of their having enjoyed themselves so much on dear Annie's birthday. Will you thank dear Kate for her letter, and say that I am so busy making preparations for our departure that I have no time to answer it, but I trust (D.V.) to be able to write to both my mother and her from Odessa, where we shall probably be detained for some time before our embarkation? Will you also say the same to Mrs. Turner when you write, and thank the Colonel for his letter? I see he expects soon to be ordered abroad; I sincerely hope it will not be to the Crimea. I hope you had a pleasant visit to Dublin and found them all well. I am delighted that Mrs. Webb has at last succeeded; she deserved it, poor thing! after all her trials and patience.

Did you succeed with the German governess? I hope she may be an acquisition. I should like all the dear pets to be able to speak both French and German well. I am glad you heard from Roach, and that he escaped the cholera which had been committing such ravages. The contents of your box seemed to have sold very well; was it the last of the series? I was sorry to find by a letter Byron got from his friends that poor young Jordan had been killed in the trenches; he does not give the date. I wonder if it was the night I was taken; he was the last person I spoke to before I was taken. I am glad your pecuniary affairs are so flourishing. Do you still keep a sum in the bank? I don't require any at present; I have ample to take me to Odessa, and if I want any I can draw there. I am much obliged to General Pennefather for his kind recollection of me, for it is a long time since I last saw him; he had only rejoined the army a short time before I was taken, and I had not been able to call on him. Our weather here has been very hot; to-day is the first wet day we have had for a long time; people have been praying for rain, which is very much wanted for the crops. Many thanks for your timely caution about those shocking wolves (so like you, my darling pet!), but I don't think they abound here, as this is not a wooded district. I am sure the advice must have amused the person who has to read my letters before they are delivered, and which, in this instance, was the Governor's English governess. I sent a message in a letter one of our party wrote to Mdlle. Radzewitch at Simpheropol, and begged her to ask the person to whom I gave the two letters I wrote to you there what he had done with them, as they had not been received by you. I suspect he never sent them, and that it was the same case with those written by me at Sebastopol during the bombardment. I anticipate much pleasure from our visit to Moscow, which I would rather see than St. Petersburg or any other city in Russia. We go to Moscow by the express permission of the Governor, in order to let us see it (it being out of the direct road to Odessa), but we must pay the expense of the détour ourselves. This indulgence is confined to the eight military officers, but does not extend to the other six prisoners, who are either in the Transport or Commissariat Service; they go on direct to Toula. Our escort to Moscow is to be Count Boutourlin, who speaks English nearly as well as I do, and is a very agreeable, well-informed person besides. I am in a difficulty about my luggage, as, when travelling by diligence, they only allow you 29 pounds, and charge very high for the surplus. I shall get rid of all the rubbish out of my portmanteaus and make them as light as possible. I don't like parting with my bed, which has been such a friend to me, but I think must get rid of the mattress in order to reduce the weight. Tell dear little Annie, with my love, that I hope she behaved well in church, and was not locked up in the organ-loft. I am so glad to hear that C. K. has been so kind and generous to you. God bless anyone that is! I am happy to hear that F.'s farms are doing so well and repaying his outlay. The crops in this part of the country are very fine; their harvest will commence about the middle of July.

June 29.

I dined yesterday with the Governor, and found that our idea that we were to start on July 1 was a little premature, as we are not to go for a fortnight or three weeks. This is certainly very disappointing, but we must have patience. The cause given for this delay was that the Emperor was anxious before we were exchanged to ascertain whether any officer would prefer remaining in Russia to going home, and we all assembled at Government House this morning for the purpose of signing a paper to that effect; none of us, however, gave a preference to Russia. While there I had the gratification of getting your dear letter of June 12, forwarded through Rev. Mr. Gray. I am indeed grieved to hear that you have not yet got any of the numerous letters I have written to you since the one of May 7 from Ekaterinoslaw. I am afraid those I sent through the Governor of Kharkoff and Varnesch were not sent; they are kept to be copied and translated, and are then neglected to be forwarded. Count Boutourlin declares all I have sent to the Governor here have been forwarded. I shall send this through to Mr. Gray, of Moscow, who has kindly offered to forward letters, although *contre les règles*. I had a kind letter yesterday from Mr. Merrillies, St. Petersburg, to whom I wrote soon after my arrival here, hearing that he had heard news of you which came from Mr. Knalleke, the Foreign Secretary for the Bible Society in London. He says he forwarded to you on June 18 my letter to him, and has kindly offered to forward our letters to each other. His address is M. Archibald Merrillies, Négocien at St. Petersburg. I will send an answer to your last through him by this post, so as not to lose a chance. I wish now to concert our plans, so that we may meet as soon as possible after my arrival in England. I cannot expect now to arrive at Constantinople before the middle of August, which will give you, I hope, ample time to have an answer to this awaiting me at Constantinople, addressed to the care of the British Consul-General (who, on second thoughts, would, I think, be more accessible than the Ambassador), the letter to be kept till called for, and a duplicate to be sent to the regiment in the Crimea, in case of our being taken there before going to Constantinople. In this letter you could propose any plan of your own or modification of mine. From Constantinople we are almost certain of being sent home by a return steam transport, touching at Malta. On arrival at Malta, I will (D.V.) write to you viâ Marseilles, which will probably reach two or three days before our ship gets to England. What I propose is, that as soon as you get this letter from Malta, that you start for Dublin and stay with your mother, as a telegraphic message will reach you there so much sooner than at Weston, where so much time is lost between Duleek and Drogheda. On landing in England—probably at Portsmouth—I will telegraph at once to you at Sidney Terrace (I am sure they will forward it to Weston). I will await your answer by telegraph, and you must tell me when you will be able to start for London viâ Holyhead, and where we are to meet in London, at what hotel or lodgings; you might ask A. de Lachaumette to look out for lodgings a short time before you expect me, and I could go up and take them and meet you at the train. I long for that blissful moment to arrive! Any improvement or alteration in this plan you must communicate to me. You might have a letter awaiting me at Malta, addressed to the care of officer commanding depot, to be kept till called for.

I will now say adieu, dearest, with kisses to pets, and fondest love to my dear mother and yours, and also to Kate, Annie, Louisa, and Francis; kindest regards to Mrs. Webb and C. K., and remembrances to Mrs. Caffray.

Believe me ever your most fondly attached

RICHARD.

June 29.

Let me know if Colonel Browne is with the regiment in the Crimea. I was very sorry to hear that poor

Maxwell had been wounded, but trust that he has recovered from it. I see that Lawrence also has been wounded, and Schniffner very severely hurt by a fall while riding a race, and that Guilt and Gordon have been mentioned for gallant conduct. Mr. Gray sent us from Moscow, a lot of papers and books, and the former, though old, were very interesting to us, as we had not seen them before. I read in them the account of my dead body being found ; I can well imagine what a shock that must have been to you. I also read Lord Raglan's first despatch about the affair in which I was taken, in which there are two or three errors. Previous to the sortie of the Russians in which I was taken they had made another, which I repulsed (after a sharp fight) with the detachments of 77th and 87th Regiments ; this repulse is stated in the despatch, but it is said that the troops were under the direction of Major Gordon, R.E., on that occasion, which is quite a mistake. Gordon (an old friend of mine, and with whom I have been on duty several times, and more zealous or braver officer never stepped) was certainly with us, and was severely wounded, but I commanded the party, took them out, remained with them the whole time, and brought them back after we had repulsed the enemy. I was close to poor Vicars, of 97th, when he was shot while gallantly leading on his men. The French have a proverb *Les absents ont toujours tort*, and that is the reason, I suppose, I did not get whatever credit was due for the affair. If I have an opportunity, I shall point out the error to Lord Raglan, and try to get it rectified, and in the meantime you have my authority for explaining it to any of my military friends. Tell dear Annie that I am much obliged to her for having written to me, although I have not yet got her letter, but I hope it will soon arrive. I will now say adieu, with affectionate love to my mother, Kate, Annie, Francis, and all your dear family, when you write. Love and kisses to all the dear pets, and kind regards to C.K.

  Believe me, dearest Ellie,
    Ever your most affectionately attached
        RICHARD.

          RIASÁN,
          July 11, 2 *a.m.*

MY DEAREST ELLIE,

  Although it is 2 o'clock in the morning, and that I am just returned after a six miles' drive from a house in the country, where we dined and spent the evening, I must write you a letter, even if a short one, before going to bed, as I have an opportunity of sending it to-day to Moscow, to be forwarded from thence by Mr. Gray. We only heard yesterday morning that a Russian Captain, having been taken prisoner by us lately at Sebastopol, was sent back by Lord Raglan with a request (being, I suppose, in want of Engineer officers) that he might be exchanged for Captain Montague, which has been acceded to, and Montague starts at 10 a.m. to-day by the diligence for Moscow, *en route* to Odessa, and has promised to give this to Mr. Gray *en passant*, with a request that he would forward it, so I trust you will get it safe in about three weeks.

 I took advantage of Montague's return to our camp to write a long letter to Simpson, thanking him and Roach for their kindness in having written to you after I was taken; this occupied me till one, till it was time to get ready to go to Colonel Kobanieff, who dined at three, and where we spent a very pleasant day. His family consists, besides his wife, of a young cadet home for the holidays, a younger boy of ten, two lady-like girls of eighteen and sixteen, the younger very pretty, and a little dot of three years with blue eyes and curly light hair like our pet Sophie, which resemblance caused an immediate friendship between us, carried on my part by the intervention of my watch, as at present the young lady only discourses in Russian. The second young lady, Mdlle. Julie, is an accomplished musican, and we enjoyed quite a musical treat, as their music master, an Austrian who resides in the house, is a first-rate performer; and we had solos and duets, and a great variety of music, but chiefly from the 'Prophet.' There was also an exquisite Germon duo, called the 'Erl-könig'; do you know it? It is founded on a German superstition: a father is riding through a forest with his son in his arms, and the demon-king tries to entice his son away; the boy sees and hears him, but the father does not, and tries to sooth his child, and at the end of the ride finds him dead in his arms. The music represents the dialogue between the three and the galloping of the horse very well. The instruments were two grand pianos and a harmonica, which I never heard before, but which is a beautiful instrument, and can imitate either separately or together fourteen different instruments, and when all the stops are out it is just like a full orchestra. It is played with the hands just like a piano, and by the feet as if you were playing an accordion; when played in company with the piano it had a beautiful effect. We had a (word illegible) dinner-party with champagne, and what is now dearer in Russia, porter—*specialement pour Messrs. les Anglais*. The salon is a very good room, and there was such a nice floor *en parquet*, that the young ladies thought that it would be a pity if there was not a little dancing, so the music master struck up some of Strauss' music, and polkas, valses, and quadrilles were the order of the night, in which latter only I indulged. I had always fancied that we had succeeded in making that dance a very mild, amusement in England, but to witness dancing made easy you must go to Russia, for the first preliminary in forming a quadrille is placing as many chairs as there are dancers, where the couples are to stand, or rather sit, for they only stand while actually dancing. A most convenient storm of thunder, lightning, and rain, kept us till twelve, when we were allowed to depart, as we had a river to cross by boat on our way home. At the first ferry we came to they told us they were rather doubtful about the strength of the rope by which they hauled across; they would try and take us over if we liked, but the chances were that we should make a voyage of discovery down the Okce, which kind offer we declined and drove to the next, where we got across all safe, and now, having got home, I shall say good-night and God bless you! I trust I may hear from you to-day, I will (D.V.) write again soon. Give my fondest love to my mother and all at home, and kisses to the darling pets.

Believe me,
Ever your most affectionately attached
RICHARD.

P.S.—A lovely morning and quite light.

RIASAN,
July 16, 1855.

MY DEAREST OWN ELLIE,

Yesterday I had the happiness of having your dear letter of June 14 (sent through Lord Blomfield) handed to me by the Governor, together with two packets containing all the letters you sent to the camp after I was made prisoner—in all eight letters, viz., 23rd, 27th, 31st of March, and 3rd, 14th, 15th, 19th, 24th of April;

and although the dates were old, you can imagine what delight it gave me to receive them.

Our living here is very moderate; my share for the last half of June only amounted to $7\frac{1}{2}$ roubles, or £1 5s., which included wages and washing, but then we don't drink wine, and dine out generally three times a week. Drosky-hire, which we indulge in a good deal, is also moderate here; the charge for a one-horse drosky which holds two is 10d. an hour; a set-down to the Governor's, who lives about quarter of a mile from the town, is 4d. if you take one off the stand, or 6d. if he comes to the house for you. If you take them five or six miles into the country, and keep them for half a day, not beyond twelve at night, they charge from 5s. to 6s. 8d. The drosky is a low light carriage on four wheels like a single-seated phaeton; some of them have hoods for bad weather. The chief fault in them is that the seats are sometimes too narrow for two people to sit comfortably in them.

I long to hear your answer from Lord Panmure to your letter relative to the exchange of prisoners. They told us here on June 29 that the English Government had proposed the exchange, and that the Russian Government had consented to it, and if so, I can't understand the reason of the long delay in our departure. I was sorry to find by one of your letters sent to the camp that both Lieutenant-Colonels are to remain abroad, which I did not know before. I suppose, therefore, if we are landed in the Crimea from Odessa, that I shall be detained there; if so, it will cost me a good deal to buy horses and a fresh field-kit. Under these circumstances I do not think I shall part with my bed, although the carriage of it in the diligence will cost a good deal.

I am afraid that the fearful loss that our regiment

sustained on June 18 will cause a number of officers to be sent out. I wonder if the Colonel has any intention of re-joining. I wrote to Cox on June 30 to apprize them of my existence, and I will (D.V.) do the same the end of this month. I hope you do not allow yourself to run short of money, nor to want anything that may conduce to yours and the children's comfort, for we, thank God! are, comparatively speaking, very well off now, as my pay is not stopped, and I wish you would assist your mother a little, as I know it would give you such pleasure. I hope Louisa enjoys better health than she has done lately. Give my love to them all.

I feel very grateful to all my friends for all the kind interest they took in me when they heard of the report of my being killed. Fancy poor faithful Grouney writing to you! I feel that very much; I hope he is still at the depot and not sent out. Did I ever tell you that my sword, which Baron Osten Sacken wished to send you, could never be found? I suppose the rascally Greeks sold it; he sent them out of Sebastopol on account of it. The proprietor of the Governor's country house here is a Mr. Ruminy, uncle of my friend the (word illegible) of Baron Osten Sacken. I met him once at the Governor's; he says he often hears from his nephew, so I begged to be remembered when he next wrote. He says his nephew has a large property in Siberia, with a gold-mine on the Ural Mountains, but that he has run through a great deal of money keeping a yacht and other extravagances. The Governor and I are great friends; he always says when I come: 'Ah! mon cher, pourquoi ne venez vouz pas plus souvent?' and embraces me *à la Russe*, which latter ceremony I would gladly dispense with; he is, however, an exceedingly kind-hearted man, and I like him very much. I am to have his portrait before I go, which I must certainly have hung up at Weston. Fancy my delight! Byron, who has just returned from dining at the Governor's, tells me he has another letter for me from you, enclosed in one to himself from you, at which he was highly delighted, saying that it is very *comme il faut*, and that you are *très polis*. He always gives me now your letters without reading them, as he can rely, he says, on your *sagesse* that you will not touch on politics. I must go now and look after my letter.

You ask me about clothes. I assure you I am very well off. You must know that before leaving Simpheropol to start on our journey each officer was furnished with a suit of clothes by the Russian Government—viz., a gray great-coat, which I shall keep as a curiosity, a pair of brown cloth Cossack trousers, which I have had cut down into modern shape, and which make a capital pair of morning trousers, a brown cloth jacket which I have turned into a waistcoat, and a very nice pair of light boots, which I use as dress ones. I have had besides made a black cloth paletot, which is my dress-coat, as the dinner-hour, being generally three o'clock, people appear in morning costume. I have also got a light pair of shepherd's plaid trousers and a holland coat for morning wear this hot weather, and I have taken the braid off my black trousers and turned them into dress ones again, so you see I am very well off. I will now say good-night, as it is very late.

July 17

A most lovely day. We dine to-day at Colonel Kobanieff's, where there is a fête, it being his eldest daughter's birthday, and I hope we shall hear some more music. The Governor and Mme. de Novisilicheff are to be there. I am glad we are not going to have such a day as this day week, when we were last there. I will now say adieu! God bless you, my love! Let us hope that we may soon meet. Kiss the pets for me; tell them that papa hopes that he will find them grown, and good children, and that they love him as much as ever. Give my fondest love to my mother, K., A., and F.; kind regards to C. K. and Mrs. Caffray.

Ever your most affectionate
RICHARD.

CHAPTER VIII

LIFE IN CAPTIVITY AT RIASAN

RIASAN,
July 24, 1855.

MY OWN DEAREST ELLIE,

Last Sunday (one of the post-days here) the Governor dined out, but yesterday he sent for me to dinner, as he had letters for me, and on arrival I had the pleasure of receiving your dear letters of July 4, forwarded through Mr. Anderson; June 24, sent by post; and April 28, sent through the English camp. They were, indeed, a great treat to me; many thanks to you for them all, and especially for your unwearied kindness in writing to me so often, and never missing an opportunity. Your letters, as you can well imagine, afford me the greatest happiness here, and I was so thankful to find by yours of July 4 that you, the dear children, and all at Weston continued in good health, thank God! with the exception of my pet Sophie being a little delicate; but I trust that (D.V.) with the aid of Dr. Hudson's prescriptions and care, she will in time gain strength, and that her constitution will not suffer from the effects of a tropical climate. I am so glad to hear that you all derived so much benefit from the sea-bathing and air at your nice cottage at Betty's Town; how you must have enjoyed your favourite amusement of gathering shells! how happy, indeed, I should have been to have joined you! but let us hope that is a pleasure to come, and that it may not be long delayed, although, strange to say, we hear nothing further about our departure. This delay appears very extraordinary, but I suppose there are official reasons for it.

I must now tell you what we have been doing since my last letter to you of 16th and 17th. On that latter day we were at a large party given by Coloned Kobanieff in celebration of his daughter's birthday. We sat down forty to dinner in the dining-room, besides ten in the veranda adjoining. Among the company were the Governor and his wife, the General of Militia, and Marshal of Nobility of the province, and several other swells. We had a capital dinner—champagne, claret, and Burgundy, and delicious melons at dessert from the Colonel's garden. The Colonel and his wife, according to the old Russian custom, did not sit down at dinner, but walked about attending to their guests, the Colonel, with a bottle in his hands, filling all glasses he found empty. In the evening we had some very good music and singing, and when most of the people had left, dancing with a select few; we were not allowed to go till after supper, our droskies having been sent back when we attempted to make a start before. The supper was merely a repetition of the dinner, with the addition of porter for the English, without which they imagine we can't exist. I besides dined twice last week with the Princess Tcherkatzky, who, with her only daughter, lives about four miles from here. Her husband died Governor of Simbirsk, and was a clever man and highly respected. They are very nice people; they both speak English, the daughter, who is about twenty, quite fluently, and is very conversant with English literature. Their grounds are very pretty, and laid out in the English style more than any place I have seen in the country, and behind the house there are some very extensive woods (which are scarce in this neighbourhood) with drives through them, and the last day I dined there we drove and walked through them after dinner, and the Princess showed us through her farmyard, where they were stacking large ricks of rye, the harvest being nearly over here. The corn crops are very fine, but the oats quite a failure. The Princess and her daughter have had the whole management of the property for the last month, having had to dismiss their steward for roguery. She told me that some friends of hers at St. Petersburg had, on the part of Dr. Law, British chaplain, requested her to show me attention, which she, however, had already been kind enough to do before receiving their letter. I drank at their house some of the most delicious tea I ever tasted—yellow tea brought over-land from China; it is, however, very dear, costing twenty roubles, or £3 6s. 8d., a pound. I must now conclude with kisses to the dear pets, and fond love to all at Weston.

Believe me, dearest Ellie,
Ever your fondly attached
RICHARD D. KELLY.

RIASAN,
July 26, 1855.

MY DEAREST ELLIE,

I had intended, if I had been ordered to rejoin in the Crimea, to speak to Lord Raglan about the error in his despatch of the affair in which I was taken, in saying, while referring to the first sortie made by the Russians that night, that the troops on that occasion were under the command of Major Gordon, R.E., while the fact was they were under my command the whole time, as, after having visited the sentries early in the night, I never left that part of the trench until the attack was made, which I was expecting every minute, and which I was prepared for; and not only were the arrangements for the reception of the enemy (and which I afterwards saw by the despatch were highly approved of) made by my orders and under my superintendence, but I accompanied and commanded the party that sallied out of the trench and repulsed the Russians, in which affair poor Vicars was killed and Gordon wounded. Gordon, a capital officer, was next senior to me, and he gave me every assistance, and his aid was most useful, as he knew every inch of the ground; but I was the responsible person for the whole affair, and was actually present, and am therefore entitled to whatever credit is due. I feel a little jealous about it, as I see the Queen was pleased to express her approbation of the conduct of the troops on that occasion, and may not have another opportunity of distinguishing myself. Now that poor Lord Raglan is dead I don't know what steps to take, unless I speak to General Simpson. Was not poor Bale wounded again on June 18? I am most anxious to know how our poor wounded fellows are going on, and for some news about the regiment. I don't think the Colonel will remain long. Byron and all the rest of us are as well as possible. We bathe a good deal this hot weather. Adieu, with fondest love to all and kisses to the pets.

    Believe me, dearest E.,
      Ever your affectionate
         RICHARD.

P.S.—Please send the enclosed to Cox.

RIASAN,
August 2, 1855.

MY OWN BELOVED ELLIE,

Yesterday I was again made happy by receiving through Mr. Gray your dear welcome letter of July 12, and I was indeed rejoiced to learn by it that you were in the enjoyment of such excellent health, also that dear Ellie and Annie and the darling boy were so well, and that pet Sophie had benefited so much by Dr. Hudson's prescription. I shall be most anxious to hear the result of your visit to Dublin, and to learn what Dr. Hudson thinks of the child. I am very glad Mr. Gray sent you my letter to him of June 19 acknowledging the receipt of yours of May 14, but I wonder you have not received the letter I wrote you in reply a day or two after, and which I sent through the official channel, which I suppose must have caused the delay.

I cannot understand what the French Government are to do in the relief of the English prisoners; they, more thoughtful than our Government, took care to get all their own officers and men exchanged nearly two months ago. Captain Herman, who was detained here with us, left this on June 10 for Odessa, and there is now not a French prisoner in Russia who was taken prior to June 18. If our release depends on the exertions of the committee in Paris one may be here for the next six months. The French Government won't exert themselves for English prisoners—that should be the business of our own Government; this explains the long delay in our exchange, which to us appears so unaccountable, for when we were first informed of our intended exchange on June 28 the Governor told us that he thought that in about two, or at the most three, weeks we should be off, and five weeks have now elapsed without the Governor hearing anything further on the subject. I suppose Captain Ramsay had not answered your letter about the exchange when you wrote, as you do not mention it; it is very odd his delaying so long to do so. The idea of a further detention here after having had our hopes so raised is very miserable to me, as I have already sufficiently felt the loneliness and irksomeness of a life without occupation and separated from all those I love. If I had remained in the Crimea I might have been made C.B., as I see Colonel Bunbury (33rd) has been, who like me commanded the regiment as Major.

But it is sinful in me to repine. I have been shown great mercy and my life wonderfully preserved when I little expected it, and I ought, and hope I do, feel grateful to the Giver of all good for them, and I trust that He may be still further graciously pleased to restore me to you before long, for I do indeed ardently long to be with you all again. I have, however, like yourself, my love, my apprehensions that if we should be sent to Odessa we should all go in the first instance to the Crimea; and then, as I see by the papers that the 34th have been very short of officers since their terrible loss at the assault on June 18, I shall probably have to remain for some time, as leave of absence except on score of ill-health will be difficult to obtain. But, however, something may occur to prevent our going by Odessa, and even if I do return to the Crimea I shall be in the path of duty, and God, if it is His holy will, can protect me there again as He has done before.

August 3.

For the last three days we have had some very heavy thunder-showers, which have cooled the air a good deal, but the weather is still very hot. We have just had the pleasure of reading Galignani's papers from July 1 to 15, sent to us by Mr. Gray, and have read the details of that unfortunate assault of June 18. What a mismanaged affair it seems to have been, and what a number of valuable lives uselessly sacrificed! Our poor regiment must have suffered greatly. The names of the officers killed and wounded were just those you sent me, but I cannot find the number of men killed and wounded. I think Gwilt must have been in command, as I see his name mentioned in the despatch; he deserves a Brevet majority, as this is the second time his name has appeared. Montague left this on July 11, reached Moscow next day, stayed there twenty-four hours, arrived at Kharkoff on 20th, and left on 22nd for Odessa viâ Pultawa and Nicolaieff on the *Bug*, which is, I suppose, the same route we shall take. I must conclude for to-day, as I am going with Count Boutourlin to dine at Princess Tcherkatzky's. I hope (D.V.) to finish and post this to-morrow; till then adieu, dearest.

I am sorry to see among the list of the killed the name of poor Captain Forman, of the Rifle Brigade, whom we knew at Barbadoes, A.D.C. to Sir William Colebrook.

RIASAN,
August 7, 1855.

MY BELOVED ELLIE,

I am delighted to be able to announce to you that the order of our departure from this has at length been received here, thank God! I met the Vice-Governor in the gardens yesterday evening, and he told me that he had received the order by Sunday's post. He has despatched a courier to the Governor, who is absent on a district tour, to inform him of it, and he expects his return about the 13th, and in that case we shall probably leave this per diligence for Moscow on 15th, accompanied so far by Count Boutourlin (?), who is to be our cicerone at Moscow; from thence to Koursk, which is as far as the *chaussée* extends, about nine miles. We travel by diligence, passing through Toula and Orel; and from Koursk to Odessa we travel by telega, passing through Kharkoff, which is about half-way from here; and from thence our road will be by Pultawa, Elizabethgrad and Nicolaieff. I suppose our journey will last about three weeks, and almost the entire road, except in the neighbourhood of Kharkoff, will be new to me, which is something, although I should have greatly preferred going by the route of Warsaw and Berlin, as that would have assured our return to England in the first instance, whereas at present we shall be perfectly ignorant of what orders we shall receive till the arrival of the vessel to embark us at Odessa. I, however, earnestly hope that we may be allowed to go home in the first instance, even if only for a short time; if for nothing else, we shall all want to get fresh kits.

If I am permitted to see you and all the dear ones again, what happiness that will be to me! God grant it may be so! Do not forget to have letters for me both at our camp at the Crimea and also at Constantinople addressed to the Consul-General. I will write to you (D.V.) *en route* to Moscow through Mr. Gray, and from Kharkoff through Mrs. Braillard. I send this through Mr. Merrillies, as I am writing to ask him to send any letters that may arrive at St. Petersburg for me after our departure from this to Odessa, to the care of the Chevalier di Kischione, Austrian Consul-General. I have received no letter from you since your last of July 12, which I answered on the 4th. I trust, however, I shall get another before I leave this. Would you kindly write to Byron's uncle and tell him this news, and say that his nephew is quite well. I am afraid we shall find it very hot work travelling in the telegas; the weather has been very hot for some time past, and we have had frequent thunderstorms. They say this is one of the hottest summers they have had in Russia for many years; we seldom go out in the middle of the day, but bathe almost every evening in the river, and generally walk in the gardens afterwards. There are to be some races here to-morrow, trotting matches in droskies, which they say will be worth seeing. I must call on the Princess Tcherkatzky before I go; they are one of the nicest families here, and have been very kind and hospitable to us. I must get some melon-seeds from them to bring home. I never tasted finer melons than those you get about here. We owe our introduction to the Princess to Count Boutourlin, her cousin, who has been very friendly to the English, and is a very well-informed, agreeable man; he is first cousin to the Princess Woronzoff, who married Lord Pembroke. I don't know what to do about taking my bed and bedstead with me; they only allow a passenger by diligence 20 pounds of baggage, and charge 2d. per pound for extra weight, which is immense, and will be almost their value by the time we reach Koursk; but, then, if I go to the Crimea I shall find it very awkward being without bedding, which perhaps I shall not be able to get out there, or, at least, will have to pay very high for it, so I am puzzled what to do, and wish I knew what our destination was to be.

You will find a sketch of the journey we are about to take in a book called 'The English Prisoner in Russia,' being a narrative of his captivity written by Lieutenant Royer, the First Lieutenant of H.M.S. *Tiger;* it is very light reading, but may give you some idea of how we all have to travel. He does not give the distances, but he only took nine days from Odessa to Moscow; but then he not only travelled day and night, but *en courier*, which is much quicker than we shall go, and he had besides no stoppages at the Government towns, and he had only one carriage, while we shall take four with twelve horses, which will cause delays on the road.

I must now conclude, and I hope you will kindly excuse this short letter, but I hope to write to you again in a few days. Give my affectionate love to my dear mother, sisters, and Francis, and to all the dear pets, with kisses. God grant we may soon meet! How I long for the time to come that I may embrace you all again! Kind regards to C. K. Love to all your people. Remember me to Mrs. Caffray and all friends.

Ever your affectionately attached
RICHARD.

P.S.—A Lieutenant James, R.E., arrived here this morning from Sebastopol, where he was taken on July 12. He came by Waronstock, and said that all the English soldiers there had already left for Odessa. Out of seventeen French officers taken in the assault of June 18, twelve had died.

RIASAN,
August 11.

MY BELOVED ELLIE,

I am happy to say that we start to-morrow (sooner than we expected) by diligence for Moscow, where (D.V.) I hope to put a postscript to this letter to tell you of our safe arrival, and then deliver it to Mr. Gray for the purpose of being forwarded to you. The Governor returned from his tour the night before last, and we dined with him yesterday, when he officially informed us of our departure to-morrow for Odessa viâ

Moscow, which, although it is out of the direct route, we were allowed to visit for the purpose of seeing it, and he told me, moreover, that, as I was a superior officer, my travelling expenses for this détour would be defrayed, excepting the cost of my extra baggage by diligence, which, as I have determined to take my bed with me (in case of our having to go on to the Crimea), will cost me about £2 10s.; but that is better than giving up my bed, which I could not replace at that price. We shall probably leave Moscow on the 15th, and may expect to reach Odessa about the end of the month. From thence I am afraid there is but little doubt that we shall go on to the Crimea, as Captain Frampton got a letter yesterday from his friends saying that they had written to General Simpson to request that he would grant him leave to return home on urgent private affairs. Although this will be a sad disappointment to both of us, for when I thought that we should go to Berlin and Warsaw, and before I knew that both Lieutenant-Colonels were kept in the Crimea, I fully expected that I should have the delight of seeing you once more, even if only for a short time, yet we must submit to the will of our heavenly Father, and trust to a continuance of His mercies which He has so abundantly bestowed on us. So I trust you will keep up your spirits, my darling Ellie, and do not fret yourself with anxiety about me. I have the consolation of knowing that I am in the path of duty, and, if it is His holy will, God is able to protect me through all dangers.

I have been disappointed at not receiving any letters from you by the last two posts. Your last, dated July 12, I got on August 1, and answered it on the 4th. I wrote also on the 7th acquainting you with the order for our departure having arrived.

Koursk,
August 18, 1855.

My dearest Ellie,

I am happy to say that we five (Captain Duff, 23rd; Frampton, 50th; Lieutenant Clowes, 8th Hussars; Byron, and self; the others are following) arrived here all safe and well, thank God! this morning, having left Moscow at 6.30 p.m. on the 14th. I wrote to you from Moscow on the 13th, the day of our arrival, and sent the letter to Mrs. Gray, who told me she forwarded it the next morning, and I hope you will duly receive it. She had no letter for me, but I begged her, in case any should arrive, to forward them to Odessa (where perhaps we may be detained some time), to the care of the Chevalier di Kischione, Austrian Consul-General. I trust I may receive one there, for your last, which was dated July 12, I got on August 9, and am anxious to know how you and the dear children are going on, and what arrangements you have made.

We left Moscow earlier than we expected in order to take advantage of the diligence to Toula, which left that evening. However, we managed to see as much of Moscow as we probably could in that short time. Mr. and Mrs. Gray were kind enough to act as our cicerones (Count Boutourlin being unable to do so from illness). Our first visit was, of course, to the Kremlin, with which we were very much interested. 'Kremlin' is a Tartar word, signifying 'citadel'; and the Moscow Kremlin comprises a large space surrounded by only embattled walls, and in the interior are several churches, the palace, arsenal, treasury, senate-house, and several other public buildings. It is entered by three gates, outside which are small chapels, with candles constantly burning before images and paintings, and before these a crowd is always to be seen bowing and crossing themselves. One of these gates is called the Sacred Gate, and no one is allowed to pass through it without taking off his hat. There is an image of the Virgin over it, which is supposed to have checked the French invasion in 1812, and although it was struck by a ball it was not overthrown. The palace, although a plain building outside, contains some noble apartments magnificently furnished. The throne-room in particular is very splendid; the roof and pillars, which represent palm-trees, are one mass of gilding, with magnificent chandeliers and candelabra, which had a splendid effect.

George's Hall is also a noble room, but more simple; the ceiling was white, relieved by stars of the different Orders of Russian knighthood, represented in gold and different colours in the various compartments. The walls of this room are lined with marble, having on it in gold letters the names of different regiments that have distinguished themselves. The doors of the different rooms were beautiful specimens of handiwork, being inlaid with different sorts of wood, brass, and mother-of-pearl. The floors were all *en parquet* of different patterns, which they do exceedingly well in Russia. In one of the rooms was a most magnificent chimney-piece of malachite and gold; there were not many paintings, but there were some beautifully done in sepia. A very interesting part of the palace was the old part of it, formerly occupied by Peter the Great. The rooms are arched and low, and the arches are painted in bright colours; the old furniture is still preserved in them, and contrasts by its plainness with the magnificent furniture in the modern part of it. We were much disappointed at not being able to see the treasury, it not being the day for showing it; it contains the regalia and jewels of the Crown, all the Emperors being crowned at Moscow, together with several interesting relics of Peter the Great and Charles XII. of Sweden.

In front of the arsenal, which we also could not see, are ranged several enormous guns taken from the Turks, together with all the French field artillery taken during their retreat from Moscow in 1812. We ascended the tower of the Church of S. Isaac Vasiliski, from whence we had a view of the whole city, which lay spread out at our feet, and the atmosphere being so clear and unobstructed by smoke we were enabled to see it to great advantage.

Moscow is certainly a fine city for Russia, and contains some handsome public buildings, such as the Foundling Hospital, University, and new cathedral (building), but I was disappointed in the size of it. It contains about 400,000 inhabitants, but to say (as I have heard) that it covers as much ground as London is ridiculous, for it certainly is not more than twenty-four miles round. Before the fire of 1812 the houses were almost all of wood; they are now of brick and most of them stuccoed. The best houses are on the boulevards, which encircle the city, and form a beautiful public walk some miles in length. The most striking object in the view is the number of churches (they say 365), which are to be seen with their domes and spires either glittering with gold or of iron painted green, which give a very lively appearance to the city; the domes of those in the Kremlin are gilt, and on the highest tower of the one we ascended are a large peal of silver bells, which give a very sweet tone. It was from this tower that, when they were ringing for the accession of the present Emperor, one of the bells fell, killed some of the ringers, and was broken by the fall. This was considered a very bad omen at the time. At the foot of the church stands the great bell of Moscow with a great piece broken out of it, the effect, I believe, of an earthquake many years ago. Outside the sacred gate of the Kremlin stands the most curious church in Moscow; from its fantastic architecture it is called the 'pineapple church,' the dome being made to represent pineapples, melons, and other fruits, and painted in the most gaudy colours, with frescoes of brilliant colours painted on the walls. It was built by order of Ivan the Cruel, who, having asked the architect when it was finished if he thought he could excel it, and on being answered that he thought he could, had his eyes put out in order to prevent his doing so. We also visited the Petersburg Gate, which is a very handsome triumphal arch like that at Milan, and has a chariot of Victory drawn by eight horses at the top; and the riding-school, supposed to be the largest room in Europe, is supported by pillars. It is large enough to drill with ease inside it a regiment even in winter, as it is heated by stoves. After all our sight-seeing we partook of an early dinner on the 14th with Mr. and Mrs. Gray; the dinner being an English one was quite a treat to us; it consisted of roast-beef, and a magnificent turkey and fruit tarts, etc.

They have several very good rooms in the house, which also contains a very nice chapel and school, the whole being supported by the Russian Company in London. I like both Mr. and Mrs. Gray, from what I saw of them; she is young and pretty, and very lady-like. She was a daughter of the Archdeacon of the Bahamas (I did not hear his name). Sir Robert Bateson is her uncle by marriage; she has four little girls, two of them in London. We saw the youngest, a pretty little thing of only twelve months old, who only understands

Russian. Mrs. Gray intends going to England as soon as she can get a passport, in order to bring back her other two girls. She first goes to London, then to the Isle of Man, and lastly to her sister's at Sir Robert Bateson's near Derry. We left Moscow at 6.30 p.m. on the 14th by diligence for Toula, a distance of 124 miles, which we reached at the same hour next day, the journey having been performed very slowly. The country about Toula is some of the prettiest I have seen in Russia, being well wooded. Toula, where we slept on the 15th, is celebrated for its iron-works and Government manufactory of arms, which, however, is not allowed to be seen by strangers. I bought you as a specimen a small ring inlaid with gold, which might answer as a guard-ring. I also got you at Moscow a small plain malachite bracelet, and a little filigree bracelet made in the Caucasus, which I hope to have the pleasure of bringing home to you myself; but if that should be denied me I must try and find some opportunity of sending them home from the Crimea.

We left Toula at 2 p.m. on the 16th in two carriages drawn by three horses, each called tarantasses. They are covered like a tilt-cart, and although they have not springs, the body is placed on two long poles, which are very elastic, and you are not nearly so much jolted as in a telega, and on the *chaussée* you are just as comfortable and go faster than in a diligence; there are no seats in them; you must sit on your portmanteaus, and with the aid of cushions and cloaks you can arrange yourself very comfortably and sleep soundly. We reached Orel at 10 a.m. on 17th (114 miles), left at 4.30 p.m., having halted there to change our conductor, and reached this (98 miles) at 8.30 this morning; here we are to get a fresh officer to conduct us, and we are now waiting the

Governor's orders as to when we are to proceed to Kharkoff (120 miles), and we hope to do so this evening, and also that we may get tarantasses and not telegas, as the latter being open, we should be exposed to the dust and heat of the sun, besides being much rougher, which is a consideration, as the *chaussée* ends at Koursk.

We hope to be allowed to stay at Kharkoff (which is half-way to Odessa) three or four days, in order to repose ourselves and get our clothes washed. There I intend asking Mrs. Braillard to send you this through her sister in London. The officer who brought us from Moscow told me the Governor there told him that we were to go direct to England, and that by the terms of our exchange were not to serve against Russia for a year; but I don't believe a word of this, as I don't think our Government would ever consent to such terms. We shall probably not know our destination till we are on board ship at Odessa, and we must only hope that it may be England. I will now say adieu, trusting to be able to conclude this at Kharkoff.

Ever your most affectionate
RICHARD.

KHARKOFF,
August 20, 1855.

MY DEAREST ELLIE,

I add a few lines just to say that we got here safely at one o'clock this morning, having left Koursk about the same hour yesterday, instead of 3 p.m. the previous afternoon, as was intended, but there was great *delay in getting an official to accompany, and making out the necessary papers.* We were so fortunate as to be allowed to take on our tarantasses as far as this, by which we got less dust than we should have done had we gone in telegas. We have now accomplished about half our journey, having travelled 881 versts, or about 588 miles, from Riasan. Pultawa will be the next large town through which we pass; from thence to Odessa is about 400 miles, with hardly a place where we can get anything to eat beyond black bread and eggs, except in the towns of Elizabethgrad and Nicolaieff. We do not yet know when we are to start, as we have not seen the Governor, General Kakoskin, but we are anxious to be allowed to stay here two or three days for a little rest, and to get our clothes washed. I have not yet seen Mrs. Braillard, but I hope to send off this through her by the first post. If possible I will write from Odessa, and hope I may be able to give you good news. Till then, adieu, my dearest love.

Ever your most affectionate

RICHARD.

P.S.—I have just seen the Lieutenant-Governor, Count Seiwers. It is with great difficulty that he allowed us to stay till to-morrow; it appears they have orders to send us as quickly as possible to Odessa. I am afraid, from what I hear, we shall have to go from thence to the Crimea, but we must trust in God; He is able, and I trust will protect me as heretofore, and in His own good time will restore me to all those I love so dearly. I have seen Mr. Braillard, who posts this to-morrow. He tells me my letter to you of June 29 has reached you. I trust I shall get letters from you in the camp. Adieu!

Governor's orders as to when we are to proceed to Kharkoff (120 miles), and we hope to do so this evening, and also that we may get tarantasses and not telegas, as the latter being open, we should be exposed to the dust and heat of the sun, besides being much rougher, which is a consideration, as the *chaussée* ends at Koursk.

We hope to be allowed to stay at Kharkoff (which is half-way to Odessa) three or four days, in order to repose ourselves and get our clothes washed. There I intend asking Mrs. Braillard to send you this through her sister in London. The officer who brought us from Moscow told me the Governor there told him that we were to go direct to England, and that by the terms of our exchange were not to serve against Russia for a year; but I don't believe a word of this, as I don't think our Government would ever consent to such terms. We shall probably not know our destination till we are on board ship at Odessa, and we must only hope that it may be England. I will now say adieu, trusting to be able to conclude this at Kharkoff.

Ever your most affectionate
RICHARD.

KHARKOFF,
August 20, 1855.

MY DEAREST ELLIE,

I add a few lines just to say that we got here safely at one o'clock this morning, having left Koursk about the same hour yesterday, instead of 3 p.m. the previous afternoon, as was intended, but there was great delay in getting an official to accompany, and making out the necessary papers. We were so fortunate as to be allowed to take on our tarantasses as far as this, by which we got less dust than we should have done had we gone in telegas. We have now accomplished about half our journey, having travelled 881 versts, or about 588 miles, from Riasan. Pultawa will be the next large town through which we pass; from thence to Odessa is about 400 miles, with hardly a place where we can get anything to eat beyond black bread and eggs, except in the towns of Elizabethgrad and Nicolaieff. We do not yet know when we are to start, as we have not seen the Governor, General Kakoskin, but we are anxious to be allowed to stay here two or three days for a little rest, and to get our clothes washed. I have not yet seen Mrs. Braillard, but I hope to send off this through her by the first post. If possible I will write from Odessa, and hope I may be able to give you good news. Till then, adieu, my dearest love.

Ever your most affectionate
Richard.

P.S.—I have just seen the Lieutenant-Governor, Count Seiwers. It is with great difficulty that he allowed us to stay till to-morrow; it appears they have orders to send us as quickly as possible to Odessa. I am afraid, from what I hear, we shall have to go from thence to the Crimea, but we must trust in God; He is able, and I trust will protect me as heretofore, and in His own good time will restore me to all those I love so dearly. I have seen Mr. Braillard, who posts this to-morrow. He tells me my letter to you of June 29 has reached you. I trust I shall get letters from you in the camp. Adieu!

CHAPTER IX

RELEASED

H.M.S. 'FURIOUS,'
August 31, 1855.

MY DEAREST OWN ELLIE,

Thank God I have the satisfaction of telling you that I am once more free and on board a British man-of-war. We (Frampton, Duff, Clowes, Byron and self) arrived at Odessa on the night of the 29th, and embarked yesterday, together with fourteen soldiers of different regiments (four of 34th), who were all who had arrived at Odessa, on board the boats of the *Furious*, and I am now writing in Captain Loring's cabin, where I am comfortably installed, and whose reception has been most kind and hospitable. H.M.S. *Dauntless* arrived yesterday from the fleet before Sebastopol, with orders to relieve the *Furious*, which is to proceed to Malta for repairs, and Captain Loring has proposed to me to take us as far as Constantinople, as if he transferred us to the *Dauntless*, we might remain on board a fortnight or three weeks before an opportunity offered of sending us to Balaklava, while at Constantinople there are opportunities weekly, if not daily. We expect to start at about 3 p.m., after having finished coaling the *Dauntless*, and to arrive in about two and a half days. When arrived there I must report myself to Lord William

Paulet, the Commandant at Scutari, who will most likely give us orders to proceed by the first opportunity to Balaklava, unless he allows us a little delay at Constantinople to get fresh kits, as some of the officers are without a scrap of uniform.

I had the pleasure yesterday of getting your dear letters of July 20 and August 1, which were given me by Mrs. Cischini. I was indeed glad to receive them, as it was just a month since I had heard from you. I regret, my dear Ellie, that in my letter of June 29 I wrote in such sanguine terms of the prospect of coming home direct when exchanged, instead of returning to the Crimea, as I am afraid they are for the present doomed to be disappointed; but at that time I was not aware that both Lieutenant-Colonels were kept out in the Crimea, but thought that if on arrival in the Crimea I should find Browne in command of the regiment, I should be sent home to the depôt as a matter of course; and as to getting leave, I am afraid that nothing but wounds or ill-health would enable an officer to return home, and that private affairs, except some very extraordinary case, would not be listened to, and I think, under the circumstances (except some special case arises), should not be asked for. I know, my darling love, what a disappointment and sore trial this will be to you, and to me also, but after mature reflection I have come to the conclusion that I could not with honour ask to leave my regiment on service, except something very urgent should require my presence at home. I must do my duty in that state of life to which it has pleased God to call me; and as I am in the path of duty I humbly hope and pray that His protection may be extended to me, and that, as heretofore, I may again be preserved through all the perils and dangers of the field, and be permitted before long to have the happiness of being restored to you and the dear children with the consciousness of having done my duty. If I find on arrival at Constantinople that I have to return to the Crimea, I must try and provide myself with two horses, as I shall probably get them cheaper there than in camp; this, with other articles I shall require, such as sword, shako, etc., will cost me, I suppose, from £100 to £120, so I must have that sum in Cox's hands, as I shall have to draw on him.

On leaving Odessa I found I had thirty-six Russian gold half-imperials left (about £39), and as I could not get them exchanged for French or English money, and knew that I should lose considerably by changing them at Constantinople, I gave them to Cischini, who promised to get his banker, Mr. Ernest Mahls, to give a bill of exchange on London for the amount, which is to be sent to Cox to be placed to my credit. I dare say I shall lose a little by the transaction, as exchange on England is very high at Odessa, but I expect to get at least £28 for it, and I have written to Cox to let you know as soon as he receives it. I shall be delighted to get your letter at Constantinople. Nothing could be kinder than M. Cischini's reception of me. He took us to his house and introduced us to his wife, a very pretty young woman, to whom he has been only lately married. He also took us to Mr. Mahls, his banker, who changed our Russian paper-money for gold without any charge, which would not have been the case if we had gone elsewhere.

I am so glad you and the dear children have derived such benefit from your bathing at Laytown, and that dear Sophie is herself again; also that your mother and Louisa paid you a visit there, and I hope the latter has derived benefit from it. I was very sorry indeed to hear that she still continues to be such a sufferer. Give my love to them both. I gave Byron his letter. I wrote to you *en route* from Moscow on the 13th, and lastly from Kharkoff on August 20, both of which I hope you have received. We stayed three days at Kharkoff, although the Lieutenant-Governor, Count Seiwers, wanted at first to send us off the next day. I told him that you never got the letter that I gave him for you when I passed through in May last, at which he looked very confused; I don't believe he ever sent it.

We dined twice at Kharkoff with our kind friends the Braillards; they intend leaving Russia next summer for good, as they do not like the country, and residing at Geneva. We left Kharkoff for R—— (word illegible) on the 23rd, and arrived the next day. The country was the prettiest I have passed through in Russia, with a great deal of wood and some fine single trees scattered about, giving the country a park-like appearance. Pultawa is a pretty little town with a fine building, the military college, in the centre of the grounds, attached to which is a handsome monument surmounted by a gilt eagle in honour of the Battle of Pultawa, where Peter the Great defeated Charles XII. of Sweden; the field of battle is close to the town. We left Pultawa for Odessa on the evening of the 25th, a distance of 370 miles, which we took three days and four nights to accomplish, arriving at Odessa on the night of the 28th, although we stopped only to change horses and for meals. We passed through Elizabethgrad, but not Nicolaieff, as, it containing a dockyard, we were not allowed to go through it, but had to make a détour; we crossed both the Dnieper and the Bug. As far as Pultawa I travelled in a tarantass, or covered carriage on wooden springs, but beyond that got nothing but telegas (?) or the common post-cart of the country, which are quite open and which are without springs, and in which you are obliged to sit on your luggage and are jolted about dreadfully; the whole way was across a sandy plain, and the dust was terrible, penetrating into all our portmanteaus, etc., and made us look like chimney-sweeps. When at Odessa we heard of the victory gained by the Allies on the Tchernaya on the 16th, in which the Russians confessed to a loss of 1,300 men; but you will have, of course, seen all the details in the papers before this.

'FURIOUS,' AT SEA,
September 1, 1855, 10 *a.m.*

DEAREST E.,

We expect to arrive in the Bosphorus at 11 a.m. to-morrow. We left Odessa at 4 p.m., and so far have had a most lovely smooth passage with every prospect of its continuance. The Captain intends stopping off the naval hospital at Therapia, about fifteen miles from Constantinople, in order to take invalids on board, and so we shall have to go down to Constantinople in a steamer or boat and take up our quarters in some hotel, and then I must cross to Scutari and report to the Commandant. I will close this letter now, and send it by the ship's bag in order not to lose a mail, and will write again when I have seen the Commandant, and know what our fate is to be. I hope on receipt of this you will write to me at the camp, and send me some papers as before, and, above all, my dearest love, for my sake do not allow yourself to be cast down by this present disappointment, but continue to put your trust in that omni-*potent as well as all-merciful God, who has so graciously* protected me hitherto from all perils and dangers, and will, I trust, continue to do so, and in His own good time restore me again to all those I love so dearly. You may rely on it that if I can come home with honour I will do so, but you would not wish any reflection to be thrown upon my character. God bless you, my darling! Give my affectionate love to my dearest mother, Kate, Annie, and Francis, and love and kisses to all the pets.

Believe me,
Ever your most affectionate
RICHARD.

HÔTEL DE L'EUROPE, CONSTANTINOPLE,
September 5, 1855.

MY OWN DEAREST ELLIE,

My last letter to you I posted on September 2, the day of our arrival here in the *Furious* from Odessa. We were landed that morning at Scutari, and I immediately reported myself to Lord William Paulet, the Commandant, who allowed us a few days to procure what we stood most in need of, and to get our clothes washed, which we have had no opportunity of doing since we left Kharkoff, and we are to proceed to the camp on the 6th, to-morrow, but I do not know yet by what steamer. I hear Colonel Browne has not yet arrived in the Crimea, and that Goodenough is in command of the regiment, and, as I shall succeed him in it, that will make it the more difficult for me to get away; indeed, I am afraid I have very little chance of that at present; but do not allow yourself to fret about it: God overrules all things for the best. I must do my duty, and I trust He will protect me and shield me from all danger in the discharge of it. The Commandant here has not the power of giving leave to England; it can only be granted by General Simpson, they say; besides, a Court of Inquiry will be held on me to inquire into the fact of our having been made prisoners, which can only be done in the Crimea. I intend getting a few articles here to make up my kit; I find I cannot get here either a sword, shako or great-coat, all of which I want; and if I cannot get them at a sale in camp, must have them sent out from England. I must trust to getting horses in camp, for here they are very scarce and dear. I shall, however, take with me a saddle and bridle and a pistol. I drew on Cox for £30 on the 3rd. I inquired for letters both at the British Consul-General's and at the post-office, but could not hear of any at either place. I suppose they have been sent on to the camp, where I hope I shall get them. The last I have received from you were dated July 20 and August 1, which I got at Odessa; you mention in those having written to me on July 18 to camp, and July 25 here. The English mail is due here to-day, and I trust I shall have the happiness of hearing from you by it.

CONSTANTINOPLE,
September 7, 1855.

MY DEAREST ELLIE,

I cannot leave this place without writing another line to you. I hope you have received my letters of 2nd and 5th announcing my arrival here from Odessa. Byron and I expect to go on board ship for Balaklava to-morrow, and I am going over to Scutari to-day to find out what ship we are to go in, and when she sails. I hope it will not be before the afternoon, for the English mail is expected in to-morrow morning, and I hope to have the happiness of getting a letter from you by it. Your last, received at Odessa, was August 1; I have received none since. We are next door to the post-office here, and the postmaster is very civil, and says he will keep any letters there may be for me. I met at the hotel here Brigadier-General Storks, who is to succeed Lord William Paulet as Commandant here. He has been very kind and friendly to me, and has advised me strongly to apply to General Simpson to get an error in Lord Raglan's despatch relative to the affair in which I was taken rectified, as it is therein stated that the troops (detachments 77th and 97th Regiments), by whom the first of the enemy's sorties on that night were repulsed, acted under the directions of Major Gordon, R.E., whereas, not only were the arrangements for the reception of the enemy on that occasion (and which were highly approved of) made by my orders as senior officer of the trenches, but under my immediate superintendence, and I never stirred from the spot until the Russians made their attack upon us, both in front and flank, and then I accompanied the detachment of the 97th Regiment under Captain Vicars that charged the enemy that attacked us in front, and drove them to the bottom of the hill, on which occasion poor Vicars was killed (I was close to him) and Gordon was badly wounded, and I believe we were the only three officers out. I don't know who sent in the report of the affair next day. Gordon couldn't have done so on account of his wound, or I know he would have mentioned that I was in immediate command of the troops, for he was with me the whole night. He, however, got promoted for it, as it was the most serious sortie that the Russians had then made, and we were attacked by very superior numbers; the Captains of the 77th and 88th detachments also got promoted, and I am confident that if I had not been so unfortunate as to have been taken while endeavouring to collect the men for the repulse of their second sortie that night, I should have been made a full Colonel or C.B. for it. I have written accordingly a very strong letter about it, which I hope may do something; but I am afraid they don't like altering despatches, and I am not very sanguine of success. General Storks has also advised me to apply to Lord Harding for permission to allow the time I was prisoner of war count towards getting my full colonelcy in three years, and I shall certainly try it.

I have just returned from Scutari. I don't know what ships sail to-morrow, but I shall know in the morning. I saw Peel, who was not looking at all well; he sails to-day for England in the *Imperatrice*, as also do several of our poor fellows who were wounded on June 18, and whom I saw embarking; they all said they were very glad to see me again. I saw Hon. Captain Bourke, of the 88th; he told me our Bourke expected soon to get a staff-officer of pensioner-ship in New Brunswick, and was to go on half-pay. I have also seen Rotten, of the Artillery, who went out with us in the *Apollo;* he inquired kindly for you. This place is crowded with officers of the Turkish contingent, chiefly officers of the company's service. They get enormous pay; a Second Captain of artillery told me he got £800 a year, and a Lieutenant-Colonel of infantry gets £1,200, while I get little more than £300. The weather here is very hot.

September 8.

Still without an order to go up; they say now there will be no steamers till the 10th. I am tired of staying here, and this place is very expensive. I got to-day a French sword, with brass scabbard and belt, for £4, which is not dear for Constantinople. I hear the English mail is just in, but the letters won't be given out till to-morrow. I trust I shall get one from you, as I am most anxious to hear from you. I send you by this mail a little box containing a malachite bracelet and a silver bracelet, made in the Caucasus, which I got for you at Moscow; also an iron and gold guard-ring, a specimen of the manufactures of Toula. I have registered the parcel, and trust that it may arrive safe, and that you will like them, and that I may have the pleasure one day of seeing you wear them.

September 9.

I have just had the pleasure of receiving your scrap of August 25, which, although short, was most welcome. I think you must have either posted it before the time, or it has taken a long time coming, for it has been sixteen days on the road, and I used to get letters in camp in less time. I do not anticipate being able to get leave, nor under the circumstances do I think I could well ask for it.

RICHARD.

September 9, 10 p.m.

P.S.—After I closed my letter to you I went over to the Quartermaster-General at Scutari to find out when the *Niagara* sailed, and there found that she had broken her windlass and will not be able to sail before the 12th, so we asked to be sent by the first ship that was going, and they will let us know to-morrow. As I was crossing the harbour I saw a steamer, when I said to Byron, 'That must be the *Adelaide* if she is here,' and on our return to the hotel I found the cards of Captain Young and Captain Murray, R.A., and to my great delight they both came and dined with me, and have just left. I was very glad to see them, especially Murray, as he had seen you and the dear children, he said, only five weeks ago, all looking well and happy. God grant I may have that pleasure before long! Captain Murray has got the command of a troop of Horse Artillery in the Turkish contingent, which gives him £1,000.

September 10.

This morning we heard the good news of the Malakoff having been taken, but without any particulars as to the loss, etc.; the south side will now soon be in our hands, and God grant this terrible siege will soon be over. I have just been at the post, and they tell me that a print, unless rolled round a stick, gets very crushed in the post, so I will keep it for another opportunity, and will send the seeds by next mail, I hope. Once more adieu, my dearest pet; love and kisses to all.

Ever your most affectionate
RICHARD.

I am to go up to-morrow in the *Indian*. Two Russian line-of-battle ships have been destroyed in Sebastopol by the French.

'ADELAIDE,' CONSTANTINOPLE,
September 11, 1855.

MY OWN BELOVED ELLIE,

I have just had the happiness of receiving yours and my mother's dear long welcome letters of August 27 to 29. I am afraid I shall not have much time to give you a line in reply to-day, as this morning we got our orders to embark this afternoon on board the *Indian* for passage to Balaklava. Byron has gone on board with all our baggage, and I came on board this ship with Captain Murray to dine with Captain Young, and after dinner a steam-tug is to come alongside to take the troops on board the *Adelaide* (artillery and sappers) on board the *Indian*, when I will go with them. They say we are to sail to-morrow morning, but I doubt it; we are to tow a vessel of navvies to Balaklava, which will take us at least two days. Lieutenant-Colonel Gaisford, 72nd, called on me this morning; he is on board the *Indian*, having come out from England in her, but I shall be in command, as I am senior to him.

I dined on board the *Adelaide* last night with Captain Murray; he is to be attached to the Turkish contingent, and is to remain at Scutari for the present. He tells me his pay and allowances are worth £1,000 a year to him. No one could be kinder than Captain Young has been to me. He wanted me yesterday to come and dine on board as his guest, and if we had not been going so soon I think I would have done so, as this hotel is frightfully expensive—13s. a day, without extras.

5 *p.m.* An order has just come on board to say that the *Indian* will not be ready to take her troops on board before 2 p.m. to-morrow, and I suppose we shan't sail before the 13th; these delays are too bad. I have now been here ten days, and have been eight times to the Quartermaster-General's office trying to get a passage, and have been bandied about from ship to ship. It seems as difficult to get a passage to the Crimea as to get away from it once you are there. I suppose you have heard of the glorious success of the Allies on the 8th and 9th; the whole of the south side of Sebastopol is in our power. After two days' tremendous bombardment, the Allies stormed on the morning of the 8th; the French carried the Malakoff, and repulsed an attempt on the part of the Russians to retake it, but they failed to carry the Little Redan. We attempted the Great Redan, but failed, losing, it is said, 200 men; next morning, however, we tried again and carried it, and the Russians evacuated the whole of the south side, leaving behind the whole of their guns and material and 6,000 prisoners, and suffering immense loss; they were obliged to retire by the head of the harbour towards Inkerman, as the bridge they had across the harbour was destroyed by the gale on the 8th inst. The French loss is estimated at 5,000; they had five Generals

killed and twelve wounded; Bosquet was severely wounded. Several Russian ships have been set on fire, and the whole fleet must fall into our hands or be destroyed. We have not yet received all the details of the affair, but I am afraid our loss has been very severe, especially the 34th Regiment, as the Light Division had to storm the Redan. What anxious hearts there will be at home waiting for the list of the killed and wounded! God help them in their trouble! Now that the south side of Sebastopol has fallen, I think all trench-work, which I consider the most disagreeable and dangerous of all duties, will be over, as I can't see how we are to undertake the siege of the north side. I think the Russians will have to abandon their position, as I don't think they can maintain and victual their army there during the winter.

'ADELAIDE,' CONSTANTINOPLE,
September 12, 1855.

MY OWN DEAREST ELLIE,

I despatched a letter to you yesterday, fearing we might have to sail this morning, but an order came on board yesterday evening to say that the troops on board the *Adelaide* would not be transhipped to the *Indian* till 2 p.m. to-day, so I have time to write my letter to you and (tell you of) my arrival here on 2nd inst. I slept on board here last night, as I was not able to get on board the *Indian*. In my letter of yesterday I gave you my reasons for not asking for leave to go home, as I did not think it consistent with my duty. If General Simpson, however, offers to allow me to go home, I shall not refuse it; but situated as I shall be on arrival in the Crimea, being in command of the regiment, I do not think that in honour I could ask for leave; I should be afraid of my character suffering if I did.

I must see General Simpson on arrival, as I wish

to speak to him about getting Lord Raglan's despatch of March 24th altered, and about having the time I was prisoner of war allowed to count towards my full colonelcy. I have written strong letters on both subjects, and General Storks thinks I am sure of succeeding. I wonder what has become of Colonel Browne; I suppose he has got more sick-leave; no one knows anything about him here. As regimental Lieutenant-Colonel on full pay, I am ineligible for any staff-appointment, so there is no use applying for one. I was so delighted with the good accounts you gave of the dear children, and am so glad to hear that they are all so well, and that dear Sophie is strong again; kiss our darling boy for me, and tell him papa is much obliged for his letter, and hopes he may come home to mamma and him. I was so glad to hear in my mother's letter that the children got on so well with Miss Lebel, and that she is so attentive to them. Will you tell my mother, with my love, how much obliged I am for her interesting letter of August 29th, and that I am glad that she at last got mine of July 25th? I am sure Annie will enjoy her visit to Bath; I hope she had fine weather for her journey. I was sorry to hear that you had had such heavy rain in Ireland, and that Frank's crops had suffered from them. We have had delightful weather here, only rather hot. I hardly know what I shall want if we stay a winter in the Crimea until I get to camp. I have all the flannels and warm things I took out with me, but I want a great-coat, chair, pocket-knife, cooking apparatus, horse-clothing, and cleaning-things, pack-saddle (if we take the field), but perhaps some of these articles I may be able to pick up at auctions in the camp. I will not forget to deliver your messages of remembrance to those in camp; but I almost dread to meet the regiment again, as I am afraid both officers and men will have suffered severely in the two terrible assaults on the Russians of the 8th and 9th.

TRANSPORT 'INDIAN,'
September 13, 1855.

MY OWN DEAREST ELLIE,

I embarked yesterday at 2 p.m., and we sailed at four; cleared the Bosphorus before dark; had a sharp squall in the night, with heavy rain, thunder, and lightning; and are now enjoying delightful weather and a smooth sea, and hope to be at Balaklava early to-morrow morning. I am afraid there will not be much for me to do on arrival in the Crimea, as a few hours ago we spoke a steamer on her way down from the Crimea, who told us that the whole south side had fallen, and that not a Russian was to be seen, although it was believed they still held the north side, from which, of course, we must expel them, and I hope I shall be allowed to see the last of it. We have on board a company of artillery, and one of sappers, together with drafts of convalescents from the hospital at Scutari, returning to join their regiments, from nearly every corps in the Crimea. We have thirty-one officers on board; among them is a Captain Williams, of 60th, a son of Colonel Williams, R.A., who died in Barbadoes of yellow fever; he tells me that his sister, who married Lieutenant-Colonel Handcock, 97th Regiment, is living in camp with her husband. We heard a report that the 90th and 97th Regiments suffered severely in the assault of the Redan; I trust her husband escaped. *I sent you* four letters from Constantinople, viz., on 2nd, 6th, 10th, and 12th; I hope you have got them all. I trust (D.V.) to post this to-morrow at Balaklava. I wonder if I shall find the 34th in Sebastopol; I hope to get letters there from you. Pray send me out newspapers as usual. Adieu till to-morrow, when I hope to finish this letter. I send the lock of hair you asked for; it got very thin while in Russia; you must send me one in return. I wish very much I had a good daguerreotype portrait of yourself and the pets; I should prize it highly.

BALAKLAVA,
September 14.

We got here at 7 a.m. to-day, but could not get inside on account of the harbour being so full. I, however, went on shore and reported myself to the Commandant. The *Indian*, I believe, will not go into harbour till to-morrow evening; but I shall do my best to push up to camp to-night. I hear the loss was tremendous in our storm of the Redan; 155 officers were killed and wounded. Our regiment, I am thankful to say, had only one officer—Mr. Laurie—wounded, but the 97th have suffered very severely. Lieutenant-Colonel Handcock, 97th, was killed; his poor widow is going home to England. I met Captain Hamilton of the *Diamond*, who came out with me from Malta, who told me the news; he brought her down to Balaklava. We have entire possession of the south side of Sebastopol, but the Russians blew up all their forts and ships before leaving. Their loss was estimated at 30,000 men, the English 2,000, and the French about 1,200. The Russians still occupy the north side, and occasionally fire on the south side, and very nearly killed General Airey; his orderly's horse was killed by a shot. I must now conclude, as I have to go on shore to post this letter. With fond love to all and kisses to the dear pets,

Believe me,
Ever your most affectionate
RICHARD.

CHAPTER X

BACK IN CAMP

                                Light Division Camp,
                                  September 16, 1855.

My dearest own Ellie,

In my last short and hurried letter to you of 14th instant, I mentioned my arrival that morning at Balaklava in the *Indian*. I will now go on and detail what has occurred since. Rowan, having come on board that afternoon, offered to take up part of my luggage that evening and get me a horse to ride up. I accordingly landed, and rode up to camp that evening, and met with a very warm reception from all hands; the men turned out and gave me three cheers on seeing me come up, which, as you may suppose, pleased me very much. I never saw any place so improved as our camp—good roads all through it, plenty of water, a capital mess-house in which we write and read the papers. Simpson and Goodenough have also a hut to themselves; they have given me a marquee which will be larger and more comfortable than my double tent. I am sleeping at present in poor Joey Jordan's tent until my marquee is ready, and I dine among my friends. I don't know yet with whom I shall mess. Poor Bullock has gone home wounded, and Chatfield is dead of cholera. I called on Colonel Straubenzee, of the Buffs, our new Brigadier. He is a most gentlemanly man, and told me I should find the regiment in excellent order, and spoke highly of Goodenough as a commanding officer.

Sir W. Codrington inspected our regiment yesterday, and was very much pleased. He also visited our hospital, where are a number of our poor wounded men, several of them amputated. One poor fellow had lost both arms and another received a most severe wound from a large-sized grape-shot, which went through both his cheeks and then lodged in his neck. While I was there, a poor man of the name of Brophy, of the Grenadiers, who had lost an arm, beckoned me to come and speak to him, and shook me by the hand, saying: ' I am glad to see you back again, sir; I was with you the night you were taken, and it was you that did your duty that night.' I heard he distinguished himself in the repulse of the sortie that night, and bayonetted one of the chiefs of the Albanians that attacked us that night. I also called on Sir W. Codrington, and gave him my letters about the error in Lord Raglan's despatch, which he said he would forward and accompany with his own recommendation; but he did not hold out much hope of my wishes being attended to, as he thought General Simpson would not like altering a despatch of Lord Raglan's, especially relating to an occurrence that took place so long ago. I am certainly unfortunate, as if I had been able to have left Constantinople on Thursday, the 6th, as I should have done if the *Niagara* had not broken down, I should have been in time to have commanded the regiment at the assault of the 8th, for which Goodenough will probably get a C.B., although his regiment, being in reserve, never left the trenches, and

BACK IN CAMP

sustained comparatively a small loss—six killed and fifty-seven wounded (including two officers). I have, however, the satisfaction of knowing that my own regiment, both officers and men, consider that I did my duty that night. Roach says he has often overheard the men talking about it at their cook-houses. I called on General Simpson, but he was out inspecting the guard. I saw, however, Sir R. Airéy, who was very civil to me, and I intend calling on General Simpson again.

I had the pleasure of receiving, on arrival in camp, your two dear letters of July 17 and July 25, which last was sent through the British Consul-General at Constantinople, and by him, I suppose, forwarded on here. Browne, I hear, now wishes to sell, as he finds he is not fit for foreign service, but has the modesty to ask £1,000 above the regulation; but no one, I believe, will give him a farthing. I hear he got an attack of gout the very day before he intended sailing, and even sent out his horse by the ship he intended going in.

You can have no idea what a state Sebastopol is in at present. I rode in there yesterday evening with Roach. We went through the Malakoff, which was quite in ruins, as the Russians had sprung a mine before retreating, and the ground was covered with guns and fragments of carriages. The town was terribly shattered by our late cannonade—not a house which had not the roof and walls pierced through. My old quarters, the hospital, was very much shattered. The English occupy Karabelnaïa, or the Government part of the town, situated to the east of the dockyard creek; the French occupy the west side of the town, nearest the sea. They say there have been nearly 4,000 guns taken in the town by the Allies, and the distribution among them is to be as follows: The French (having the largest force) are to have half, or five-tenths, the English three-tenths, and the Turks and Sardinians one-tenth each.

You hardly hear a shot fired now; the Russians occasionally throw shot and shell into the town from the north side, and the other day killed the horse of Sir R. Airey's orderly. We don't fire a shot at them or disturb them in any way, although they are hard at work preparing their own batteries and adding fresh ones on the north side. I suppose, according to our old practice, we shall allow them to go on making fresh Redans and Malakoffs, and when they have made them nice and strong we shall open trenches against them and take them after another year's siege. Every Russian ship or steamer has been either burnt or sunk, and their loss in men and money must have been tremendous. Their hospitals were found full of dead and dying, which they abandoned in their retreat. For two days after the evacuation of the town none of the troops were allowed to enter on account of the explosions, as the Russians set fire to or blew up most of their forts and public buildings. Fort Hall is a heap of ruins. All sorts of reports are floating about camp—one that the Light Division is to go to Corfu for the winter, another that the 3rd and 4th Divisions are to take the field, but I don't believe any of them. I am to dine with Sir W. Codrington to-morrow, when perhaps I may hear something.

September 17.

DEAREST ELLIE,

I have been all day at an auction in the 88th camp, and bought a very nice gray pony for £9 10s., which I intend making my charger. I also bought a pack-saddle, horse-clothing, head-stall, etc., and waterproof sheet for horse, the whole of which cost me £3 10s. I also bought a military bridle, holsters, and some things for my tent; also a pair of saddle-bags. The prices I paid I forget, but I will have the auction bill to-morrow, when I will let you know. I had the pleasure on returning to camp to get your dear letter of August 31. I have not yet seen General Simpson, but I do not anticipate being granted leave, as I know that Daff and Clowes applied for leave and have been refused. But, my dearest love, make your mind easy; we undergo no danger, as there is no trench work. I am off to dine at the General's, and will, D.V., finish my letter on my return.

LIGHT DIVISION CAMP,
September 20, 1855.

MY DEAREST ELLIE,

I heard a telegraphic message was received from England yesterday, directing that nothing further should be destroyed in Sebastopol by us, and that the docks, which we had mined and were going to blow up, should be spared. This looks pacific, and I shouldn't be surprised if they were to try and patch up a peace in the winter. God grant they may succeed. I rode into Sebastopol on the 18th with Colonel Brownrigg. We went through the Redan, and were able to judge of the formidable nature of that work, which caused the two assaults on it of our brave fellows to be failures. Besides the guns in its front, it was flanked on both sides by heavy batteries, which swept the whole ground with a cross-line of grape, besides the musketry fire from a numerous garrison in the work. In the face of this, our men had to drag away a formidable abattis composed of branches of trees placed in front of the ditch, then cross a deep and wide ditch by ladders, and then, rearing the ladders against the parapet, enter the work by means of them. In spite of all these obstacles, several penetrated into the Redan, but not being able to be supported, on account of so many ladders having been broken, were driven back by the numerous garrison.

We went this time into the town of Sebastopol, every house of which was nearly in ruins from the destructive cannonade lately kept up on it. I saw my old quarters in Fort Nicholas. Although the Russians did not blow up this fort, they set the floors and everything combustible in it on fire, and it presented a very blackened appearance. The French were all the time throwing rockets into the north fort, which did not, however, reply. General Pelissier was driving in the town in an open carriage with two artillerymen as postilions, and attended by a numerous staff. The Buffs now occupy the sailors' barracks in the dockyard. Before they came in they found it full of wounded, abandoned by the Russians, and in a very neglected state.

We have just returned from a parade of the division for the purpose of witnessing the distribution of Crimean medals. Only a small proportion were received, and they were distributed among the regiments that first went out, so the 90th, 97th, and ourselves did not get any this time. I hear none of them are engraved with the recipients' names, which is a great shame. They say the army will have prize-money granted to them for the taking of Sebastopol. I am going to send in a claim for £16 or £18 for the things I lost when I was taken, such as greatcoat, pistol, sword, etc.; also a claim of 5s. a day for the ten days I was kept at Constantinople waiting for a passage. My marquee is dug out, and I am having it boarded, and when that is done I shall move in. I bought at auction yesterday poor Colonel Unett's greatcoat for 16s., a lantern for 8s., and three pairs of doeskin gloves for 11s. I have not yet succeeded in getting a charger, but am on the look-out for one. I am afraid that, having already received field-allowance on first joining the army, I am only now entitled to it from the date of my rejoining, instead of from the commencement of the quarter. I have, however, referred the case to the Military Secretary. If I do not get it, I must draw on Cox, as I am reduced to a few shillings; but it is very difficult to get bills cashed here.

September 21.

I had the pleasure to-day of receiving your dear letter of September 4-5. I hope you will soon receive my letters from Constantinople, which will ease your mind as to my being in any danger, and will, I trust, convince you of the necessity of my remaining here for the present. Many thanks for your wish of sending me out things. I hardly know what I want till I get settled in my marquee, when I shall find out by degrees; the things I think of are red braid for trousers, a pair of hunting-spurs, a knife and telescope, flannel binders, one or two chamois-skins, some warm gloves (not fur), lined with leather in the palm, so as not to wear out when carrying a stick. I don't think I want anything more. I have not yet commenced house-keeping for myself, not having an article of either eatables or drinkables; and having partaken of the hospitality of kind-hearted Roach almost ever since I have been in camp, I don't think it will be of much use asking you to send me out any, as it will be two or three months before they arrive, and perhaps I may not be in the Crimea then, and the rations are now very good. Sir R. Airey visited our camp yesterday. I saw him and spoke to him about the error in the despatch; he said he would speak to General

Simpson, but did not hold out any hope of its being altered; they do not like disturbing things that have once been settled, and perhaps they think I am wishing to detract from Colonel Gordon's merits, than whom a better officer does not exist. But in my letter I merely stated the simple truth. I was on the spot and commanded the whole time during the repulse of that sortie; I had been expecting them for hours, every arrangement was made by my orders, and I accompanied the detachment of the brave 97th (certainly not seventy men) that drove a much superior force down the hill. Thank God I have plenty of witnesses to corroborate the truth of what I have said. I will not speak of my own regiment, as they may have a natural bias towards their commanding officer, and can only speak of what they heard; but going through the 97th's camp to attend an auction to-day, two of their men said to me, 'I am glad to see your honour back safe,' and when I said, 'Where did I know you?'—'Sure you took us out, sir, the night poor Captain Vicars was killed.' And the other said: 'And it was well in the front you were, sir, anyhow.' This came spontaneously from them, for I had never spoken to them in my life before, and would have passed them by without knowing them. I know that, excepting the assaults, this was as smart an affair as took place during the whole siege, and the loss of life on both sides was very great. The Queen issued an order praising the conduct of the troops engaged. Major Gordon got his brevet-lieutenant-colonelcy for it, and the officers commanding the 77th and 88th their majorities, and the Adjutant of the day, poor Marsh of the 33rd, who was afterwards killed, was promised a brevet-majority as soon as he got his company; while I, who commanded in the whole affair, am passed over because, when at the next attack I, in the execution of my duty, was in advance of my men, had the misfortune to be wounded and taken prisoner.

I am glad you like Miss Lebel so much, and that she gets on so nicely with the dear children; I am sure she will be of the greatest use to them, and I am delighted to hear they are so good and give so little trouble. How happy I shall be when I see all your dear faces again! I am glad Ellie has begun music—I hope she has a taste for it; has Annie begun to learn? I am sorry you have had such cold weather; ours to-day has been a little warmer although showery.

9 p.m.

We have just returned from Divine service, which was performed by the Chaplain to the 1st Brigade; he has sometimes afternoon service at General Straubenzee's quarters. Sir W. Codrington was on parade, and told me he had forwarded my letters about the despatch, etc., to General Simpson in time to go by the mail of the 18th. I hear the field officer on duty is not now stationed in the town, but in our old trenches outside, in charge of the guns, stores, etc., in the batteries. The Russians yesterday kept up a sharp fire on the barracks in the dockyard occupied by the Buffs, and I hear two or three of the poor fellows were killed. The fleet have been sounding with boats in the night, and I hear have discovered a passage between the sunken ships and Fort Constantine, by which ships can enter one at a time; but I do not think they will try to force a passage, as when in harbour they would be exposed to the fire of Russian batteries which they could not reach with their guns. In the evening I took a walk with Roach, and we visited the Malakoff and Redan, and finished by going through the trenches of our right attack, and revisited the spot in the mortar battery where I was made prisoner.

The trenches, however, have been greatly advanced and extended since then. I never saw such a scene of complete destruction as the Redan presented, the Russians having exploded the magazines on evacuating it—guns, carriages, masses of timber, and gabions strewed about in every direction. In the Malakoff I saw an unfortunate dead Russian still lying unburied. I picked up a few bullets in the Redan and Malakoff which I hope to bring home to you; I have also got a Russian silver medal for you. I met several acquaintances in the works, who congratulated me on my release, among others M. Las Casas, a French officer, one of our fellow-prisoners; Captain Loring of the *Furious*, who brought us from Odessa; General Dawes, R.A., and Brigadier-General Trollope, of 62nd, formerly of 36th. I find my duty to-morrow is to superintend road-making by a party of the Light Division, and I have to be up at five, and I will say good-night.

September 24, 9 *p.m.*

DEAREST E.,

I got back at 5.30 from our road-making, which commenced at 6 a.m. The men were employed digging trenches on each side of the railway to prevent its being carried away by the rains in the winter; 9,000 men of the Guards and 2nd Division were also employed in making a regular macadamized road 30 feet wide to Balaklava, which, if finished before the winter, will be of incalculable benefit. The day was most lovely, warm and clear, so I quite enjoyed the riding about. I called on Dr. Linton, whose tent was near where we were; he begged to be kindly remembered. I also met Mr. Adair, 1st Somerset Militia, but now in the Guards; he told me Lord Hardinge had been very ill from a paralytic stroke. This road-making looks very much as if we are to remain in our present position during the winter; indeed, I think under any circumstances we shall not take the field before next spring. The Duke of Newcastle, who is out here now, is reported to have said that he thinks peace will be made in the winter. God grant it may be so, and that I may soon rejoin you and the dear children, which is my prayer day and night. At present, however, the French from the town and the Russians from the north side are firing at each other as if they had no idea of peace. Captain D—— of the 48th has called on me; you may recollect his dining with us at Grenada when he was A.D.C. to General Wood; he is a very agreeable person. I saw Duff of 23rd to-day, who was my fellow-prisoner; he applied for leave to go home to get a new kit, but was refused and told he must equip himself out here.

LIGHT DIVISION CAMP,
September 27, 1855, 9 *p.m.*

MY DEAREST ELLIE,

The mail from England was due to-day, but has not yet arrived; but I hope it may to-morrow, and that I may have the pleasure of getting a letter from you. To-morrow I am to be employed road-making again; I shall be on duty till 5 p.m., and shall only have to-morrow evening and a few hours in the morning to answer your letter. My last to you was the 25th, and not much has been going on since. The weather has been very variable: yesterday was a very cold day with north wind; to-day was warm and pleasant. Things going on much as usual in Sebastopol: the Russians hard at work on their forts in the Naider (?), and a daily cannonade going on between them and the French in the town. The French, they say, are going to throw up a battery of fifty guns, to fire on Fort Constantine, and perhaps the fleet will take a part in the attack on it. The regiments have been allowed to send carts and horses into our part of the town to carry away anything that might be useful in camp. However, very little that was portable was left behind, and the chief spoils have been planks, doors, windows, boilers, etc., and such articles of furniture as were too cumbrous to be carried away. Among other things they brought me a fine large box, which will do in place of my old saddle-box. An extraordinary rumour prevails in camp, and which is generally believed, that there has been a revolution in St. Petersburg, that the Emperor Alexander has been deposed and has fled to Moscow, and that his brother Constantine has been proclaimed in his stead. This, they say, has been the work of the war party, who are very dissatisfied with the progress of the war and the losses Russia has sustained; if all this should unfortunately turn out to be true, I am afraid it will be very much against any prospect of peace. I have laid in a small store of sherry, brandy and beer at what are considered moderate prices for this place, namely, the two former at three shillings, and the latter one shilling, a bottle. When you are sending me out anything, please to send two red night-caps, same as I had before, also some postage-stamps. I called on Colonel Evelyn yesterday, but did not find him at home. Lieutenant-General Markham is, I hear, going home sick, and is to have a sale on the 29th. I have another horse to buy yet. It is very expensive work getting up a fresh kit. Poor Brine, I hear, was obliged to go to Scutari very ill. I will now say adieu till to-morrow (D.V.) when I trust to have the happiness of hearing good news from you.

September 28, 9 *p.m.*

The mail is not in yet, though I heard to-day it was telegraphed as having arrived at Kamiesch, and if so we shall not get our letters till after the closing of the mail to-morrow, which is a pity. I have been all to-day engaged in road-making, and was fortunate in having a most beautiful day for it. The road, I hope, will be finished before the commencement of the bad weather in November. There are 3,500 troops and 500 navvies employed on it every day; it will be a good road 30 feet wide when finished. I saw poor Colonel Lysons of 23rd yesterday; he was being drawn about in a little Russian carriage taken out of Sebastopol. He was wounded in the leg ir the last assault, and the ball is still lodged in the muscles of the thigh. The —th had fifteen officers killed and wounded that day; our poor wounded, I am happy to say, are going on in general very well. The wounds of one of our officers, young Laurie, showed a tendency to erysipelas two or three days go, but to-day I am glad to say he is doing better. Our sappers are to commence to-night a battery on the remains of Fort Paul, to consist of six 68's and three 13-inch mortars to silence Fort Katherine; they ought to have done so long before. The Russians fire now a good deal on the town, and the Buffs and artillery have evacuated it in consequence of losing men. There was an explosion yesterday in one of the batteries of the town, by which fifteen or sixteen men of the 68th Rifles were more or less hurt. A [word illegible], or infernal machine, as you would call it, of which there are a number buried in the earth all over the place, exploded on being trod on, and communicated with a magazine which blew up. Next week our division furnishes no working-parties, but directs all its energies to drill. I must try and ride up the Tchernaya

Valley as far as Basdar, about seventeen miles off, before the fine weather goes; I hear it is a most lovely ride.

10 p.m.

I have this moment received your dear letter of September 11 and 12, which I did not expect to get till to-morrow. My beloved Ellie, I feel for and pity you from the bottom of my heart, as I know well the misery and anxiety you must have undergone in hearing the news of the assault on the 8th, and being ignorant whether I was present at it or not; but I am confident that you have applied to the only real Source of comfort, and trust that our gracious Father has given you strength to support you in your trouble, and that ere long you received my letters, which would allay all anxiety about my safety. I trust, my dearest Ellie, that you know too well my affection and attachment for you to be sure that nothing but a strict sense of duty, and what I consider to be due to my character and that of my family, keeps me at present out here. If I had not done so, I feel I would have failed in the one and suffered in the other. If you had heard, as I have, the sneers that have been made upon such of the prisoners as asked for leave, although they were refused! ' To ask for leave after spending a pleasant time in comfort and safety in Russia, while we, who have been doing their duty, and exposed to hardship and dangers in the trenches, don't ask for it!' This was the style of their remarks, and I felt happy that they couldn't be applied to me. Nobody thinks that we shall take the field or do anything this autumn; in fact, we are making every preparation for staying the winter here, and if general leave is granted I will try and take my share of it; but I trust I may not do anything that will disgrace my character, or make my children after me ashamed of it, and I think that leaving my regiment at present, situated as I am, would be so. If Colonel Browne had been here in command of the regiment, the case would have been very different, but I cannot refuse to take either the honour or responsibility thrown on me by such a command, but rest assured of one thing, that, humanly speaking, I am as safe now here as if I were at home, and will most probably be so till next spring, and before that we perhaps may have peace.

I shall indeed be glad to see F. Smith again, and hope he will give me good accounts of you and the dear children. I am afraid this letter will not reach you till after he has sailed, but if anything should detain him I should like a little crock of butter sent out, as it is very scarce and dear here—2s. a pound. Do not forget to send me in your next a lock of your and the dear children's hair; I want to see if the colour has changed. I must draw on Cox for £30, as I owe £20 for my pony and other things I bought at auction, and as there is no money at present in the Commissariat chest, Roach cannot advance me my field allowance for October. Poor Roach has been suffering from diarrhœa for the last two or three days, but I hope a little medicine will set him right again. I am indeed glad to hear that Louisa is so much better of the pain in her side, and I trust she may have no increase of it; give her, Lady Dillon, and Mrs. Webb my love. I am glad Francis' crops are so good, and trust he may have fine weather for getting them in. It is such a comfort to me to hear that the dear children, thank God, continue so well; it is a great blessing. Although you don't speak of yourself, I trust you too, my love, are in good health. I am delighted to hear that our dear boy is such a favourite with everyone from his good temper; I trust he may never lose it.

Captain Jordan has had the ball extracted from his jaw by a practitioner in London; it was so firmly set in that he had to drag him round the room before he got it out with the forceps. His brother, who had been very ill, had to go on board ship at Balaklava for change of air, and is now better. I will now say good-night, and give you a closing postscript in the morning.

September 29.

Good-morning, my dearest Ellie; this is another lovely fine day. Did I tell you that Captain Corbe Talbot has come out here as A.D.C. to Sir R. Airey, but I have not seen him yet? I trust that by your next letter I shall hear that you have received some of mine, and that you will be more cheerful and less anxious on my account. At present, I assure you, I am incurring no danger, and our situation is infinitely better and more comfortable than it was last winter. Give my most affectionate love to my dearest mother, Kate, Annie, and Francis, and kindest regards to Miss Keys, and kisses and fond love to all the dear children, and believe me, dearest Ellie,

Ever your most devotedly attached
RICHARD.

LIGHT DIVISION CAMP,
October 1, 1855.

MY DEAREST OWN ELLIE,

The English mail is due to-day, and I trust to have the happiness of receiving a letter with good news of you and the dear party at Weston, and also to hear that you have received my first letter from Constantinople, which will set your mind at ease about my safety, although, indeed, your not having seen my name among the list of killed and wounded that was telegraphed home would have had the same effect.

The weather continues to be most lovely, dry, and warm. Colonel Evelyn, of the 20th, called on me yesterday, and we took a walk to Cathcart Hill, and looked at the neat burying-ground of the 4th Division. Sir G. Cathcart, General Goldie, and General Strangways, of the artillery, and a number of other brave officers who have fallen, are buried there; and there are stones with inscriptions in English and Russian, in order that their tombs may be respected after we leave the country, erected to almost all of them. All this has been done since I left the camp. We have also erected a stone to our eight poor fellows who have died in the Crimea. While standing on the hill, to our great regret, we saw the largest pile of buildings in Sebastopol, known as the sailors' barracks, but used latterly by the Russians as a hospital, in a sheet of flame; before night they were totally consumed, and nothing but the bare walls left standing. It appears that some of our men, not 34th, who were on fatigue there, very carelessly lit a fire on the floor of one of the lower rooms from which the planking had been removed, and the fire communicated with one of their small mines, which blew up and set fire to the whole building, and two men were unfortunately killed by the explosion. These mines are scattered all over the place, and it is a wonder more accidents have not occurred; the troops are now forbidden to enter the dockyard for fear of accidents.

Evelyn is now regimental Lieutenant-Colonel, and expects ultimately to have the regiment when Colonel Horn is made Major-General; he has never missed a day's duty since he has been out, and commanded his regiment on June 18, and applied to be made C.B. for it; but, as his regiment never left the trenches on that occasion, he was refused. He feels the refusal, for Lieutenant-Colonel Street, 57th, brother of Street of the artillery, who was not at Alma, but acted as Brigade-Major at Inkerman, and then went home on sick-leave, and has missed almost all the trenches, was made C.B. just by asking for it when he was at home. I believe leaving your regiment and going home is the way to get the good things, after all. There is a report that, of those officers who have been six months in the Crimea, a proportion of them will get three months' leave in the winter, with a free passage home. If this proves true, and that I am able to get it, I will certainly try for it. You will have seen that the Queen has granted an additional clasp for Sebastopol; rumour also says that we are to have a gratuity of six months' pay, which I hope may prove true. You will be glad to hear that I have been allowed my field allowance for the quarter I joined in, so I have now six months', or upwards of £40, due to me. I only heard this this morning; if I had known it before, I need not have drawn on Cox for £30, which I was obliged to do on the 28th, to pay for my pony and other things I bought by auction at the 88th camp, the bill for which came to £28 3s. I also bought the same day from Captain Maynard, 88th, a very pretty and strong brown pony for £17, for which I gave him a cheque on Cox. My two ponies, which are all I require out here, have cost me £26 10s., which is not dear; altogether, including what I paid at Constantinople, my kit has cost me about £50; but, then, I have sold the French saddle, which I did not like, for what I gave for it—£3. I have applied for 5s. a day for the ten days I was detained at Constantinople, which I expect to get. I have also sent in a claim for £19, for the loss of my sword, coat, and pistol, which I lost when I was taken; this will have to go home to be decided on by the Secretary at War, and I suppose in three or four months I shall get about half. You must recollect that I have drawn, altogether, £77 from Cox, viz.: £30 at Constantinople, £30 here on the 28th, and same day a cheque for £17 for pony; but, then, he ought to receive about £30 from Odessa to my credit. I have now quite sufficient money in hand to carry me on to the end of the year, so you can dispose of whatever balance there may be at Cox's as you think best.

11 p.m.

Just returned from dining with General Straubenzee. Mrs. S. is an agreeable person. Colonel Bunbury, commanding 28th; Captain Watson, commanding 7th Fusiliers; and his A.D.C., Mr. Newton of the Buffs, composed our party. We had a capital turbot for dinner, which we enjoyed very much; we were all talking of our supineness in wasting the time and actually doing nothing. The French General, D'Allonville, with his cavalry, has had a brush with the Cossacks, and taken six guns 200 prisoners and some waggons at Eupatoria. The French will get the whole credit of the campaign; they call us the British contingent. All our cavalry is to go to Scutari for the winter, and accommodation is to be provided there for 6,500 horses. I took a ride to-day to see the Ouvrage Blancs, which the French twice failed to take last February, but which afterwards they took the same day as the Mamelon; they were firing from them on the Russian forts the other side of the harbour, and the Russians returned their fire, but as long as I stayed made very bad practice. There is no mail in, I am sorry to say, and I shall have to send off this letter without acknowledging one of yours. Good-night, dearest; it is very late.

October 2.

Another lovely morning. No mail, I am sorry to say, and I shall be obliged to close this without acknowledging one of yours; I trust, however, it may come in to-day, and that I may have good news of you, and that you are less anxious about me. General Markham has gone home sick, and Brigade-General Garrett has got the 2nd Division *pro tem.*, and Lord William Paulet, from Scutari, the vacant brigade.

I have now exhausted all my gossip, and will conclude with affectionate love to my dear mother and all at home, and kisses to the darling pets. Can little Sophie read yet? Adieu, my darling Ellie, and believe me,

Ever your most affectionately attached

RICHARD.

LIGHT DIVISION CAMP,
October 3, 1855.

MY DEAREST OWN ELLIE,

Yesterday, only a few hours after the mail for England closed, I had the pleasure of receiving your dear letter of September 14 and 15, and indeed it afforded me great delight to find that not only you, the dear children, and all at Weston were in good health, but also that your natural anxiety about me was set at rest by not finding my name included among the casualties on the 8th, and also by having received my first letter from Constantinople.

You ask how it was we did not succeed at the Redan; I believe the whole affair was very much mismanaged. They say the Redan should not have been attacked at all, except as a feint; for once the Malakoff was taken, the

Redan must fall as a matter of course, and if it was to be attacked, it should have been with a much greater force, and columns should have followed in succession, pushing each other on till the place was taken; instead of that, a part of the Light Division was sent at it first, unsupported, and when they were driven back, the 2nd Division was sent in the same way, and failed likewise. The French, in their attack on the Malakoff, followed one another like waves of the sea, and although their first attack took the Russians quite by surprise, as they were at dinner, not expecting an attack in the middle of the day, yet they soon received reinforcements, and very nearly drove the French out again; and so hard pushed were they that Pelissier applied to General Simpson for a division, but was told none could be spared, although the 1st, 4th, and Highland Divisions were in reserve, and did not fire a shot, and either of them could very well have been spared; it was a great pity, as the English could then have participated in the honour of the only successful attack made in the day, while now the French get the whole credit of the business. I am also sorry to say that I have heard from various credible sources that many of our men on that occasion did not behave as well as they ought to have done; stormed the place, and got up the ladders into the Redan gallantly enough; but when inside they found a party of Russians firing at them from behind a ditch, and instead of rushing on them and driving them away, they could not be got, in spite of the example and efforts of their officers, to leave the shelter of the traverses (?), from which they kept up an ineffectual fire on the enemy. It is the long time they have spent in the trenches, where they have always (been) taught to keep under cover, and shelter themselves from the enemy's fire, that has wrought this change in the natural daring character of the British soldier. It is to be hoped that when we again take the field he will recover it again. A brigade of the 4th Division (the first) consisting of the 20th, 21st, 56th, and 63rd Regiments, under Brigadier-General Hon. A. Spencer, 44th Regiment, embarked to-day in steamers. Report says they are to proceed with 30,000 French under a French General, to try and take Fort Kinburn, a very strong fort the Russians have erected at the mouth of the Dnieper, and commanding a passage to Nicolaieff, their great dockyard. They have taken mortars with them, and the fleet and gunboats are to accompany the expedition. I hope the Russians will not hear of the expedition in time to send reinforcements there. If they take the fort they are to winter there, and will be in rather a perilous position, situated between the garrisons of Odessa and Perekop. From all I can learn, I don't think that, when we take the field next spring, we shall attempt to force their position on Mackenzie's Heights, as they have made it too strong; but we shall probably try and turn their position, by landing a force at Eupatoria, and marching from thence on Simpheropol, by which their communications will be quite cut off from Perekop.

To-day I distributed on parade the Crimea medals (122) that we received to each officer, N.C.O., and as far as they would go among the men who landed here before December 31. There are 320 men altogether of the first arrivals who are entitled to them, and as we have yet 200 to receive, it will be some time before it comes to my turn. The officers who got them were Simpson, Scott, Byron, Wyse, Cochrane, Chapman, Roach, Rowan and Dr. W——.

I took a ride yesterday down what the French call the

Grande Ravine, which leads to the head of the dockyard creek, passing by the way the ruins of what must have been once a very nice country house, with gardens and vineyards attached, but all completely laid waste. Such are the horrors of war. I also went over the French trenches on their left attack; such a network of trenches and batteries I never saw. This evening I rode to the plain of Balaklava, where the Light Division races were going on, and then along the Tchernaya to the field of battle of Traktis, but had not time to view it very closely. Roach's dysentery still continues, I am sorry to say, and is weakening him a good deal; I think he is quite right to try and get home. Poor young Laurie of ours, who was wounded by a shell on September 8, is, I am sorry to say, not doing at all well; he has had erysipelas round the edge of the wound for the last week, and it is sloughing very much, and I am afraid he is sinking under it. Although only a flesh wound, yet I think he was not in a good habit of body. The poor boy is only eighteen, and seems a nice lad; he has a brother out here in the 4th Regiment, which will be some consolation to his friends. I will now say good-night, my love.

October 4.

This day has been very changeable; the morning was very wet, so that we could have no parade, but it afterwards cleared up and turned out very fine, and General Straubenzee had a drill for mounted officers, and practised them in taking up points and distances preparatory to a brigade field-day which is to come off to-morrow. Byron, when out with a working-party to-day, in front of our old trenches, discovered near one of their rifle-pits three infernal machines, as we call them, of the Russians. They are square iron cases filled with about 50 pounds of powder, buried in the earth, with a tube projecting, which when trodden on gives way under your foot, and the pressure breaks a small glass ball filled with nitric acid contained in the tube, which sets fire to a match communicating with the powder, and explodes the machine. It is by one of these that poor Best was supposed to have been killed on June 18, as his body was never found. I believe the Russians buried those machines in all directions about their works, and it is very fortunate that so few accidents from them have occurred. Byron dug his three up, and brought them safely into camp.

My tent, I am happy to tell you, is much more comfortable than last winter; it is dry, the floor boarded, and the sides lined with waterproof canvas. I have two chairs, a dressing-table, writing-table with drawers, bed and cupboard: what do I want more? I have a very good dug-out stable roofed over, so the ponies are very comfortable; and I am building a cook-house. If you could meet with a neat plain horsewhip, you might send me one, as it would be very useful. Will you thank Miss Keys for the slippers she so kindly worked for me? although I do not require them, as the ones I brought out with me are still in good order. Thank Annie also, with my love, for the nightcaps she is making for me, and which, although I do not use one, I will value for her sake.

My stock of relics consists at present of balls and grape-shot found in the Malakoff and Redan, a Russian musket, helmet and two swords, also a silver medal and ribbon, given for the Hungarian campaign of 1849; and I have spoken to some Frenchmen, who are the owners of the plunder, to bring me a silver cup of St. George and one of the pictures of the Virgin which are to be found in every room in a Russian house. I will try and pick up as many relics as I can, and hope to have an opportunity of sending them home to you. I am glad Mrs. Gray has arrived safe home. I wish you could meet her; she is a nice, pretty person. I was very much interested by the letter you forwarded me on August 16. Many thanks for all the trouble you took in copying out Colonel Campbell's letter about the mistake in the despatch. I hope my explanation will be as well attended to.

Since writing to you I have just bought a Russian officer's chair with handsome plate for five shillings, and another sword of different shape for four shillings; so I have now quite an armoury. . . . William Jordan has just come up from Balaklava, where he had been on board ship for change of air for a month; he is looking much better, and his brother is, he says, to join the depot on the 22nd. The Adjutant-General, I hear, has written to Maxwell to ask him when he will be fit to go out again. I think it is very hard that he is not sent to the depot as well as the other wounded officers. Captain Shaw has arrived at Balaklava in the *Ripon*.

The Queen has sent two silk handkerchiefs, hemmed by herself, to be given to two wounded men in each regiment. We got ours to-day, one black and the other coloured, and very neatly worked; they are to be given to Sergeant Smith of the Grenadiers, who was wounded in eight places, and to Private Boyce, who has had both his arms shot off. We hear to-day that the French corps which left this for Eupatoria soon after the fall of Sebastopol have crossed the Belbek and dispersed three Russian regiments. If this be true, and that the French can take and hold Simpheropol, the Russians outside Sebastopol will be quite cut off from their resources, as the French will be between them and Perekop.

Poor Laurie is a little better to-day, I am glad to say, although very weak; they are apprehensive that gangrene is commencing in his wound, which is a bad symptom, but I trust it may not be so. I will close for to-day, and (D.V.) give you a postscript in the morning.

October 6.

DEAREST ELLIE,

This appears to be a fine morning. The Frenchman brought me the cross yesterday, but asked such an absurd price for it (£6) that of course I would not buy it. I am afraid you will be hardly able to read this . . . so I shall conclude, as I have no more news. The fleas are very troublesome in the tents just now, but I hope the winter will kill them. We are also infested by mice, which run over everything.

Give my most affectionate love to my dear mother, Kate, Annie, and Francis, and kisses and love to all the dear pets, and love to your mother and Louisa. Kind regards to C. K. and to nurse, and believe me, dearest Ellie,

Ever your most affectionate
RICHARD.

October 8.

Yesterday we had Divine service, and afterwards the Sacrament was administered in a hut, at which several officers attended with myself. William Talbot called the other day to see me, but I was out; he saw Roach, however, who said he was looking very well. He said Lord Luton had left him £10,000 by his will, which was *a great thing for him;* they have no children, I hear. Roach's complaint was something better yesterday. When he goes home, as he has offered to take a box for me, I intend sending in it some of my Russian trophies, which are a soldier's helmet, an officer's shako, three soldiers' swords of different sorts, a small painting of three very warlike-looking saints, taken out of a house in the town, and lots of bullets, grape-shot, and buttons; the silver medal I think I will send you by post. There is a report that the French division sent from Eupatoria have crossed the Belbek and dispersed three Russian regiments. A brigade of English light cavalry is to join them. If they can penetrate to Simpheropol and hold it, they will cut off the Russian troops outside Sebastopol from Perekop, whence they receive all their supplies, and will make them abandon their strong position at Mackenzie's Farm. I believe it is decided that the Light Division are to remain in their present ground during the winter. If the promotion caused by Browne's retirement goes in the regiment, Chapman will get his company, and I am thinking of giving the adjutantcy to Byron, who is the only Subaltern fit for it, and I think with a little application he will make a very good Adjutant.

I have been employed all the forenoon, from eight to twelve, in charge of the plunderers of the Light Division, getting planks and timber and sheet-iron for roofing out of the town, which is all that is to be got there now. I have to go again on that duty at 2 p.m., and hope to be back about six. I have just had the pleasure of getting your dear letter of September 21 and 22, which I must defer answering till my return.

That paragraph about me in the Malta paper was a very extraordinary one; I wonder who put in so cool a lie, as I never even applied for leave, feeling that it would be both dishonourable and useless to do so.

I got the papers—many thanks for them; Mr. Roger's book I thought rather meagre and flimsy. I met at

Constantinople the person who said he wrote the book for him, and he told me they only got £70 between them for it, which is but small encouragement. I wish you could send me the paper with the account of the assault of June 18, in which it is said a regiment showed the white feather; it was certainly not the 34th, as no regiment could have behaved better than they did on that occasion, as they did not retire till ordered to do so by Colonel Lysons, 23rd, who succeeded to the command of the storming column on the death of Colonel Yeo. They were ordered to retire because it was found impossible to force the abattis placed in front of the Redan, consisting of trees and branches piled up on one another and fastened on by chains and stakes, and which should have been destroyed by the fire of artillery before the assault, but were neglected like many other things. The assault on June 18 was a far more difficult thing than that of September 8. On the former occasion the men had to go exposed to fire for a much longer distance, as our trenches were not then so advanced. The abattis was perfectly unbroken; the last assault it was shattered to pieces by our artillery, and the works of the Redan were much less injured on the first occasion than they were on the last. Out of eleven officers who went out with the regiment on June 18, nine were either killed or wounded, and out of 400 men, 240 were killed or wounded. This loss is, I think, proof sufficient that the regiment did their utmost, and that it was no fault of theirs that they did not succeed. Poor Laurie had a bad night last night; I am afraid he is sinking fast. His brother is out here in the 4th Regiment, and it will be a comfort to his friends to know that he has met with every care and attention possible.

I must conclude, as it is just twelve, and I was up

before six, and on horseback riding about for eight hours. I shall not have time to give you a postscript in the morning, so, with kisses to pets and love to all,

Believe me,

Always your most affectionately attached

RICHARD.

LIGHT DIVISION CAMP,
October 12.

MY OWN BELOVED ELLIE,

I am afraid, indeed, our attack on the Redan was greatly blundered, and that the assault should have been made with a much greater force, and our men—that is to say, the young soldiers—did not fight as well as they should have done; we have too many recruits in the army at present, and most of them, I am afraid, of a bad class. Our regiment was never called on to leave the trenches that day, so is not involved in the disgrace at all. We have heard nothing positive of what we are to get for the capture of Sebastopol, except an additional clasp to the medal, which I suppose we shall get about a year hence, as one fourth of the medals have not been issued yet. The ribbon is not very pretty—light blue with yellow edge. I have seen out here some very pretty miniature medals and crosses of the Bath to wear with undress uniform, which look very well. If they make me a C.B., as they did Gordon for March 22 (which I don't expect they ever will), I shall get one of them.

Many thanks for the papers, all of which I got. My two servants—Cormack, my groom, formerly Harman's servant, and whom I like very much, he is so willing; indeed, till yesterday he has been my only servant, but on that day I got Gregg, who had been servant to the chaplain of the division, Rev. Mr. Ede, who leaves for

England to-day. Mr. Ede gives him a very good character, and says he is a very fair cook, which Bullock, poor fellow! was not certainly. Bullock, I am glad to say, is out of hospital, and at his duty as hospital orderly at Balaklava. Both the horses are very well, and I like them very much; the gray is a little fidgety, and I must get a martingale for him; they are both perfectly steady with troops. I continue to mess with Roach, who is the same good, kind-hearted fellow as ever. I am sorry to say, however, that he still suffers from dysentery, which I think is weakening him a good deal; I shall be glad when his September pay-list is finished, in order that he may go home on sick-leave. He has offered to take a box for me, so I intend sending you my Russian trophies. I shall ask him to send them by long sea from London or Portsmouth if he touches there, and I hope they may arrive safe. Roach has promised me his poultry when he goes, consisting of a cock and five hens; they were given him by Saunders, and the hens are capital layers, and we have fresh eggs every morning for breakfast; they will be a valuable present, and it is very kind of him giving them to me instead of selling them. I am so glad you like the presents I sent you, and that the ring fits you; these rings are sometimes used as egg-cups in Russia, which are a very scarce article, they generally using wineglasses; they are, however, not so valuable as you suppose, as the whole of them did not cost £5. I must not forget to send my portrait of Novosillekeff in the box with Roach, and I should like you to get it newly framed and hung up at Weston. I have posted to-day and registered a little box containing a small silver medal and ribbon given for the Hungarian campaign of 1849, which was taken in Sebastopol, also a small brass clasp of a book.

What a severe article that was in the *Times* of September 29 against General Simpson! I wonder if he will throw up the command. They also made a hit at General Codrington, but I think without reason, as no one has worked harder or better than he has; he was at Colonel Airey's auction to-day when I was, and appeared very much out of spirits. We are very busy making roads about our camp, and building cook-houses and guard-houses of stone and brick; our men make the bricks, and we have made a kiln to burn them in; the timber, sheet-iron for the roofs, and windows come from Sebastopol, which will soon be stripped. Several of the officers have commenced building. I am glad the melon seeds arrived safe, and I hope they may succeed, but I don't recollect ever seeing water-melons either in England or Ireland; they are delicious in Russia, and thrive best on sandy soil.

I am so glad you approve, under existing circumstances, of my having returned to the Crimea; indeed, I think I could not with honour have acted otherwise, although it was a severe trial to refrain from asking leave to go home to see you after all that had taken place, but probably I should have been refused, and then indeed I should have regretted having ever asked. There is a report here that all officers who were out here last winter, and remained out without leaving, are to have three months' leave and a free passage given them; but they are to pay ten shillings a day for their living on board, and they say that in the infantry this will only include seventy-nine officers in the whole army. But these are only reports; nothing official has come out about the leave. Roach heard from Maxwell yesterday; he was staying at B——. The Adjutant-General had written to him about a fortnight before to ask him if he was ready to go out again, to which Maxwell replied that he was not sufficiently recovered from his wound to enable him to do so, and hoped he would be allowed to remain till October 14, the end of his original leave. I think it is very hard that Maxwell is not allowed to go to the depot. Gwilt, I hear, has leave till January, Homan till November 14, and Jordan till November 30. Poor Sitwell, I hear, has returned from Madeira a perfect wreck. He writes that he is dragging out a miserable existence. Laurie, you will be glad to hear, is much better; he made a wonderful rally the last few days, and his wound looks much healthier, and they now consider him out of danger, and that he only wants nursing. Perhaps you would like to know the number of the killed and wounded we have had out here up to September 8:

	Field-officers.	Capts.	Subs.	Sergts.	Cpls.	Drs.	Pvts.	Total.
Killed	0	2	3	1	1	0	69	76
Died of wounds	0	0	2	3	1	1	43	50
Total died	0	2	5	4	2	1	112	126
Wounded	2	7	7	17	14	2	272	321
Grand Total	2	9	12	21	16	3	384	447

This is altogether exclusive of those who have died from disease, who amount to a much greater number.

I saw Colonel Hale, of the 82nd, the other day in our camp, who told me that Colonel and Mrs. Maxwell with their large family had gone to Spa in Belgium to economize, but found it nearly as dear as at home. Edward Roper's brother, Captain Roper, of the 47th, is out here. I sent him a message the other day to say I was here and would be glad to see him, but I am afraid it was not delivered to him, as I have not seen him yet. I will, however, try and make him out. He has a very good appointment at present as one of the superintendents of roads, with 7s. 6d. a day extra pay and forage for three horses.

I will now say good-night, and (D.V.) will give you a P.S. in the morning.

October 13, 7 *a.m*.

Good-morning, my dearest Ellie. This is a most lovely morning! Do you drive out often at Weston? I wish you had a little phaeton and horse of your own; you could very well afford it. When does Annie return from Bath? Is her school quite given up? I hope Francis had a good harvest this year, and that prices were remunerative. I will now conclude, with much affectionate love to my dearest mother—who I hope continues well—Kate, Annie, Francis. Kisses and love to the dear pets, and don't let them forget me. Kindest regards to C. K., and thanks for her present. Remember me to Mrs. Caffray, and above all, with fondest love,

Believe me, dearest Ellie,

Ever your fondly attached
RICHARD.

LIGHT DIVISION CAMP,
October 18, 1855.

MY OWN DEAREST ELLIE,

I have had the happiness of just receiving your welcome affectionate letter of October 3, containing the precious lock of your hair, for which, indeed, I am obliged, and value it highly. I am surprised that when you wrote you had not received my letter of September 18, as by the same mail which brought me your letter of October 2 I got an official letter of the 5th, acknowledging one of mine of September 21. I trust, however, you found a letter from me at Drogheda, and also that, on your arrival at home, you found the dear children and all at Weston well. I am sure our darling boy must be very fond of you; it were strange if he were not, after all the care you have taken of him.

There has been no news lately of the different expeditions that have left this army. Large fires have been seen for several nights lately on the heights occupied by the Russians over the Tchernaya, and most people think that they have been destroying their huts and stores preparatory to a retreat. It was, however, telegraphed to General Simpson from London, viâ Russia, that news had been received viâ Berlin that the Russians threatened an attack on our position, and to be on his guard; many think this is a Russian ruse to prevent our sending away any more troops to threaten their communications: if so, it has had the desired effect, for a Highland Brigade and a Light Cavalry, that were to have gone to Eupatoria, have been countermanded, and we have resorted to the salutary method of having parade at half-past five in the morning, when the whole army is under arms. If, however, the Russians do attack, I think they will meet with the same reception that they did on August 16, and get soundly beaten, with but little loss to ourselves, as our position is not only naturally very strong, but is also well fortified. I confess, however, I should like to see the Inkerman plateau occupied by some troops, for the greater part of the French who were in camp there have left for Eupatoria, and have not been replaced yet. As for us the position of the troops has not been changed since the place has been taken, and the third (the strongest division in the army) and fourth remain still on our extreme left, where, now the siege is over, they can be of no use, as we are perfectly safe from any attack in that direction, and if we were attacked on the right, it would be two hours before they could come up in time to support. But 'happy-go-lucky' has been the motto of the Generals of this army; they have not shown much foresight as yet. General Simpson, for a wonder, was seen out to-day actually inspecting the Inkerman position, and I hope some good may come of it. We hear that the Emperor Alexander is expected shortly to visit his army here. This morning, about half-past seven, they sent a shot into our camp, which certainly took one of the longest ranges I have heard of—out here, at least. It was fired from their lighthouse battery, from the north side, which is situated on some heights at the head of the harbour, at least three miles off; it went over the whole of the camp and pitched at the extreme end of it, close to the door of Sergeant Baker the hospital-sergeant's hut, where it buried itself nearly 5 feet in the ground. It must have been fired from a gun with great elevation to go that immense distance. The shot was dug out, and it weighed 27 pounds, and is now at my tent door. These random shots thrown from elevated guns very seldom do any mischief, as they could only kill one man, even if they hit him, as, from the height they come down, they bury themselves when they strike the earth, and don't bound.

October 19.

DEAREST E.,

I know you will be glad to hear that I have had an answer to my letter about the mistake in the despatch, and also to my application that I might be allowed to reckon the time that I was prisoner in Russia as part of the three years' service as Lieutenant-Colonel required before promotion to Colonel; this they have granted, and they say that my letter correcting the despatch will be duly recorded—whether with a view to any ultimate benefit time will show. I will wait patiently till the next serving out of honours takes place, and if I find that I am left out, while those who never quitted the trenches at the late assault of the Redan are promoted or, decorated, I shall apply again; as I know Major Gordon, R.E., got either a lieutenant-colonelcy or a C.B. for that night—indeed, I am not sure that he did not get both, and if you have kept the *Times* paper I should feel much obliged if you would look carefully through the Gazettes after April 6, and let me know the date of Gordon getting his lieutenant-colonelcy and C.B. He was afterwards made, for his subsequent services, a full Colonel and Queen's A.D.C., which he well deserved. I send you in another envelope a copy of General Yorke's letter, as well as of those I wrote, as I dare say you would like to see them; you will see that General Yorke's letter, though dated October 6, was received yesterday by General Simpson.

We had a long brigade field-day to-day, also yesterday. The weather continues delightful. We have got up two more huts for the men, which will enable me to hut altogether two companies. I am glad to say that the French are sending a division to-day to their old ground at Inkerman. If well manned, no enemy should take that position from us. The Medical Board was held on Roach to-day, and he is to have six months' sick-leave, and expects to leave this by the steamer of the 27th. I am glad he is going home, as he has certainly been very much weakened by his dysentery. I send a box of relics home by him.

You will be sorry to hear that poor Sitwell died on the 2nd. I dare say he found death a happy release, for in the last letter he wrote to the regiment he said that he was dragging on a miserable existence.

I am delighted to say that it has just been published in orders that a telegraphic despatch has just been received from Sir Edward Lyons, stating that the expedition to the mouth of the Dnieper has perfectly succeeded; the three forts commanding the entrance to the river were bombarded and forced to surrender with 1,390 prisoners, and the fleet have now entire possession of the entrance to the river, and I dare say before long we shall hear of an attempt being made by the gunboats and [word illegible] vessels of light draught of water on Nicolaieff, and if they can destroy the dockyard and vessels building there it will be a great blow to Russia, as it is where all her Black Sea fleet are built. These expeditions will, I think, oblige the Russians to detach troops from this army, and prevent them from undertaking anything serious here. I will now say adieu, and will give you a postscript in the morning.

October 20, 6.30 *a.m.*

DEAREST E.,

I have just returned from an hour's drill, since 5.30. It is a lovely morning indeed; we are most favoured by weather. I hear the Russians suffered most severely at the repulse of their assault on Kars. The Turks fought uncommonly well. Four thousand Russian muskets were picked up, and 300 prisoners were made, and it is said they carried off 5,000 wounded.

I think you will find that Gordon's lieutenant-colonelcy was dated April 24, and Captain Rickman, 77th, who was with me that night, got a brevet-majority for it on that date; so I wish you would search in the *Times* of April 25: I think you will find Gordon's name.

I must now conclude with kisses to the darlings, and affectionate love to my dear mother, Kate, Annie, and Francis, and kind regards to C. Keys and to Mrs. Caffray.

Believe me, dearest Ellie,
Ever your most affectionate
RICHARD.

LIGHT DIVISION CAMP,
October 22, 1855.

MY DEAREST OWN ELLIE,

Since I had the pleasure of writing to you on the 20th, nothing very particular has occurred. The Russians have made no attack on any part of our position, nor do I think they intend doing so, although it is reported the Emperor is with them; but I fancy they give out these reports of attacks as a sort of ruse to induce us, if possible, not to detail any more troops to harass them in flank. If they do attack, they are certain to be beaten with heavy loss, as our position is very strong, and I am glad to say the French within the last few days have sent up more troops to Inkerman. We have again commenced erecting a battery on the ruins of Fort Paul to fire on the Russian forts on the north side. We have certainly taken our time about it. The Light Division got lots of drill the latter end of last week. On the 20th we had regimental drill at 5.30 am., brigade drill from 10 to 12, and at 2.30 p.m. we had a grand field-day, with all the ten regiments of the division under Sir W. Codrington, which was a very pretty sight and lasted till past four. This week our regiment has 300 men working on the road to Balaklava, and the rest of the men are employed in making roads, building houses, and putting up huts in the camp. The cook-house of the right wing is, I am glad to say, finished, and the flues draw remarkably well; we took the boilers out of the Russian barracks in Sebastopol. Our brick-makers have been very successful in making their bricks hard enough to resist the fire. The 23rd put up an oven in their kitchen, but unfortunately, from the bricks not having been sufficiently burnt, the whole thing came down when the fire was lighted. We are also commencing a stone guard-house, Quartermaster's store, and wash-houses for the men and bake-house for the hospital. All other regiments are doing the same more or less, so when we leave the Crimea we shall leave behind us some substantial proofs of our occupation. I only hope our building will not be interrupted by any change in the fine weather we have lately had. Yesterday was a very bleak, cold day, but to-day is warm again, the wind having come round to the south; it threatens, however, rain very much. Roach expects to leave for England on the 27th, and to-morrow I must commence packing up the box of relics I intend sending you by him. I shall miss him very much when he goes.

We are expecting soon again to hear news from the expedition that went to the mouth of the Dnieper, and are anxious to learn if they were able to go up to Nicolaieff, but I am afraid they were not strong enough for that.

Dearest E.,

On my return from riding I had the happiness of receiving your long and affectionate letter of October 5 and 6. Many thanks to you for it. I was so happy to find by it that you were no longer in such a state of wretched anxiety about me, as you very naturally were in when I was out here before; but there is now really, thank God, no cause for apprehension, and, please God, we may yet be restored to each other before very long.

It was certainly very gratifying to me on my return to meet such a reception from the men, and I hope I may always merit it. My two ponies do me very well for the work I have here; I have ridden them both on parade, and they are as steady as rocks with troops. The gray is a little fidgety sometimes when you want him to stand still, and I ride him, in consequence, in a martingale. If we take the field next spring, I shall buy a stronger one to ride. Leander is still in the regiment, and is in the enjoyment of very good health, although looking rather rough from being out all last winter; he is the property of young Peel, who bought him from H——.

I have every reason to be satisfied with my servants. Gregg is a very steady man. I have not yet tried his skill in cooking, as Roach's servant always cooks for us; but his former master, the chaplain, told me he cooked very well. You will be glad to hear that my new kitchen was finished to-day, and that the chimney draws uncommonly well, and will be ready for his *coup d'essai* on Saturday. I am very sorry, for poor Mrs. Maxwell's sake, that her husband has been ordered out again. It is very unfair to him that he should be sent out of his turn; every officer at the depot should have gone before him. When he does come out I hope we shall mess together. I was very much grieved to receive by this mail an account of the death of poor Bullock at one of the hospitals on the Bosphorus on the 16th, of chronic dysentery. By the last accounts I heard he was so much better that he was able to return to his duty as orderly. Both the servants I brought out with me are now gone. It was very kind of Maxwell to offer to bring out a box for me, and thanks for thinking of the shako and forage-caps for me; the former I find is hardly worn out here now, but the latter I wanted very much, as my present one is getting very shabby. Many thanks for all the things you intend sending me out by Campbell, all of which I am sure will prove useful. I have not yet heard of the arrival of the *Queen of the South*, but I hope I soon shall. I shall be very glad indeed to hear of my stray box on board the *Royal Albert*, but, unfortunately, she has gone with the expedition to the Dnieper, and no one knows when she will return. I only hope I may get my box safe at the end of her cruise. I am glad they are going to send us out a draft, and especially some Captains, of whom we are very short; and there are several at the depot who have either never been out at all or only for a very short time; they ought to be sent out before any of the wounded.

Thank Kate, with my love, for the braid she sent me; it will do very nicely. Kiss my dear pets Ellie and Annie, and thank them, with my love, for being so kind as to hem handkerchiefs for papa; I shall be very glad indeed to get them, and, if possible, will write them a letter next mail thanking them. How very kind of your Aunt Sophie to send such nice presents to the children! The map of the sugar-plantation was a very appropriate present for our little creole: does it bring sugar-cane to her recollection? Dear Daddah must be very amusing to you with his games and tricks; what is the colour of the frock that Miss Keys gave him? You say that he and Sophie are quite well; I hope nothing is amiss with the other two. I am glad Ellie has a taste for music, and hope Annie will acquire one also. It is very odd that R. Lloyd does not write to you; I must write to him myself and send it through you. There was nothing in the papers brought by this mail about the promotions or honours for the army on account of the capture of Sebastopol. I suppose they will come by the next mail, which will bring the Gazette. If I see that officers are decorated for the Redan who never left the trenches, and that I am passed over, I shall certainly write a strong letter, and try and get it backed by Sir William Eyre and General Simpson now that they have admitted that it was I, and not Major Gordon, who commanded on that occasion. In justice I should get the same rewards that were given to Major Gordon; in fact, every officer almost who had any sort of a command that night, that wasn't killed, has been promoted except myself. Even the officer, Lieutenant Marsh, 33rd, who was my Adjutant that night, was promised a brevet-majority as soon as he got his company. I am afraid our share of prize-money will not be very large; report says that we shall have a quarter's field allowance given us instead. I find the serge suit very useful, and wear it every day; it saves my other clothes.

The last that was heard of Colonel Browne was that he was staying at Sir G. Douglas's, and going to balls. Douglas, I hear, intends paying us a visit shortly in his yacht, with young William Scott, late of ours. He leaves Lady Douglas with her mother at Gibraltar. I am very glad Bourke has so comfortable a berth at Jersey; I am sure Mrs. B. is delighted to have a little gaiety. I see Dr. Lawson has left the Ordnance Medical Department for the line. I hope they will like Malta. I have heard Captain Hammond, R.B., spoken of out here in the highest terms, both as a Christian and an officer. Poor Vicars, also of the 97th, was another noble Christian character; no one could have led on his men more gallantly the night he was killed. I was close to him when he got his death-wound; in fact, I was the only one of the four officers that went out with the 97th that was not hit. Poor Browne is not in the Crimea; he is either at Scutari or gone home; I hear he was very ill. You ask about my wound: my hand is slightly marked in the back where the bayonet entered, but not at all in the palm where it came out; the bayonet came in about the middle of the back of the hand, between the . . .

[The remainder of this letter is missing.]

CHAPTER XI

SECOND CRIMEAN WINTER

LIGHT DIVISION CAMP,
October 25, 1855.

MY DEAREST ELLIE,

I have just finished packing up my box with the Russian relics, of which I enclose a list. Roach goes on board to-morrow, and is to sail in the *Emperor* on the 27th; she is what they call a direct ship—that is, she makes no delay at Scutari, and only coals at Malta—and therefore ought to arrive at Spithead on November 14; so look out for her arrival in the *Times*. I have given Roach an envelope directed to you, and he has promised on arrival at Portsmouth to drop you a line in it saying when the box will leave Portsmouth by long sea for Dublin. I have directed the box to you at Duleek, to be forwarded there by rail from Dublin; but on receipt of Roach's letter you can write to the agents and give your own orders about it; I only hope they will arrive safe. Novosillekeff's portrait is wrapped tight round a roller to prevent injury; the picture of the saints is done up in paper; mind that in the little cardboard box with buttons there are also three cartridges, so be careful of fire, and keep them out of the way of the children. It is most fortunate for the road-making and building that we are still favoured with the most splendid weather, although the nights and mornings begin to be very cold.

I took a ride yesterday to the monastery of St. George, which is built on a shelf in the cliffs overhanging a little bay. The building is now used as a convalescent station or sanatorium, although the monks still reside in a part of the building and use their neat chapel daily; they are rationed by our Government. The monastery is very substantially built of stone, and has a terrace with little gardens in front, which contrast very prettily with the bare and savage appearance of the bold cliffs on either side. The day was lovely, and we enjoyed a very extensive sea-view, enlivened by numerous vessels.

Two days ago I got a message to say that a parcel which had been lying for a considerable time for me at Kazatch was then at head-quarters, and requested me to send for it. I, thinking it was the missing box from the *Royal Albert*, borrowed a mule, put my pack-saddle on it, and sent my orderly down with it; the parcel turned out to be an old mackintosh and a brown holland coat, neither of them worth much nor belonging to me. I fancy they must have been left behind either in the *Furious* or the *Dauntless* by some of the other prisoners, and directed to me. However, on its way back the mule shied, and the orderly managed to tumble off and let him go, pack-saddle and all, and he has not been heard of since, nor I suppose ever will be. The mule belongs to Roach's servant, and if not found I will have to pay him his value altogether. It is a most provoking accident. Roach says during his leave he must go to Ireland, both to Dublin to see Mr. Hamilton, and a friend of his at Balbriggan, and he has promised me that he will go from there to see you at Weston. He is to write to you to give you notice of his coming, and perhaps my mother, if not inconvenient, could make out a bed for him for a night. He has promised to write to me how you are looking and the children, especially his friend Daddah.

I am so sorry that I shall not be able to accompany Roach on board to-morrow, but, unfortunately, I am in charge of the working-parties on the roads, which will keep me employed till 5 p.m. He has left me all the furniture of his tent, among which I shall find many useful things. Brigadier-General Shirley, 88th Regiment, is going home on leave, and Colonel Lysons, 23rd, gets the command of the 2nd Brigade in his absence, and I shall be then senior field-officer in the Light Division. The brigade of the 4th Division that went to the Dnieper is coming back again, as the French are going to garrison during the winter the forts that were taken there. The Russians have blown up the forts on the opposite side of the river, and by the last accounts the French were making a reconnaissance towards Nicolaieff, but I am afraid they are not strong enough to take it. Last Saturday, when we had a drill of our division, there was also a review at the same time of the French Imperial Guard on the plain near Balaklava, and they, seeing such a large body of troops out at the same time, thought we were certainly going to make an attack, and turned out a large body of troops—cavalry, artillery, and infantry—in readiness. It made them show their force, which was larger than we supposed. I myself don't think they have any intention of retiring as long as their provisions hold out.

The mail is late; it has not arrived to-day as it ought. I trust to-morrow, however, that I shall have the pleasure of getting one of your dear letters with good accounts. I will now say good-night, as it is nearly ten, and I have to be up at five. God bless you!

October 26.

DEAREST E.,

I was on the roads to-day in charge of working-parties from eight to four. The day was very fine and warm, and I enjoyed it very much, and on my return home had the happiness of getting your long affectionate letter of October 9 and 10, together with equally affectionate ones from my dear mother and Kate, and they all contain such interesting news; in fact, I never had a more delightful budget. I also received that comfortable bandage which you so kindly worked and my mother sent out for me. Many thanks to you both for it!

I don't think the Light Division will take the field this winter certainly, but we have not yet heard of any leave being granted to the officers, and only hope it may prove true. It would indeed be happiness to see you all again. When I go to Constantinople, I hope either to send or bring you a table-cover and other articles from the bazaar. I would have got you some when last there, only I had no means of sending it. Many thanks for the things you are sending me from Hibbert. Maxwell, I have just heard, is not coming out now, but is to go to the depôt, as in all fairness he ought to do, and I am very glad of it both for his and Mrs. Maxwell's sake, although personally I shall miss him very much. Thanks for the silk, but as my former stock was not exhausted I did not suffer for the want of it. I am sorry to hear that Colonel Ward has been so ill. I hope you have heard since that he is better; he would be such a loss to his family. How kind of my dear mother thinking of sending me the *London News;* it is so like her usual generosity, but I am sorry she has put herself to the expense, for not only do we take it at the mess, but Chapman also takes it and lends it to me. I will, however, keep all the numbers. I must write and thank her both for it and for sending the binder. My hair is not falling off or getting thinner, you will be glad to hear. I have not yet heard of the arrival of the *Queen of the South*. I shall wait patiently till I see the honours awarded for the late assault, when, if I get nothing for March 22, I will send home a respectful remonstrance, backed by Sir W. Eyre, whom they say is to be our new Commander-in-Chief. We hear that these promotions are not to appear before November 9.

Roach bequeathed me a very nice table of walnut-wood, a little bit of plunder which he made on first arriving at Balaklava. It is a very neat article of furniture for a camp; being polished (which we are not), enables me to send one of my tables to the kitchen. I had my first dinner cooked in the kitchen to-day, and find Gregg is a very good cook and that he makes capital soup. The kitchen chimney draws admirably, and perhaps, if the winter is very cold, I may occupy the kitchen as being the warmest place. The cook-house for our right wing that we have finished is considered quite a model kitchen in the camp; it is certainly the best in the Division, the brickwork is so good and the flues draw so well. But our brickmakers and layers are better than our masons, as endless critics assert, and I am afraid with some truth, that our back wall is a little out of the perpendicular, and that some fine day it may come down by the run, and to prevent so terrible a catastrophe I intend supporting it by building a woodhouse at the back, which I hope will have the desired effect.

SECOND CRIMEAN WINTER

Light Division Camp,
October 29, 1855, 7 *p.m.*

My dearest own Ellie,

I have deferred commencing my letter to you in hopes of hearing of the arrival of the mail, and of having one of your dear letters to answer, but unfortunately it has not yet arrived, and as I have not much news of my own to give you, you must excuse this letter not being as long as usual. Our fine weather still continues, and although we make no use of it for field operations, yet it has been of the greatest advantage to us for making our roads, which, if it lasts for a fortnight longer, will, I think, be entirely completed; and in order to insure their being so, our early morning parades have been discontinued, to allow the men to begin work earlier on the roads. Our own camp-buildings are also slowly progressing, it being difficult to find fatigue-parties for them, as we have so many men on public working-parties.

The night before last a handsome Russian church in the town, built after the model of the Temple of Theseus, with a colonnade of pillars all round, was burnt, whether by accident or by Russian shells was not known. It was, however, a magnificent sight when the fine proportions of the building, with its colonnade of pillars, was lit up by the flames. You will be glad to hear that Brine called to see me yesterday, having just returned from sick-leave to Scutari; he is much better, though still a little weak; he is now attached as engineer to the Light Division. Mrs. Brine was quite well when he last heard; she is staying with his father. I also saw to-day Lieutenant James, R.E., who has just returned from Russia, where he had been prisoner. He arrived at Riasan only a few days before we left; he told me he had been treated with great kindness by Mr. de Novosillikeff, and that Madame had told him to tell me that she had received your letter with the bracelet, for which she thanked you very much, but Mr. James did not bring your letter to me; perhaps, however, it may yet arrive.

The English part of the expedition to the Dneiper has returned. The French are going to occupy Fort Kinburn during the winter; after taking the forts, they sent an expedition up the country to gain intelligence, which recorded that Nikolaieff and Cherson were too strongly occupied to be attacked with any chance of success. I suppose, therefore, nothing further will be done this winter, as in another fortnight we may expect the rains.

Laurie expects to be sent home next Saturday; he walked to-day for the first time, with the assistance of a stick, but is very weak. However, he only wants air and nourishment now.

I have heard nothing more of my claim for the things I lost when I was made prisoner; I suppose it has been referred to the Secretary at War. I wish you would send me by post a braid guard-chain for my watch, as the one I have is nearly worn out.

I must write on the other side a short note to the pets, to thank them for hemming the handkerchiefs for me; you will read it to them.

The *Queen of the South* has not yet arrived. Good-night, my love; I will give you a postscript (D.V.) in the morning, and I hope you will kindly excuse this stupid letter.

CAMP NEAR SEBASTOPOL,
October 29, 1855.

MY OWN DARLING CHILDREN, ELLIE, ANNIE, LITTLE PET SOPHIE, AND MR. DADDAH,

I have been long intending to write you a letter, for I am afraid the last letter I wrote to you when I was in Sebastopol with the Russians never reached you. I was so glad to hear from mamma and grandmamma and Auntie Katie, by their last letters, that you were all so well and had been such good children, and getting on so nicely in your lessons with Miss Lebel, and that you are kind to one another, and affectionate to your mamma and grandmamma. This news made me very happy indeed, and I trust that you pray to God to send you His grace to keep you good children, for without that you cannot long continue so. Mamma tells me that Ellie and Annie have been so kind as to hem handkerchiefs for me. I am very much obliged to you for it, and shall be very anxious to get them and to see how nicely you have done them. I hear that Ellie is fondest of reading, Annie of working, and little Sophie of playing, and Daddah of pretending to be John Kelly—all very good things in their own way, and each at its proper time. Mamma, I am sure, has told you that I have returned from Russia, where I was so kindly treated, and have got back to the same camp I was in before, and live in a tent, very like the one I once wrote to you about, only more comfortable. You will, I am sure, be glad to hear that there is no fighting going on now, for the town we were fighting about has been taken; only hardly anyone can live there now, for the houses which were once very fine ones, built of stone, are so full of holes made by cannon-balls that they are quite destroyed. There are no women or little children in the camp, but there are cocks and hens, and two goats to give milk, and they are so tame that when it rains they will walk into the first tent they see, and stay there till the rain is over. There is also a young dog called Malakoff; he is such a funny little fellow, and barks and plays with the goats all day. I must not

forget the two cats, a black and a gray, that go round the
tents paying visits, and stay about two days at a time;
they are on a visit to me now, and the black cat is asleep
on my bed. I am glad to see them, because they catch
the mice, which are very troublesome. Sometimes they
run races over the top of my tent, when they make
such a noise. Mamma, I am sure, will be kind enough
to read this to you, and give every one of you a
sweet kiss from me with my love. Good-bye, my dear
children; God bless you all, and keep you good and well
in soul and body. I trust I shall always hear good
accounts of you, and that in God's good time we may be
all spared to meet again in health and happiness.

I am,
Your most affectionate papa,
R. D. KELLY.

October 30, 6.30 *a.m.*

Good-morning, dearest Ellie. This is another fine
day; we have had no rain for nearly five weeks now,
so you may fancy what splendid weather we have
had for making roads, and also for field operations, if
they had chosen to make use of it. Mr. James was told
they would hardly believe in the fall of Sebastopol when
the news arrived in Riasan. The Russians thought
it never would be taken. He told me they had hardly
any troops but Militia in Odessa, but that he met about
5,000 of the Grenadier Corps coming from Poland
when he was on his way to Odessa. The Generals here
are, I think, a little jealous of all the distinction General
Windham has got, and attribute it to his having asked
the reporter of the *Times* to dine with him the day
after the assault, who puffed him up; they say also
he should never have left the Redan himself to ask

for reinforcements, but have sent an officer. However, it can't be denied that he was the only General Officer who entered the Redan, or, I believe, even left the trenches, and that he deserves credit and distinction for that alone.

Give Kate her little note. I hope you will be able to make out my little note to the pets. Give them my love and a kiss, and kind regards to Mrs. Caffray; also love to your mother and Louisa when you write. I have sent love to all at Weston by Kate.

Believe me,
Always your affectionately attached
RICHARD.

I hope the mail will arrive to-day, and bring me a letter from you.

LIGHT DIVISION CAMP,
November 1, 1855.

MY DEAREST OWN ELLIE,

I must give you a description of the internal arrangement of my marquee, as you wish. A marquee differs from a bell-tent in being long instead of round, and having a pole at each end to support it, instead of one in the centre, and it is much larger, and consists of one tent inside another, the outer being made of canvas and the inner of bed-ticking; and between the door of the outer tent and the curtain of the inner there is, of course, a space, making a sort of anteroom; but my tent being sunk about 3 feet, this is chiefly taken up by the step. The sides of my pit are lined with waterproof canvas to keep out the damp, and the top makes a sort of shelf running all round the tent. I have a bank of earth thrown up all round the tent between the inner and outer canvas, which helps to keep it warm, and a good trench outside to carry off the rain. I am also building a porch with a raised door and two windows, which I hope will be finished to-morrow, and that it will be a great addition to my comfort. The curtains of the inner tent, now that it has been dug out, do not, of course, reach to the ground, and consequently I must have them lengthened by adding a piece of canvas or tarpaulin, to enable them to keep out the wind in the winter. My furniture is arranged as follows: On the right, immediately as you enter, is my dressing-table, covered with black waterproof canvas, and having good-sized drawers, in which I keep my stationery, writing materials, etc.; under the table is a cask of beer, on top of which are ranged my boots; my bed extends from the table to nearly the end of the tent, just leaving sufficient space at the head to stow away a carpet-bag, etc. I have plenty of blankets, and use one of my railway rugs for a quilt; the other I was obliged to put on one of the horses, as I only brought one set of horse-clothing.

I use a large leather cushion I bought at Toula for a pillow, as your dear pillow makes such a nice seat for a hard-bottomed wooden chair I bought at A——, which I always use. Opposite the dressing-table and on the other side of the tent-pole, just leaving a gangway sufficient for one person to pass, is the table I am now writing at, which is also my dining-table. It was given me by Roach, and is of polished walnut, and a very handsome affair for a camp; the top of it turns round, and underneath is a drawer, which is useful. This table is across the tent; under it is a packing-case with my clothes for present use, and in front of it my chair, a very strong affair, with wooden back and seat and iron legs, which fold up. Next to the table along the tent are my two portmanteaus, one on top of the other, which serve either as a seat or a sideboard; then come the wooden arm-chair made by our carpenter, a stupendous affair, very like a porter's chair, which, as I seldom sit in it, I greatly grudge the room it takes; next is a small cupboard made out of a box, in which I keep my breakfast-things, bread, cheese, etc.; finally, at the head of the tent, next my bed, used to stand my fine Sebastopol box, painted green, but as Roach wanted a chest to take home his clothes in, I gave it to him. A pile of packing-cases occupies its place, and on top of them I keep my uniform and clothes I wear every day. Round each tent-pole I have clasps with hooks, on which are hung my sword, pistol, lantern, dressing-gown, and other paraphernalia; between the two poles a cord is stretched, on which I hang my towels. So now I think I have given you a full and complete inventory of all my furniture, and I think you will admit that I am tolerably comfortable.

I believe a tent with fire is much warmer than a hut without fire, but the great puzzle is what to burn in a tent during the winter. I hear charcoal is not to be issued, and without it braziers are no use. To use a stove you must either bring the pipe outside through the door of the tent, which would be very inconvenient, or the pipe must be carried outside underground through the bank of the tent, when I am afraid the stove would infallibly smoke for want of proper draught. I am seriously thinking of committing the extravagance of sending home for one of P——t's army stoves, as being in a tent without fire in the winter in this climate would be misery. The fuel used in this stove is a preparation of cocoanut, and they say it gives out neither smell nor smoke. The hospital stoves have come, and I am going to have one lighted in my tent to see what sort of heat it throws out; you can also cook with it. The stove, with 102 pounds of fuel, sufficient for thirty-four days, costs £4 5s., packing-cases and all included; but what deters me is the expense of the fuel, which is 1s. 6d. a pound, and a pound lasts eight hours for warming and four hours for cooking—thus, warming the tent alone in the winter would cost at least 1s. 4d. a day, which is enormous. I fancy a hut will be nearly as cold as a tent in winter, only you will have much more room in it; but from what I see and hear I don't think any more officers will be hutted this year, and only about half the men.

I am sure I shall like the knife as you ordered it, but I am afraid the spurs at 4s. will be too small to put over long boots, for which I require them. I will, however, let you know when I get them. What shall I do with Roach's slippers now that he has gone home? How I should have enjoyed visiting the model of Sebastopol with you! Could you make out the position of our camp on it? I was delighted to get the children's hair. Ellie's is indeed lovely; Sonny's is something like Sophie's; let me know which of his sisters he is fondest of. I am glad he shows such an affectionate disposition, and I hope it will grow up with him. I am delighted to hear that you have lost your headaches, and trust you may not have any more of them, for I am sure they were all nervous and brought on by anxiety.

November 2.

DEAREST E.,

The mail which was due yesterday has not yet arrived, and I am afraid will be late. On October 30 I dined with General Codrington; we had only a small party, as besides himself and his A.D.C., Captain Ponsonby, of the Guards, there were only Goodenough and myself, an officer of the 90th, and Lord James Browne of the 7th, a brother of the Marquis of Sligo; he was with me the night I was taken. The next morning I was employed on the roads from 6 a.m. till 5 p.m. I thought we were going to have a change of weather, it looked so threatening, but the clouds blew off, and for the two following days we have had a most disagreeable sirocco wind from the south, which blows about quantities of dust; but I dare say when it goes down it will end in rain, for we cannot expect this unusually (long) spell of fine weather to last much longer.

My porch is progressing, and I hope it will be finished to-morrow. I am afraid, although I have a glazed door and a window to it, it will darken the tent greatly. I saw General Codrington on business yesterday, and took the opportunity of showing him the letter I had got from the Horse Guards, when he told me he thought I was clearly entitled to receive some mark of approbation, as my juniors had been promoted, and that if I was not included among the promotions shortly expected for the capture of the place to write him a strong letter on the subject, which he would back, so I must wait in patience. I had a visit yesterday from Mr. Adair, of the Coldstreams, whom you may remember as Captain of the Somersetshire Militia at Plymouth; he came to make a sketch of the tomb of a cousin of his in the artillery who was killed in the trenches and buried in the graveyard behind our camp. He tells me that Hinton has had a paralytic stroke, and is obliged to wear a moustache to hide his mouth being crooked; it is a great pity, for he was a nice-looking young man. Villiers went into the Turkish contingent, but has left it. I see a Medical Board is ordered on Talbot; he was looking very well when I saw him a few days ago, but I hear he has had a quarrel with Sir R. Airey, and that, I dare say, gave him a sudden illness. Nothing has been going on here lately; there was a heavy explosion from the central bastion (in the part of the works occupied by the French), but I have not heard whether any mischief has been done. There is a report that the French Emperor is going to confer two crosses of the Legion of Honour in each regiment out here, on whoever, whether officer or soldier, shall be recommended by the Commander of the Forces. I see by the orders that I am to be road-making again to-morrow, so I must close this to-night; I shall not have time to write a postscript in the morning, as I must be off by half-past six. I have just had a note from Stewart, dated October 31, on board the *Queen of the South* in Kazatch Bay, where she had arrived on the 29th; he says he doesn't know when they are going to Balaklava. They have several officers of other regiments on board, but he does not mention Colonel Daubeny.

I have just tried one of these Crimean stoves lighted in my tent for the last hour, and I do not think they answer at all; they throw out so little heat. I shall, therefore, not order one, but trust to getting charcoal. I wish, in the next box, you would send me out some candles, as they are very dear here (2s. 6d. a pound), and the allowances are not nearly as liberal as they were last winter, for I only get seven candles a month; so send me out a good supply, as I want them here more than tapes and buttons. I regret to say the mail is again late, and has not yet arrived. I hope, however, to-morrow to have had the pleasure of hearing from you.

I will now conclude with affectionate love to my dear mother, Kate, Annie, and Francis. Kindest regards to Miss Keys, and kisses and love to the dear pets.

Believe me, dearest Ellie,
Ever your affectionate
RICHARD.

LIGHT DIVISION CAMP,
November 5, 1855.

MY DEAREST OWN ELLIE,

Last Saturday, the 3rd, when I returned from the working-party I had been on all day, I had the happiness of getting your two dear long letters of October 16 and 18, together with the *Times* paper, but neither the *Illustrated News* of the 20th nor the two books which you and Kate were so kind as to send me. I trust, however, I may receive them by the mail that is due to-day. How very kind of you to write me a second letter in order to answer mine of October 2.

This is the anniversary of Inkerman. I don't think it likely the Russians will make a similar attempt again, as they will have far less chance than they ever had before. The reports from the spies say they are emptying their magazines, and sending their contents to the rear, which looks as if they intended retiring; but, on the other hand, they are busy throwing up batteries and fortifying their position, but that may be only for a feint. I think it a great pity that we don't try and strike a blow at Nikolaieff now that we are masters of the mouth of the Dnieper, but we must secure Odessa first as a base of operations.

Our weather has continued wonderfully fine, but for the last week we have had a sirocco wind blowing from the south, which has made it quite close and sultry, but I think when the wind changes we shall have rain. I had a long day on the roads on Saturday, but the day was very fine and I enjoyed it. I brought a feed for the pony, some bread and cheese and a bottle of cider for myself. The roads are progressing slowly, considering that there are 10,000 men at work on them every day, but I think they are on too grand a scale (30 feet wide). On making the road near where we were at work there was a very interesting discovery made some time ago of the remains of an ancient Greek temple, with some coins before the Christian era; there was also found a flat stone, the channels cut in it, and round it were vases of earth : this is supposed to be for the sacrifice of human victims, and the vases were to contain their blood, probably. Colonel Munro of the 39th, who is a great antiquarian, has charge of the excavation. I dare say a sketch of it will be given in the *Illustrated*.

My whole establishment, I am thankful to say, are in perfect health. The gray pony, which was lame for a few days, is all right again now. I generally rise at 6.30, breakfast at 8.30 on tea and something that is left from dinner—or fried pork, if any; lunch on bread and cheese, and dine at six on soup, which my servant makes very well, and either Irish stew or beafsteak pudding, according to whether the rations are fresh beef or mutton. Should it be salt beef, which I do not like if it could be avoided, I open a tin of preserved meat, which are sometimes very good and sometimes quite the reverse. I have not time to go to Balaklava, as every third day we are on the roads, and the other days my time is fully occupied with business and writing, and seeing my friends occasionally. Besides, anything out of the way costs immensely dear, such as eggs 2d. apiece, candles 6d., sugar 1s. a pound. I have always a cup of coffee at 8 p.m. I find candles a very heavy item, as I generally sit up late writing, and it begins to get dark now very soon, and the allowance of candles is not half what we used to get last year. There is no form of letter requisite to draw a balance out of Cox's hands; just write to him to send the amount to you, whatever it is, in a bank-post-bill. Mrs. Straubenzee is differently situated from you, my love. In the first place she has no children; next, her husband is a General Officer, and can command much more accommodation and comfort than I can. He has both a marquee and a hut at his disposal, has stables and coach-houses built for him, and is surrounding his premises with a wall to make him more private. This I can't do, as we haven't the space in our camp. But with all this, Mrs. S. is exposed to a great many discomforts to which a lady must find it hard to submit. I know, my dear Ellie, that you can rough it with anyone, and that you would willingly submit to any hardship to prove your love to me; but, believe me, it is best for both of us that you should remain where you are at present. I can well imagine what you went through in that agonizing time in April; it showed the deepness of your attachment to me, and God grant you may never be exposed to such a fearful trial again. I hope I shall get the books by the mail due to-day, but not in yet. I have just read 'Sunny Memories,' by Mrs. Beecher Stowe, and liked it very much. I have never heard of the other. I should be very glad to pay off Goff and charge as soon as we have saved the money, but could not think of applying Mrs. W.'s money for that or any other purpose.

I must conclude with affectionate love to all, and kisses to pets. I will give a postscript if the mail comes in.

Ever your affectionate
RICHARD.

LIGHT DIVISION CAMP,
November 8, 1855.

MY DEAREST OWN ELLIE,

So far as I can form any opinion of events, I should say that, if we have a successful campaign next year, and are able to wrest the Crimea from Russia, we will not do anything more in this quarter of the globe.

I do not suppose we shall be so foolish as to try to penetrate into Russia. The Brigade of the 4th Division has returned from Kinburn, but are still on board ship at Kazatch, and they say are to form part of an expedition which is to be despatched very shortly to Kaffa to take possession of it, as a highroad leads from thence to Simpheropol.

I have heard a report that the Commission has valued the English share of the guns and stores taken at Sebastopol at a year's pay for the whole army, but this I very much doubt. The poor fellow Boyce who lost both his arms got a neck- and not a pocket-handkerchief hemmed by the Queen, and so will be able to use it. It will indeed be a happiness, if God allows it, when we meet again to relate to each other all we have seen and heard and gone through since we parted. God grant that happy time may soon come! I am glad Campbell got the box safely; I suppose he has only gone as far as Malta. It was very remiss of Hibbert not sending out the first box you sent him. What excuse did he make for it? Stewart joined us on the 6th; Colonel Daubeny, I hear, has also landed, and I will call on him. He has not yet sent me the parcel, nor did he leave it at the parcel-office at Balaklava, whither I sent for it. I suppose Maxwell will arrive in a week; I shall be glad to see him, and will pay him for the whip. The laced-boots that you sent me I received in a box sent into Sebastopol, and are capital boots and fit me very well. The long-boots I bought were second-hand and not very good, but they will do to keep me out of the mud. I wish you would send me a new pair of laces for my laced-boots. Warm clothing for officers has arrived, consisting of fur-coats, caps, gloves, and long-boots, but we are to pay for them this time. The prices are not known yet. Last year the price of a fur-coat was £8, too much to give; the tweed coat lined with rabbit-skin (which I intended for you), the Turkish fur pelisse, and all the warm clothing I had from Government, were returned into store when I was taken, so I have only now my great-coat and an old pea-coat.

How very kind of my mother to send me an opera-glass from Malta! so like her usual thoughtful generosity. I must write and thank her for it. I hope it will be a nice one; they are certainly more portable than a telescope, and are clearer for a short distance of two or three miles, but they have not the range of a telescope. Laurie embarked yesterday in the *Andes;* he was very weak, but I hope will gain strength during the voyage.

My dear pet, I have never difficulty in making out your letters, you always write so well and clearly, but I am afraid you sometimes have great trouble to decipher my crossings.

I intend making Byron Adjutant; I think he is sharp enough if he will only apply. I trust you heard from your mother and Louisa, and that you received good accounts. That was a most audacious robbery at Annsbrook; no doubt the discharged servant was the robber. My porch is finished all but a little tarpaulin to put on where it joins the canvas of the tent, and it adds greatly to the warmth and comfort of the tent; the glass door, however, which I got in Sebastopol, has lost several panes, and I find it difficult to replace them. I am going to try a stove at the far end with a pipe going outside through the bank, and I hope it will not smoke. Flies, to my great annoyance, abound here everywhere. I was working on the roads yesterday near some old French camp, and on getting off my horse for a few minutes I was covered with them; they came out of the old rubbish. I am glad Miss Lebel's room is comfortable, but I am afraid it will be very cold in winter without a fire; I suppose, however, she dresses in the nursery, and the children could have your room as a schoolroom in the winter. Our weather still continues most lovely, although a little cool morning and evening, though I have not yet felt the want of a fire. The roads, I am glad to say, are expected to be finished this week, when the men are to be employed making roads about their own camps and getting up huts. It is expected that two locomotives will be ready to run on the railway this week, which will greatly facilitate the bringing up of stores.

Sir W. Codrington assumed the command of the army yesterday, and Sir J. Simpson goes home I hear to-morrow. They did not give the command to Sir C. Campbell, as he was not conciliatory enough with the French, and he would not serve under Codrington, who was his junior. Lord William Paulet is to have the Light Division; I hear him very favourably spoken of. Captain Bourke, who was on his Staff, has rejoined his regiment, the 88th; General Barnard is to have the 2nd Division, and General Windham is to replace him as Chief of the Staff. Before spring the army is to be divided into two corps of 20,900 men each: General Barnard is to have the right corps, consisting of 42nd Highlanders, 1st, 2nd, and Highland Division, and Sir William Eyre the left, composed of 3rd, 4th, and Light. They say he is a great Tartar and very bad-tempered. I have just seen in General Orders that my claims for losses have been allowed, and that I can get it paid on application to the commissariat, so I will try and remit you a bill for £20 by the next mail.

7 p.m.

The mail due to-day is not yet telegraphed, so we have no chance of it to-day. I went to-day to see the specimens of warm coats which are to be issued to such officers as like to pay for them. There are three sorts—first, seal-skin (not real) lined with cloth inside; second, pilot-cloth lined throughout with fur; and third, a tweed coat lined with rabbit-skins, like what we had given to us last winter. They are all good articles except the last, which I do not think will resist wet, and the prices are moderate —viz., £3 5s. for each of the first two, and £1 9s. for the last. I think I will treat myself to one of No. 2, as I shall require a warm coat; samples of the boots, caps, and gloves have not yet arrived. Did I ever tell you that we have put up stones in the Light Division burying-ground to the memory of all our officers that have died out here? One was put up first to Jordan and another to Lawrence, killed on June 6, and to the five poor fellows who fell before the Redan on the 18th, and we are having one cut now to poor Ramsey. The officers of the Light Division Provisional Battalion at Malta have put up a slab to the memory of Reay, who was highly respected by them, in the cathedral at Malta.

It is said, on the authority of Colonel Munday, of the 33rd, whose brother is secretary to Lord Panmure, that there is an iron star, made out of the captured guns, to be given for the trenches; but it is not yet fixed what amount of service in the trenches an officer must have done to entitle him to it. This will give much greater satisfaction than the clasp given for the capture of the place merely to those who happened to be present in the Crimea on September 7. It is also said that an Order of Merit for distinguished conduct is to be instituted. We have just been told that our letters must leave the camp in future at 6.30 a.m. instead of eight; I shall not, therefore, be able to give you my morning postscript in future, but must close at night. The mail, I hear, is in, but has only brought the official despatches. Sir W. Codrington is to be Commander-in-Chief, General Barnard is to have the Light Division, and General Knowles, who commands the camp at Aldershot, is to succeed him as Chief of the Staff. I hear Browne is out in the *Gazette*.

I must conclude with kisses to pets and affectionate love to all.

Ever your affectionate
RICHARD.

LIGHT DIVISION CAMP,
November 15, 1855.

MY OWN DEAREST ELLIE,

I have just had the happiness of receiving your long affectionate letter of October 26 and 27, and it gave me such pleasure to hear that you, the dear children, and all the dear party at Weston were so well, and that you were not suffering now from headaches, but were in good spirits and reconciled to our long separation, which I trust, however, may only prove temporary. Believe me, dearest, it was entirely against my own inclination that I advised your not coming to Therapia to see me, but for the reasons I have already given you I thought it best that we should both remain as we are for the present. The mail that was due on the 12th only arrived to-day; *that due to-day has not yet arrived.*

November 16.

DEAREST E.,

I had written so far yesterday, when I was interrupted by a terrific explosion, the ground shook under my feet as in an earthquake, the things were thrown down in my tent, some of the tent-hooks broken, and part of the side of the porch blown out. I at first thought a Russian shell had burst close to the tent, and was congratulating myself on my escape, when, on going out to see what was the matter, I heard another tremendous explosion and such a sight as presented itself. The air was filled with a dense cloud of smoke and dust, in the midst of which were hundreds of the largest shells, rockets, shrapnel, bursting and sending their splinters in all directions, and the noise of so many shells bursting at once was like a tremendous cannonade. In front of this cloud were about 100 frightened artillery horses that had broken loose, and they came rushing through our camp knocking down some of our men, and many of the horses themselves being thrown down by the tent-ropes. These were followed by a crowd of equally frightened artillerymen, all rushing from the explosion. When the panic had a little subsided, we found that the magazine of the French siege-train, 300 yards in the rear of our camp, in which was stored an immense quantity of powder (a good deal of it Russian), had exploded—how, is as yet not known, probably through some gross carelessness—and the fire unfortunately communicated with the English magazine in the English artillery park, full of live shell (they say at least 1,000), shrapnel and rockets, which also blew up and set on fire a quantity of gun-carriages and timber, and also the timbers (?) of the huts which were thrown down by the explosion; the fire raged till 8 p.m., and it was dangerous to approach it to try and extinguish it, as the ground was covered with live shell and rockets which had not gone off at the first explosion, but were thrown to a distance, and were sent off separately as the fire reached them. The loss of life among the French and in the Light and 2nd Divisions by this deplorable accident has, I am sorry to say, been considerable, besides a number of wounded and immense destruction of property. The greatest loss was sustained among a party of the division under Goodenough, who were making a road close to the artillery park when the explosion took place, and they had to run for shelter with the shells bursting all round them (a much heavier fire, while it lasted, than any that came from the Redan). When order was a little restored these men performed the hazardous service of moving out of reach of the fire such shells as had not exploded, and you may fancy how dangerous it was when some of the shells had to be dropped because they were too hot to be carried in the hand; English and Zouaves were working together, and vied with each other as to who should show most fearlessness. We lost one poor fellow in camp, and I believe our loss is less than those of the other regiments, as the greater number of the shells went away from our camp. I have just heard that the Light Division lost ten killed and sixty-nine wounded; the Artillery one officer, Mr. Yellånd, and seven men killed, and two officers (one of whom, Mr. Dawson, lost a leg) and forty men wounded. The loss of the 2nd Division I have not heard. Several shells burst in and over our camp; a piece of one went through my servant's tent and broke his bed. Dyer's tent behind mine and the orderly tent were both thrown down by the explosion, the poles having been broken. The rooftree of one of the hospital huts was also broken by the explosion, rendering the hut useless, and all the huts were shaken or damaged, more or less; the mess hut had the chimney partly thrown down, and nearly the whole of the side of one of our new cook-houses was blown out.

The huts in the neighbourhood have suffered greatly; the whole of the French hospital on the opposite side of the ravine was thrown down, and I hear a great many of the poor patients were injured; indeed, in every camp in the division you see huts thrown down and in ruins. A number of horses, frightened by the explosion, broke loose, and have not yet been recovered. Colonel Evelegh lost his horse this way; Major Bruce of the 23rd had his horse cut in two by a shell. Several of the artillery horses are still about; they had their harness on at the time, which was greatly injured. Some of the escapes were wonderful: a shell fell on the tent of Captain Travers, of the Artillery, and burst, tearing his trousers and wounding his servant in the calf of the leg; another burst in a mess-hut of the 33rd, when there were three officers in it, and blew out the side of the tent without doing them any injury. We were at one time apprehensive that the commissariat stores of our brigade would be burnt, as the fire went very close to them; and they are full of forage, fuel, and provisions, which would have been a great loss. Fortunately there was little or no wind; but what we were most apprehensive about was our powder magazine, the wind-mill (which has been so often given in the *Illustrated News*), which was about 300 yards from the fire—in fact it was between two fires, as a French commissariat depot was in flames beyond it; this mill contained between 40 and 50 tons of powder. The wooden roof was actually lifted up by the force of the explosion, and came down again in its place; and although two burning fuses of shell fell close round it, most providentially none fell inside. If it had blown up the consequences would have been awful; the whole of the division would have been blown into Sebastopol. We expected the Russians would have taken advantage of our disaster, and have attacked us this morning, and we were under arms before five, and quite ready for them if they had tried. Fortunately for us the ammunition that blew up was siege ammunition, which we don't now require. I visited the scene of the disaster this morning; it was a sad sight. Several bodies of Frenchmen and horses were lying close round the site of their magazine, and the ground was covered with bullets, fragments of shell, of gun-carriages and wheels, and ruins of huts. Deplorable as this accident has been, we ought to be thankful that more lives were not lost, considering the imminent risk that everyone near the place ran, and the destruction of both life and property was not so great as that caused by the storm of November 14 last year.

LIGHT DIVISION CAMP,
November 21, 1855.

MY OWN DEAREST ELLIE,

Many thanks for sending me the *Gazette* with Gordon's promotion, which was, just as I thought, on the same date that Captain Rickman, who commanded the 77th that night, got his; they were both promoted for the same affair. Gordon got his C.B. subsequently, and also A.D.C to the Queen and full colonelcy, and no one deserved or earned his promotion better. He was one of the most hard-worked officers of the army. He has lately rejoined from England, and called upon me a short time ago, and I was glad to see he had recovered from the wound he got on March 22. I got by last mail the two books 'Sunny Memories' and 'My Brother's Keeper,' which you and Kate kindly sent me; many thanks for them. The first I have read and like very much. I suppose they were detained at the post-office, which they have a right to do with books when they think the mail is too heavy. If we are to take the field next spring I think I will ask Boyce to buy me an opera-glass at Malta, as they are more portable and easier to use on horse-back than a telescope. If we take the field I shall want a few other things also—a new tunic which comes into wear next April, also a pair of trousers strapped with leather. We shall probably have to send an officer in a day or two to Scutari with warm clothing for the invalids there, and, if so, I shall be extravagant enough to ask him to buy me a Zante quilt for my bed in winter; they are made of wadded silk, and are very warm and light, and cheaper than a buffalo robe, costing from fifteen to twenty shillings. This is the first winter's day we have had, and it has been very cold with hard frost, but, fortunately, no wind, and my tent, with both curtains down, and a good fire in the stove, was very comfortable. I have made an improvement in my tent by putting a railing round it of old tent-poles and iron hooping. The ropes of a marquee stretch out much more than those of a bell-tent, and people are constantly tumbling over them of a dark night, and not only may hurt themselves, but their fall shakes the tent like a young earthquake. The railing, however, will stop all these calamities. We had our first snow last night; it was not very deep, however, and was away with the morning sun. The mountains are, however, covered with it, and look very beautiful.

I called this morning to see how Mrs. Straubenzee fared after the explosion. They were in a woeful plight: their chimney was partly thrown down, and their hut greatly shaken by the explosion, and poor Mrs. S. was slightly wounded herself in her foot by a splinter; they were living and sleeping in one room while repairing the damages of the other. I have lent him one of our best masons to rebuild his chimney, and he has promised me when he has done with it a glazier's diamond, which, as I have got glass, will enable me to fill up the empty spaces in my glass door, and make the porch much more snug and comfortable for the winter. The porch is a great comfort, as, when complete, the door will have twelve panes besides a pane above and a slide-pane at each side of the porch. This gives me so much light that on a cold day I can write with the door shut, while in a tent you must have it open.

November 22.

Good-morning, dear Ellie! This is a mild morning and favourable for building. Cumberland Row, as the line of houses at the upper end of our camp is called, is progressing rapidly; it consists of ten houses of various styles of architecture, but all very comfortable. In front is the main road of our camp, which we have just finished, and in front of that again is the omnibus-hut, or menagerie, which is in process of erection, and will be 72 feet long and 24 feet wide, and is to contain three Captains and ten Subalterns. The Captains will have a pen each, and the other five will be for the Subalterns, two in each compartment, which will be 18 feet long and 9 feet wide, where they will be very comfortable, the greatest objection being that all conversation will be heard from one end of the hut to the other. I have also commenced an orderly-room, as I find it very cold writing in the tent without a fire; it will be a very handsome edifice of white Inkerman stone from Sebastopol, pointed, and 12 feet square inside, with a good chimney, fireplace, and white stone mantelpiece, and I have an idea, if I find it very comfortable when finished, of shifting there and making the marquee the orderly-room. I took a long walk with Maxwell this afternoon through the dockyard and to the ruins of Fort Paul, which the Russians blew up on their retreat. We have constructed a 10-gun battery on them, but with what view I can't say, as it has not yet been armed. The docks are magnificent structures, and capable of containing very large line of battle ships; the lower ones are filled with water from the harbour, and the upper ones from the Tchernaya by means of a conduit leading from the aqueduct. We have sunk shafts in them ready to blow up at a moment's notice. In the water near Fort Paul they have thrown nearly thirty or forty field-pieces, which they did in their retreat. When they leave the north side we can easily fish them up and send home as trophies. By-the-by, the report from headquarters is that they are retiring. I hope it may be true. They were, however, working away at the north side as busy as possible at their old trade of making batteries, as if they were going to stay for another year.

LIGHT DIVISION CAMP,
December 3, 1855.

MY DEAREST ELLIE,

Very little of interest has occurred since my last to you, posted on the 1st. The weather has been very inclement, and still continues so: rain and sleet by day and sharp frost by night, with heavy gales of wind. Our church parade was interrupted yesterday by heavy showers of sleet; evening service is, however, performed in a hut, as the members attending are limited. I find that they have no more in store of the warm pilot-coats for officers, lined with fur, at £3 5s. each; so I have taken a tweed monkey-jacket, lined with rabbit-skin, like what we had last year instead. It is not anything like as warm or comfortable, but it only costs £1 9s., and it will do very well. Wyse, of our regiment, goes home to-morrow on leave till February 29 on very urgent private affairs, his father being in a dying state, and several leases will fall in by his death which will require Wyse's presence at home, his elder brother being in India. I take the opportunity of sending by him a small box with bits of the white stone of which the sailors' barracks, the principal one in Sebastopol, are built; they were used as a hospital during the siege, and I was taken there at first and remained there two days, during the whole of which time eight doctors were cutting off legs and arms as hard as they could from daylight till dusk in the room (*salle des amputations*) in which I was confined, and it was only separated by a partition from the part in which I slept; and although I could not see the operations performed, yet I could distinctly hear all the cries and groans of the poor wounded, for they did not use chloroform. Upwards of 500 wounded Russians, they told me, were brought into that hospital alone the night I was taken. This white stone all comes from the Inkerman quarries, and works up very nicely, as you can saw it like wood or cut anything out of it; so you may have an inkstand, or, better, a mortar for holding matches, as you have seen them made out of the Maltese stone, which is very like it, and have 'Sebastopol' cut on the stand of the mortar; or have a *presse-papier* made, with a grape-shot polished on the top, and 'Sebastopol, 1855,' cut on it. Wyse has promised to leave it at 4, Sidney Terrace, for you, and to call on your mother if he can. I like Wyse very much; he is a very gentlemanly, well-principled young man; his uncle is the English Minister at Athens. His family are from Waterford, and are Roman Catholics. I also put in the box to fill it up a few small bullets which I picked up about the trenches, a metal screw to hold the fuse of a shell, and a Russian 30-kopek piece, value about a shilling, wrapped up in paper. Although these are trifles, I hope you will get them safe. I received yesterday from headquarters your letter of August 3 returned from Riasan, and which I suppose was the last you sent there, as I think I must have now received all the letters you wrote to me in Russia. I was very glad to get it, although of so old a date, for it shows what deep affection you have always evinced for me, and how anxiously you wished to share my captivity in Russia, although, for your sake, I am glad you were not called upon to do so. The grand military steeple-chase, open to all officers of the allied armies, came off to-day; I did not attend, as I had a good deal of writing to do in the orderly-room, but good sport was anticipated. One of the stewards was the Vicomte de Tournon, a Frenchman of good fortune, and who has a capital stud of horses in France. He had a great desire to see the progress of the siege, but as the French do not allow amateurs to accompany their army to the field, to gain his purpose he was obliged to enlist in the Chasseurs d'Afrique, in which he is now corporal, and has been appointed standing orderly to Pelissier, whom he accompanies everywhere. I see by the paper that Westhead has been entertained at a public dinner at Wolverly, near his father's place, upon which occasion he made some very absurd speeches; among the decorations of the room in which the dinner took place was Westhead's forage-cap, which was shot through by a musket-ball at the time he was wounded.

I am delighted to hear that Annie is better, and that she has already felt some relief from an ointment Dr. Toynbee has given her. Tell her, with my love, that I often wear her cap, and find it most comfortable.

I have not half answered your letter, but I must conclude as it is now late—past 12 o'clock. I have had to write to-night other letters besides to you; among others, to Miss Nightingale, who is in a peck of troubles because one of her nurses wants to marry one of my sergeants at Scutari, which she does not at all approve of, nor do I. Tell Kate I hope to answer her letter by next mail. With kisses to the pets and love to all,

Believe me,

Ever your affectionate

R. D. KELLY.

December 4, 1 *a.m.*

Raining in torrents; I must pop into bed.

LIGHT DIVISION CAMP,
December 13, 1855.

MY DEAREST OWN ELLIE,

On the 11th, the day after I despatched my last letter to you, the mail came in, and I had the pleasure of receiving your affectionate letter of November 24, giving me the gratifying intelligence of your safe arrival at Weston, and finding the darlings and all the dear circle there so well. What a fine little fellow our darling boy must be! I am glad they were all so pleased with the presents you brought them, and especially that they enjoyed my letter. I haven't material at present for another letter, but you may tell them, as they are fond of hearing about animals, etc., that Dr. Dyer has got an owl which has splendid eyes, and is quite tame and eats mice, and that Malakoff was lost for a whole week and found in another camp and brought back. I am so rejoiced to hear that my mother's cough is so much better, and I trust she will not increase it this winter, but be prudent and not expose herself to cold or damp; her life is too precious to us all for her to risk it. That was certainly a most curious and interesting meeting that you and Annie had with Dr. and Mrs. Cameron; it is delightful to think how my father was beloved by all who knew him. I think Dr. Cameron is quite right in accepting a situation in Ceylon to one in the Crimea, the emoluments are so much greater. I wish I had the chance of commanding a regiment in India; I should like it very well, as in about five years I would save enough to clear off all the encumbrances on Mucklon. Do not fancy, my love, that I have any chance of being a General Officer for some time; there are too many full Colonels in the army, and I cannot expect to be a full Colonel for upwards of two years. I don't think they have any intention of giving C.B.'s or any more rewards to the army, as all the reports we heard about these honours have proved false, so I must only be patient and do as well as I can without it. We are to have 100 more medals given us in a day or two, but that number won't complete the men who came out in the first instance with the regiments, so my turn has not come yet.

I am so glad you completed yourself and the chicks with warm things for the winter; it is money well laid out. I told you in one of my former letters that I intended getting a warm fur coat, price £3 5s., for the winter. Well, on applying for one at the Quartermaster-General's stores I was told there were none, that only a few had arrived, and that they were all issued, but that they were expecting more; but although it is three weeks ago they have not yet arrived. I suppose they will arrive about the beginning of spring, when they will be of no use. It is fortunate I have my old pea-coat still with me. A third of the army is still without warm clothing, notwithstanding all the experience of last winter. Our winter is now commencing in earnest; to-day is a real Crimean day; yesterday was a delightfully mild one, a south wind blowing which dried up the mud and was making the ground quite dry, when at 6 p.m. it began to rain and poured in torrents till twelve. I never heard heavier rain except in the tropics; my tent was dripping, and I had to spread a waterproof sheet over different things to keep them dry; fortunately, the rain did not come on the side of my bed. The wind then changed suddenly to the north, and it froze very hard with drifting sleet, and a wind that pierced through you; the canvas of my tent this morning was as stiff as a board from the frost.

What a nice day's amusement the children had at Somerville! it was really very kind of Miss S. asking them all. I am glad they enjoyed themselves so much; I hope they behaved well. Which did they prefer the most—the magic-lantern or the Christmas-tree? I suppose the latter, as it contained presents for them.

LIGHT DIVISION CAMP,
December 21, 1855.

MY BELOVED ELLIE,

Our winter has commenced in real earnest, and for the last three days we have had excessively cold weather. On the 19th the thermometer in the day was three degrees below zero, accompanied by a piercing cold north wind. We had sixteen men frost-bitten that morning on parade, and that night an unfortunate artilleryman, who fell down drunk, was found frozen to death. That afternoon I walked with Maxwell on the Woronzoff road, which was like glass, and we might have skated the whole way into Sebastopol. The road was covered the whole way with fatigue parties, French and English; loaded with firewood, and many a poor [fellow] fell under his load from the slippery state of the road. I dined that evening with Lord W. Paulet, the General of our Division, and, although I was well wrapped up, had a most excessively cold walk, both going and returning, and even at dinner some of the party put on their great-coats it was so cold. In my tent ink, water, etc., were frozen solid. Lord William's A.D.C. is a Mr. Poulett, brother to Lord Hinton; he told me that his brother had not a paralytic stroke, but suffered from a dreadful abscess that extended from his shoulder to his spine.

Only fancy my ingratitude, when mentioning the different articles in the box sent by Campbell, to omit thanking you for the handsome and most comfortable slippers you sent me; but really I was so pressed for time, having deferred commencing my letter in hopes of the mail arriving, that I did not say half what I should; I hope you will forgive my neglect. The slippers fit me beautifully, and are very handsome, especially the small pair, which I have carefully put up for summer, and wear the large pair, which just fit my foot when enveloped in three pairs of worsted socks, which is my [word illegible] during the present cold weather. I assure you, my love, I value them highly as being your work, and they are so handsome and comfortable besides. I have given Maxwell my old worsted slippers that you made for me; he wanted a pair to wear inside long boots, and these just answered him. I hope the box sent by Roach arrived safe. Did he send you a note in an envelope I directed for him? I hope he will come and see you when in Ireland as he promised. I hope you have also received the white stone I sent home by Wyse and the mits from Bayne. Master Arthur seems rather fond of mischief and practical jokes which, though great fun to him, are not so to others; he should be firmly checked in it, or else some day he will do some mischief that we shall all regret. I am sure he is a great pet from his open, frank disposition; but he mustn't be spoilt or allowed to have his own way. I am so delighted to hear that dear little Annie is such a good child, and becoming more of a favourite; she has deep feeling and strong affection. How kind of my mother giving the children winter frocks, and also paying half the expense of my coat! she is indeed generous and liberal. I hope the man at Drogheda is a good photographer, and takes likenesses well. I think ours would make a nice group if they could only be induced to sit still.

I am afraid there is not much chance of peace at present, although there is so much said about it. The pretensions of both parties are too high at present, and the Russians have not yet been sufficiently beaten to make them sue for terms. Admiral Lyons has gone from this with the greater part of the fleet, and they say he is to be summoned to Paris to attend a Council of War to be held on next year's campaign. Sir W. Codrington will, they say, also attend. An English prisoner, who escaped the other day from Mackenzie's Heights, says the Russians are in great force there, and well supplied with provisions.

The French Government have placed at the disposal of the English several crosses of the Legion of Honour. Our regiment's share is three—two for officers, and one for a non-commissioned officer. Sir W. Codrington has named Simpson to receive one, who certainly deserves it, and I have recommended Gwilt and the sergeant-major for the others; it will certainly be a coveted distinction. I am so glad you have made a friend in Miss Somerville, as she appears so very amiable. There does not seem much to choose between the two candidates for Meath; both are as bad as possible. Let me know what French books you are getting. Our land-transport corps have almost shut up; they say they are losing 500 horses a day for want of proper shelter for them. The officers' baggage-horses are now employed in bringing up provisions for the camp. I do not think of anything that I require at present, unless you could send me a comforter to wear round my neck; it mustn't be too large, as I would wear it inside my jacket instead of a stock. The candles will be very acceptable when they arrive, as my allowance is only seven a month, and I burn one a night and pay sixpence apiece for the extra ones. Brine paid me a visit to-day, and tasted your cake, and begged me to tell you it is delicious; he expects Mrs. Brine out on a visit to him, as she says she is most anxious to take a house in Sebastopol. He must build a house for her, as at present he has only [a] small room. Poor thing! she will have to go through a great deal of discomfort. Mrs. Straubenzee's maid is a great annoyance to them—always grumbling and wanting to leave; she can't rough it as well as her mistress.

I must now conclude, my dearest Ellie, with affectionate love to my dearest mother, Kate, Annie and Francis, and kisses and love to all the darlings.

Believe me,
Ever your most affectionately attached
RICHARD.

LIGHT DIVISION CAMP,
December 23, 1855, 8 *p.m.*

MY OWN DEAREST ELLIE,

That Psalm you mentioned, xci., is indeed beautiful, and very applicable to my case, as, indeed,

I feel that I have been wonderfully protected against danger, which no merely human aid could have warded off; and may God give me grace to have always a grateful sense of His mercies to me! I hope Francis may get the farm, as it seems to be such a desirable one. Compensation in money is only given in cases of severe wounds, and to get it I should have had to be examined by a Medical Board, and as my wound was healed long before my return to the Crimea, that could not be done. We have heard nothing here about the distribution of Turkish medals to the British Army. I think I mentioned to you in my last about the crosses of the Legion of Honour that the French Emperor is going to distribute amongst us. I don't think our Government intend distributing any more honours to the army, so I think I will forward my claim without waiting any longer. Many thanks both to you and my mother for the books you are so kindly sending me. 'The Caxtons' is a most interesting and well-written novel; I read it at Riasan, and liked it very much. 'The Gambler's Wife' I have never read. We send all books when each has read them to the mess hut, that they may be circulated among the other officers.

It gratifies me very much to hear of the continued accounts that you and my dear mother give of the dear children. I am rejoiced to learn that they are all in such good health, and happy together, although, of course, like all children, they must occasionally have disputes; in these, I fancy that Mr. Daddah is the cock of the roost, and that his sisters give in to him without similar reciprocity on his part; he must not, however, be allowed to have too much of his own way. With all his little domineering and waywardness, I am sure his fine, generous temper and affectionate disposition must endear him to everyone. I am delighted to hear that Ellie and Annie are getting on so nicely with Miss Lebel, and are such good children. This is dear pet Sophie's birthday. God bless her and grant her many happy returns of them! Tell her, with a kiss, that this is papa's prayer and wish for her, and he hopes that when he next sees her she will say some of her hymns for him. I am so glad Mrs. Caffray is not going to leave you; she would be a great loss. I suppose Mr. Daddah's goat is now laid aside for the superior attractions of the cart and horse his grandmamma gave him. What nice presents she is always making the children!

This is quite a mild day, and thawing rapidly. We had afternoon service in the camp of the 90th; Lord William Paulet, his staff, and a number of officers attended.

This is a cold, raw, foggy day, but I think it will freeze hard in the night. To-morrow will be Christmas Day. God grant you all many happy returns of it, and that we may all pass the next together! Do you remember how we hardly hoped to have the pleasure of spending our last together at Plymouth? I am to indulge in the luxury of a goose to-morrow for dinner, and my servant is going to try and make me a plum-pudding, only there are no raisins to be had. I will, however, drink to the health and happiness of you all.

Will you, as I have not had time to write by this mail, thank my mother for that nice Christmas-box she sent me in that handsome scarf, which arrived so appropriately and was just what I wanted, so you need not send the comforter I wrote for? also thank her for her affectionate letter, which I hope to answer in a few days; it was so good of her sending the scarf. I got all the *Times* you sent, and their scraps; many thanks for them. I hope your mother and Louisa were quite well when you last heard; I am glad they are going to spend a little more time with their friends in the County Longford. Give my love to them when you write. I got the boot-laces; many thanks. I am so glad you have commenced singing again, and with such a nice companion as Miss Somerville. I have not yet had an answer either from the War Office or the agents to the letters I wrote about the £92 19s. 9d. being credited to my account. Have you heard anything about it? I have been detained so long in the orderly-room writing officials for the mail that I have had very little time to finish my own, and now they are waiting to take this to the post, and although I have not half answered your letters, I must delay doing so till next mail. God bless you, my dearest love! and with my affectionate love to my dearest mother and all at Weston, kisses to the dear pets, and kind regards to C. Keys, Miss Lebel, Mrs. Caffray,

    Believe me to be,
      Ever your most affectionate
         RICHARD.

        LIGHT DIVISION CAMP,
         December 27, 1855.

MY DEAREST OWN ELLIE,

  I do not put much faith in all the rumours of peace that we hear of in the papers, although, if Russia accepts the terms said to be proposed to her by Austria, I don't see what we can require more; but I don't think Austria is acting in good faith, nor do I think Russia is sufficiently humbled to sue for peace. We have heard to-day that the fall of Kars is unfortunately confirmed; the brave garrison was obliged to surrender from want of provisions, the men being so weak from hunger that they could hardly hold their firelocks. General Williams and all the English officers were made prisoners, but are to be exchanged immediately. Omar Pasha, who, after his victory, was advancing to the relief of Kars, has been obliged to return. I am afraid this capture of Kars will be a great blow to the Turkish campaign in Asia. Some of good authority think here that, if the war is renewed next year, the ensuing campaign will not be in the Crimea, but on the banks of the Dnieper, in the neighbourhood of Nikolaieff. I have not yet heard of the arrival of the *Batiania*, by which Hibbert sent the things you got for me in London. I had one of the tongues my mother sent me in Hibbert's box dressed for dinner with a fowl on Christmas Day, and it was very good ; I am reserving the goose for another day. My servant made me a very good plum-pudding, which I enjoyed. The men had excellent dinners on Christmas Day ; the band, especially, had fowls and geese roasted and baked, and one company had an entire sheep roasted whole, and all had plum-pudding. They have all plenty of money now—in fact too much, some of them.

The orderly-room is not finished yet. The frost has retarded building very much, but, excepting there being more space, I doubt its being more comfortable than a tent, except perhaps in stormy weather, when the flapping of the canvas is very disagreeable ; with a good fire in the stove I can keep the tent comfortably warm, except in very cold weather. The two cats generally sleep in my tent ; they lie between the two curtains close to the stove-pipe, and are very cosy. The omnibus hut is finished, and the officers are moving in ; the rooms are a good size, and are well-lighted, but I am afraid they will find them very cold unless they line them with paper and put oakum into all the chinks. Christmas

Day and yesterday were fine bracing days with warm sun and no wind, and, although frosty, very agreeable. To-day we have had a regular Black Sea fog, enveloping everything in a cold, clammy mist that is very penetrating. I dine to-night at General Straubenzee's, and will therefore say adieu for the present, as it is time to dress for dinner.

Leeson, who went on duty to Scutari, has not yet returned with my Zante quilt. The docks have not yet been blown up; the miners have to come on ships, which present great difficulties.

Good-morning, dearest Ellie! this is a fine, clear morning without fog. We had only a family party at General Straubenzee's last night—only himself and his brother, who is his A.D.C. We had the remains of the Christmas dinner—stewed turkey and fried plum-pudding —which were very good. I heard no news except that Sir J. Simpson, on his return home, met Lord Panmure at Haslar; he turned his back on him, considering he had been badly treated by him.

The French, it appears, blew up their share of the docks on the 22nd. The Russians fire constantly both on the docks and on the town, and appear to be training new gunners, which they can do with impunity, as their fire is never returned. Colonel Turner is the new Commandant in place of General Windham, and they have broken all his windows by shells and sent some through the roof of the house next his. I got the boot-laces all right; many thanks. I don't know that I want many things now. I have at last got a fur coat, cloth outside, from the Quartermaster-General's store, for which I am to pay £3 5s., and also from the same place a very good pack-saddle, well stuffed, with bridle, head-stall, and luggage-straps, for £2 5s.; and I shall perhaps write to Hibbert to send me a candle cooking-lamp, which, they say, are very useful. As Biggars in Drogheda has my measure he might make me a pair of strong Wellington boots, which you could send me when you have an opportunity, and also an india-rubber or gutta-percha water-bottle, as mine were sold. I can't think of anything else at present.

LIGHT DIVISION CAMP,
December 31, 1855, 5 *p.m.*

MY OWN DEAREST ELLIE,

I hear that the mail is signalled, and I trust to have the happiness of acknowledging one of your dear letters before the post closes at seven. And sure enough, just as I had finished these lines, the letters arrived, and I have had the pleasure of receiving your dear one of December 14 and 15, and was delighted to receive such good accounts of yourself and all the dear ones at home.

We have got a new chaplain, a Mr. Smith, to our brigade, who preached his first sermon yesterday, which I liked very much. After evening service Maxwell and I took a long walk with Colonel Lawrence and Dr. Fraser, of the Rifles; the former has only just returned from a long sick-leave, and has been appointed to command the Brigade in the 2nd Division. He is a most excellent, religious man. He told me that he took up my duty in the trenches when I was taken prisoner, and while the flag of truce was going on for burying the dead, Colonel Estcourt, the Adjutant-General, came down, and was lamenting my fate, when Colonel Lawrence told him it was not yet certain; he, however, thought it was confirmed, and telegraphed my being killed. After he was gone, but still during the truce, Dr. Fraser told me that he met a Russian officer, and asked him if I was a prisoner in their hands, to which he replied I was; and information was immediately sent to General Estcourt. I heard the other day from Jordan. Gwilt, Warry and Harman are still prevented by their wounds from joining. They find it very difficult to get recruits. Jordan was sent, however, to Dublin, where he got sixty-seven volunteers from the Cavan Militia, all little sturdy fellows. Bob has arrived at Malta in the *Culldon;* the ship took fire when they had been out four days, and burnt for one and a half hours when, fortunately, they got it under. I don't think either Bob or Campbell will have to come on till spring to the Crimea. Our weather continues very cold, but fine and healthy and very bracing. The Brigade marched out to-day and drilled for an hour.

They have just come for the letters, so with kisses to the dear pets, and affectionate love to all,

Believe me, dearest Ellie,

Ever your affectionately attached

RICHARD.

LIGHT DIVISION CAMP,
January 4, 1856.

MY DEAREST OWN ELLIE,

There is but little news here, everything going on quietly, and drilling and rifle practice being the order of the day. There is a general impression abroad that we shall leave the Crimea in the spring; that Sebastopol having been destroyed there is no object to be gained by staying; and that the Russian position is too strong to be attacked. It is all supposition, however, as to where we shall go; many think Asia Minor, as we could easily throw a strong force on the Circassian coast, and advance some way in the country long before the Russians could receive reinforcements. I don't think the French, however, will join us in campaigning in Asia Minor; perhaps they will occupy the attention of the enemy by an attack on Italy. I hope our land transport will be in an efficient state by the opening of the campaign, which it is far from at present. Their horses are now obliged to be not worked to get them in order for the spring, and the provisions and forage are now brought up from the railway depôt to the divisional stores by the regimental battalion horses and those of officers. Colonel Wedwell is now in charge of the land transport during the absence, on sick-leave, of Colonel McMurdo, and they say when he took over the department there were 4,000 horses that were returned on paper not forthcoming, so they could not have been very well looked after. The corps is also very much in want of men, and each regiment in the Crimea has been ordered to furnish fifty men to be attached to them, which will reduce the army by 3,000 effective men; but it is better to have a smaller army efficient than a larger one without the means of moving. Lord Panmure, Colonel Lawrence told me, hopes to have every infantry regiment completed to 800 rank and file by spring, but I doubt whether he will be able to accomplish it, as recruiting is getting so slack at home. We shall want 250 to complete, and I don't think the depôt can send fifty. Jordan, however, got sixty-seven volunteers from the Cavan Militia the other day, which is some help. I hear a very good account of the campaign has been published by Major Hamley, R.A. It came out originally in *Blackwood's Magazine*, and if you could get it, I should be obliged if you would read it.

It rejoices me to hear such continued good accounts of the darlings that they are good, well and happy. God bless them all! I suppose you will defer going to Dublin till your mother returns, and then I hope you will stay there some time and get all you want, not forgetting the frame for Novosillekeff's picture. I am glad you will then be able to pay Roper £100 of his bill, which ought to satisfy him for a year. You will find this a very dull, uninteresting letter, but I have no news, and I have not one of your dear letters to answer.

The two brigades had a great snow-balling match to-day in the ravine, and the snow-balls were flying about like hail.

With love and kisses to the pets, and kind regards to Miss Lebel and Mrs. Caffray,

Believe me, darling Ellie,
Your most affectionate
RICHARD.

P.S.—I have written to Hibbert to send me one of Clarke's cooking-lanterns, which do lighting and cooking at the same time; price — with eight packets of candles—35s.

LIGHT DIVISION CAMP,
January 5, 1856.

To Major-General Lord William Paulet, C.B.

MY LORD,

I do myself the honour of addressing you under the following circumstances :

On September 18 last, immediately after rejoining my regiment on my release as prisoner of war, I addressed a letter to the Commander of the Forces, through Lieutenant-General Sir W. Codrington, then commanding the Light Division, pointing out a mistake affecting myself that had occurred in the despatch, dated March 24, of the late Lord Raglan reporting the repulse of the Russian sortie on the night of March 22, in which it was stated that the troops engaged in the repulse of the first of these sorties were under the direction of Major Gordon, R.E., whereas they were under my immediate command, and my statement having been confirmed by Sir W. Codrington, it was forwarded by the then Commander of the Forces, Sir J. Simpson, to the Commander-in-Chief. On October 6 an answer was returned by the Military Secretary admitting the error, and stating that my letter should be duly recorded. Since that date a number of officers have been promoted for services in the field, and some junior to myself— Campbell (80th), Wetherell (Guards)—have been promoted over my head, while in my case a bare acknowledgment that an error has been made has been considered sufficient, and even this rectification has not been published in the *Gazette*, as has been the case in other instances, both previous and subsequent to my letter, when errors or omissions have been made in the despatches. Had the affair been considered of no importance, or had no officers been rewarded for it, I should have been silent as to the error; but when I saw that Her Majesty was graciously pleased to express her approbation of the conduct of the officers and men engaged on that occasion, and that, as a mark of it, Major Gordon, who was supposed to have had the command of the troops, and Captain Rickman, 77th, also under my orders, received brevet promotion, and that the late Lieutenant Marsh, 33rd Regiment, who acted as my Adjutant, was, I am informed, promised a brevet-majority on his obtaining his company, I had hoped, having taken an equal share with these officers in the repulse of the enemy, and having had, in addition, as senior officer, the entire responsibility of the defence of the trenches, that, when the mistake was admitted, I also would have received some mark of Her Majesty's approbation, unless some reason existed to the contrary, of which at present I am not aware.

[To show the responsibility of the post that I had the honour to hold, I may mention that, from Prince Gortschakoff's account of the affair published in the *Invalid Russe*, it appears that the trenches of the right attack were attacked that night by the following force, viz.: four companies of Greek Volunteers, 260 sailors, and the 6th Battalion of the regiment of Minsk, amounting altogether to at least 1,200 or 1,000 men who attacked us in front, while at the same time we were attacked in the rear by part of the force sent against the French trenches adjoining our own, and who, after having entered them, turned to their right into our own. The guard of the trenches under my command consisted of 1,200 men, 400 of whom were posted in the 21-gun battery, considerably in the rear of the advanced trench, and who did not take any part in its defence; of the remaining 800, 300 were employed as a working party, leaving 500 men alone immediately available for the defence of a trench about 1,500 yards long. I beg to state that I was not taken by surprise, as, from the fierce assault that commenced early in the night on the French trenches, I anticipated that an attack would probably be made from them on our right flank, and to guard against such an attempt I had thrown out a company of the 77th Regiment under Captain Rickman, in extended order, supported by a company of 88th.

N.B.—In the letter I sent I omitted this last paragraph as I was afraid of making it too long.]

In Lord Raglan's despatch of March 27 it will be found that Major-General Sir W. Eyre, the General of the day, was pleased to express his entire approbation of the dispositions I had made for the defence of the trenches, and Lord Raglan's despatch of March 22 will show that these dispositions were perfectly successful, for it states that, although the enemy attacked us in front and rear at the same moment, he was repulsed on both points. When the attack took place, I, together with Major Gordon, accompanied the detachments 97th Regiment that sallied from the trench and repulsed the party that attacked us in front, on which occasion Major Gordon was so severely wounded as to be obliged to leave the trench and return to camp. Far be it from me to undervalue the services of so distinguished an officer as Major Gordon, but I may fairly ask, What did he do on that night more than I did? We both shared the same dangers, but on me and not on him rested the responsibility as senior officer. Yet, when it was supposed that he held that position, he was promoted, although, when the mistake was pointed out and admitted, a bare acknowledgment of the error is considered a sufficient recompense for me.

My friends, in whose opinion I desire to stand well, will naturally think that some reason must exist for this distinction. It surely cannot be because I had the misfortune to be wounded and taken prisoner during the second attack of the enemy, made later during the night, on our extreme left. If such be the case, I can only say that I was taken when in the active discharge of my duty. As soon as I heard the firing on the left I proceeded thither with a reinforcement of the 7th Fusiliers, and having gone alone a little in advance in order to rally the guard of the trenches, I fell in with a party of Albanians, by whom I was knocked down and bayoneted, and but for the humane interposition of a Russian officer (who in doing so received himself several blows of butt-ends) would most probably have been murdered by these savages as I lay on the ground.

I regret being obliged to weary you with these details, but I cannot help feeling strongly at having been passed over in the way I have been, and I accordingly trust you will have the goodness to forward my letter for the favourable consideration of the Commander of the Forces, who had previously kindly promised to support my claim.

I have etc.,
R. D. KELLY.

CHAPTER XII

RUMOURS OF PEACE

Light Division Camp,
January 18, 1856.

My own dearest Ellie,

Last night I had the happiness of receiving your welcome letter of December 27 and 29, and was thankful to find by it that you and all the dear circle at Weston were in the continued enjoyment of good health. I am sure, my dear Ellie, that you very naturally think it strange that I should not have asked for leave to come home when so many other officers had obtained it, and I now, when, alas! it is too late, bitterly regret that I did not do so, as I am afraid it has caused you great pain and anxiety, but I trust you will believe me when I say that nothing but a sense of duty has kept me here. You can easily imagine that if I could have followed my own wishes and inclinations how eagerly I would have flown to you, but I own I was afraid that by so doing I might suffer in the estimation of my superiors, and that reflections, perhaps just, perhaps ill-natured, might be cast on me. It might be said of me: 'He was absent during all the hard work of the siege, and now, after rejoining, he wishes to go away again and leave others to do his duty.' I know I am very sensitive to public opinion—it is one of my many weaknesses; but at the time I acted as I thought was right, although it cost me many a bitter pang. I now think that I have perhaps acted overstrictly, and that I might have asked for leave as well as another; and this thought has given me great pain, for I fear that by my irresolution I have not only deprived you and others, as well as myself, of happiness that you had a right to expect, but have caused you unnecessary anxiety, and have given grounds for some to suppose that I am not so anxious to come home as others. But you, my dearest Ellie, will, I am sure, from your long-tried affection for me, do me the justice of believing that that at least was never the reason, and will excuse and forgive me for having, under the circumstances in which I was placed, allowed my duty as a soldier to prevail over that of a husband and father.

It is now too late to ask for leave, as none is granted beyond February 29; and within that time it would be impossible for me to do more than get home, only to return immediately. We must still put our trust in that merciful God who has been so good and gracious to us, and hope that His care and protection may be continued to us, and that before long, in His own good time, we may be reunited. I fervently hope we may soon have peace, which would give me an opportunity of leaving the army without discredit; but I am afraid there is but slight chance at present, as I do not think Russia is sufficiently humbled to make her accept the terms offered by the Allies, nor that Austria or Prussia will be induced to assist in compelling her to accept them by force. The plan for the ensuing campaign, if formed, is kept a profound secret here, and it is only conjectured that a part of the force will be sent into Asia Minor. A considerable force must, however, remain to garrison Balaklava and Kamiesch, where we have such a quantity of stores and material—at least, till they are embarked. Rumour has named several divisions as likely to proceed to Asia. I have not heard, however, ours mentioned yet as among the number. The 1st Corps, under Sir C. Campbell, will, it is said, consist of 1st, 2nd and Highland Divisions. Every exertion is being made to get the Land-transport Corps into working order, but they are still deficient of a great number of horses. Officers have also been warned to provide themselves with pack-saddles and field-equipment, which I have already done. I am glad Captain Bourke arrived home safe. My pony has quite recovered from the kick he got, and is in capital condition, and carries a beautiful coat. My other pony has been usefully employed in bringing up wood from Sebastopol, of which I have now an abundant supply, quite sufficient to last to the end of the winter.

LIGHT DIVISION CAMP,
January 24, 1856.

MY OWN BELOVED ELLIE,

What a state of excitement the wholy army has been thrown into of anxious hope that the news may be true, and yet of fear lest it should be too good to prove so, by a report that has been received here, not generally believed, that Russia had accepted the terms of the Allies, and that peace will soon be concluded! I first heard on Tuesday that Admiral Fremantle at Balaklava had heard from Admiral Gray at Constantinople that a telegraphic despatch had been received there from Vienna stating that Russia had accepted the terms proposed by Austria on the part of the Allies. Still, the news was thought so improbable that few credited it, and the general impression was that an error had been made in the despatch, and the word 'not' had been omitted; that it should have been 'not accepted.' Yesterday it was reported on good authority that Marshal Pelissier had officially communicated the same intelligence to Sir W. Codrington, which seems to remove all doubt on this subject. We are now anxiously waiting the arrival of the English mails to confirm the good news; the one due on the 21st has not yet arrived, and another is due to-day. God grant the news may be true! Oh, what a happy prospect, to be able to see your dear face again, and the dear children, and all whom I love most on Earth! I trust we may not be doomed this time to disappointment.

Even if peace should be happily concluded, it will take our army some months before it can leave this with all its stores and encumbrances. I wonder where we shall be sent to. What speculation the future presents! I, humbly trust that a happy and speedy meeting may be in store for us; but we must not repine. We have been wonderfully blessed, and we must be patient and wait God's own good time. I, however, have been castle-building, and I hope my plans may not prove visionary. If this news should be happily confirmed, it is my intention (D.V.) to ask for leave as soon as possible—say to April 30 next—and to travel by Marseilles and Paris, and to ask you to join me at Paris, and to spend a few days there with me. Would not that be a nice plan? If I got leave, I would write to you by the mail before I started, telling you when I was going to embark. On receipt of that letter, I would propose your going up to your mother's in Dublin, as there you would get letters and messages from me sooner than at Weston. I would also (D.V.) write to you from Constantinople and Malta, and on reaching Marseilles, if practicable, send you a telegraphic message, or, if that is impossible, a letter, the receipt of which should start you for Paris; and in the meantime you might write to your friends the Whites, who I dare say would look out for lodgings for us; and the way to meet in Paris would be to ask Mrs. White to leave at Galignani's English Library, 18, Rue Vivienne (where I would call immediately on my arrival in Paris), a note with her address, which I do not know, and I would call there and learn particulars of you, or perhaps have the happiness of finding you there. You should try and persuade Francis to be your escort, and if Kate would accompany you what a nice addition she would be to the party! This plan seems almost too fraught with happiness to be realized. If circumstances should prevent you joining me at Paris, I should make no delay there, but proceed straight to London, where I must go, and look for the pleasure of joining you there. I shall, however, hope to find a message at Paris in case you can't come, saying where we are to meet in London—I suppose at your old lodgings in Jermyn Street; but I do hope you will be able to come to Paris. What delight it gives me making all these plans! I firmly trust we may not again be doomed to disappointment.

I have not much other news to give you. There was a rumour that the 3rd Division were to go to Kertch, which, if the war continues, would certainly require to be reinforced, as it is very much exposed to attack by the Russians; but I suppose nothing more will be done till this news is confirmed or not. The Russians made an attempt a few nights ago to cross the Tchernaya with pontoons, but were repulsed by the French pickets; and as they were not in force, I suppose it was only done to try the vigilance of the French pickets. They continue, however, their fire night and day on the town, but do very little mischief.

Our weather since I last wrote has continued damp and foggy; we had no such mild weather last winter. The fogs perhaps have been the cause of the delay of the mail. I hope it may arrive to-day. Mrs. Brine, I hear, has arrived, but I have not seen her yet. I, however, must call. I have also heard that Dr. and Mrs. Powell have arrived out here; but I don't know where they are stationed.

8 p.m.

I am happy to say that both the mails have arrived, and that I have had the delight of receiving your two dear letters of January 4, 5 and 8, and also your scrap of the 9th, sent in the *Times*. Many thanks for them all, and also for the nice comforter, which I also safely received.

LIGHT DIVISION CAMP,
January 27, 1856.

MY OWN BELOVED ELLIE,

The mail due to-day is not yet signalled, but I trust it will arrive with the confirmation of the happy news of peace, the rumours of which, I am happy to say, gain strength every day, although the Russians still continue to fire on the town. The latest reports say that the terms proposed by Austria on the part of the Allies were accepted by Russia on the 16th inst., and that it was stipulated that the Crimea should be evacuated by our armies within forty-five days of the signing of the Articles; but I doubt very much whether we could embark our army with all its stores and encumbrances in that time. Sir William Codrington was in our camp on the 26th, and we asked him what he thought about the reports of peace, when he said he had sent a despatch announcing it that Marshal Pelissier had received, which he considered almost as good as official, but that he himself had heard nothing from our Government, which is very extraordinary. They say both the Ambassadors, French and English, at Constantinople have had it announced to them. In fact, everyone implicitly believes it, and we are all anxiously looking for the official confirmation, which I am afraid, however, will not arrive before the mail of Thursday next, the 31st. Oh, how thankful we should feel to the Giver of all good for having so unexpectedly put an end to this dreadful war, and thus, I trust, having the happiness of being restored to one another! It appears almost too much happiness to be realized.

5.30 p.m.

I am happy to say the mail has just arrived, and I have just had the delight of receiving your long affectionate letter of January 11 and 12. We have also received papers of January 15, and I see that the *Times* of that date states that the Russians have only partly accepted the propositions of the Allies, and that they have refused to cede the required territory on the banks of the Danube, or to promise not to fortify the Aland Islands; and without both these terms are agreed to, I suppose we shall not make peace. Whether Pelissier's despatch is a later date than the 15th, and that the Russians subsequently accepted those terms, I can't say; although the reports here say that the terms were accepted at St. Petersburg on the 16th, which, of course, would not be known in London till the 17th at the soonest. God grant the report may be true, but we must be prepared for disappointment in this as in many other things of this life. The mail due on the 31st will, however, I suppose, clear up all doubts as to peace, as January 18 was the latest date to which the Russians were given to give their answer. Of course, till it is known positively that there is peace, I can't apply for leave; and till you get my letter saying I have got leave, you, of course, will not take any step about going to meet me. I trust my next letter will give you some decisive news one way or the other, for nothing is worse than being kept in suspense; and God grant it may be favourable news! If the news of peace is confirmed I shall apply for leave, and if I get it would like to go home by Marseilles and Paris, in order that I might have the happiness of meeting you there and our seeing Paris together.

February 1, 5 p.m.

DEAREST E.,

I was sent for this morning by Sir W. Codrington to speak to me about my leave, and I regret to say he could not grant it at present, as he said the reports of peace are not as yet sufficiently confirmed to allow of his permitting any officer to leave the army at present. He told me he knew nothing officially about the peace, only what he saw in the papers; and he did not know whether Russia had accepted the terms proposed by Austria unconditionally, or only as a basis for further negotiations. He received me very kindly, and I am sure when peace is once confirmed I shall have no difficulty in getting leave. We must submit to this trial with patience, and wait till it is God's good time to restore us to each other; and let us pray that the rumours of peace may be well founded. I don't know what to make of the reports in the papers. The *Times* of the 17th says the Russians have accepted the terms unconditionally, and in the leading article of the 18th advises the public not to put too much confidence in the reports. However, if Russia tries to shuffle off after having accepted the terms of Austria, I think Austria is bound to declare war; and if so I think one campaign, if successful, would finish the war. Let us hope, however, that all will happily end in peace. How we shall long for the next accounts, as I suppose something decisive one way or the other must be known at home by this time!

We have got quite a return to winter again. The rain turned to snow last night, and we have now a white world and cold weather once more.

I will now conclude, with affectionate love to my dear mother, Kate, Annie and Francis, and love and kisses to all the darlings. Kind regards also to Miss Lebel and Mrs. Caffray, and, with fondest love to yourself,

Believe me,
Ever your most affectionately attached
RICHARD.

LIGHT DIVISION CAMP,
February 4, 1856.

MY OWN BELOVED ELLIE,

Since I last wrote to you on the 1st, nothing of particular interest has occurred. We are still anxiously expecting the confirmation of the happy news of peace. By the latest papers that we have received—those of January 19—it seems as if they almost doubted the news being true, and that they suspected some duplicity on the part of Russia. We, however, in the Crimea are very sanguine about it, and think that the French Emperor would not have permitted a notification to be affixed in the Bourse at Paris, that Russia first accepted (*pur et simple*) the terms proposed by Austria, if such had not been the case. I suppose, however, the English Government will take care to know for certain whether there is to be peace or war before the meeting of Parliament, in order that it may be announced in the Queen's Speech, which we are anxiously looking for, and which in ten days, I suppose, we shall receive. I presume that the acceptance of these terms by Russia will lead to a negotiation to settle the details, and that in the meantime an armistice will be concluded. At any rate, I think it will take some time before the Crimea can be evacuated. I suppose you were equally astonished and delighted to hear of the reports of peace, and although we have been both greatly disappointed at my not being able to get away on leave immediately to see you, yet if these joyful rumours are happily confirmed, how thankful we should all feel that you are now spared so much anxiety on my account, and that—please God!—before long there is every prospect of my having a happy meeting with you and all the other loved ones at home.

The mail due to-day was not telegraphed till 5 p.m., so there is no chance of having one of your dear letters to answer this evening, nor have I much news of interest to give you, so I am afraid you will find this letter rather a stupid one. We have had a return of our winter weather. Yesterday and Saturday were very disagreeable days, very high wind with heavy showers of snow, hail and sleet, and hard frosts at night. To-day, however, was very fine and calm, with a bright sun. Maxwell and I had a long walk towards the Redan. While we were out, Fort Nicholas (the largest fort in Sebastopol, and in which I spent some time as a prisoner) was blown up by the French in three successive explosions. The report was not at all loud: you saw an immense black cloud go high up in the air, and when that cleared away nothing but a heap of rubbish remained on the spot where Fort Nicholas once stood. To show you the great force the sun has, even now I can tell you that I pulled a yellow crocus in full blow this afternoon growing in the snow.

Lord William Paulet is busy making the inspection of the different regiments of his division. While inspecting the 23rd this morning, an unfortunate accident occurred to Colonel Bonbury, who commands them. The ground being very slippery from the frost, his horse slipped and fell on him, and, the horse being large and he a heavy man, he was very much bruised, although, fortunately, no limb was broken. A dreadful murder has been committed in the 77th Regiment. A poor wounded artilleryman was in the hospital, and he was attacked by one of the hospital orderlies with a crowbar; he broke his arm the first blow, and killed him with the second. On being asked, he could give no motive for the horrid deed, but said he was actuated by an impulse which he could not resist; he has been tried by a general court-martial and will, it is generally supposed, be executed. Out here we say that one of the strongest symptoms of peace is that General Windham, the Chief of the Staff, has shaved off his beard. Did I tell you that Dr. and Mrs. Powell have gone back to England with invalids in the *Thames?* Gordon, Westhead and Harman have all been ordered out to Malta. I wonder how Cassidy manages to keep so long at the depot, for I see he is no longer rifle-instructor. I got a letter by last mail from Hayter and Howell, telling me that my box had left on January 10 in the *Edina*, so I hope I shall soon receive it. They directed the letter to Colonel Kelly, 88th Regiment, so I did not get it till next day. I suppose they thought I ought to be a Connaught Ranger from my name. I hope your cow has turned out a good milker, and that she has given you a good calf. Have you ever heard from Phillips whether he has sent me out my coat or not? for I have heard nothing about it. He should have let me know by what ship he was sending it. This is the last of my stamped envelopes, and I should be much obliged by your sending me a few stamps as sometimes they are very difficult to get out here; the post-office at present is quite out of them. I hope to-morrow the mail may arrive, and that I may have the happiness of getting good accounts of you all. I trust the dear pets are well, and that they will escape very severe colds this winter. Do Ellie and Annie write yet?—that is, are they out of pot-hooks and hangers? Has little Sophie mastered her letters yet? I presume Mr. Daddah is excluded from the room during school-hours, or else he would make too great a 'tappage' with his hammer. I trust he is as well as ever. The bugle has gone for the letters, so I must conclude in haste, with affectionate love to my dear mother and all at home, and kisses to the dear pets; and with warmest love to your dear self,

Believe me, dearest Ellie,
Ever your most affectionately attached
RICHARD.

LIGHT DIVISION CAMP,
February 6, 1856.

MY OWN BELOVED ELLIE,

Yesterday morning, on my return from the Redan, where I had been on duty, I had the happiness of finding that the mail was in, and of receiving your affectionate letter of January 19. I can easily imagine how you and all the dear circle at Weston must have rejoiced at hearing the glad tidings of an expected peace, and how your hearts were filled with gratitude to our Almighty Father for having heard our prayers and granted so fair a prospect of being soon restored to each other. I think we both, as well as the public in general, were a little too sanguine on first hearing the news that peace would ensue immediately on acceptance of the proposed terms by Russia. I see now by the further information given in the English papers, that although it is most probable that peace will be shortly concluded, yet at present it cannot be considered as positively certain, and that negotiations must be entered into involving a great deal of discussion, in which Russia will do all in her power to try and modify the terms, and all this will cause delay; but, still, I think peace will be the result, as it is absolutely necessary for Russia, and Austria and France are both anxious for it, and although England is less anxious for peace than the other Powers, as being better prepared to put out her strength by sea and land this year than she was last, and has her character for military and naval renown to retrieve, France having as yet monopolized the lion's share of the glory. Should, however, Russia accept in good faith the proposed terms, no such selfish consideration would, I trust, prevent England from being satisfied with them also, and thereby putting a stop to the frightful waste of blood and treasure that the war has hitherto cost. But we must still exercise a little more patience till all these points are settled, which, I suppose, will be before the meeting of Parliament; as until he gets this information I don't think Sir W. Codrington would give leave for any officer beyond February 29.

A rumour is prevalent here that the negotiations for peace are to be held in either Paris or London, and that an armistice is to be granted till March 31, by which time the negotiations must be either finally concluded or broken off; and I think it is very probable that some arrangement of this sort will be made. I should like to know very much what you think of the proposed rendezvous in Paris, in case I should get leave, as I shall most probably receive your answer to this letter before there is any chance of my leaving this; and if you thought it feasible, and that it could be done at a moderate expense, I should very much like to gratify both myself and you by making the trip. I don't know, however, what balance Cox had up to December 31, nor if that sum would last you till March 31. I have drawn nothing from the agents since the cheque for £3 I sent to Campbell for the opera-glass. I have still sufficient money in the Paymaster's hands. I can fancy what delight you must all have been in at Weston when Francis returned home with the good news, and how your faces must have beamed with joy and thankfulness.

LIGHT DIVISION CAMP,
February 11, 1856.

DEAREST ELLIE,

The mail, I am sorry to say, is not telegraphed, so I am afraid I shall not have the pleasure of answering one of your dear affectionate letters. I have not much news to give you, as nothing of importance has occurred since the 8th, when I last wrote. Our weather continues wonderfully mild for the season. Yesterday was a lovely day, and our brigade paraded for Divine service in the open air without winter clothing, and we did not feel it at all cold. Afternoon service was in the chaplain's hut. Mr. Seddall, 33rd, acted clerk and organist, playing on a seraphine as a substitute for the organ. At morning service the bands of the different regiments play. We are anxiously looking for the Queen's Speech to give us some insight as to whether we are to have peace or war. We shall not, however, receive it before the 14th. I think the Allies will give the Russians till April 1 to come to terms, and if by that date a treaty of peace should not be concluded in all respects satisfactory to us, that the war will be proceeded with. God grant, however, that peace may be concluded, and that I may have the happiness of being restored to you and all who are so dear to me! Oh, how I long for that moment!

I saw in the *Times* a statement that the Russian Government had despatched on January 18 an order from St. Petersburg for the cessation of hostilities. However, if such should be the case, the messenger cannot have arrived here yet, for hostilities have by no means ceased, and the firing to-day on the part of the Russians has been heavier than I remember for a long time past. They have been firing regular salvoes from their batteries; what provoked them a good deal, I dare say, was seeing Fort Alexander go up in the air, which the French blew up at ten o'clock to-day in very neat style with Russian powder. I was out riding at the time, and saw it go up with a tremendous explosion; the wind blew all the smoke and dust over the north side, which, I dare say, prevented their batteries from opening fire for some little time after. There only remains now the quarantine fort and the remainder of the sailors' barracks to be blown up, which I suppose they will try and get on with as fast as possible, in order to have them all destroyed before peace is concluded.

We are endeavouring now to get as many prize guns as we can out of the town, and I saw one of them upset to-day in a ditch in the Woronzoff ravine. It was a Russian 36-pounder, and was drawn by fourteen artillery horses. They, however, kept too close. The ditch, breaking under the weight of the gun, over it went, dragging one of the shaft horses into the ditch with it, which, after a good deal of trouble, was extricated without injury. The gun will give them a good deal more trouble to get out. The Light Division, I was informed to-day, are not now to go down to Balaklava, which I am very glad of, as it would have been a great nuisance moving, now that we are so comfortably settled. Our regiment, however, marches down to Balaklava to-morrow to exchange at the ordnance stores our present Miniés for an improved weapon—the Enfield rifle—with which the whole army is to be armed. You see, although there is a prospect of peace, we still continue our preparations for war. This exchange of arms will be a long business, and will keep us the best part of the day at Balaklava. I hope, therefore, the weather will be fine. This evening threatens rain. I called on Saturday on Mrs. Brine, but found she was staying at Balaklava on a visit to some friends.

I have just finished a very interesting little work by Dumas, the 'Maître d'Armes,' being the memoir of a French fencing-master who was in St. Petersburg during a most interesting period, just at the commencement of the reign of the Emperor Nicholas. It forms one of the numbers of the Travellers' Library, and has been very well translated by the late Marquis of Ormonde, and I think if you could get it to read you would like it. It is very short. By the way, I have not received Mr. Russell's letter, which you so kindly sent me; I am afraid it has gone astray. I see by the papers that Buckley has joined at Chatham. Have you heard anything more about our baggage at Plymouth—whether it can remain there or not? I trust you paid your intended visit to Dublin to your mother, and found all well at Sidney Terrace. It is a long time since you have seen them. I suppose Wyse will be about starting now to rejoin.

With kind love to my dear mother, Kate, Annie, and Francis, and loves and kisses to all the darling pets, kind regards to Miss Lebel and Mrs. Caffray, and affectionate love to yourself,

>Believe me, dearest Ellie,
>>Ever your fondly attached
>>>RICHARD.

>LIGHT DIVISION CAMP,
>*February* 15, 1856.

MY OWN PRECIOUS ELLIE,

The papers, I see, still continue very sanguine about peace, although the Queen in her Speech expresses her determination to continue the preparations for war till peace is actually concluded, in which I think Government are perfectly right. I see Lord Clarendon in his speech entertains a doubt as to the sincerity of Russia, but I think the Emperor has gone too far now to recede, as if he did he would add Austria to the number of his enemies, and he would weigh the consequences well before doing that. So I hope by the end of this month we shall hear of an armistice being concluded, and that then I may be permitted to fly to you. I do not think we shall get prize-money for Sebastopol till later in the year, if we get it at all, for it must be first voted by Parliament.

Our weather, though a little cold and raw to-day, continues wonderfully mild for the season, and a great contrast to last winter; you, on the contrary, seem to have had a very hard winter, and I am sure you suffer very much from cold when you sit up so late of a night writing to me—you ought to go to bed earlier. The day before yesterday was very fine and the ground quite dry and clean, so Maxwell and I took a long walk to the central bastion and the Russian works on the French side of the town, which, although very extensive, are not, I think, so strong as those of the Malakoff and Redan. The French have removed almost all the guns from their share of the works, but the greater part of ours still remain in the embrasures; we are, however, beginning to think seriously of removing them, and as a first step our regiment has been selected to make a road from the Redan to the Woronzoff road, about two miles, for the artillery waggons to travel on. This, I suppose, will take us about three weeks to complete, the whole of them working every week-day from seven till four, and during all this time I shall not be able to have a parade or an inspection—enough to ruin a regiment; and when I remonstrated about our regiment being exclusively employed, I was told that I ought to consider it as a compliment that we were selected, because we required less drill than the other regiments in the division, so I must put up with it. We commenced yesterday, and if they continue to work as well as they did then, I hope we shall get it done under the time. The field-officers take it in turn to superintend the work; it will be mine to-morrow.

Both Wyse and Scott, I hear, intended applying for an extension of leave, but as they did not do so through me I fear they will be refused. I hope you saw Wyse in Dublin, and, if he is to join on the 29th, that you sent anything you had for me by him, as I would be certain of receiving them quicker that way than any other. I have not yet heard of the arrival of the *Edina*, which was to have left on January 10, but I received a communication from Hayter and Howell, dated January 31, stating that they had shipped the parcel for me on board the *Clyde*, which I suppose are my trousers from Johnstone; the new clothing for the regiment is also on board the *Clyde*. I am glad to tell you I got by the mail last night

Russell's 'Letters from the Seat of War' that you so kindly sent me. I am so glad they have arrived, as I began to be afraid that they had gone astray in the post-office. I will take great care of the book, as I am sure I shall find it very interesting.

If the regiment is ordered home, I will certainly try and get a passage for my brown pony, he is such a pet and so handsome; he is admired by everyone, and keeps such a beautiful coat. I am very sorry to hear of Mr. Despard being so ill; I hope change of air will do him good. I am delighted the children gave their money spontaneously to Biddy, poor little things! I must conclude in great haste, as they have called for the letters. Love to all and kisses to pets.

Ever your affectionate
RICHARD.

LIGHT DIVISION CAMP,
February 17, 1856.

MY DEAREST OWN ELLIE,

Imagine my delight yesterday evening on opening the *Times* of the 29th that you sent me by last mail, and which I had not time to open before, finding in it your dear scrap of January 31, which, as I got it on the same day as I received your letter of the 30th, proves that it only takes two days from Drogheda to be in time for the mail. I am so glad you got my letter of January 14, and that you are sanguine about the prospects of peace, which from all accounts I think is very probable, and that our hopes may be realized. God grant this may be the case, and also that the chance of war with America, which seems threatening in the distance, may be averted! I trust that the present disputes between the two Governments may be terminated by mutual concession.

I have commenced my letter to you to-night although Sunday, as we have just been informed that to-morrow we are to be reviewed by Sir W. Codrington, which will be a splendid sight, as I dare say there will be 30,000 men in the field. The orders are not yet issued, so I am ignorant of the time and place, but I dare say it will take us the greater part of the day, and that I shall not have much time for writing when I return. On my return from church this afternoon I was surprised at getting a note from Campbell announcing his arrival on the 16th at Balaklava from Malta with Mr. Villiers and a draft of sixty-seven men. They are to march up to camp on the 19th. Were you not sorry to see in the papers the loss of the poor old *Apollo* in the Dardanelles, where she ran ashore in a snowstorm and became a total wreck, and, what was most dreadful, the unfortunate captain blew out his brains as soon as it happened? It was a most melancholy affair!

I was out with our regiment making the road from the Redan yesterday; the men worked uncommonly well, and I believe another day will finish what they thought would take a fortnight to do. The Assistant-Quartermaster-General of the division said it was the best piece of road-making he had seen in the Crimea, and Lord W. Paulet complimented me on it to-day after church. It has been made to facilitate the getting the Russian guns, etc., out of the Redan, for the artillery are to begin in earnest at that work to-morrow, as they say there are nearly 1,000 guns to be shipped for England, and part at Balaklava and part at Kazatev, to which latter place a brigade of the 4th Division is to be sent immediately to construct wharves. In the Redan yesterday the artillery were busy unspiking the Russian guns, and either drawing the charges or firing them off into the parapet. They were almost all double-shotted, with a round shot and a charge of grape. When the barracks and aqueducts are blown up (which is shortly to be done), the destruction of Sebastopol as a military and naval post will be complete.

I have at length received my answer to the application I made to the Horse Guards through Lord W. Paulet. I send you a copy of the letter, which you will be sorry to hear is unfavourable, Lord Hardinge having altogether refused to admit my claim to promotion. He seems to be under the impression that I applied for the rank of Colonel, whereas I did not, or did not intend at least, to claim any particular reward, but to receive some distinction for an affair in which, whilst I commanded, my juniors alone were promoted. However, people are very apt unconsciously to overestimate their own services and to think more highly of them than others do, and no doubt I have done the same, so I shall not write any more about it; and if any of our friends should speak to you on the subject, don't you say that I have any grievance to complain of. I hear the Horse Guards have determined now not to let any officer retire on full pay till he has completed thirty years' service, so when the war is over, if I am spared, I must only retire by selling out. I hear also they will not give substantive rank to brevet field-officers under ten years' service, so Harman will not be able to get it at present. Our parade to-morrow is to be at 8.30, as we have to be on the ground in rear of the Guards' camp at ten.

I will now say good-night, and hope (D.V.) to have the pleasure of answering one of your dear letters to-morrow if I have time. The 7th Fusiliers have private theatricals to-morrow night, to which I have received an invite, and think I shall go.

February 18.

DEAREST E.,

This turned out such a desperate morning, with snow and sleet, that the review was countermanded. Only the 6th Division of Infantry were to have been reviewed—no artillery, nor sappers, nor the 11th Hussars, the only regiment of cavalry left in the Crimea, all the others being at Scutari. You must not be annoyed at my claim being refused at the Horse Guards; I never expected to be made a full Colonel. The expressions I used in my letter were, 'I hoped that some mark of Her Majesty's approbation would be conferred on me,' and I thought I was entitled to be made a C.B. If, however, I should be spared to come home, I will try and make a personal application at the Horse Guards, which perhaps will be better than writing. This limitation about the retired full pay affects me more seriously, as unless I remain eight years longer in the army I must sell out, and in these times it is very difficult to get anything beyond regulation.

This day has become much colder since the morning; it is now freezing hard, with a piercing cold north wind. No sign of the arrival of the mail, and I am afraid we shall not have it to-day. General Straubenzee has just paid me a visit; he wants to get the bands of the different regiments of the brigade to play together as one band. He is very confident about peace, and expects that the preliminaries will be very soon signed. I hear we are to be joined by three more subalterns from Malta in a few days, so we shall soon have plenty of officers. Lord W. Paulet issued a division order to-day praising our regiment for the manner in which they made the road from the Redan, and said the Quartermaster-General of the army concurred in the praise. With most affectionate love to yourself,

        Believe me,

                Ever your most devotedly attached

                            RICHARD.

                        LIGHT DIVISION CAMP,
                            February 25, 1856.

MY OWN BELOVED ELLIE,

        The only two events of importance that have occurred since I wrote to you on the 22nd are the execution on Saturday morning of that unfortunate wretch, Private Day of the 77th, for the barbarous murder of an artilleryman while in hospital, and the grand review of the British infantry, which took place yesterday. The first spectacle, I am glad to say, I was not obliged to witness. A company from every regiment in the army (except the Highland Division, from its being so far distant) attended, and I hear the prisoner met his fate in a seemingly very unconcerned manner, and walked to the gallows with as firm a step as any of the escort who accompanied him. When his body was cut down, it was buried in a grave at the foot of the gallows.

The review yesterday was a very fine sight, although many were surprised at Sir W. Codrington so far imitating the French as to hold it on a Sunday; but I believe the reason given was that there could be more men present on that day, as there were no fatigues, and as the ground was then in good order they were afraid change of weather might spoil it. We left our camp about a quarter-past eleven, and did not return till half-past four. The day, though fine, was raw and cold, and the sun did not shine till just as we were returning. The whole of the infantry, except a brigade of the Highland and a brigade of the 3rd Division, were present, and it was supposed there were about 26,000 on the ground. The troops were first inspected by Sir W. Codrington, who rode down the line accompanied by Sir Colin Campbell and a numerous staff, among whom were several French and Sardinian officers, and we afterwards marched past in quick time both in open and quarter-distance columns, by divisions, commencing by the 1st Division, the Guards leading. The marching past was a magnificent sight, for the whole army followed by successive companies, something in the shape of a horse-shoe, so part of them were marching parallel to each other, although in different directions, and thus we had a good sight of each other in marching past. The bands of each brigade were formed into one monster one that played while the regiments of the brigade marched past. Our tunes were, the first time 'Ciascune lo dice,' from the 'Figlia,' and the second tune 'The Huntsman's Chorus.' The Guards looked very well indeed, and marched past steady as a wall; they were very strong. The Grenadier Guards had ninety-six men in a company. The Highlanders also looked splendid in their bonnets and kilts, and marched past beautifully; but the 1st Brigade Light Division got the credit from several of having marched past the best of the whole lot.

Marshal Pelissier was present in his carriage and four (for he is unable to ride), attended by a numerous escort, some of whom were Algerine Spahis in their picturesque costume of snowy-white turbans and bernous. The Marshal seemed to take great interest in the review, and was seen attentively examining one of our new Enfield rifles. The whole army looked uncommonly clean and healthy. I was sorry to hear a report on the ground that the peace conferences would not take place because England and France had refused to admit Prussia to take a part in the negotiations; but I was glad to find that it was not generally believed, and I don't know how it could have come, as the submarine telegraph has broken down, and the latest papers received don't mention a word of it, and I hear that General Windham, the Chief of the Staff, a very good authority, feels most confident about peace, so I trust it is merely a false report. I hope also it will soon be settled one way or the other, so that we may be out of suspense, which in many ways is very inconvenient. If we are to have war, I must at once write to Johnstone for a tunic, as on April 1 the tunic will be taken into wear. I am in hopes, however, that I may be able to defer getting it till I go home on leave, and trust that in that happy anticipation I may not be disappointed.

We had almost a hurricane here on Friday night and Saturday, and part of the gable wall of the orderly-room, which I at one time thought of occupying as a quarter for myself, was blown in. Fortunately, no one was hurt; my tent, although it shook and flapped greatly, weathered the gale bravely, and I am sure my marquee is warmer in wintry weather than a hut. On or about March 10 next there are to be great shooting-matches throughout the whole army, and prizes are to be given for the best shot, consisting chiefly of tobacco and cigars, the remnant of the Crimean Fund. The distance is to be 300 yards, and for each company the first prize is to be 25 pounds, the second 20 pounds, and the third 15 pounds, of tobacco. The prize for the best shot in the brigade is to be 25 pounds of cigars. In addition, Sir W. Codrington and his staff give the following prizes to be competed for by the whole army, viz., first prize, £5; second, £2 10s.; third, £2; and so on, each diminishing 10s. down to the sixth prize, which is 10s. These will excite a good deal of interest, as the men begin to take great pleasure in the weapon, which is now really as good a one as can possibly be made.

Some indiscreet correspondent of a newspaper at Kertch has sent home and had published a detailed account of our position at Kertch, with the strength of fortifications, garrison, etc., which has roused the indignation of Sir W. Codrington, and a strong order has been published to-day calling on all officers either to abstain from giving such information or to request their friends not to publish it, and threatening newspaper correspondents that if they are guilty of similar indiscretion they will be expelled from the camp. No news of the *Edina*; she has been a long time out. I hope she may soon arrive, as my stock of preserved soups, chocolate, etc., is getting very low indeed. I am reading now the 'Polish Lancer,' one of the books you sent me. It is a very interesting tale, founded chiefly on incidents of Napoleon's invasion of Russia in 1812.

Colonel Browne is, I hear, now at Gibraltar, as also Sir G. Douglas and his wife. This is a very dull, stupid epistle, but I have, unfortunately, none of your letters to answer, and I have in vain racked my brains to find something interesting to tell you, but cannot, so will conclude with affectionate love to my dear mother and all at Weston, and kisses to the dear pets; and with most affectionate love to your own dear self, believe me, dearest Ellie,

Ever your most devotedly attached
RICHARD.

Light Division Camp,
February 27, 1856.

My own beloved Ellie,

Maxwell and I had a very nice ride yesterday. We went to the extreme left of our position, tied up our horses at the French guard-room, walking through the Russian works from the Bastion de Mats (or flagstaff) and Fort Alexander, nearly to the Quarantine Fort, which is at the mouth of the harbour opposite Fort Constantine, and the strength of the works and the labour that must have been employed in their construction is surprising. From Fort Alexander they had a stone loopholed wall running for a long way in front of their works, but which was not completed when the siege commenced. Fort Constantine was amusing itself while we were there in throwing shells in the direction of the Redan. On our way back it began to snow, although the wind was from the south, and during the night it snowed very heavily, and we have quite a white world this morning; and to-day it has done nothing else but snow and sleet, which, the wind being still southerly, thaws almost as soon as it falls, making the ground dreadfully sloppy, and before to-day the ground was so dry and clean.

Many thanks for preparing the box for me. I suppose you intend sending it by Wyse, who will be here in a few days now. I am happy to tell you that the *Edina* has at length arrived, and that yesterday I had the pleasure of receiving all the nice things you sent me in the box. The soups, potted meats, candles, jam and bottle of cordial, sugar and biscuits, all arrived perfectly safe, and were very acceptable, but I am afraid the plum-puddings, which you kindly took such pains with, are quite spoiled by mildew. The box must have been put in a damp place,

I suppose. It is very provoking, after all the trouble and expense you went to about them. However, I am going to try to-day if any part of them is eatable, and I will let you know to-morrow the result. My curry powder is quite exhausted; I hope you sent me a supply in Wyse's box. Many thanks for all the good things you sent me by the *Edina*; they are a great addition to my store.

I must order a tunic from Johnstone. When the regiment leaves the Crimea, I will try if possible to take my ponies with me, as they are both very good-looking and in beautiful condition. My groom Cormack is the best I have ever had since I have been in the regiment. He takes such good care of the horses, and I have never once had occasion to speak to him. The brown pony is my favourite; he is so handsome; everyone admires him, and he is so good-tempered and full of fun. I shall not bring my bed with me when I go on leave, as I must travel light and take as little luggage as possible, as they charge so high for it on foreign railways.

I hear we are to have another review on Sunday of the whole of the army in the Crimea; they say it is for the distribution of the Legion of Honour, but I hope Sir W. Codrington is not going to imitate the French by holding all his reviews on Sundays. I forgot in my last to mention a pleasing incident which occurred at the last review: When Major Browne, 44th, who lost his right arm and part of the fingers of his left at Inkerman, was not able to salute Sir W. C., he, observing it, took off his hat to him and made him a low bow.

I must now conclude for to-day, as I am going to the Rifle Theatre after dinner.

February 28.

DEAREST ELLIE,

We had a very pleasant evening at the Rifles last night ; the acting was capital. I enclose you the bill. The scenery was not quite so well painted as at the Fusilier Theatre, but the ladies' dresses were better, having been sent from Malta by Lady Exmouth, mother of Captain Pellew, who is the manager ; we had also glee-singing by their band, and a Highland fling danced by one of their men went off capitally. Sir W. Codrington, Lord W. Paulet, and both the Brigadiers were present, and after the performances were over we all adjourned to the Rifle mess-hut, where we had a capital champagne supper, when Sir W. Codrington's health was drunk, and he returned thanks in a neat speech, saying he always looked back with pleasure to his connection with the 1st Brigade, to which he said he owed his appointment to the command of the army. The mess-hut was very tastefully decorated with flags, and with transparencies, beautifully executed, of Sir W. Codrington's crest and of the breastplates of the different regiments in the 1st Brigade.

I tried yesterday at dinner some of the plum-puddings you so kindly made for me. I had to cut off a good deal of the outside, which was mildewed, but the centre was still good, and I had some of it fried, and it was excellent; I never tasted a more delicious pudding. To-day the weather is most delicious ; the sun is as warm as in May at home, and is thawing the snow fast, so we shall have the ground very sloppy for some time. Dwyer, I am sorry to say, has not been well lately; he has been suffering from ague, and has gone to-day on a fortnight's leave to stay with his brother in the 14th on the heights above Balaklava, and I hope the change of air will do him good. No one could be more devoted to the care of his patients than he has been.

I have just received your dear letter of the 13th from Dublin, and fully sympathize with you in your disappointment at my not being able to get leave as soon as I expected, for I felt it bitterly myself. I trust, however, that (D.V.) this happiness is only deferred till the end of March, for, thank God! I see that the accounts by this mail are very pacific, and I hope we shall shortly hear of peace being concluded. Let us exercise our patience for a few weeks more, and then, please God! we shall be rewarded by being united again, never, I trust, to be separated again on this Earth. I like the route you have chosen for the journey to Paris—it is the quickest you could take, but I am afraid you will find it very inconvenient travelling by yourself; I wish you had somebody to accompany you. I am very glad you went to Dublin and stayed a little time with your mother, and I hope she accompanied you back to Weston. I am delighted to hear such good accounts of the darling children. I trust that the peace when concluded will not be so short-lived as they seem to anticipate. I think it will take a long time before Russia can recover from the heavy sacrifices she was obliged to make during the war. I am more apprehensive of a war with America, although I was glad to see that the last accounts were more pacific. War with America would indeed be a dreadful calamity for both countries.

I hope you found your mother, Louise, and Aunt Anne all well. Give them my kind love, and say that I shall indeed be glad to see them again. How much I wish I had been able to send darling Ellie some little souvenir on her birthday, but (D.V.) on her next I may be able to do so. What nice books you sent her! How kind of your mother giving her one!

February 29.

After writing to you yesterday evening, I took a walk with Maxwell, and we came across the ridge just in time to see that magnificent pile of buildings, the sailors' barracks in Sebastopol, but used as a hospital by the Russians during the siege, blown up. There were several explosions, causing loud reports, and sending up columns of smoke and dust, which reduced the once stately pile to a mass of ruins; the mines were fired by galvanic batteries. The Russians threw two shells from Constantine Fort in that direction, but without doing any harm, as, of course, no one was near the building at that time. There is a report prevalent that an officer of the 31st was shot on Tuesday last while out shooting in the Tchernaya Valley by the Russian riflemen, but I am inclined to hope it is not true, as no one seems to know his name. The Russian sentries, however, do fire on everyone they see shooting in the valley; it is a most cowardly practice, for it does no good, and is little better than assassination.

Best and young Stewart and Villiers, two nice lads, were shooting yesterday at the head of the harbour, when a field-piece was fired at them from the north side with a round of canister-shot, which flew all about them, but fortunately did not strike them. Wyse has applied for an extension of leave till April 2 to settle his affairs, which I have forwarded. Scott is expected in a day or two. I heard from Hibberd by this mail that he had shipped for me on the 10th instant a cooking-lantern, with 10 pounds of candles, by the *Cape of Good Hope* steamer. I heard from Jordan, asking Farrel's direction that he might send him an amended discharge; I gave him the address. If Farrel does not get it in due time, he should write to the depot again about it. Jordan is under orders for Malta. I am going to ride now to Kamiesch with Maxwell and Campbell, and will say adieu till evening, when I hope (D.V.) to give you a P.S.

We have just returned from our ride to Kamiesch; the distance is about twenty miles there and back. We had a lovely day starting, but a heavy snow-shower coming home. The town of Kamiesch is at present larger than Balaklava, and consists almost entirely of wooden huts erected by the French. The number of cafés is surprising, where I believe ten shillings is the charge for lunch alone; a large theatre is also in course of erection, and there are shops and stores of all sorts. I believe things are cheaper there than at Balaklava, the market being glutted. The harbour is larger than Balaklava, but not so crowded with ships; the wharves were covered with Russian guns and anchors ready for shipment to France. On our way home Campbell met with an accident, which, although painful, it was fortunate was not worse. We were riding pretty briskly, when a Frenchman came full gallop in the opposite direction, and came into collision with Campbell and struck him above the instep. I thought horse and man would have been knocked over, and Campbell was in such pain that he was not able to sit on his horse; fortunately, just at the spot we met a cart belonging to Colonel Bunbury, of the 23rd, returning home, into which we put Campbell, and took off his boot, which gave him great relief, and the sergeant in charge of the cart took charge of his pony, and half an hour after our return I was glad to see Campbell able to ride into camp.

There has been a rumour flying about the camp that the order for the armistice has arrived, but, as I see nothing about it in orders, I don't believe it. I see in the orders that one hundred medals are to be issued to the regiment. I am afraid this will not quite complete the men who came out originally with the regiment, so it will not come to my turn yet.

I must now conclude, with affectionate love to my dear mother and all at home, loves and kisses to the darling pets, and kind regards to C. K., Miss Lebel and Mrs. Caffray; and with warmest love to yourself,

    Believe me, dearest Ellie,

        Ever your affectionately attached

            RICHARD.

CHAPTER XIII

THE ARMISTICE

LIGHT DIVISION CAMP,
March 2, 1856.

MY OWN BELOVED ELLIE,

This is the eighth anniversary of our happy marriage, and, although chequered by some sad and trying events, on the whole what eight happy years they have been to us! Each year has increased our regard and affection for each other, which the possession of our darling children has firmly riveted. We have shared largely in the bounty of a merciful God, and I trust that there are still many happy years in store for us, and I trust that before long we may commence enjoying them. I told you in my last of the report prevalent that the order for the conclusion of an armistice has been received out here, but that I disbelieved the report. I, however, now find that it was better founded than I expected, as I hear that on the 29th ult. General Windham met a Russian flag of truce at Traktir Bridge to settle the terms of the armistice, and the only point now to be arranged is the extent of neutral ground to be enjoyed by both parties, and when that is fixed I suppose the terms will be published in general orders, and that then we can explore every corner in Sebastopol or shoot in the Tchernaya without being exposed to the risk of the Russian bullets. This armistice certainly looks more like the confirmation of glad tidings of peace than anything I have yet heard, and I trust that peace itself will soon follow, as it was determined that no armistice was to be granted until all the concessions required from Russia had been acceded to by her, and then I hope there will be no difficulty about my getting leave to go home. It is an odd thing, however, that Sir W. Codrington has refused the extension of leave to April 30 that Wyse asked for, although he wrote a very strong letter saying it was absolutely necessary for the settlement of his family affairs on his father's death, and that if he could not get it he would have to sell out, and the necessity of his remaining at home was supported by a letter from his lawyer. However, I suppose that they thought that he already had had sufficient leave, and I trust that I may be more fortunate.

I mentioned in my last the blowing up on the 29th ult. of the naval barracks in Sebastopol, and I regret now to say that it was attended with a fatal accident. One of the mines (which, I suppose, was fired by a fuse instead of by the galvanic battery) was a long time in going off. Major Rankin, one of the Engineers employed, who had been through the whole siege without being touched, thought the fuse had gone out, and ran to the mine to see if it was so, but when he got there found it still burning, and told some sappers who were with him that they had but a minute to run, and commenced to do so himself, when directly the mine exploded, and he was buried in the ruins of the building, and it took some hours' digging before they could find his body, which was completely crushed. The sappers fortunately escaped. It was a most melancholy accident.

We seem now as if we had got rid of winter for a

season, and are now in spring, for, except on the hills, the snow is quite off the ground. The sun at church parade this morning was quite hot.

6 p.m.

After evening service it was such a lovely evening that Maxwell, Campbell, and I took a walk. At starting we met poor Major Rankin's funeral-party just returning from the Engineers' burying-ground, which is close to our camp. We afterwards met Colonel Lysons, 23rd, who commands the 2nd Brigade in our division, and I was talking to him about the armistice, peace, etc. He says he expects the former will be signed in a day or two. The Russians are to keep the line of the Mackenzie Heights, and not to come down into the valley; while the Tchernaya is to be our boundary, which we are not to cross. At the meeting at Traktir Bridge the other day to arrange the preliminaries, a Russian General said to the French negotiator: 'Well, I suppose, as everything is nearly arranged, we had better not fire on you any more.' 'Oh, not at all,' said the Frenchman; 'you had better go on as usual till everything is concluded, for it makes no difference to us, as you never hit anything nor do us any harm.' The armistice is to be for thirty days, but Colonel Lysons thinks that before ten days we shall hear of peace being concluded, and he says that it has been arranged that, except a force to be left in Turkey, regiments will go back from whence they came, which will be Corfu for us, to which I shall not object. I hope the mail may arrive to-morrow, and bring me one of your dear letters, although I well know how much disappointed you will be at my not being able to get leave when I expected it.

March 3.

DEAREST ELLIE,

The prospects of peace look more and more favourable by every mail, and I anxiously look forward to being able to leave this by April 1 to join you. It was announced to-day in orders that, pending the arrangement of the terms of an armistice to last till March 31, hostilities are to cease on both sides; but neither party is to pass the outposts. Yesterday I heard there was great fraternization going on between the English, French, and Russians along the Tchernaya, and exchange of tobacco-pipes for crucifixes, etc.

I see the funds have fallen again on account of the intention of Government to make a fresh loan, but no doubt they will rise again as soon as peace is declared. I am so glad you found on your return the dear children happy and well and our darling boy recovered from his little attack. How smart he must look in the handsome frock sent him by C. K., who is very generous to him! I am sorry that the Sebastopol stone has been done so badly and cost so much. I wish I could have got it done in Malta, where they are accustomed to work in that sort of stone. They have called for the letters, so I must conclude in haste, with love to all and kisses to pets.

Ever your most affectionate
RICHARD.

LIGHT DIVISION CAMP,
March 6, 1856.

MY OWN BELOVED ELLIE,

Our winter, instead of nearly ending, feels as if only just commencing. We have not yet had severer weather than has prevailed for the last three days. The ground is covered with snow more than a foot deep. It is blowing a regular gale of wind, and every half-hour a heavy shower of snow or hail, and at sea the weather must be very severe indeed, and I am afraid that our mail, due to-day, will be several days late. Sunday last was a most delightful day, and in the evening the sun was so warm that I found walking with an overcoat quite oppressive. Next morning (3rd) was raw and cold, and towards evening it began to blow, and blew all night very hard, with heavy showers of snow and sleet. The next forenoon it cleared up so much that Maxwell and I determined to take advantage of the armistice to explore the creeks at the head of the harbour, where we could not have entered before without incurring the risk of a shot from the opposite side. We started, and proceeded along Careening Bay, and were pursuing our way to the head of the harbour, when a thick sea-fog came on, shrouding the whole of the harbour in mist, and with it a heavy snowstorm, which forced us to turn back; and from that time till now the weather has continued the same—constant squalls from the north, with piercing cold winds and heavy showers of hail and snow.

Yesterday was a bitter day. I was field-officer of the day, and had to patrol along the course of the aqueduct in the Tchernaya Valley to see that no infractions of the armistice were committed by any of our troops. I started on foot, for it was impossible to ride, on account of the depth of the snowdrifts, but was not able to get further than the brow of the cliff overlooking the valley, as the snow was so thick and driven so fast by a cutting wind that I couldn't see twenty yards before me; and as it was unlikely that anyone except on duty would be out on such a day, I returned to camp, and so long as the squall lasted had some difficulty in finding my way. In the intervals between these squalls it was fine enough, although very cold, and our men yesterday afternoon took advantage of one of these intervals to enjoy a grand snowballing match, right wing against left, officers and all, the right being protected by a strong line of fortifications thrown up of snow. The contest was carried on with great spirit by sound of the bugle for upwards of an hour, in the course of which several prisoners were made on both sides. It is now while I am writing blowing most tremendously, and I am afraid we shall have bad accounts from sea. We have papered our mess-hut with views from the *Illustrated News* and *Punch*, which give it a very cheerful appearance. As an improvement, grotesque heads from *Punch* are very artistically pasted over the principal figures in the large pictures from the *Illustrated*.

Scott has rejoined from leave in the *Medway*, and has been at Balaklava for the last three days, but the weather has been so severe that he has not been able to come up.

5 p.m.

Scott has just arrived, looking very well. He tells me that indignation at home against Lords Lucan and Cardigan and Sir R. Airey, caused by the publication of Sir J. Macniell's report, is very great. I think the two last will lose their situations, and deservedly so. Colonel Wetherall and Captain Mackenzie, A.Q.M.G., have just been telegraphed for to go home to give evidence before the Committee of the House of Commons appointed to inquire into the subject. Colonel Wetherall, having charge of the land transport corps, can't be spared till the return of Colonel McMurdo. We have five Subalterns just arrived in the *Columbo* from Malta. I had heard their departure from Malta was countermanded, but here they are. The wind has changed to the south-west, and, although still blowing a gale, it has become much milder, and is now raining in torrents, which will soon clear away all our snow. Have you ever read the sermon called 'Religion in Common Life,' preached by the Rev. Mr. Caird at the church of Craithie before the Queen and Prince Albert, and which they commanded to be printed? Maxwell lent it to me, and I found it a very excellent and practical discourse, most eloquently and forcibly written.

March 7.

To show what a changeable climate this is, I will tell you that last night, when I went to bed about twelve, it was quite mild, the wind blowing from the south-west and raining hard; but before morning the wind chopped round to the north, rain turned to hail and afterwards to snow, with which the ground is once more covered, and this is almost as severe a day as any we have had during the winter, for the wind blows hard from the north and is piercingly cold. The weather in the Black Sea since the beginning of the week must have been frightful, and I am afraid we cannot expect our mail for some days.

The news by the next two mails will be very interesting, as I see the Conferences were to have commenced on February 23, and by the mail due on the 10th we ought to hear something about their proceedings. Scott tells me that the report before he left England was that Lord Palmerston had sent instructions to Lord Clarendon in Paris not to accept any terms that the country would not be satisfied with, for, even if France did not join in the war, England was quite able to carry it on by herself. I hope, however, that we shall not do anything so rash, for even if we were a match single-handed for Russia, yet I am afraid the other Powers would eventually join Russia against us, as we might naturally be considered the only obstacles to peace in Europe. The issues of peace and war are, however, in the hands of an all-wise and omnipotent God, who will rule all for the best, and in His hands we may safely leave it.

5 *p.m.*

I have just returned from a walk with Maxwell through the Karabelnaïa suburb. It was tolerably fine though cold; the wind had gone down greatly, but on our return it commenced to snow fast, which is likely to continue, as the air seems full of it. This weather will interfere with various amusements which were to have come off next week. On the 10th the different shooting-matches for prizes throughout the army were to have come off; and on the 11th there were to have been athletic games for the men, such as jumping, running, etc.; and on the 17th the Light Division spring races were to take place, but unless the weather changes for the better they will all have to be postponed.

Believe me, dearest Ellie,
Your most affectionately attached
RICHARD.

LIGHT DIVISION CAMP,
March 13, 1856.

MY OWN PRECIOUS ELLIE,

The English mail arrived on the 11th, and I had the delight of getting your two dear letters of February 22-23 and 23-24. How kind of you to write me a second letter to let me know that you had received mine of the 8th, which I am so glad reached you in time to be answered! We, like yourself, are anxiously awaiting the result of the Conference, which must now soon be known, as it is said the French Emperor is anxious to be able to communicate news of peace to the Senate at their opening session, which was to take place on the 3rd inst. Most people here seem to think that peace is almost certain, especially as the armistice, which was communicated out here by telegraph, was agreed on after the opening of the Conferences, which is looked upon as a good sign. It is also stated that Russia has agreed not to maintain Nicolaieff as a dockyard or arsenal, which is a great concession on her part; it is said, however, on the other hand, that she will make a struggle to retain Kars in her possession, which, of course, the Allies would not permit for a moment. I think if the Allies demand from Russia an indemnity for the expenses of the war there will be a split over that point, as I don't think Russia has the money to give; but I do not consider that the Allies have a right to demand it, as it was not included in the terms proposed by Austria. God grant that all may end well, and that I may have the happiness of being soon restored to my affectionate, true-hearted Ellie!

To-day I am on duty as field-officer, but as I have not to visit the neutral ground I shall soon be back. In spite of the strict orders against officers crossing during the armistice the line of the aqueduct, I hear that General Windham, the Chief of the Staff, caught the other day no less than eight officers, among whom were two Generals, Garrett and Trollope, transgressing, some led away by following game, others by a wish to speak to the Russians across the Tchernaya. I have not heard what is to be done with the culprits. Among the rest was a black lady from Jamaica, Mrs. Seacoal, who for some time past has established a restaurant near Kadikoi, and where she charged rather more than West Indian prices. She was also principal medical officer to the army works corps or ci-devant navvies, and at the time of the cholera last summer used to prescribe pomegranate-juice, which was an almost never-failing specific. This lady, I hear, attracted great attention on the part of the Russians, most of whom, I dare say, had never seen a negress before. One gallant Russ took one of the sacred medals that they wear as relics round their necks and threw it across to her, and she, not to be outdone in generosity, threw back a bag full of tobacco.

I hear it is settled that the 3rd Division are to relieve the French outposts at Baidar very shortly, and it is reported that we are to relieve theirs on the Tchernaya; if so, I hope they will allow our division to remain in our present camp. Dwyer has gone to England on medical certificate; I trust the change will restore him to health.

What is the reason of my mother wishing to give up Weston? Is it that she finds it too damp for her? I sincerely trust her health is not failing. I got all the papers you and Kate kindly sent; tell her I am very much obliged to her for the *Punches*. I am reading now the 'Gambler's Wife'; it is very interesting, and the characters extremely well drawn. Many thanks for Miss Ward's letter, which I return; it is a very agreeable one. She is a steady, kind friend. I am glad the Colonel was better, but very sorry that Mrs. W. was likely to have cataract; it is a dreadful misfortune. The Boyce whom she mentions as having lost both his arms was not her friend the Lieutenant, but a private in the regiment of the same name.

By the reduction of 30 per cent. in the fares of French railways and steamers in favour of English officers, I could get home viâ Paris as cheap as by a transport steamer to Spithead, and from London to Paris by return ticket, and in much less time, which is a great consideration, as I would have the happiness of meeting you sooner. I shall indeed enjoy our being together by ourselves for a short time, but after that I shall be anxious to see the darling children and all the dear ones at Weston. You must remember me kindly to Lowey next time you write to her.

Dearest E., the mail has arrived very punctually the day it was due, and I have had the happiness of receiving your dear letter of February 26-27. I was indeed rejoiced to find that dear little Annie was better of her severe attack of feverish cold, and trust that she has had no relapse. I send the poor little thing a few lines to comfort her. Thank God she is better! We have indeed abundant reason for deep gratitude for the many mercies we have received from a bountiful God.

I will now conclude with affectionate love to my dear mother, K., A., and F., loves and kisses to the dear pets, and kind regards to Miss Lebel and Mrs. Caffray; and with affectionate love to yourself.

Believe me, dearest Ellie,
Ever your most devotedly attached
RICHARD.

LIGHT DIVISION CAMP,
Patrick's Day, 1856.

MY OWN BELOVED ELLIE,

I have not much to communicate since my last of the 13th. Our weather, though fine and clear, has for the last four days been most piercingly cold, as we have had hard frosts with a very high wind from the north, which penetrates through everything; indeed, it has blown quite a gale, and I am afraid the mail due to-day will be some days late. We are now paying for the fine weather we enjoyed at the beginning of the winter in November. I have heard no more rumours or 'shaves' flying about the camp, nor shall we have any, I suppose, till the mail comes in.

On Thursday last the armistice was formally signed by the English, French, and Russian Generals at Traktir Bridge; before that it was only a provisional arrangement. The bounds have also been extended to the banks of the Tchernaya, which is to be the line of demarcation between the two enemies. A great crowd, I believe, were present at the interview at Traktir Bridge, and the Russian General, I heard, treated them to champagne. There has been great fraternization and interchange of little presents going on between the troops on each side of the river. Several Russian soldiers crossed the river and came as far as the French camp on Inkerman, and one, indeed, yesterday evening came into our camp, or, rather, was brought in as a prisoner by the Provost-Marshal, who found him wandering about; he appeared in a terrible fright, as if he expected to be shot. I sent him to the General, who sent him back to his own army. On the 15th Maxwell and I took a ride all through the French part of the town, which he had not yet seen; it is almost entirely a mass of ruins, and the few houses that are still in good repair are occupied by the French as cafés. I must try to get you, if possible, a Russian crucifix as a relic.

Yesterday Sir W. Codrington had three divisions—1st, 2nd, and 3rd—out at the monastery to practise bivouacking and cooking in the field, but it turned out so cold that, after marching past, they were all sent home again, and we met them returning. I suppose it will be the turn for our division next.

As perhaps you would like to know the strength of the British Army out here in case we are obliged to make another campaign, I give it to you as follows: Strength of the British Army in the East on March 7, 1856—Fit to take the field, 52,000; servants, batmen, and soldiers attached to Land Transport Corps, 11,000; Land Transport Corps, 5,000; medical staff, etc., 630; reserve at Malta, all fit and waiting for transport, 5,000—total, 73,630. This includes four regiments of the British German Legion at Kulalie, one Swiss regiment at Smyrna, and the cavalry on the Bosphorus, but no part of the Turkish contingent under General Vivian.

The Queen has sent out such a lot of nice books for the men to read, intended as a Christmas gift for her army; there are 786 different works, and many of the most popular are in duplicate. I have got one of the catalogues nicely bound, which I hope to bring home to show you what a nice selection she has made. I hear that the Russians complain that they have to pay very heavy prices for luxuries on their side of the river—champagne 27 francs a bottle—and they wish that during the armistice they could be supplied from our canteen. The athletic games are to come off on the 19th, when a great deal of amusement is anticipated.

I enclose a little note for Annie Louisa which I had not room for in my last letter. Although the sun is bright to-day, the wind is bitterly cold and quite pierces through you. We have had a hard frost for the last four days; I hope the weather may soon change for the better. No chance of the mail to-day. I think next Thursday's mail, the 20th, ought to bring us some decisive news from Paris; God grant it may be favourable! I am getting quite impatient, and longing for the moment when I shall be able to join you and all the other dear ones that I so ardently love. Please God it is not far distant!

  Believe me, dearest Ellie,
    Ever your most affectionately attached
              RICHARD.

P.S.—Love to all your dear people.

THE ARMISTICE

Light Division Camp,
March 24, 1856.

My own darling Ellie,

Saturday last was the anniversary of my most Providential escape from the jaws of death. What a year of mercy I have had since then, and how grateful I should feel to the Lord for His goodness in sparing me then and giving me further time for repentance, instead of cutting me off unprepared in the midst of my sins as He might have done! We have indeed great cause for thankfulness in the many mercies we have received, and we must not repine at minor misfortunes or drawbacks, as we consider them, to our happiness.

The French received telegraphic intelligence by this mail of the Empress Eugénie having been safely delivered of a Prince yesterday. Imperial salutes of 101 guns were fired (by) both English and French artillery in honour of the event, and at night the French camps were illuminated by immense bonfires. This must have caused great happiness to the Emperor, as it will serve to consolidate his throne.

On the 22nd Maxwell and I rode down to the valley and along the banks of the Tchernaya; there were not many Russians out, but I got enclosed little crucifix from one, which I wish you would give to dear Annie, with my love, as a little souvenir of her kindness in making me such a nice cap and vest. I wish it was better worth her acceptance, but any rubbish coming from Russia is now prized, and it will do to hang at her watch-chain with her other charms. Tell Kate I have got a little consecrated medal for her, but it is too heavy to send in this letter, and I must wait for another opportunity. The way these things are got across the river is as follows: The Russian does up the cross in a ball of clay and throws it across, and a coin is sent in the same way in return from our side. I was unfortunate in my first throw, as I was on horseback and did not want to dismount. I asked a Frenchman standing by to do up the money in clay and throw it across; he, however, did not use force enough, and it fell in the river, so I had to make a second venture, which was more successful. While we were there a carriage came down to the Russian bank, in which were a general officer and two ladies, one of them nicely dressed in a plaid dress, and they were attended by a Cossack and a chasseur in a handsome Albanian dress, who interpreted for them that they wished to exchange gold coin with some English officers of the Guards who were on the opposite side, and which I believe they did. I hear that when the armistice was signed at Traktir Sir W. Codrington attended as a spectator, when a Russian officer went up to him, not knowing who he was, and asked him to exchange whips with him, which he did.

Maxwell, I regret to say, is now laid up with boils, which are very painful, but I hope he will soon be better. I shall feel the loss of his society in my walks and rides very much. I can well understand, my love, how ardently you wish for my return home, if only to be relieved from the daily anxiety that you suffer on my account; but we must patiently wait for God's own good time, which I think will not now be long in coming, and that you will soon have your 'peace and war and paper' back to bother you. We cannot decide anything about my selling out or remaining in the service until I return home and see how affairs stand. I am very glad your mother thought our dear boy so fine a child, and hope he may continue to improve. I don't think they will be able to do away with purchase in a hurry; it will be a great hardship to me if after all my service I shall only receive the regulation price I gave for my commissions.

I have just returned from the racecourse; it was a lovely day for the sport, and there was a sight which will not often be seen again. There were, I suppose, at least 60,000 English, French, Sardinians, in every variety of military costume, scattered all over the plain; there was also a fair sprinkling of Russians on the opposite bank, but not nearly as many as I expected. A number of French officers crossed over and were riding and conversing with the Russians, but neither English nor Russians left their proper side of the stream. The French had erected a pavilion, surmounted by the flag and adorned with boughs; in front was posted a guard of honour, and there was a strong escort of Circassians besides. Sir W. Codrington, on the contrary, was attended by a few of his staff and a single hussar orderly. Several French officers and soldiers sported the Crimean medal given by our Government. I have only just received mine, and have not got the Sebastopol clasp yet. The racing was very good, but the French, as you will be surprised to hear, have carried off the chief honours. The first race, a pony race, for which forty-nine started, was won by an officer in the Chasseurs d'Afrique (T. Roper started a pony for this race); the next race, a steeplechase, was also won by a Frenchman, the Vicomte Talon.

APPENDIX

To Lieutenant-General Sir W. Codrington, Commanding Light Division.

LIGHT DIVISION CAMP, CRIMEA,
September 15, 1855.

SIR,
   I have the honour to request that you will submit to the Commander of the Forces, with the view of his recommending it to the favourable consideration of the Commander-in-Chief, this my application to be permitted to allow the time that I passed as prisoner of war in Russia until I rejoined my regiment in the field on exchange—viz., from March 23 to September 14, 1855—to count towards the three years' actual service requisite towards obtaining the rank of Colonel in the army, I having been in command of the regiment as Lieutenant-Colonel at the time I was taken. I am induced to make this application as my absence from my regiment was involuntary on my part, and occurred whilst I was in the actual discharge of my duty, I having been taken prisoner under the following circumstances: On the night of March 22, 1855, I was the field-officer in command of the trenches of the right attack, on which occasion the enemy made a sortie in force on the right of

our advanced trenches, which was successfully repulsed by the detachments 77th and 97th Regiments, acting under my immediate direction. About an hour afterwards the enemy made another attack on the left of our trench. I proceeded to the spot immediately on hearing the firing with a detachment 7th Fusiliers, under the Hon. Captain Browne. I went a little in advance of this party, intending to collect the guard of that part of the trenches and unite them with the detachment of the 7th in an attack on the enemy, when I fell in with a party of six or eight Greeks who had penetrated into the trench, and who, from the darkness of the night and their being dressed in sheepskin coats such as were worn by our soldiers, I mistook for our own men, and, being entirely by myself, was knocked down, wounded, and taken prisoner by them. I beg to state that on my being exchanged at Odessa I rejoined my regiment in the Crimea with the least possible delay; I therefore trust my application will be favourably entertained.

I have, etc.,
R. D. KELLY,
Lieutenant-Colonel 34th Regiment.

Answer to above.

HORSE-GUARDS,
October 6, 1855.

SIR,

Having had the honour to lay before the Field-Marshal Commanding in Chief the letter which was forwarded from Lieutenant-Colonel Kelly, 34th Regiment, detailing the circumstances under which he was taken prisoner on the night of March 22 last when field-officer in command of the trenches of the right attack before Sebastopol, with a view to the time during which he was prisoner—viz., from March 23 to September 14—being allowed to count as part of the three years' service as Lieutenant-Colonel required to qualify him for the rank of Colonel, I am directed by his lordship to acquaint you that, as it appears from Lieutenant-Colonel Kelly's statement, which is confirmed so far as respects the sortie of the enemy and the command held by that officer by Lieutenant-General Sir W. Codrington, that his capture was in no degree to be attributed to any fault or imprudence on his part, and that he was actively engaged at the time in the discharge of his duty, his lordship considers it fair that Lieutenant-Colonel Kelly should be allowed to reckon this time, and the decision will therefore be recorded. I have also laid before Viscount Hardinge Lieutenant-Colonel Kelly's letter, which was forwarded by you, explaining that there was an error in the despatch in which this sortie was reported, the troops engaged on that occasion having been stated to have been under the direction of Major Gordon, R.E., whereas they had been under his (Lieutenant-Colonel Kelly's) immediate superintendence; and I am to acquaint you that, as Lieutenant-General Sir W. Codrington states that Lieutenant-Colonel Kelly was field-officer in command on the occasion, the letter in question has been duly recorded.

I have, etc.,
(Signed)   C. YORKE.

To General Simpson, etc.

Letter from Mr. John Laurie.

SURREY HOUSE, HYDE PARK PLACE,
December 28, 1855.

SIR,

I cannot resist thanking you for all your kindness and attention to my son, Lieutenant J. D. Laurie, who arrived safely on Friday last at Portsmouth by the *Indiana* transport. His wound is indeed a severe one, and Medical Board give every facility for its recovery. I hope he is now out of danger, as the moving caused it to inflame. Your calling upon him daily at the camp gave him much satisfaction, as it proved that he did his duty, and as he has been reported twice wounded, it will be a great source of satisfaction to him through life to know he was esteemed by his Colonel. He is now looking forward again to join the camp as soon as he gets the use of his leg, which shows his courage and his desire to distinguish himself in the honourable profession he adopted. His brother, Lieutenant J. W. Laurie, of the 4th, was a great comfort to him; he writes he is unlucky enough not to be hit. Hoping you will be spared as a blessing to your regiment and an honour to the service, where, I hear, you live in the hearts of the officers, and once more thanking you for your kindness to my son,

I am, sir,
Your obedient servant,
JOHN LAURIE.

LETTERS RELATIVE TO THE REPORTED DEATH OF COLONEL KELLY.

To Mrs. R. Kelly, from a Private in the 34th Regiment.

PRESTON,
April 11, 1855.

MRS. KELLY,

I hope you will excuse my freedom in writing these few lines, but in consequence of the report of the death of our brave Colonel, who fell in leading in the regiment on the night of March 22, and I could not tell you how sorry we felt at the loss of the best friend ever we had or ever would have again; but how, in consequence of the glorious news of this morning's paper, that our brave Colonel was only wounded slightly and taken prisoner, and knowing how you would feel at the lost (loss) of the best of men in the account of the last week's newspapers, so I took the liberty on seeing this day's paper to let you know, as I thought it might reach you before you would see it in the papers, and I can assure you that the letters came here from the regiment that the praise of the way the Colonel brought up the regiment is past anything, and also says that only for him the Allies would have lost the advance works.

Lieutenant Jordan was killed on that night, and Captain Jordan (?) was wounded, and Lieutenant Ramsay was wounded. We had Major Goodenough here for two days; he is gone away. We got orders this morning for a draft of one Captain, two Subalterns, three sergeants, one drum, and sixty men to proceed (word illegible).

I would be very happy to send you any news you would wish to know any time. And thank God our brave Colonel is living, and Mrs. Mallen hopes you and all your family are well.

We remain your humble servants,
JOHN AND MARY MALLEN,
34th Regiment.

To F. J. Kelly, Esq., from Mrs. Westropp.

29 P.P., CHELTENHAM,
Wednesday.

MY VERY DEAR FRANCIS,

I have been in tears, in sorrow, in sad affliction since Thursday last. I feared your dear brother was quite gone. You were all before me—the delicate mother, the poor wife, the attached sisters and brother, the four little beings unconscious of their severe and irreparable loss. That excellent man Colonel Fitzmaurice sent me the enclosed this morning, and Mr. Palmer telegraphed me the same. I sent to the station and had a telegraphic message sent to Mr. Singer asking him to forward this good news to Weston. I only heard this at ten o'clock, and I sent a gentleman to have it telegraphed to Mr. Singer; I could not manage it in any other way. They told him the news would reach Dublin by twelve o'clock this day; but this letter will not for some days longer. Oh, how I wish to fly over with it to comfort you all! May God Almighty do so! What you have all suffered! I hope the Russians will keep the poor fellow, for he will be out of all danger.

I am very poorly. I was ill on hearing this in the dreadful *Times* newspaper, and am so unwell that I go up to London to see Dr. Latham. Write to me at 118, Gloucester Terrace, Hyde Park. Tell me how your dear family are. If you have heard this good and blessed news before you heard from Mr. Singer, tell me all. I scribble this from my bed. With love true and sincere,

Yours,
A. WESTROPP.

To Mrs. Colonel Kelly.

EAST INDIA HOUSE, LONDON,
April 12, 1855.

DEAR MADAM,

I was heartily rejoiced on reading in the papers of yesterday, and again in the official despatch of Lord Raglan, dated 'Before Sebastopol, March 27' (published in all the morning papers of April 12), that Lieutenant-Colonel Kelly was alive. I confess I gave him up. I can fully enter into your feelings; but you are a soldier's wife, and I am sure you will patiently submit to the fate of war, and thank Providence for His great mercy in sparing your husband's life in the sanguinary and dangerous affairs in which he was engaged on March 22. The Lieutenant-Colonel did his duty nobly, and was obliged to succumb. His wound, I hope, is not at all serious, and soon, no doubt, he will be perfectly restored to health.

I fear you will be disappointed with the reply I make now to the queries put in your letter; but I think you would like to peruse the accompanying letters enclosed, which I value (especially that of your kind and considerate husband), and will be obliged for their return when no longer required. We have had no letter from Lieutenant Byron, of the 34th, now a prisoner in the hands of the enemy, since January 8, the date of that sent to you—nor do I think he is permitted to write to his friends here direct, because no letter has come to hand yet except through the British camp; nor from Captain Frampton, of the 50th Regiment, and Lieutenant Clarke, taken captive on December 20 with my nephew; and I am constantly inquiring at the army agents (Cox and Co.) and elsewhere. Colonel Clarke, of the Quartermaster-General's Department at the Horse Guards, is an uncle of Lieutenant Clarke alluded to, and I have had two interviews with him on the subject of the British officers taken prisoners in the Crimea; but he could not give me any intelligence of his nephew, nor do I think he knows where he is; but my impression is that several British officers and soldiers are at Simpheropol. Colonel Kelly would be placed, I should say, in the north fort at Sebastopol, where he would receive the best medical attention and consideration from the Russians. Make up your mind to be satisfied on this score. You cannot write to Colonel Kelly direct with any chance of your letter reaching him. He may be removed already from Sebastopol into the interior or elsewhere, but you might try the chance of a letter to him through Major Simpson or Captain Gwilt, of the 34th.

I could not at present advise your proceeding to the Crimea or Russia; it would be costly, laborious, and hazardous to your health to make the attempt. We have not written to the missing Lieutenant (see Army List), being under the impression that no communication by post would reach him, and, besides, no one can say where he now may be, such is the risk and chance of warfare. You might with propriety consult (by letter) Lord Panmure, War Department, London, and I am sure you will meet with a prompt reply to any questions put by you. Colonel Kelly would not remain long at Sebastopol, but this would depend on his health.

In the first letter we had from my nephew (which is with his father), he said he received every consideration from the enemy.

Believe me truly yours,
W. BYRON.

To Mrs. Colonel Kelly, but to be opened by any Member of the Family.

DROGHEDA TERMINUS (whilst the train
is waiting to start),
Tuesday, 5 *o'clock*.

Mr. —— cannot deprive himself of the great gratification of informing Mrs. Colonel Kelly that at mid-day a telegraph marked within, stating that Colonel Kelly is alive, but slightly wounded, and a prisoner in the hands of the Russians, which he hopes to be true.

On another Scrap of Paper, written in Pencil.

You will please read enclosed to Mrs. Colonel Kelly, and break the news to her. It came by telegraph, and I believe it to be true, but yet there are sometimes mistakes, so use the necessary caution.

Copy of Telegram enclosed.

MAGNETIC TELEGRAPH OFFICE, DROGHEDA.
DUBLIN TO DROGHEDA.

BALAKLAVA,
March 27, 1855.

Colonel Kelly is not dead; he is only wounded slightly. He is a prisoner in Sebastopol. I heard the news from James McCann, Esq., M.P.

To F. J. Kelly, Esq.

LONDON,
April 10, 1855.

MY DEAR FRANCIS,

The second edition of Monday's *Times* has just appeared, and contains as follows, 'Colonel Kelly is a prisoner and slightly wounded,' and I hasten to let you know. If I knew his wife's address, I would send either the paper or a telegraphic message, but sincerely do I congratulate you all on this (word illegible) news.

You see, Lord Raglan was right and the *Times* wrong.

Pray present my best regards and kindest wishes to Mrs. Kelly and your sisters, and

Believe me,
Yours very sincerely,
W. WYNDOWE.

APPENDIX

Copy of a Letter to A. W. Kinglake, Esq., M.P., Author of 'History of the Invasion of the Crimea,' relative to the Sortie made by the Russians on the Night of March 22, 1855.

18, RUE PORTE NEUVE, PAU,
October 7, 1868.

SIR,

Having observed in a footnote to the last page of the fourth volume of your 'History of the Invasion of the Crimea' that you would welcome any communication respecting the Battle of Inkerman or subsequent events down to the close of June, 1855, I am induced to address you on a matter personal to myself regarding the part I took in the repulse of the Russian sortie on the night of March 22, 1855, on which occasion I was in command of the trenches of our right attack, and in the second of the assaults made on us that night was wounded and unfortunately taken prisoner ; and as it was the only important affair beyond the ordinary routine of trench duty that I was engaged in during my service in the Crimea, and considered of sufficient importance to receive from Her Majesty the Queen a special commendation of the conduct of the officers and men engaged in it (some of the former under my command having received brevet promotion in consequence), I am anxious that an error affecting myself that occurred in Lord Raglan's despatch, dated March 24, 1855, relative to this affair might be rectified in a history which is so eagerly read by military men and all others who take an interest in the services of our army in the Crimea, should you deem the subject worthy of notice : for I do not wish to magnify my services, but merely to state facts as far as I know them, and to do justice as far as is in my power to all engaged.

The despatch referred to states 'that on the night

in question the detachments 77th and 97th Regiments, although suddenly attacked by the enemy both in front and rear, repulsed them at the point of the bayonet,' etc., all of which is perfectly correct; and it then goes on to say that these troops were under the direction of Major Gordon, Royal Engineers. That is the statement that I complain of, for not only were the dispositions to meet the flank attack of the Russians (which I had foreseen) ordered by me without suggestion from anyone, but were carried out under my personal superintendence, and you will find it stated by Lord Raglan in a subsequent despatch, dated March 27, that Major-General Eyre (the late Sir William Eyre), who was general officer of the trenches on the night in question, highly eulogized the dispositions I had made. But I was also present with the detachments 77th and 97th Regiments when the attacks both in front and flank (which were nearly simultaneous) were made, and, together with Major Gordon, R.E., accompanied the detachment 97th Regiment, who, at the bidding of that noble soldier Hedley Vicars, sprang over the parapet and charged with the bayonet the Russian force that was attacking us in front; and on the fall of Captain Vicars, who was shot by my side, and after having driven the Russians into the ravine in our front, I brought back the detachment of the 97th into our trenches, being the only officer of those who accompanied them who was not either killed or wounded on that occasion, Major Gordon having been severely wounded in the arm soon after leaving the trench while gallantly cheering on the men, and Captain Vicars' Subaltern being also wounded.

Far be it from me to disparage the services of so distinguished an officer as Major (now Major-General) Sir W. Gordon, K.C.B., an old and valued friend of

APPENDIX

mine, and for whom I entertain the highest regard. On that night we were together all the time till he was wounded, and I was much indebted to him for advice and assistance; but while we both equally shared in the repulse of the Russian attack, I am sure he would be ready to admit that the command of the troops actually engaged, and the disposition of them for the defence of the trench, devolved on me as commanding officer, and not on him as directing Engineer.

At the risk of being considered tedious, I will, to make this evident, give you a statement of what actually occurred that night, so far as it came under my observation. At the usual hour on the evening of March 22, 1855, I went on duty to the trenches of the right attack as senior field-officer and in command of the guard, about 1,200 strong, consisting of detachments from each regiment in the Light Division. Of these, about 300 of the 7th, 23rd, 19th, and 33rd Regiments, under the second field-officer (whose name I forget), were placed in reserve in the 21-gun Battery; 300 more, taken in proportion from all the regiments in the division, were employed under Lieutenant-Colonel Tylden, R.E., as a working party, extending the right of our advanced parallel to meet in the middle ravine (Ravin de Carenge), the left of the trenches which the French were constructing to our right towards the Victoria Redoubt; while the remaining 600, under my immediate command, lined the parapet of our advanced trench from the middle ravine on our right to the Woronzoff road on our left (about 500 yards long), and, as well as I can recollect, were posted in the following order from the right—97th, 77th, 88th, 34th, 90th Rifle Brigade. On my arrival in the trenches I was warned both by the officer I relieved, Colonel Farren, 47th Regiment, and Major Gordon, the directing Engineer, that I might expect an attack on our trenches that night, as the Russians were making a serious attack on the French trenches on our right, and Gordon at once kindly offered to accompany me whilst I posted my sentries outside the trench, an offer I gladly accepted, as he was so well acquainted with the ground, and I was anxious that our working-party should not be surprised.

When we had finished posting the sentries, I went along the whole line of our trench to see that all the detachments were on the alert. When I returned to the right of our trench, I observed from the direction of the firing that the Russians had succeeded in carrying the French trenches after an obstinate resistance, and felt sure that they would then turn to their right and try to sweep along the rear of our trenches, and to guard against that I extended the detachment 77th Regiment, under Captain Rickman, in skirmishing order, with their left resting on the right of our trench, so as to cover our right flank, supporting them with the detachment 88th in line, and at the same time sending my Adjutant, Lieutenant Marsh, 33rd Regiment, to the 21-gun Battery to ask for reinforcements of another company to replace those two detachments in defence of the trenches in front. I recollect Gordon saying to me at that moment (for our acquaintance was of long standing), 'Kelly, you have done just what was right.' We were together close in rear of the detachment 77th Regiment, and the leading files of the Russians who had carried the French trenches and were trying to sweep along ours had just commenced firing on us, when we heard a loud volley fired just in front of the right of our trench, succeeded by a ringing cheer, as Captain Vicars, 97th, following only the dictates of his gallant spirit, leaped over the parapet and led his small detachment of not more than seventy or eighty men against the Russian column. Gordon and I at once followed the 97th over the parapet, but he was almost immediately severely wounded in the arm by a musket-ball while gallantly cheering on the men. I ran after and overtook Vicars, and we were running side by side, and I was in the act of speaking to him, when he got his death-wound from a musket-ball, and his Subaltern, an officer, I think, of the name of Hammond (who had risen from the ranks, and who had been sergeant-major of the regiment), having been also wounded, I, being the only officer left with them, brought the detachment back to the trenches after having driven the Russians into a ravine in our front.

The composition of the column that attacked us in front, according to the Russian despatch, was as follows —viz., four companies Greek Volunteers, under Prince Morovli, 260 sailors, and the 6th Battalion of the Regiment of Minsk, the whole under the command of Captain Bonditscheff, of the navy, and forming a force, so far as I could judge, of at least 800 men. The extreme darkness of the night must have prevented them from seeing with how small a force Vicars attacked them, for they certainly made no attempt to stand, but, after firing a volley into our trenches, retired in column at the double, their rear files turning back to fire as they ran, and it was by one of these shots that poor Vicars was killed. Their speed was perhaps accelerated by the cheers of our men and by the 'Advance!' sounded repeatedly by a gallant little bugler of the 97th who was well in front, and whose name I unfortunately did not ascertain before I was made prisoner, as it had been my intention to have mentioned him in my report next morning. On my return to the trench I had the satisfaction of finding that the attack on our right flank, which had been going on while I was outside the trench, had been gallantly repulsed by the detachment 77th Regiment, under Captain Rickman, and that the detachment 7th Fusiliers, under the Hon. Captain Browne, had arrived from the 21-gun Battery to reinforce us.

I should imagine about an hour had elapsed after the repulse of these attacks, when our attention was roused by hearing heavy firing and loud cries proceeding from the centre and left of our advanced trench. The same Russian column that had been repulsed on our right must have gone round to our other flank to try if they would meet with better success in an attack in that direction. I immediately directed Captain Browne to accompany me to the left with his detachment of Fusiliers, and he moved them off by fours from the left for that purpose; but as that part of the trench was in process of construction, their progress was much impeded by stones and other obstacles, and their files opened out a good deal, so I told Captain Browne that I would go on before and see how matters were, and begged him to bring on his men as fast as he could in a compact body. I never saw him again, but heard he was soon afterwards killed while leading on his men. His Subaltern, Lord Richard Browne, was the only officer who at the court of inquiry, that was subsequently held to ascertain the cause of my being taken prisoner, was able to give any evidence concerning what had become of me that night, for by an extraordinary fatality nearly every officer with whom I had been in close contact since the commencement of the Russian attack was either killed or wounded that night, and it was first supposed that I had been killed, and a report of my death was sent to my wife.

On arriving at the mortar battery about the centre of

our trench, I met Lieutenant Jordan with a party of my own regiment, the 34th, and he told me that he was afraid the Russians had penetrated into our trench a little further on. I told him to get his men together, that the 7th Fusiliers were coming up, and that we would try and drive the Russians out again. The poor fellow was killed after in the successful attack made on the Russians by the 7th and 34th, together with the working-party, who, under Lieutenant-Colonel Tylden, R.E., had stood to their arms, and were by him led to the attack. I had gone on only a little beyond where I had left Lieutenant Jordan, when I saw a group of seven or eight men standing in the trench, and who, the night being so dark, and from their being dressed in goatskin capotes, very like the sheepskin coats then worn by our men when on duty in the trenches, I mistook for my own regiment, and I went up to them and told them to fall in with the party under Lieutenant Jordan. Their first exclamation undeceived me, and I thought my only chance of safety was to shoot one of them, when perhaps the others would bolt. I had not drawn my sword that night, but carried in my hand a thick stick which I always took with me into the trenches; I, however, dropped my stick and pulled my revolver out of my belt, and put it to the head of the man nearest to me and pulled the trigger, but unfortunately, as I then thought, the safety-catch, which I had neglected to push before coming into the trenches, was on, and the pistol did not go off, and while I was lowering the pistol to release the catch I was knocked down by blows from butt-ends of muskets, and while on the ground was bayoneted in the shoulder and calf of the leg and through the left hand, and knocked about a good deal on the head. None of my wounds were, however, severe, and most providentially all their muskets were at the time unloaded, for, as I afterwards heard from Russian officers, they had discharged their muskets before leaping over the parapet, and had not reloaded when I came up. But, under Providence, I owe my life to the humane interposition of a young Polish officer who stood over me whilst on the ground and warded off the blows of butt-ends, receiving several himself that were intended for me. The number that were stabbing at me at the same time was also in my favour, as they got in each other's way. I learnt afterwards that my captors were Albanian Klephtis, savages by nature and robbers by profession, of which they soon gave me a proof by stripping me of everything but my clothes, my watch, which to my surprise they overlooked, though it was in the breast-pocket of my coatee.

I was first taken before Admiral Pamphiloff, who commanded in the Redan, and who received me very kindly, gave me a cup of tea and a forage-cap of his own to replace mine lost in the struggle. He then sent me to the hospital established in the naval barracks in the dockyard, where I had my wounds dressed and remained two days, and was there joined by Captain Montague, R.E., who was taken prisoner the same night. While I remained in the hospital amputations were being performed from dawn to dusk by the Russian surgeons; and I shall never forget the dreadful moans and shrieks of many of the poor wounded Russians, they not being supplied with chloroform to deaden the pain. They admitted having sustained a loss of 1,000 killed and wounded that night. I was afterwards removed to Fort Nicholas, where, with the exception of three days passed on board a ship in the harbour, I remained during the rest of the time I was in Sebastopol. I was while in captivity treated with the greatest consideration, both by Prince Gortschakoff and Baron Osten Sacken, who was the Commandant de Place of Sebastopol, and who kindly supplied the meals of myself and the officers confined with me from his own table, and generally by every Russian officer with whom I was thrown into contact.

I have now sufficiently wearied you with a long and egotistical story, for which I trust you will pardon me. It is not intended, of course, for publication; but I want to appeal to you as to one who, I am sure, wishes to be, so far as lies in your power, an impartial writer of history on a matter touching my reputation as an officer, to show that the troops who repulsed the first of the attacks made on us by the Russians on the night of March 22, 1855, were under my directions, and not, as stated in Lord Raglan's despatch, under those of Major Gordon, R.E., who, I am sure, if appealed to, would confirm my statement.

I think it right to add that, on my return to the Crimea in September, 1855, after having been exchanged as prisoner of war, I addressed General Sir James Simpson, then commanding our army in the Crimea, relative to the alleged error in Lord Raglan's despatch, and was informed in reply by the Military Secretary of Lord Hardinge, then Commander-in-Chief, on October 6, 1855, that as it had been stated by Lieutenant-General Sir William Codrington, who was at the time in question the General of my division, that I, and not Major Gordon, was field-officer in command, my letter explaining the error had been duly recorded; but no correction of the error was (as is usually the case) subsequently published, and consequently the outside world are still under the impression that the merit of the repulse of that Russian attack is due to Major Gordon, and not to me.

Your history, however, will remain a standard work open to all, while despatches are peacefully slumbering in the dusty pigeon-holes of the War Office.

R. D. KELLY.

Copy of Mr. Kinglake's Reply.

28, HYDE PARK PLACE,
October 12, 1868.

SIR,

I have the honour to acknowledge the receipt of the statement which you have been so kind as to address to me on the subject of the sortie of March, 1855, and I desire to offer you my grateful acknowledgments for the clear and interesting narrative thus imparted to me. You may be sure that when I touch that part of the campaign I will not fail to let it appear that you were in command of the troops which repulsed the enemy.

I have the honour to be, sir,
Very faithfully yours,
A. W. KINGLAKE.

THE END

Elliot Stock, 62, Paternoster Row, London, E.C.

www.ingramcontent.com/pod-product-compliance
Lightning Source LLC
Chambersburg PA
CBHW031129160426
43193CB00008B/78